GW01142461

12.00

Universal language schemes in England and France 1600-1800

JAMES KNOWLSON is in the Department of French Studies at the University of Reading, England.

For centuries Latin served as an international language for scholars in Europe. Yet as early as the first half of the seventeenth century, scholars, philosophers, and scientists were beginning to turn their attention to the possibility of formulating a totally new universal language. This wide-ranging book focuses upon the role that it was thought an ideal, universal, constructed language would play in the advancement of learning.

The first section examines seventeenth-century attempts to establish a universal 'common writing' or, as Bishop Wilkins called it, a 'real character and philosophical language.' This movement involved or interested scientists and philosophers as distinguished as Descartes, Mersenne, Comenius, Newton, Hooke, and Leibniz.

The second part of the book follows the same theme through to the final years of the eighteenth century, where the implications of language-building for the progress of knowledge are presented as part of the wider question which so interested French philosophers, that of the influence of signs on thought. The author also includes a chapter tracing the frequent appearance of ideal languages in French and English imaginary voyages, and an appendix on the idea that gestural signs might supply a universal language.

This work is intended as a contribution to the history of ideas rather than of linguistics proper, and because it straddles several disciplines, will interest a wide variety of readers. It treats comprehensively a subject that has not previously been adequately dealt with, and should become the standard work in its field.

Universal language schemes in England and France 1600-1800

JAMES KNOWLSON

UNIVERSITY OF TORONTO PRESS

TORONTO AND BUFFALO

© University of Toronto Press 1975

Toronto and Buffalo

Printed in Canada

Library of Congress Cataloging in Publication Data
Knowlson, James.
Universal language schemes in England and France, 1600–1800.
(University of Toronto romance series; 29)
Bibliography: p.
Includes index.
1. Languages, Universal – History. I. Title.
II. Series: Toronto. University.
University of Toronto romance series; 29.
PM 8009.K57   499.99   73-81759
ISBN 0-8020-5296-7

IN MEMORIAM

FRANCIS FREDERICK KNOWLSON

1905–1972

Contents

Acknowledgments / xi

Introduction / 3

1 / A language of real characters:
the intellectual background / 7
The first language of mankind / 9
From secret to universal writing / 15
Languages, language, and real studies / 27

2 / Early schemes for a common writing / 44

3 / The philosophical language / 65
Descartes and Mersenne / 65
The universal character as a mirror of reality / 72
John Wilkins's 'real character and philosophical language' / 98
A brief look at Leibniz / 107

4 / Ideal languages in the imaginary voyage / 112

5 / The eighteenth century:
origins of language, general grammar, and a universal language / 139

6 / Pasigraphy in the 1790s / 150

7 / Signs and thought / 161

8 / The Idéologues and the perfect language / 183

Appendix A
Gesture as a form of universal language / 211

Appendix B
Checklist of schemes of universal writing and language in the seventeenth and eighteenth centuries / 224

Notes / 233

Bibliography / 270

Index / 292

Illustrations

PLATE 1
Francis Lodwick *A Common Writing* London 1647
28–9: the Gospel according to St John, chapter 1,
in Lodwick's universal character / 60

PLATE 2
George Dalgarno *Ars signorum* London 1661
95: first page of the Latin-universal character lexicon / 89

PLATE 3
George Dalgarno *Ars signorum* London 1661
118–9: first chapter of Genesis in Dalgarno's universal character / 90

PLATE 4
John Wilkins *Essay towards a Real Character and a
Philosophical Language*
London 1668, 387: description of the real character / 92

PLATE 5
John Wilkins *Essay towards a Real Character and a
Philosophical Language*
London 1668, 395: the Lord's Prayer written in the real character / 93

PLATE 6
John Wilkins *Essay towards a Real Character and a
Philosophical Language*
London 1668, 415: attribution of sounds in Wilkins's
philosophical language
to various categories of ideas / 94

PLATE 7
George Psalmanaazaar *An Historical and Geographical
Description of Formosa*
London 1704, facing 267: the Formosan alphabet / 127

PLATE 8
Joseph de Maimieux *Pasigraphie, ou premiers élémens du
nouvel art-science*
Paris 1797: title page / 154

PLATE 9
Joseph de Maimieux *Pasigraphie, ou premiers élémens du
nouvel art-science*
Paris 1797, 4–5: index of link words and phrases / 158–9

PLATE 10
John Bulwer *Chirologia, or The Naturall Language of the Hand*
London 1644, 151: gestural signs and their meaning / 213

Acknowledgments

In the course of writing this book, I have received help and advice from so many professional colleagues and personal friends that a list of all those to whom I bear some debt can no longer even be contemplated. I am particularly grateful, however, to my former professor, George Lehmann, for his guidance in the very early stages of this work and for his constant encouragement, to Haydn Mason and Robert Fargher for kindly correcting some errors in an earlier version, and to Vivian Salmon and the late Bernard Rochot, who have shared discoveries most generously.

The material that is used in this book was collected mainly in the British Museum; the Bodleian Library; Reading, Glasgow, and Sheffield university libraries; the library of the Royal Society of London; the National Library of Scotland; the Bibliothèque nationale, the Bibliothèque Mazarine, and the Bibliothèque de l'Institut national in Paris. The courtesy and assistance of the staffs of these libraries have made what was necessarily a lengthy task less onerous than it would otherwise have been. At various times I have been helped financially by the Research Boards of Reading and Glasgow universities and should like to express my gratitude to both of them. The book has been published with the help of a grant from the Humanities Research Council of Canada, using funds provided by the Canada Council, and with the help of the Publications Fund of the University of Toronto Press. The editorial staff of the University of Toronto Press have been extremely helpful and I am particularly indebted to Dr R.M. Schoeffel for his kindness and courteous advice. My debt to my wife is too great to be satisfactorily acknowledged. Finally, and less usually, I should like to thank the London refuse-collector who helped me to retrieve a section of the manuscript of this book from Harlesden rubbish-tip, when it had been found on a train from Oxford to London and thrown into a bin on Paddington station! Let us hope that it was worth his trouble.

Reading

Universal language schemes in England and France
1600-1800

Introduction

Most books concerned with the history of the universal language movement concentrate primarily upon artificial languages constructed in the past hundred years or so.[1] If they look back at all into the more remote past, it is to single out the early suggestion of Descartes for a language based upon the 'true philosophy' and the proposals of Leibniz for a *characteristica universalis*, sometimes adding a brief mention of one or two other schemes, such as those of Dalgarno and Wilkins in the seventeenth century, or of Faiguet and Delormel in the eighteenth. It is, of course, only natural that writers on this subject should have devoted their attention to the more modern would-be universal languages, since they have been chiefly concerned with assessing the linguistic qualities and defects of these constructed languages and with judging their suitability for international adoption.

The artificial languages which will be treated in this book were, on the other hand, all constructed before the great period of modern linguistics, and the claims that they make on our attention are totally

NOTE: Full bibliographical details of works referred to may be found in the checklist or bibliography. A short title in the text or notes followed immediately by a date in parentheses indicates that bibliographical details may be found in the chronological checklist (Appendix B) under that date; details of works indicated by a short title may be found under the name of the author in one of the sections of the bibliography. Bibliographical details are provided in the footnotes only for works not included in either the checklist or the bibliography.

different from those made by languages formulated more recently. Professor J.R. Firth has pointed to a relationship between seventeenth-century plans for a universal language and subsequent attempts at standardizing scientific nomenclature,[2] and several scholars have followed Firth's lead by investigating the relations between these early efforts at language building and contemporary developments in science, education, and philosophy. For instance, studies devoted to the various influences affecting English prose style in the mid-seventeenth century, to the origins and early years of the Royal Society, to the relations between Puritanism and science, and to the exchange of ideas between the Czech educational reformer, Comenius, and a number of English scholars, have all thrown some light on the role that universal language was thought to play in the advancement of learning at that time. Many students of the history of ideas in the seventeenth and eighteenth centuries will have been struck, and possibly surprised, by the keen interest that was taken in this subject by so many distinguished scientists and philosophers, some of whom regarded the institution of a 'real character and philosophical language' (to use Bishop Wilkins's term) as likely to contribute in a most fundamental way to the progress of knowledge.

Two recent studies have already made a substantial contribution to our knowledge of this field. Paolo Rossi's important *Clavis universalis arti mnemoniche e logica combinatoria da Lullo a Leibniz* considers seventeenth-century schemes of universal language as a continuation of the search for an *ars combinatoria* (although he unaccountably ignores Mersenne's work in this field). The second book, Paul E. Cornelius's *Languages in Seventeenth- and Early Eighteenth-Century Imaginary Voyages*, contains much material on the search for a *lingua humana* (the primitive language of mankind before Babel) and on the relationship between the idea of a universal or philosophical grammar and the construction of these imaginary languages. Cornelius, however, presents an over-simplified, hence distorted, picture of the complex factors that led to a wide-spread interest in universal language in the middle years of the seventeenth century. This over-simplification arises mainly out of an almost obsessive concern for the influence of Chinese character-writing, which was of importance, but by no means exclusively so. Far more reliable are recent articles by Vivian Salmon which will be referred to later. Much research remains to be done on this period, yet a stage has now been reached when a fuller and, one hopes, a more accurate account of the universal language movement in the seventeenth century can be given.[3]

By contrast, eighteenth-century thought on this subject has been almost entirely neglected,[4] and it therefore seems desirable to follow through the theme of radical linguistic reform and its implications for the progress of knowledge into the final years of the eighteenth century. For in the 1790s, particularly in France, there was a considerable revival of interest in the possibility of formulating a universal 'philosophical' language. This interest derived largely from contemporary sensationalist theories on the relationship between signs and thought, and is reflected not only in a fresh outburst of what were termed *pasigraphies*, but also in a sometimes surprisingly modern discussion of the whole question of signs and thought, as well as in an analysis of some of the fundamental problems involved in the construction and adoption of an artificial, *a priori* language. French philosophers as distinguished as Destutt de Tracy, de Gérando, Garat, Laromiguière, and Maine de Biran participated in this discussion, and, if initial enthusiasm for the idea tended to blind some of these thinkers to the obstacles that lay in the path of a radical reconstitution of language, and led them to over-estimate the impact that such a reform would have on the progress of knowledge, it also stimulated a highly critical examination of the motives, claims, and methods of the language planners that in many respects remains perfectly valid today.

A subject of this nature, straddling as it does several disciplines, could clearly be dealt with in a variety of ways. The approach adopted here, for example, is very different from that of the logician or the student of the history of linguistics. My hope is that any reader concerned with the history of ideas in the seventeenth and eighteenth centuries will find interesting and valid a book that sets out primarily to consider the relevance of universal language schemes to certain important preoccupations of scholars at that period – particularly to their over-riding concern with the progress of knowledge.

The vastness of the field and my own limitations have meant restricting this study to the language schemes of English and French writers, excluding thereby the work of Kircher and Becher and above all that of Comenius and Leibniz. There is, in fact, some discussion of the ideas of these scholars but it is confined to what seemed strictly necessary for a proper understanding of the chosen theme of the book. In this way, I hope to have provided some guide to future scholars who might be interested in pursuing this enquiry beyond the modest limits laid down here.

1/A language of real characters: the intellectual background

In the sixteenth and early seventeenth centuries Latin served scholars of different European countries as a virtually international language. Its use had been consecrated by tradition and its unique position in Europe was maintained because it provided a repository of ancient learning and remained a requirement for admission to the clergy, the professions, and the 'Republic of Learning.' In theory then, if not always in practice (for speakers sometimes tended to differ so much in their pronunciation of the language as to be mutually unintelligible),[1] scholars and clerics, statesmen and diplomats, merchants and travellers were able to communicate with their counterparts in other countries by using this common tongue. Needless to say, the remarkable convenience of possessing such an international language did not pass unnoticed at the time, and in the sixteenth century tributes to Latin were frequent on this score. For instance, in the *De tradendis disciplinis* of 1531 Juan Luis Vives was already commenting upon an established position when he wrote that 'such a language as that universal one, just suggested, should be sweet, learned and eloquent ... Such a language it seems to me is to be found in the Latin tongue, above all those languages which men employ; above all which are known to me.'[2] And, a little later in the century, Pierre Belon writes in his *Portraits d'oyseaux, animaux, etc.* in 1577, 'Une compagnie d'hommes villageois ... un Breton, Basque, Escossais ne s'entreentendraient l'un l'autre d'autant que la langue de chacun est estrangere à l'autre. Mais s'ils estaient hommes lettrez et qu'ils parlassent le langage lettré dont l'on use en leur religion, alors chacun s'entre-entendra parler. Combien donc est advantagé l'homme lettré sur le mechanique.'³

Yet, in spite of the fact that the classical language remained in constant use throughout educated Europe, by as early as the first half of the seventeenth century many scholars, philosophers, and scientists were beginning to turn their attention towards the possibility of formulating a totally new universal language composed of real characters, which, it was hoped, might ultimately replace Latin, first as a form of common writing, then perhaps even as an auxiliary spoken tongue. Interest in this proposal arose partly out of an awareness of the problem of communicating with people who spoke non-European languages – an awareness that grew as the reports and journals published by travellers and missionaries introduced readers to the seemingly strange languages of the Far East or West. A second factor adding to interest in this idea was a changing language situation that will be examined more fully later.

But few of the distinguished thinkers who gave serious consideration to this question – and their names constitute a most impressive list which includes Descartes, Peiresc, Gassendi, Mersenne, Comenius, Newton, Boyle, Wilkins, Ward, Petty, Wallis, Ray, Willoughby, Kircher, and Leibniz – would have lent it a second thought had they regarded the real character *merely* as an alternative means of communicating with men of different language-speaking communities. For the new character soon came to be thought of as superior to existing languages in a number of important respects. Usually it was praised as being simpler, briefer, and more regular, hence easier to learn, remember, and use. Sometimes, when it reached a spoken form, it was even said to be more harmonious than other languages; but later in the seventeenth century it was also described as more directly representative of the natural world. For, while hoping to preserve its advantages as a common writing, later scholars sought to provide a universal character that through the actual composition of its 'words' would accurately mirror the various qualities of natural things and the relations between them. In this way, language would not only be a means of acquiring knowledge; it would itself *be* knowledge, since each 'word' would provide an accurate description of the thing signified. Finally,

Leibniz and certain eighteenth-century philosophers aimed to construct a universal character that would express, through the combinations of its signs, the most profound and complex affiliations of our ideas, making the new character into an instrument of both analysis and discovery. It is this development from a very rudimentary form of 'common writing' to a highly ambitious, sophisticated language of science and philosophy that I intend to trace in the opening section of this study. Before looking though at the schemes of universal language themselves, let us consider some of the factors that led to the development of such schemes or that were in some measure responsible for the particular routes that the language planners came to follow.

THE FIRST LANGUAGE OF MANKIND

The second chapter of Genesis recounts how, while God was creating the world, he brought every beast of the field and every fowl of the air before Adam 'to see what he would call them: and whatsoever Adam called every living creature that was the name thereof.' Following this, for many generations 'the whole earth was of one language and one speech.' Until man's pride brought upon himself the confusion of tongues at Babel, he possessed a common language, which was widely thought to have been formed by Adam under the guidance or direct inspiration of God.

It has often been taken for granted that, because various thinkers in the seventeenth century expressed similar hopes for the institution of a universal language or real character, they were all in agreement as to the kind of language that they had in mind and the uses to which it might be put. It is now clear that such was by no means the case, and some of the divergences of view can be glimpsed through the varied reactions to the Genesis version of the origins of language.

Most projects of universal language in the seventeenth century do, in fact, refer at some point to the confusion of tongues at Babel, their authors often claiming that the new character or language would in itself provide a remedy for this curse. In a letter to Samuel Hartlib in 1646, Robert Boyle wrote that the new scheme for a common writing that Hartlib was then engaged in publishing 'will in good part make amends to mankind for what their pride lost them at the tower of

Babel,'[4] and, five years earlier, John Wilkins had described the perfecting of such an invention as the only way to unite the seventy-two languages of the first confusion.[5] Similarly, in France, Jean Douet wrote in the *Proposition présentée au roy, d'une escriture universelle* (1627) that 'la diversité des langues qui sont parmi cet univers, qui prirent leur origine au temps de Nembrot, edifiant Babel, est le troisieme fleau,' a curse which, he argued, his system of universal writing could at first render less serious, then with time entirely remove.[6] Similar claims to 'remedy Babel' are to be found in most of the better known schemes of universal language. The frequency of such references seems to bear witness to the fact that the Genesis story proved to be a lively stimulus to the universal language planners, though on occasion it may well have become little more than a routine claim, made by inventors who were often at the same time their own publicists.

The Biblical account of the state of man *before* Babel portrayed a situation in which mankind was united by a common language into one people, undivided by differences of race, nation, colour, or creed. For this reason it offered an ideal of religious harmony that was fundamental to many of those Christians who, in the middle decades of the century, were striving to bring about the reunification of the churches. Many of these reformers, belonging to Protestant groups located in various countries throughout Europe, regarded the invention and adoption of a universal language as likely to remove one of the greatest obstacles to the religious harmony that they had so much at heart. The brief account given in Gilbert Burnet's biography of William Bedell,[7] who was Bishop of Kilmore in Ireland, suggests that the scheme undertaken in the late 1630s by a certain Reverend Johnson, with Bedell's active encouragement, was conceived primarily as a religious endeavour.[8] The ideal of a return to an earlier religious harmony was particularly dear to the Moravian reformer, Johann Amos Komenský (Comenius), and to many of his supporters or associates in different countries. In the *Via lucis* (1668) Comenius looked forward to the invention of a 'language absolutely new, absolutely easy, absolutely rational, in brief a Pansophic language, the universal carrier of Light.'[9] Pansophia, it should be explained, was for Comenius 'a single and comprehensive system of Human Omni-Science,' that is, a system of all the things under Heaven, which we can know, say, or do. Only by the formulation and general adoption of a truly pansophic language, Comenius believed, could 'the commonwealth of men, now torn to pieces, be restored, a single speech be granted again to the world, and the glory of God increased by so splendid a method.'[10]

A similar vein of muted evangelism may be found in the works of many of the English language planners. One should however distinguish between their general interest in the spreading of the Christian gospel and Comenius's vigorous and specific call for a pansophic language that would unite, or rather *reunite*, men into a single religious commonwealth. This distinction is particularly necessary in view of recent attempts to identify Comenius's ideas with those of English universal language planners in the middle years of the century, a subject which will be discussed more fully in a later chapter.[11] Research on the origins of the Royal Society brings this distinction into a rather clearer light,[12] since none of the English scholars who were engaged in the search for a universal character, either loosely under the auspices of the Royal Society (Ward, Wilkins, Petty, Boyle, Hooke, and Lodwick), or outside it (Beck and Dalgarno), were very closely concerned with furthering Comenius's pansophic plans. Only Hartlib strongly supported both Pansophia and the efforts to construct a universal character and language. Although the French scholars who took an interest in the provision of a universal character, Mersenne, Descartes, and Peiresc, had their own vision of a form of universal science, and despite their sympathy for certain of the Moravian's ideals, they were not actively involved with Comenius in furthering his dreams of Pansophia.

For Father Philippe Labbé, who described his own version of the universal language as 'l'instrument général pour établir le commerce et planter la Foi Chrétienne par toutes les nations de la terre,'[13] the evangelical aim was clearly a dominant one. But more frequently it took its place alongside other more secular objectives. So George Dalgarno's *Ars signorum* (1661) was described by its author as most useful for 'civilising barbarous Nations, Propagating the Gospel, and encreasing Traffique and Commerce.'[14] Similarly, John Wilkins wrote in his *Essay towards a Real Character and a Philosophical Language* (1668), 'Besides that most obvious advantage which would ensue, of facilitating mutual *Commerce*, amongst the several Nations of the World, and the improving of all *Natural Knowledge* ; It would likewise very much conduce to the spreading of the knowledge of Religion.'[15]

Yet, although the aims of the majority of the language planners differed both in direction and intensity from those of Comenius, their stated religious motive need be regarded as no less genuine[16] than the more scientific intentions that we shall consider later, particularly in view of the position occupied by many of them within the church and what might be termed the religious character of their scientific investigations, the world of nature seeming to many but a further manifestation of the work of the Divine Creator, a second book to be read alongside that of the Scriptures.

But there was another respect in which the Genesis account of the gift of language and the subsequent discussion of this question encouraged the search for a universal language. From Plato's *Cratylus* onwards, philosophical discussion of language had centred on the question whether words signified naturally or by institution only. To many Biblical commentators for whom the Genesis account described the only true origins of language, the question was whether the names that were assigned to natural things by Adam conveyed the nature or essence of these things, or whether they signified in a purely arbitrary manner. Although there were some thinkers, such as Mersenne, who considered that the names that Adam used to represent animals could just as well have been applied to stones or to trees,[17] in the main orthodox opinion tended to maintain that this original language had been at least in some way representative of the true nature of things, even though other languages might have come to signify more or less arbitrarily. In this view, man had once possessed a deep understanding of the created world that, ever since, he had been unable to attain.

In the sixteenth and seventeenth centuries there was considerable controversy as to the fate of this original catholic tongue and of the primitive letters in which it was thought to have been written down. Detective work on the tribal movements described in the book of Genesis, hypotheses, deductions, and sometimes sheer guesswork characterized the various attempts to identify in existing languages the original speech of Adam and his immediate descendants. Claims and counter-claims were made, most frequently for primitive Hebrew, but also for Chaldean, Samaritan, Scythian, and even Celtic and Teutonic. The details of this controversy, though interesting in themselves, are of relatively little importance to our theme.[18] We should, however, bear in mind that the belief that there had once been a common *lingua humana*, from which all other languages had descended, and that this common language had once provided an insight into supernatural truths, was both long-standing and persistent, continuing to influence ideas on language very late in the eighteenth century.

In the two previous centuries, numerous attempts had been made to rediscover this original language either by examining the ancient languages with a view to identifying in them common roots, or (notably in the case of the Cabalists and Rosicrucians, following in a medieval Jewish tradition) by analysing the Hebrew letters in order to arrive at the divine truths that were thought to lie hidden somewhere behind them. Such efforts both anticipated and continued parallel with the seventeenth-century attempts to formulate a universal language. In the case of the Jesuit scholar, Athanasius Kircher, the two activities were directly related, as his interest in the new common writing – a project that he himself attempted to realize in the *Polygraphia nova* (1663)[19] – arose out of a recognition of the fact that, though eminently desirable, a reconstruction of the original language of mankind was unlikely ever to be achieved. Belief in a primitive language is reflected also, as we shall see in chapter two, in a number of seventeenth-century schemes of universal language. Moreover, as Hans Aarsleff has recently shown,[20] it is necessary for an understanding of Leibniz's approach to language, and it re-emerges, in rather different form, in the work of two intriguing eighteenth-century French writers on language, Court de Gébelin and Charles de Brosses.

The majority of the seventeenth-century universal language planners had, in my own view, little sympathy for the mystic overtones of those scholars who sought to rediscover the language of Adam. They were conscious that they were pursuing a related path but in a quite different spirit. Nonetheless, the idea that there had once been a language in which names had conveyed something of the essence of the things signified was one that probably influenced some of them far more than they themselves recognized, even if the influence was only negative.

Seth Ward and John Wilkins, two of the leading figures in the search for a universal language in England, plainly regarded the primitive tongue as being far beyond man's reach and understanding, and thus unlikely ever to be rediscovered;[21] it was therefore, they suggested, quite pointless to speculate idly concerning its nature and powers. So, when the Puritan chaplain, John Webster, writing in an attack upon the universities, virtually equated a universal character with the 'Natursprache' of Boehme,[22] they treated his views with the greatest possible contempt. For in the first part of their reply, Wilkins wrote:

> The man [Webster] doth give me the freest prospect of his depth and braine, in that canting Discourse about the language of nature, wherein he doth assent unto the highly illuminated fraternity of the *Rosycrucians*. In his large encomiums upon Jacob Behem [Boehme], in that reverence which he professes to judicial Astrologie, which may sufficiently convince what a kind of credulous fanatick Reformer he is like to prove.[23]

The language of real characters that both Wilkins and Ward had in mind is thus expressly dissociated from the mystical notions of Webster and continental writers, and Ward proceeds to explain that his conception of the proposed character will be based instead upon a description of things by their qualities and their relations. Yet, even in redefining what he meant by a 'natural language,' Ward revealed that the mystical view of language had not been entirely without influence upon himself and Wilkins: 'Such a language as this (where every word were a definition and contain'd the nature of the thing) might not unjustly be termed a naturall Language and would afford that which the *Cabalists* and Rosycrucians have vainely sought for in the Hebrew.'[24]

We should, of course, beware of relating the interest of English churchmen and scientists in a universal language too closely to a tradition of continental mysticism that is best represented by the writings of Jacob Boehme, Johann Valentin Andreae, and Johann-Heinrich Alsted, Comenius's teacher.[25] On the other hand, it has been much too easy since the pioneering work of Richard Foster Jones in this field to portray the universal language projects as arising exclusively out of a strictly nominalist attitude towards language. In order to demonstrate how relevant these schemes are to the emergence in mid-seventeenth century English prose of a simple style of mathematical plainness, this over-simplified view has ignored different tendencies that also played a significant part in the movement to discover a real character. Carried to extremes, this view presented the language planners as aiming to reduce language to nothing more than the 'dead, colourless symbols' of mathematical equations.[26] This is, in fact, to misunderstand completely the momentous and extremely varied consequences that were envisaged from the invention and adoption of a universal character or language. For Comenius and Kircher certainly, and probably for Bedell and Hartlib also, the universal character was, as Paolo Rossi has expressed it,[27] both an attempt to renew contact with divine harmony in the universe and a crucial effort to bring about a reconciliation between men, that would lay the foundations for an enduring, religious peace. Yet, in a different way, the schemes produced in England in the 1660s by George Dalgarno and John Wilkins, were equally ambitious in their aims. For, as we have already noted, they intended to fashion an impressive instrument of knowledge out of language itself, with the lines, shapes, and dots of the 'real character' reflecting by their arrangement and combination the order that science was in the process of discerning in the natural world.

FROM SECRET TO UNIVERSAL WRITING

Before looking back into the sixteenth century for a precise origin for the idea of a common writing, it is important to bear in mind two of the fundamental notions upon which the development of such a project depended.

First, in the *De augmentis scientiarum*, Francis Bacon underlined an idea that had become common by the beginning of the seventeenth century: 'Whatsoever is capable of sufficient differences and those perceptible by the senses, is in nature competent to express cogitations.'[28] He went on to explain that consequently speech sounds were not the only means of expressing one's ideas, for written symbols or descriptive gestures could also represent them directly, as could be seen from the example of the deaf and dumb, and from accounts of the

Chinese, who used real characters to express not letters and words but things and notions. On the authority of earlier accounts such as Acosta's *Naturall and Morall Historie of the East and West Indies* Bacon added that real characters are used in the East as a universal written script between men speaking quite different languages. He went on to divide the different methods of communication into two distinct kinds: first, those which, like hieroglyphs and gestures (as they were then understood) seemed to bear some resemblance to the object or idea which they represented; secondly, those real characters which, like Chinese ideograms (again as they were understood at the time), bore no such resemblance and therefore signified in a purely arbitrary manner. Although Bacon maintained that, in spite of the numerous deficiencies and imperfections of language, words remained by far the most convenient means of communication, 'Yet,' he remarked, 'because this part concerneth as it were the mint of knowledge (for words are the tokens current and accepted for conceits, as moneys are for values, and that it is fit men be not ignorant that moneys may be of another kind than gold and silver), I thought good to propound it to better enquiry.'[29] So as well as outlining briefly various possible ways of representing things and notions directly, Francis Bacon pointed to a field of enquiry in which many scholars were later to work, as they derived encouragement from the example of a form of character-writing, already used as a common writing in the Far East.

Secondly, in the *De prima scribendi origine et universa rei literariae antiquitate*, a book that was first published at Antwerp in 1617 and was often quoted in the course of the century, the Dutch Jesuit, Hermann Hugo, touched upon a further theory that, in one form or another, was to be fundamental to all subsequent projects of universal language for the next two centuries. Men, he argued, receive the same concepts of things through the senses, and so the differences that arise among them must result from the terms that are applied to these concepts rather than from the concepts themselves.[30] A similar conclusion to this was sometimes arrived at by a different philosophical route. In this view, the common notions that all men share arise as a consequence of the unity of the human reason – a belief which, stemming from the neo-Platonism of the previous century, was given further authority and prominence by the place that it came to occupy in Cartesian thought. But whether the approach to the origins of our ideas was basically Aristotelian or Platonic, it was widely accepted that ideas were the same from one person to another. The problem thus became, Hugo suggested, that of representing these universal ideas satisfactorily by means of common symbols that would need to be agreed upon by everyone. If this were done, it was confidently expected that everyone would then understand each other's ideas and it was asserted (with what now, of course, appears to be very naive optimism) that disputes over words would be removed.[31] John Wilkins expressed this reasoning most lucidly when he wrote, 'As men do generally agree in the same Principle of Reason, so do they likewise agree in the same *Internal Notion* or *Apprehension of things* ... So that, if men should generally consent upon the same way or manner of *Expression*, as they do agree in the same *Notion*, we should then be freed from that Curse in the Confusion of Tongues, with all the unhappy consequences of it.'[32]

One of the chief characteristics of the sixteenth century was the keen interest that was taken in various kinds of writing by symbols: Egyptian hieroglyphs, emblems and devices, anagrams and cryptograms. In a recent book, Madeleine David distinguished between two divergent trends in emblematic writing: on the one hand, that of the symbol proper or allegorical figure (hieroglyphs, emblems, devices, *rebus*) in which a considerable latitude of expression and interpretation is often accompanied by a religious and moral intention; on the other, that of the cryptogram, with its notion of a 'message' requiring rigorous analysis in order to be deciphered.[33] Although Mlle David is undoubtedly correct in deriving the seventeenth-century works of universal writing from a cryptographic rather than an allegorical tradition, it would be wrong to disregard entirely the force of the emblematic figures, and the example of Egyptian hieroglyphs in particular, since these focused upon the possibility of a direct relationship between language and the real world. The distinction that she makes was in any case far from being as clear-cut in the sixteenth and seventeenth centuries as it might appear today, for a number of treatises of secret-writing contained sections devoted to an exploration of the meaning of 'symbols' possessing a religious significance. So, for Blaise de Vigenère, 'les Hieroglyphes des Egyptiens, Ethiopiens, Perses souverains mages entre tous les autres ... ne sont à proprement parler, qu'une manière de chiffres ... aussi que sont à peu près nos devises, dont elles sont fort approchantes; pour représenter quelque mystère de la divinité, ou secret de la nature.'[34]

With this reservation in mind, in what respects may the various sixteenth-century *polygraphies, cryptographies,* or *steganographies,* as they were termed, be regarded as leading up to the earliest schemes of common writing?

Treatises devoted to secret-writing were certainly numerous in the sixteenth and early seventeenth centuries, from Tritheim's *Polygraphiae libri sex* of 1518 and Baptista Porta's much-printed *De furtivis literarum notis* of 1563 to Gustav Selenus's *Cryptomenytices et cryptographiae* of 1624. In such works, these three authors, together with Cardano, Schwenter, and others, explored very fully the resources of *non-figurative* signs. For it is obvious that, since the cryptograms were invented with a view to communicating messages secretly, figurative signs could hardly be used. And so the various signs consisted in the main of letters ingeniously transposed, numbers, lines, dots, circles, and musical notes (juxtaposed with other rather more picturesque ways of transmitting messages by writing, for example, on the shell of an egg or on the head of a messenger!). A large repertoire of non-figurative signs existed, some of which, hardly surprisingly, were taken up and used later as the actual characters in the schemes of universal writing; slanting lines and dots that changed their position in relation to a variable line became, next to numbers, the favourite alternative to alphabetical letters in such schemes.

But the sixteenth-century cryptographies provided more than a mere fund of possible signs. Although they worked in one language only, at times they introduced signs that stood for whole words, or even whole sentences.[35] This procedure in itself, taken with accounts of Chinese character-writing, may well have been enough to suggest a form of general character, which, to quote John Wilkins, would be 'legible to all Nations and Languages.'[36] It is worth recalling that it was while he was investigating various methods of secret-writing that Wilkins first came to deal with the question of a universal character in the *Mercury*.

Jean Douet claimed that his own early system of universal writing 'imite ou plustost surpasse les Hieroglyphiques Egyptiens, les carracteres Chinois et les Nottes de Tiro, affranchy de Ciceron, commentées par sainct Cyprien.'[37] This reference to the shorthand notes of Tiro, Cicero's freedman, which had been gathered together and published by Janus Gruterus in 1602–3,[38] suggests a link between schemes of common writing in the seventeenth century and shorthand that may be worth pursuing a little further. For again, as with the cryptographies, a student like Douet would have found among the *Notae veterum Romanorum* (as the ancient shorthand notes were often termed) not only single letters representing whole words, but also a number of special signs (a slanting line, for example) standing for particular words, usually for prepositions.[39] It needed no great effort of the imagination to consider inventing a system of signs in which *all* the symbols used would directly represent common ideas. In the case of Douet, the idea of a universal writing seems to have derived from an examination of both Roman shorthand and treatises of secret-writing as well as from accounts of Chinese character-writing.[40] Again the distinction that is now clearly made between shorthand and secret-writing was often decidedly blurred in the late sixteenth and early seventeenth centuries. The first known English system of shorthand, for instance, described in Dr Timothy Bright's *Characterie* of 1588, was not only a short and swift art; it also claimed to be 'secrete, as no kinde of wryting like.'[41] It was not at all uncommon in the seventeenth century for the same treatises to be concerned both with shorthand and secret-writing, as in the case of John Willis's *Art of Stenographie* published in 1602, or Noah Bridges's *Stenography and Cryptography, or The Arts of Short and Secret Writing*, published in 1659. One recalls Samuel Pepys composing his diary in shorthand for reasons of secrecy, and John Locke's remark in his treatise on education that 'shorthand ... may perhaps be thought worth the learning, both for despatch in what men write for their own memory, and concealment of what they would not have lie open to every eye.'[42]

Although the Roman shorthand notes were not unknown on the Continent in the seventeenth century – Mersenne also drew attention to them in 1640 in a letter to Theodore Haack[43] – it was in England that the idea of a script especially abbreviated for speed writing was taken up again, developed independently in numerous published schemes, and actually used for taking down the proceedings of the law courts or for recording Church sermons.[44] It was also in England, as Vivian Salmon first showed, that shorthand writing seems to have made the most marked contribution to the development of a common writing.[45]

Most English shorthand writers aimed, of course, at providing a script in which one could record rapidly the words of a single language, whereas those who were to construct a common writing needed to assign symbols directly to ideas so that they could be universally intelligible. And yet Timothy Bright's early 'characterie' consisted largely of – to use two seventeenth-century terms – a non-alphabetical, 'verbal' as distinct from a 'spelling' character, in which certain whole words were represented by single, variable characters. Moreover, the author, according to his own account, intended his work to serve in addition as a form of universal writing, by means of which 'nations of strange languages, may hereby communicate their meaning together in writing, though of sundrie tongues.'[46] Sir William Boswell (once secretary to the future Herbert of Cherbury and British resident in the Hague) was convinced, according to an entry of 1640 in Samuel Hartlib's *Ephemerides*, that Bright's 'characterie' 'might bee notably perfected. For they are rather Reales Cherienses then those other stenographical characters.'[47]

Later entries in Hartlib's journal refer to other attempts to perfect a stenography that would be applicable to all languages, and there was certainly hope in the middle years of the seventeenth century that a satisfactory form of real character might well develop directly out of the work that was then being done on an improved universal shorthand.[48] Vivian Salmon has shown that George Dalgarno's *Ars signorum* was probably first conceived as an attempt to invent such a system of universal shorthand rather than as the character based upon philosophical classification that it was ultimately to become.[49] We may note that the schemes that were founded on philosophical classification have been plausibly linked with the idea of conceptual classes established by Bright in his *Characterie*, which, although superseded by simpler alphabetical systems, may have been known through John Willis's *Art of Stenographie*.[50] An important fact is that one of the six copies of Bright's original *Characterie* known to be still in existence belonged to Seth Ward, Bishop of Sarum,[51] to whom Wilkins, on his own admission, owed the idea of classification that lay behind the tables of his *Essay*.

There is evidence then, to suggest that, although the seventeenth-century schemes of shorthand and universal writing owe many of their resemblances to common sources in the earlier cryptographies, in England, where shorthand flourished most vigorously, developments in that art were very closely related to the activities of the universal language planners.

A third type of writing by symbols is frequently quoted by seventeenth-century scholars who were interested in the possibility of constructing a universal character. These are the Arabic numerals, which are commonly referred to as illustrating the feasibility of a common writing, a distinction being drawn between the written and the spoken form of these numbers, the former being widely understood, the latter confined to one particular language. One typical example will serve here. Robert Boyle, though later to become sceptical concerning the practicability of the universal character, wrote in 1647 in a letter to Samuel Hartlib, 'Since our arithmetical characters are understood by all the nations of *Europe*, the same way, though every several people express that comprehension with its own particular language I conceive no impossibility that opposes the doing that in words, that we see already done in numbers.'[52]

In view of the impressive example set by arithmetical numbers it is scarcely surprising that Arabic numerals should have been adopted as the symbols employed in a number of schemes of common writing, among which were Cave Beck's *Universal Character* (1657), Johann Joachim Becher's *Character pro notitia linguarum universali* (1661), and Athanasius Kircher's *Polygraphia nova et universalis* (1663). Although the combination of numbers in which many seventeenth-century mathematicians showed a keen interest contributed, as we shall see in chapter three, to the development of a real character established on philosophical principles, I should like to draw attention here only to the value of numbers as a form of notation that was universally intelligible, as well as clear, precise, brief, and regular.

The same qualities were being attributed to the new algebraic symbolism which was developing rapidly at the beginning of the seventeenth century, and was elaborated in mathematical treatises by Vietà,

22 Universal language schemes

Harriot, Oughtred, Hérigone, and Descartes. The search for a universal character was often explicitly linked with the development of algebraic notation, frequently by the language projectors themselves.

George Dalgarno, for example, in a printed prospectus announcing the *Ars signorum* (1661), explained that the way in which his character expressed 'Real Truths' 'will be easily apprehended by those who are versed in late Mathematical Writers, who have begun to follow this way, by expressing words of frequent use with real characters, and that partly because it works a more real and lively apprehension of the thing treated of, and partly for compendiousness of delivery.'[53] One of these 'mathematical writers,' William Oughtred, praised the use of notes instead of words to represent things, explaining that 'this specious and symbolicall manner, neither racketh the memory with multiplicity of words, nor chargeth the phantasie with comparing and laying things together; but plainly presenteth to the eye the whole course and processe of every operation and argumentation.'[54] Seth Ward, who became Savilian Professor of Astronomy at Oxford, and had earlier been a private pupil of Oughtred,[55] stated that it was largely through his acquaintance with the new algebraic symbolism that he came to consider whether other things 'might not as well be designed by Symboles, and herein I was presently resolved that Symboles might be formed for every *thing* and *notion* ... So that an Universall Character might easily be made wherein all Nations might communicate together, just as they do in number and species.'[56] It is significant too that many of those who were most interested in the possibility of establishing a universal character were mathematicians: Ward, Wilkins, Wallis, Pell, Newton, Mersenne, Descartes, Peiresc, and Leibniz.

In addition to these specialized forms of script, scholarship and travel accounts had, by the opening decades of the seventeenth century, furnished European readers with a knowledge (much of which turned out later to be erroneous) of several forms of character-writing which had either been used in the past or were in current use as a means of general communication among peoples.

By this time the 'myth of Egypt,' as it has recently been termed,[57] had long been established in the European mind, and with it a keen curiosity concerning Egyptian hieroglyphic writing. The discovery of

Horapollo's manuscript *Hieroglyphica* in 1419, and the subsequent growth of a large body of explanatory literature, of which two of the main works were Francesco Colonna's *Hypnerotomachia poliphilii* of 1499 and Valeriano Bolzani's *Hieroglyphica* of 1566, had encouraged an allegorical approach to the hieroglyphs that presented them, in Iversen's words, as 'pictures by means of which the initiated could manifest not the name or the form of the thing, but its very essence and true meaning.'[58]

Egyptian hieroglyphs were referred to on several occasions by those scholars who were seeking to construct a universal character. Jean Douet quoted them along with Chinese characters and shorthand notes.[59] Philip Kinder, in a letter that will be discussed later,[60] compared some of the symbols of his own universal character with them, while Cave Beck regarded them as offering merely 'a Symbolical way of writing by Emblems and Pictures.'[61] Finally, for a spokesman at the Bureau d'Adresse in Paris in the mid-1630s, hieroglyphs, like Chinese characters, would have provided a good method of forming a universal language, had they not been much too diffuse.[62] In view of the fact that knowledge of hieroglyphs was so inadequate at the time and interpretations of them so varied, it is hardly surprising that they were thought to provide a most unsatisfactory model upon which to base a clear, precise, unequivocal universal character. Cave Beck judged them unfavourably not only because they were too hard to learn and tedious to use, but also because too often one picture was displayed to the eye, only for another quite different meaning to be assigned to it.[63] Charles Sorel argued similarly in *La Science universelle* that mistakes in interpretation could be made too easily on account of the obscurity of the hieroglyphs and the multiple meanings that they were given.[64] Nonetheless, if hieroglyphs constituted an unsatisfactory model, they offered a further instance of a less specialized form of character-writing that was generally thought to represent objects and ideas, however obscurely, without recourse to the representation of speech-sounds. Moreover, an allegorical interpretation of the hieroglyphs almost certainly reinforced the example provided by the primitive language in leading a number of universal language projectors at least to hope for a new character, which, like earlier, sacred languages, would lead one more deeply into the nature of reality.

Far more generally influential as a common writing in current use among the various peoples of the Far East were the Chinese characters with which Egyptian hieroglyphs were so often associated. As early as 1569, Gaspar da Cruz, a Dominican friar, had set down a brief description of Chinese character-writing,[65] emphasizing first the direct relationship that exists between 'things' and the characters that represent them; secondly, the great number of characters that are necessary, since 'one only character signifies "Heaven," another "earth," and another "man," and so forth with everything else';[66] thirdly, the important fact that this written character provided a common means of communication for the Chinese, the Cochinchinese, and the Japanese. Da Cruz's description became better known through Juan Gonzalez de Mendoza's history of China,[67] which, since Mendoza had himself never visited that country, leaned heavily on eye-witness accounts such as those of Da Cruz and Martin de Rada.[68] By the end of the century, Mendoza's book, first published in Spanish in 1585, had appeared in some thirty editions and in all the main European languages.[69] In this work, the author drew special attention again to the universality of the Chinese characters among Oriental nations, writing that, even though these peoples speak many different languages, they can understand each other perfectly adequately through their writing, since no matter how diversely it may be pronounced, a written character represents the same idea for all of them.[70]

The publication of Father Matthew Ricci's diaries in 1615 by Nicholas Trigault in the well-known *De Christiana expeditione apud Sinas*[71] emphasized further two primary facts concerning Chinese characters: first, the universality of their written signs, and secondly, the direct nature of the relationship between object and character. Taking his cue from these reports, and following the lead of Francis Bacon, Hermann Hugo, and Gerhard Vossius, all of whom discuss Chinese characters,[72] John Wilkins wrote in his early work on communication, the *Mercury*:

> That such a manner of writing is already used in some parts of the World, the Kingdomes of the high *Levant*, may evidently appear from divers credible Relations. *Trigaultius* affirms, that though

those of *China* and *Japan* doe as much differ in their Language, as the *Hebrew* and the *Dutch*, yet either of them can, by this help of a common character, as well understand the books and letters of the others, as if they were only their own.⁷³

This idea appears to have rapidly become something of an intellectual commonplace in the seventeenth-century world of learning, and the majority of the projectors of a common writing or, later, of a character based on philosophical principles referred to the use of these characters as a form of common script in the East.⁷⁴ As late as 1681, in his first letter to the *Extraordinaire du Mercure* about a universal character, De Vienne Plancy expressed his initial surprise that Chinese characters had not been adopted throughout the world 'pour le commerce des Nations, puisqu'ils signifient immédiatement les pensées.'⁷⁵

From the frequency and nature of these references, it is clear that, by its very existence and reputation as the universal language of the East, Chinese character-writing rendered the whole idea of a common writing eminently feasible to European scholars. And, more clearly than the treatises of secret-writing or the shorthand notes, it also indicated that the only way to form a script that would be universally intelligible was, to quote John Webster (here echoing Bacon), to use characters 'which are real, not nominal, expressing neither letters nor words, but things and notions.'⁷⁶ It was not merely the general intelligibility of such a real character (as it was commonly called) that appealed to so many seventeenth-century scholars. For, as we shall see more clearly shortly, the fact that language was brought in this way into a more direct relationship with 'things' was thought to have important consequences for an understanding of the natural world and for the progress of 'real knowledge.'

Accounts of Chinese often stressed the enormous number of characters that were required when separate signs were accorded to individual things. And early in the century it was supposed that a common writing would need a similarly vast number of individual characters. Bacon believed that there would be 'as many as are radical words.'⁷⁷ Hugo certainly assumed that a large number of characters would be required, defending this by arguing that even the least educated person manages to retain in his memory the thousands of words that are used in everyday speech, and that, since the Chinese learn them successfully, there is no reason why Europeans should not do the same.[78]

Nonetheless, although, the Chinese characters recognizably had important virtues, it was not generally considered that the multiplicity and complexity of the signs were among these. For example, after further consideration, De Vienne Plancy in a letter to the *Extraordinaire du Mercure* came to the characteristic conclusion that the trouble that the Chinese had in forming and recognizing their own written characters probably explained why other nations had not taken up this kind of writing, 'les autres Peuples ne s'étant pas trouvés d'humeur à passer, comme les Chinois, la plus grande partie de leur vie dans l'étude d'une Écriture dont tous les caractères sont si embarrassés, qu'ils semblent autant de labyrinthes.'[79] To an unnamed speaker at the Bureau d'Adresse in Paris some forty years earlier the art of character-writing appeared so diffuse that it would have been abandoned long ago, even among the Chinese, had there not been in operation a form of 'closed-shop' policy that allocated the highest posts in the magistrature and in the service of the state only to those who were fully versed in character-writing.[80]

Among the English language planners, many of whom refer to Chinese characters, the most detailed criticisms are to be found in John Wilkins's *Essay towards a Real Character and a Philosophical Language* (1668). Wilkins's analysis again reveals the disadvantages of the multiplicity of characters required, and of their complex structure. But not only are the Chinese characters too numerous, too complex, and too equivocal: they are also, Wilkins maintained, not truly representative of things. For he wrote that 'Besides the difficulty and perplexedness of these Characters, there doth not seem to be any kind of Analogy (so far as I am able to judge) betwixt the shape of the Characters, and the things represented by them, as to the Affinity or Opposition betwixt them, nor any tolerable provision for necessary derivations.'[81] And, since, by this time, the search had become a quest not merely for a simpler, briefer, more regular form of common writing, but for a philosophical 'real character' that would convey something of the order of reality, the Chinese characters were judged by Wilkins deficient in the light of these requirements. In this respect, his conclusion was that 'though in some particulars they seem to found their Character upon the *Philosophy of things*, yet 'tis not so in others ... It should seem to be observed only in some few *species* of nature which are most obvious, there being reason to doubt whether they had any such general Theory of Philosophy, as might serve for all other things and notions.'[82]

Although seventeenth-century assumptions concerning Chinese character-writing thus played an important part in directing attention to the possibility of establishing a real character for universal use, they did not, indeed could not, reveal any precise, satisfactory method according to which this would-be universal character could be constructed. For Chinese could provide no solution to the key problem of how one managed to achieve brevity, clarity, regularity, and simplicity in a real character, while still adequately representing the diversity and complexity of the natural world.

LANGUAGES, LANGUAGE, AND REAL STUDIES

If the emergence of the idea of a universal character in the first half of the seventeenth century can best be understood by reference to the vogue for various forms of writing in symbols, the interest with which such an idea was received is accounted for largely by certain attitudes towards existing languages and by the demands that were being made of language in general. Even though only the briefest portrayal of such attitudes is possible here, a broad survey will go some way towards explaining why the formulation of an artificial, 'real character' was thought to have such importance.

At the opening of the century the various vernaculars of Western Europe had reached very different stages in their growth. By her relatively rapid espousal of Tuscan, Italy had set a pattern for the subsequent development of the other vulgar tongues. The growth of national consciousness and pride, and the economic needs of an expanding printing industry had further encouraged their cultivation, in spite of opposition from reactionaries in many fields. Use of the chief vernaculars in poetry, drama, the liturgy and propaganda of the Reformed Church,[83] and certain kinds of scientific books destined primarily for a non-Latin public meant that they needed to be greatly enriched by means of newly coined words (often of a technical kind) and by frequent borrowings from other languages. On the other hand, the Renaissance insistence upon a return to pure classical Latin meant that this language tended to appear to many to be increasingly unsuited to modern needs.

In France and Italy the vernacular had been regularized, until, even before the seventeenth century, it had achieved a remarkably high degree of efficiency.[84] The progress of English was slower until the middle of the century, when a profusion of grammars and dictionaries tended to add the qualities of regularity and stability to the eloquence that the language of the Elizabethans had already possessed. German was, of course, even further retarded, in spite of the works of propaganda of Martin Luther, his translation of the Bible into the vernacular, and the efforts of such a distinguished scholar as Johann Tritheim to encourage the use of the vernacular.

Yet even taking into account these differences in development, it is broadly speaking true that, throughout the sixteenth and early seventeenth centuries, the leading vernaculars of Europe gradually encroached more and more into fields which had hitherto been reserved for Latin alone. Important books in growing numbers were published in the vernacular so that by the middle decades of the seventeenth century what may be termed the language situation was already becoming more than a little confused. In particular, the danger of this situation was that publication in one vernacular of the results of experiments conducted by a distinguished scientist like Galileo Galilei,[85] or later by Fellows of the Royal Society, or members of the Académie Royale des Sciences, meant that scientists from other countries, though working in parallel fields, might be unable easily to take account of their colleagues' discoveries. This situation is one with which we are familiar today, but to the world of learning at that time such a confusion of tongues was both novel and disconcerting. Mersenne expressed this concern most cogently in 1640, when he wrote in a letter to Theodore Haack, 'Vous avez raison de dire, que ni Dieu, ni les sciences ne sont point liées aux langues, et en effect, chacune est capable d'expliquer toute chose; mais le malheur est qu'il faudrait les entendre toutes, pour participer aux labeurs de ceux qui escrivent en celles qu'on n'entend pas.'[86]

One possible solution to this growing problem was, of course, that scholars should learn several vernaculars other than their own. But educational practice in England and on the Continent was so firmly geared to the teaching of the classical language that in order to render such a solution at all practicable a major reform in the teaching of the grammar schools, *collèges*, and universities would have been necessary. As matters stood, particularly in England, the private tutor and the 'Grand Tour' (though not so named until 1670),[87] were the only means of acquiring a good working knowledge of modern foreign languages. Although the French, the Spanish, and the Italians were more familiar with each other's languages, a knowledge of English was relatively rare in these countries and few scientists and scholars had sufficient command of several vernaculars to conduct their exchanges in any language other than Latin. This was one of several reasons why the 'disseminator of information,' in the persons of such cosmopolitan figures as Hartlib, Haack, and Oldenburg, could play such an important role in the mid-seventeenth century.

Yet it was not merely the firm classical tradition of schools and universities that made learning a number of languages seem an unwelcome, as well as an impracticable, solution to the problem of communication. For the seventeenth-century scientific world had as one of its chief characteristics the desire to stress the importance of 'things' rather than 'words.' Such a view argued against the acceptance of a solution that would inevitably mean that time would be wasted in learning two, three, or more languages, instead of one.

A second solution to the problem posed by the rise of the vernacular – one which was, in fact, commonly adopted – was to republish in Latin books first composed in the vulgar tongue. And so, to take only three well-known examples, the writings of Robert Boyle, the *Philosophical Transactions of the Royal Society*, and Descartes's *Principes de la philosophie* were all reissued in Latin translations. Samuel Hartlib's so far unpublished *Ephemerides* contain numerous references to plans for the translation of works first published in the lesser-known vernaculars. Mersenne, in the letter to Haack which has already been quoted, hoped for the institution in each kingdom of an academy consisting of fifteen or twenty men who would be charged with the translation of whatever seemed worthwhile into 'la langue commune de l'Europe chretienne, qui est la Latine.'[88] Republication in Latin went some way towards solving the problem, but at the same time it created fresh difficulties and inconveniences. Most important of these perhaps was the fact that, at a time when knowledge was consciously felt to be advancing extremely rapidly in certain areas, it seemed more and more difficult to cover adequately the output in the various vernaculars, hence it was likely that important works would be passed over or would appear only years after the original versions had been published. To some translation and republication seemed then little more than a rather cumbersome stopgap.

Since it appeared at that time exceedingly unlikely that any one of the European vernaculars would rise to the status of an international language to take the place of Latin – French did not stake a serious claim to this honour until the end of the seventeenth century – there remained the tempting possibility that man might construct a wholly new, artificial universal character that would be simpler to learn and to use, more regular, and closer to the world of material realities than any of the existing languages.

There was, however, another factor that was more important than the rise of the vernacular in creating a climate favourable to the idea of a universal character – the growing feeling of dissatisfaction with languages in general and with Latin, the existing international language, in particular, that characterized the scientific and scholarly circles in which language schemes flourished.

Throughout the sixteenth and the early seventeenth centuries, the criticisms that were made of Latin, with few exceptions, concerned primarily the manner in which it was taught, rather than the language itself. And so it was often argued that far too much time was wasted in learning the language in a way that was cumbersome and relatively unsuccessful. The blame for this situation was usually laid squarely at the door of the grammarians. Consequently, various new methods were proposed for teaching the classical language in a more effective way. From Erasmus and Vives onwards, the emphasis in these proposed reforms was usually placed upon 'customary grammar': grammar should be taught only as a quick preliminary to the study of the language in the work of classical writers; the language should be used in speech and composition; and it should serve as a way of reaching the 'solid things' expressed in the ancient language. The recommendation that the rules of Latin should, in the main, be learned inductively from actual writings, and that the classical language should be used in speech and composition was stressed by Sir Thomas Elyot in *The Boke Named the Governour* in 1531, Roger Ascham in *The Scholemaster* in 1570, Scipion de Gramont in his *Abbrégé des artifices* in 1606 and Joseph Webbe in *An Appeal to Truth* in 1622.

It might at first appear that so great a concern with finding the most efficient way of teaching Latin could do little but consolidate its standing in Europe. Yet the increasing irritation aroused by the arduous, time-consuming methods of the formal grammarians is symptomatic of a greater concern for speedy access to the knowledge which the ancient language contained.

The important language reforms suggested in the middle years of the century by Comenius, took this development a stage further by associating much more closely a word and the thing it represented, and by aiming to use Latin from the outset as a means of acquiring knowledge about the world. He wrote, for example:

> The study of languages, especially in youth, should be joined to that of objects, that our acquaintance with the objective world and with language, that is to say, our knowledge of facts and our power to express them, may progress side by side. For it is men that we are forming and not parrots ... From this it follows, firstly, that words should not be learned apart from the objects to which they refer; since the objects do not exist separately and cannot be apprehended without words, but both exist and perform their functions together.[89]

Coming after the Vernacular school in his reformed educational system, the Latin school was intended to continue a child's introduction to 'real studies' by the use of new textbooks written according to these guiding principles.[90] Comenius's textbooks were, in effect, an effort to achieve a workable compromise between a traditional philological training and the requirements of the new experimental science. The language of medieval scholarship is retained but is put to a new use. Hence the 'study of things' becomes possible *by means of* the 'study of words,' rather than the one appearing to be in direct opposition to the other.

Latin was retained in Comenius's proposed curriculum partly because it provided a key to ancient learning (until such time as an encyclopedia of ancient knowledge could be compiled), and partly because it served as the only existing international language. Yet Comenius was far from regarding Latin as ideally suited to perform this latter function. He agreed with Vives that, if another better language could not be found, Latin should be used rather than any of the existing vernaculars.[91] But, conscious of the need to communicate easily with the inhabitants of the new worlds to east and west, he objected that the use of Latin greatly favoured Europeans, and that it lacked the perfection that should be found in a language worthy of international usage. For Comenius found Latin defective in several important respects. First, because of its difficulty, it required many years of study; secondly, it was full of variety in the cases of its nouns and was irregular in its declensions, in the moods and tenses of its verbs, and in its syntax; thirdly, it was poor in composite terms, hence lacking in richness; and finally, it was, he maintained, full of ambiguities, redundancies, and confusion. In view of these defects, Latin, he wrote, 'falls short of unity and simplicity, never approaches the perfection which is needed, and therefore is inadequate both in itself and in regard to the subjects of discourse.'[92] In reaction against these imperfections, as well as for the more positive reasons already touched upon, Comenius looked forward hopefully to the provision of an artificial language, 'a language absolutely new, absolutely easy, absolutely rational.'[93]

In his *Essay towards a Real Character and a Philosophical Language* (1668) – certainly the most impressive attempt in the seventeenth century to provide a universal character and a spoken version of that character – John Wilkins dwelt at considerable length on the many defects of Latin, which, he wrote, 'doth in these parts of the world supply the place of a Common Tongue.'[94] He pointed out that defects abounded in the language, in that its alphabet in one respect has too many letters and in another too few; its words have a variety of meanings; ambiguity results from the use of metaphor and idiom; and its syntax has a superabundance of unnecessary rules. Yet, he continued, 'It cannot be denied but that all these Rules are necessary to the *Latin* tongue; but this argues the imperfection of that Language, that it should stand in need of such and so many Rules as have no foundation in the *Philosophy of Speech*.'[95]

These highly critical remarks by Wilkins and Comenius should not be confused with some of the more virulent attacks that were made upon Latin in England during the Commonwealth by the more fanatical of the Puritan reformers, for whom the classical tongue was at once the language of the Papal beast, paganism, and traditional scholastic learning. The former stemmed rather from a coherent critique of language in general that needs to be rightly understood before the significance for learning of the later schemes of a 'real character and a philosophical language' can properly be appreciated. And if we look first at some of the more moderate attitudes to language found in Puritan proposals for educational reform, it is with a view to discerning a more general climate of opinion that was to some extent common to both Puritan and non-Puritan circles.

'Tongues,' wrote John Dury, 'are no further finally usefull then to enlarge Traditionall Learning; and without their subordination unto Arts and Sciences, they are worth nothing towards the advancement of our Happiness.'[96] Modern languages served only 'to Understand what others say to us, according to their custome of speaking; and to express our mind unto them significantly according to our custome.'[97] As for Latin it was useful only as a key to the knowledge handed on from the past. For John Milton, in the treatise entitled *Of Education: To Master Samuel Hartlib*, the primary purpose of learning Latin and Greek was for the 'solid things' contained in them, and Sir Thomas Urquhart commented wryly in the *Ekskubalouron* (1652), 'What I have delivered in freedome of the learned Languages, I would not have wrested to a sinister sense, as if I meant anything to their disparagement; for truly I think the time well bestowed, which boyes in their tender yeers employ towards the learning of them, in a Subordination to the excellent things that in them are couched.'[98]

Languages were to be learned, then, for purely functional reasons and language teaching needed to be suited to the practical needs of the individual: Latin would be taught therefore to the scholar, while modern languages would be learned only by the person who needed them for purposes of travel or trade. Further, since languages were considered as no more than the shell in which real knowledge was contained, no particular glory could be claimed for knowing more than was required for these practical purposes. So John Webster, a fervent Baconian and a keen admirer of Comenius's reforms in language teaching, asserted:

> If a man had the perfect knowledge of many, nay all languages, that he could give unto man, beast, bird, fish, plant, mineral, or any other numerical creature or thing, their distinct and proper names in twenty several *Idioms*, or *Dialects*, yet knows he no more thereby, than he that can onely name them in his mother tongue, for the intellect receives no other nor further notion thereby, for the senses receive but one numerical species or *Ideal*-shape from every individual thing, though by institution and imposition, twenty, or one hundred names be given unto it, according to the *Idiome* of several nations.[99]

For this reason it appeared to Webster that scholars were wasting both time and effort in acquiring what he called 'some small scantling and smattering in the tongues'; in the end they had obtained no more knowledge than they would have gained in the one language, except an ability 'like Parrats to babble and prattle.'[100]

Behind this strictly functional view of language there clearly lay a belief in the over-riding importance of the 'real knowledge' to which language should provide swift and easy access. For in the mid-seventeenth century the 'solid truths' of the new experimental philosophy were commonly contrasted with the book-knowledge and empty wordiness of much of scholastic learning. In the work of John Wilkins, William Petty, Samuel Hartlib, and Robert Boyle, for instance, the study of things was set against (to use Petty's term) a 'Rabble of Words,'[101] and 'real knowledge,' promoting the genuine advancement of learning, was contrasted with the useless disputations of a stagnant Aristotelianism.

Puritan projects for educational reform thus firmly emphasized that, in teaching, the study of words should be subordinated to the study of things.[102] Consequently John Dury wrote:

Whatsoever in the teaching of Tongues doth not tend to make them a help unto Traditionall Knowledge, by the manifestation of Reall Truths in Sciences, is superfluous, and not to be insisted upon, especially towards Children, whence followeth that the Curious study of Criticismes, and observation of Styles in Authors, and of straines of wit, which speak nothing of Reality in Sciences, are to be left to such as delight in vanityes more then in Truths.[103]

To this end, certain modifications in the existing structure and curriculum of the schools and universities were proposed. The emphasis upon real studies would affect the choice of subjects to be taught in the reformed schools. Chemistry, anatomy, botany, and gardening, for instance, would come on to the curriculum, while the older subjects would be treated in a much more practical manner, the emphasis being placed upon their importance to the advancement of learning and upon the material benefits that they could bring to society as a whole.[104] At a higher educational level, if the proposed reforms of Dury, Hartlib, Webster, Hall, Petty, Hooke, and Cowley had in fact been successful, the universities would early have become research-cum-teaching institutes, aimed primarily at providing a form of vocational training, at collecting the mechanical knowledge of the past and assembling it in accessible form, and at conducting research into many fields of natural studies.

Secondly, it was felt by Puritan reformers that young children learn best through the senses and the imagination. They believed therefore that it was wise to appeal to this natural capacity by introducing the young as often as possible to natural objects either directly or by means of illustrations. Since the mother tongue seemed to offer the easiest and most natural way of introducing the young to 'real and useful knowledge,' they argued that the vernacular should be the first and principal language in which a child should be taught. Latin would therefore either be entirely excluded from the curriculum, experimental philosophy replacing classical studies even in the universities, or, since Latin remained of some use as the language of ancient learning (not all of which could be rejected), study of it should be deferred until a later stage in the child's education, when it could be introduced in a manner much more relevant to contemporary needs. For at this point

Comenius's 'real' method of language teaching could continue to enlarge and deepen the child's knowledge by substituting Latin for the vernacular as the linguistic medium in which 'solid truths' were to be taught.

The chief aim of the Puritan reformers in this area was therefore to provide the easiest possible access to real knowledge: hence the proposed introduction of the vernacular, the deferment of Latin until a later stage in the curriculum, and certain recommended changes in curriculum and teaching methods.

Yet to certain reformers, and to a number of the new scientists and *virtuosi*, including some of those who were to form the nucleus of the Royal Society of London, these proposals took no account of the potentially grave obstacle that the use of *any* existing language, whether ancient or modern, could present to the progress of learning. Nor did they do anything to bring language into any form of closer union with real knowledge. For it is often forgotten that the seventeenth-century schemes of universal writing and philosophical language arose not only out of attitudes that were condemnatory of existing languages, but also from a keen desire to forge a new, more direct relationship between words and objects, a remarkable ambition that, has rarely been properly understood since Richard Foster Jones's early criticisms of these schemes as 'degrading' language.

The seventeenth-century critique of language had its roots in the remarks made by Francis Bacon in the *Novum organum* and in the *De augmentis scientiarum* on the 'idols of the market-place.' These particular idols, which Bacon regarded as the most troublesome of all, were the errors which all too easily could creep into the understanding through misalliances of words and things. Such errors in themselves could constitute a major obstacle to the progress of knowledge, for, wrote Bacon, 'men believe that their reason governs words, but it is also true that words react on the understanding; and this it is that has rendered philosophy and the sciences sophistical and inactive.'[105] The frequently nefarious influence of language resulted, according to Bacon, from two principal imperfections: the admission of words for things which have no existence at all in the real world and the attribution of names to objects in a confused, distorted, and quite arbitrary manner.

As Paolo Rossi has rightly pointed out, Bacon's views on language should not be regarded as revealing a fierce antipathy to language as such, though there was in his work a reaction against the sterile wordiness of the peripatetic tradition.[106] Bacon clearly realized that language was important, and that it could be either an aid or an obstacle to an understanding of the real world. In a positive sense, his ideal appears to have been a language in which a word stands for an object in a constant, unequivocal relation with it, intervening as little as possible between a natural object and its apprehension, recollection, and representation by the human mind.

Partly as a consequence of Bacon's brief consideration of the errors that can affect the understanding, existing languages came to be subjected to many adverse criticisms in the mid-seventeenth century. For example, the aim of William Petty's 'Dictionary of Sensible Words' (which was not written until 1685, but was characteristic of his general preoccupation with clarity of meaning) was 'to curtail all verbal superfluity and insignificancy, in short, to sweep away all the fogginess of words.'[107] In *A Free Inquiry into the Vulgarly Received Notion of Nature* Robert Boyle drew attention to the ambiguity of the word *Nature* and other commonly used terms to which no exact meaning could be given. Boyle's hope was that philosophers and other learned men would 'introduce some more significant, and less ambiguous terms and expressions in the room of the too licenciously abused word nature, and the forms of speech that depend on it; or would, at least, decline the use of it, as much as conveniently they can: and where they think they must employ it, would add a word or two, to declare in what clear and determinate sense they use it.'[108] More detailed criticisms of language came from the exuberant pen of the English translator of Rabelais, Sir Thomas Urquhart, who objected to the inadequacy of all the alphabets known to him: 'one lacking those letters which another hath, none having all, and all of them *in cumulo* lacking some. But that which makes the defect so much the greater, is, that these same few consonants and vowels commonly made use of, are never by two Nations pronounced after the same fashion.'[109]

But the most comprehensive critique of existing languages is to be found in John Wilkins's *Essay towards a Real Character and a Philosophical Language* (1668) in which he discussed not only the defects of Latin but the imperfections of all the languages known to him. The defects quoted by Wilkins were so numerous that only one or two of the major categories can be referred to here. Misunderstandings frequently arose, he stated, because one word often has a variety of meanings: for example, *liber*, *malus*, and *populus* in Latin; and in English the word *bill* meaning *a weapon*, *a bird's beak*, or *a written scroll*, and the word *grave* meaning *sober*, *a sepulchre*, or *to carve*.[110] The ambiguity caused by the use of metaphor and 'phraseology' (by which Wilkins meant native idioms) constituted a second major defect of language: 'This is in all instituted Languages so obvious and so various, that it is needless to give any instances of it; every Language having some peculiar phrases belonging to it; which, if they were to be translated *verbatim* into another Tongue, would seem wild and insignificant. In which our English doth too much abound.'[111]

Among the other defects noted by Wilkins were the abundance of synonyms which all languages possess, the anomalies and irregularities in their grammatical constructions, and the differences that exist between the orthography and the pronunciation of a language. Even Chinese characters were seen on closer inspection to be as imperfect as either Latin or the European vernaculars.[112] That defects were discovered in so many languages seemed to confirm Wilkins in his belief that imperfections had developed along with the languages themselves. For, he wrote:

> There are no Letters or Languages that have been at once invented and established according to the Rules of Art; but that all, except the first ... have been either taken up from that first, and derived by way of *Imitation*; or else, in a long tract of time, have, upon several emergencies, admitted various and *casual alterations*; by which means they must needs be liable to manifold defects and imperfections, that in a Language at once invented and according to the *rules of Art* might be easily avoided.[113]

Such an awareness of the faults of existing languages was by no means confined to England, although it received its fullest expression in the work of English scholars and scientists. Numerous references could be given to similar criticisms in the work of Continental writers, although the ideas of only three such scholars, all of whom were involved in the search for a universal language, are quoted here. Descartes, in a letter to Mersenne about a universal language based upon the relationships between ideas, stated that such a language 'aiderait au jugement, lui représentant si distinctement toutes choses qu'il lui serait presque impossible de se tromper; au lieu que tout au rebours, les mots que nous avons n'ont quasi que des significations confuses, auxquelles l'esprit des hommes s'étant accoutumé de longue main, cela est cause qu'il n'entend presque rien parfaitement.'[114] Mersenne himself in his *Harmonie universelle* (1636) defined the best language as that which expressed 'les pensées de l'esprit et les désirs de la volonté' as clearly and as briefly as possible.[115] And so, conscious of those defects that have arisen with the development of languages, Mersenne concluded that, since the letters, syllables, and pronunciation of these letters were quite arbitrary and meant only what we intended them to mean, one should consider the possibility that human ingenuity might indeed contrive to invent this best of all possible languages.[116] For Comenius, words were attached to things without regard for the nature of the things themselves, and so 'the basic qualities of things are not revealed either by the habit of speech or by the reciprocal harmony between things and names ... For since their words are not exactly commensurate with things, they are unable to form concepts in exact fitness to the things (of which they speak). And so for all the noise of doctrines and discussions we scarcely advance an inch in the study of wisdom: because we speak words, not things.'[117]

To propose a radical shift of emphasis from words to natural studies, as the Puritan reformers had done, did not, of course, remove the necessity for the use of language. Moreover, one may discern in the mid-seventeenth century a growing awareness among scientists of the need for accuracy in the reporting and communication of experiments. The scientist asked of language that it should be regular, clear, precise, and, above all, unequivocal. Instead he found existing languages to be full of irregularities, inconsistencies, anomalies, and illogicalities: a situation which clearly made some reform of language a matter of urgent concern.

In the *Leviathan* Hobbes elaborated upon Bacon's survey of the errors that can creep into the understanding by pointing to four corresponding abuses of language:

> First, when men register their thoughts wrong, by the inconstancy of the signification of their words; by which they register for their conception, that which they never conceived; and so deceive themselves. Secondly, when they use words metaphorically; that is, in other sense than that they are ordained for; and thereby deceive others. Thirdly, when by words they declare to be their will, which is not. Fourthly, when they use them to grieve one another.[118]

To combat these abuses, the man who seeks for truth must, Hobbes recommended, 'remember what every name he uses stands for; and to place it accordingly; or else he will find himselfe entangled in words, as a bird in lime twiggs; the more he struggles, the more belimed.'[119] He must take care also to trust words no more than they deserve, 'for words are wise mens counters, they do but reckon by them; but they are the many of fooles, that value them by the authority of an Aristotle, a Cicero, or a Thomas, or any other doctor whatever, if but a man.'[120]

Hobbes's recommendations for extreme caution in the use of words, for the need of strict definitions, and for the avoidance of metaphor at least in scientific discourse were shared by many men of science of the seventeenth century. William Petty and Robert Boyle, for example, proposed as a remedy for the worst defects of language a strict examination of the words we employ, in order to discover those which have no clear meaning, to clarify the meaning of all vague terms, and to exclude from use those words which have no real meaning at all.[121] This cautious approach to language, arising out of a concern for the clear, untrammelled expression of real knowledge, was adopted by the Royal Society and was recommended by that body as promoting a plain, precise style best fitted to scientific communications. According to Thomas Sprat, in a well-known passage of his *History of the Royal Society*, there was

> a constant Resolution, to reject all the amplifications, digressions,

and swellings of style: to return back to the primitive purity, and shortness, when men deliver'd so many *things*, almost in an equal number of *words*. They [the Royal Society] have exacted from all their members, a close, naked, natural way of speaking; positive expressions; clear senses; a native easiness: bringing all things as near the Mathematical plainness, as they can: and preferring the language of Artizans, Countrymen, and Merchants, before that, of Wits, or Scholars.'[122]

To a number of scholars and scientists in the middle decades of the century, however, a compromise solution of this kind appeared inadequate. Francis Bacon had already doubted the efficacy of definition in curing the ills of language, 'since the definitions themselves consist of words, and these words beget others.'[123] Recognition of the many defects that have grown up with language, together with the desire for a language much more closely related to knowledge, encouraged the acceptance of a further, far more radical solution, namely that a new language might be invented by men that would avoid the defects of existing languages, be regular, simple, and easy to learn and use, and represent objects and ideas directly, thus bypassing the varied sounds of speech. And so a universal character came to be placed by a large number of thinkers among the chief *desiderata* of learning.

The aim was not simply to construct a readable pasigraphy, which could be understood by peoples speaking different vernaculars, but to provide an instrument that would remedy the confusion caused by the imperfections as well as by the diversity of languages. Even the clumsy, elementary scheme of arithmetical numbers proposed in 1657 by Cave Beck, Rector of Saint Helens, Ipswich, was regarded by its author as representing an improvement upon all defective spoken languages:

This last Century of years much hath been the discourse and expectation of learned men, concerning the finding out of an *Universal Character*, which if happily contrived, so as to avoid all Equivocal words, Anomalous variations and superfluous Synonomas (with which all Languages are encumbered and rendred difficult to the learner) would much advantage mankind in their civil commerce and be a singular means of propagating all sorts of Learning and true Religion in the World.[124]

Beck's scheme, which could be learned, he claimed, in only a week of study, was intended to provide such a universal character. Father Philippe Labbé in the *Grammaire de la langue universelle des missions et du commerce* similarly envisaged his language as essentially simple and regular, avoiding the exceptions of other languages, and composed in the main of words of only one or two syllables.[125]

One of the chief recommendations of a language of 'real characters' for the seventeenth-century scholar and man of science was that, unlike all known languages, it would not impede the progress and communication of learning. This was not only because the new universal writing was to be unique in the simplicity and regularity of its forms; nor was it simply because, as a result of this invention, it was hoped that *'Arts* would arrive at a high perfection in a little space, and we might reckon upon *more time* ... to be employed in *substantial study of Matter.*'[126] The characters of the new language were to represent *directly* objects or notions of the mind that were common to all men; that is to say, a symbol or real character would stand for a thing or an idea, rather than for a sound or a collection of sounds. And so, instead of being an obstacle to learning, it was intended that a language of real characters would be an active aid to the progress of real studies. Seen in this light its appeal to those scholars who had the advancement of learning at heart becomes far more readily understandable. It was partly for this reason that William Petty suggested that boys should be taught to read and write in real characters as well as in their own mother tongue, and that John Webster wrote in 1654, 'What a vast advancement had it been to the Re-publick of Learning, and hugely profitable to all mankind, if the discovery of the universal Character (hinted at by some judicious Authors) had been wisely and laboriously pursued and brought to perfection.'[127]

Yet it was not merely the directness of the relation between the character and the thing represented that rendered the idea so attractive to many distinguished seventeenth-century scientists and scholars. It was the nature of the relation itself. For, as we have already suggested, in the middle decades of the century attention came to be focused increasingly upon the possibility of constructing a written character, and perhaps a spoken language, which would represent by the very distribution and combination of its characters either a scientific description of natural objects or a philosophical ordering of ideas. The probable reasons for this shift of emphasis to a language of scientific description or philosophical analysis will be examined in chapter three. Yet it should be borne in mind that there was no sudden change from one set of requirements to another. Universal characters continued to be published which were constructed on non-philosophical lines. And, as DeMott has pointed out, part of the difficulty with the more ambitious plans for a philosophical language lay in the need to keep the new languages simple, regular, and easy to learn and use, while still reflecting as accurately as possible the structures of the natural world.[128]

Nonetheless, it was above all the exciting possibility of constructing a real character and a philosophical language that could be directly representative of the world of material realities that aroused so much interest in the 1650s and 1660s, particularly among a group of members of the Royal Society and their associates and friends. For such a philosophically constructed language would reveal knowledge through its very terminology and, what is more, knowledge of the most up-to-date, exact, and profound kind. Hardly surprisingly, such a project appeared to George Dalgarno as 'more accommodated for an emphatic delivery of real Truths, and the grounds and precepts of Arts and Sciences, than any other Language.'[129] For, as Comenius pointed out in the *Via lucis* (1668), 'to be skilled in it shall greatly help us towards the understanding of things themselves.'[130] For this reason above any other the construction of a universal language came to be considered as of vital importance to the progress and diffusion of learning, and so, wrote John Wilkins, 'to be preferred before that [work of dictionary making] as *things* are better then *words*, as *real knowledge* is beyond *elegancy of speech*, as the *general good of mankind*, is beyond that of any *particular Countrey* or *Nation*".[131]

2/ Early schemes for a common writing

Accounts of the earliest efforts to construct a universal character usually begin with Descartes's letter to Mersenne of November 1629.[1] But, after looking at a number of the factors that first prompted an interest in this question, it seems clear that the idea of some form of common writing was relatively familiar long before that date. Vivian Salmon has referred to an early discussion of the subject in Theodore Bibliander's *De ratione communi omnium linguarum* of 1548,[2] and we have already noted that Dr Timothy Bright's 'Characterie', although conceived primarily as a method of shorthand writing, was also regarded by its author as capable of fulfilling a purpose very similar to that of early seventeenth-century schemes of universal writing.

There was thus nothing particularly unusual about the appearance in the late 1620s of the anonymous prospectus that outlined a universal character and provoked Descartes's criticism, except that in this work the desire to provide a set of symbols which would be universally intelligible had become central rather than secondary to its author's concerns. And yet, even in this respect the project was not unique, for interest in some elementary form of universal writing was far more common in the early years of the century than has generally been appreciated. Writers on China and things Chinese had drawn attention to the tremendous usefulness of a written character intelligible to men speaking different languages. Francis Bacon had alluded to the convenience of such a system of real characters in the *De augmentis scientiarum* of 1605, while in 1617 Hermann Hugo actually called for the institution of a universal character, comparing Chinese characters with a number of symbols already in use among the European nations. He pointed out that all men recognize the sign of the Zodiac that stands for Taurus, although they may differ completely in the words which they use to describe it.[3] And so Hugo concluded that 'si singulae literae impositae essent, non vocibus, sed rebus ipsis significandis, eaeque essent hominibus omnibus communes; omnes omnino homines, etiamsi gentes singulae res singulas diversis nominibus appellent, singularum gentium scriptionem intelligerent.'[4]

Claims to have answered this demand for a common writing were already fairly frequent in the second and third decades of the seventeenth century, although, to the best of my knowledge, no actual scheme appeared in print until the late 1640s. Most claimants in fact drew a deliberate veil of secrecy over their own version of the universal character, withholding all details of the principles upon which their schemes were constructed. This was done partly in an attempt to avoid the intellectual piracy that was so rife at the time, and partly in the hope of deriving some measure of financial reward, profit, or simply distinction, from an invention which appeared of the greatest importance to its originators.[5] In the form in which these earliest schemes are known to us, they are therefore no more than 'projects of projects.'[6] There were too among these early proponents of a common writing undoubtedly a number of total charlatans, whose claims were either entirely bogus or greatly overstated. Yet, although taken singly they are too slight to merit very much individual discussion, as a group these suggestions for a universal character reveal much about the attitudes and aims, if relatively little about the specific methods, of the first language planners.

The earliest projects concerned with a universal character that have so far come to light were announced or described in the 1620s. The first of these, which is both the fullest and the only one to be printed, remains nonetheless little more than a prospectus, published in 1627 and dedicated to Louis XIII with the acknowledged intention of gaining the latter's support for the scheme of an 'escriture universelle.'[7] Its author, Jean Douet, 'Sieur de Rompcroissant,' claimed that he had discovered a system of universal writing which, the title of the work informs us, was 'admirable pour ses effects, tres-utile et necessaire à tous les hommes de la terre.' Douet described the diversity of languages as the third curse of mankind. But, unlike the two other principal curses which could not be remedied – the Flood being a historical fact, and death the necessary condition of our mortal state – the confusion of tongues, originating in the time of Nenbrot with the building of the tower of Babel, could, Douet maintained, be removed by a form of universal writing, which he had been granted the privilege to discover. Since the diversity of languages was responsible for man being separated from his fellow-man as well as from much of his literary, religious, and scientific heritage, the removal of such an obstacle was accounted by Douet second only in importance to the discovery of writing and superior to the invention of printing. The emergence of the idea of a universal character from a consideration of hieroglyphs, shorthand notes, and Chinese character-writing is seen quite clearly in Douet's work, as is the inadequacy of all these three forms of writing, which are treated there as being too difficult to learn, remember, use, or interpret.

By contrast, one of the principal advantages of the new character was, Douet claimed, the tremendous ease with which it could be written, remembered, and understood. Another important virtue was the versatility of the character, which could be written either syllabically, forming words, or in what Douet called 'Figures mystiques,' like Egyptian hieroglyphs or Chinese characters. Moreover, the new character had the additional advantage of conforming to almost any system of writing (i.e. from left to right, right to left, top to bottom, in columns) and of being so composed that, it was claimed, the new characters, unlike the words of existing languages, would remain unchanged after centuries of use. Douet did not describe the precise method followed in the construction of this character, but he did reveal that it was a system of signs that could be read off by every person in his own language, suggesting that the principle was that of assigning a character or characters to words in different languages that have the same meaning. An Englishman would then read off from a universal writing-English dictionary the meaning of a particular character, which a Frenchman would arrive at by means of a corresponding universal writing-French dictionary. So cumbersome a method of translating can hardly be thought to live up to the extravagant claims made for the character, and the absence of any later, more elaborate version of the scheme suggests that Douet's pleas for support fell on deaf ears.

On the other side of the Channel, in a correspondence that took place in 1628 between Philip Kinder and William Beveridge, the vicar of Barrow in Leicestershire, there is talk of the universal character of 'our ould and learned friend Monsieur de la Champagnolle.'[8] Although virtually nothing is known about Champagnolle's actual scheme, his name crops up several times in later discussions of the subject. Several years after Champagnolle's death, which probably occurred in 1643, it is clear from Samuel Hartlib's *Ephemerides* that William Petty and Seth Ward, as well as Sir William Boswell, were involved in negotiations with his widow concerning the publication rights of his universal character.[9] Although she was asking for a hundred pounds, Petty declared firmly, after studying a short key to it, that he would be very unwilling to pay her even sixpence for it, a judgment with which, apparently, Ward was in entire agreement.[10] With this learned and radical condemnation in its wake, Champagnolle's scheme makes no further serious appearance in scholarly discussion, although Vivian Salmon has identified it as the character referred to by Ward in the *Vindiciae academiarum*, where he recounted that several books of Homer, translated into a universal character, had been shown to King Charles.[11]

Philip Kinder claimed in the letter to Beveridge that he had solved the mystery of Champagnolle's universal character. But the solution that he arrived at is far more likely to have represented his own version than any interpretation of Champagnolle's scheme. Champagnolle had stressed, we are told, the vastness of the enterprise, the cost of which '... would be many thousands, ye people to conduct some hundred for many dayes, ye books a voluminous Index, ye manner to understand ye Character painfull, till a good memorie in a large tyme had confirmed it.'[12] Kinder stressed, on the other hand, the simplicity and ease of his own idea of the universal character, which could be learned by even an ordinary man in the space of two hours. And so he went on:

I challenge you, were we both ignorant of each other's language, or were this Prototype presented unto a High-German's hands, would not you or he presently resolve it into his native language; will you reade or write extempore this Character (good catholick) ye manner is easie, expedite, for ye succeeding number and row of Alphabett coupled hand in hand, is a true methode for an artificiall locall memorie, which is most capacious, most retentive.[13]

One of the principal reasons for the ease with which, it was claimed, Kinder's character could be learned was that the symbols were assigned according to a mnemonically satisfying method, a link with the *ars memorativa* tradition which will be explored rather more fully in connection with later schemes. The character adopted by Kinder appears in fact to have been based primarily upon the use of numbers, for at the end of the letter he writes 'behould ye misterie; it is number figure; this is al and summ. Thank Pythagoras that I have slept in's lap.'[14] In addition to numbers, certain special signs were used to distinguish gender, number, and tense. The masculine was signified, for example, by a single, upright line sloping to the right, the feminine by one sloping to the left; plurality was indicated by a stroke resembling an apostrophe, while tenses were represented by a variety of symbols, some of which were inspired by hieroglyphics ('somethings we have borrowed from ye Aegyptians,' wrote Kinder).

The fourth project chronologically is of interest chiefly because it prompted Descartes's well-known letter to Mersenne rather than for any particular virtue of the universal character itself. Indeed, since the prospectus itself has not been preserved, our knowledge is confined to what may be gleaned from Descartes's passing description and criticism[15] (Descartes's own very different proposals are considered in the next chapter).

Even the identity of the author of this prospectus has not yet been satisfactorily established. In the second volume of the *Correspondance* of Mersenne[16] it was suggested that it might well be the work of a certain 'des Vallées,' mentioned by Charles Sorel in *De la perfection de l'homme*,[17] and by Tallemant des Réaux in his *Historiettes*.[18] However, in later volumes of the correspondence,[19] the former editor, Cornélis de Waard, attributed it instead to Claude Hardy, a gifted mathematician and orientalist,[20] who was well known to both Descartes and Mersenne, and this attribution has been repeated several times since.[21]

Mersenne's recent editor, the late Bernard Rochot, convincingly refuted this attribution with a number of detailed arguments that it is unnecessary to repeat here.[22] Yet it is easier at present to show who was *not* the author of this prospectus than to determine who was. In the absence of further documentary evidence it seems reasonable to return to the earlier hypothesis of des Vallées, for a number of the other possible candidates can be immediately eliminated. Jean Douet had already published his *Proposition ... d'une escriture universelle* (1627) two years earlier in French, while it is clear that the prospectus to which Descartes referred was written in Latin. Le Maire, whose ideas we shall consider in a moment, is certainly *hors concours* for he was not known to Mersenne until six years later when he first came to Paris in 1635. And no connection has as yet been established between Mersenne and Champagnolle, who was resident in England in 1628 in the county of Huntingdonshire. Of the des Vallées mentioned by Cornélis de Waard we know virtually nothing except what is recounted of him by Sorel and Tallemant des Réaux. The latter relates in the *Historiettes*:

> Il y avait à Vitré en Bretagne, un avocat peu employé, nommé des Vallées. Cet homme était si né aux langues qu'en moins de rien il les devinait, en faisait la syntaxe et le dictionnaire. En cinq ou six leçons il montrait l'hébreu. Il prétendait avoir trouvé une langue matrice qui lui faisait entendre toutes les autres. Le cardinal de Richelieu le fit venir ici, mais il se brouilla avec de Muys, le professeur en langue hébraïque, et un autre; peut-etre était-ce Sionita, cet homme du Liban, qui travaillait à la Bible de Le Jay.[23]

The reference to the claim made by des Vallées that he had discovered a *langue matrice* or primitive mother tongue renders the attribution of the anonymous prospectus to him rather more plausible, though it remains by no means conclusive. For it is obvious from Descartes's comments that the author of the prospectus had made a similar claim for his own scheme, describing it as a language from which all others were derived and of which they were mere dialects.[24] Speaking of those who put forward such a claim (and it must be conceded that des Vallées was not the only person to do this at the time), Sorel explained that they denied resolutely that this *langue matrice* was Hebrew and that they wanted one to believe that it was so secret and so mysterious that only they and the angels had access to it.[25]

As Sorel suggests, a man like des Vallées was probably deliberately surrounding his efforts with an air of mystery, as well as linking his supposed achievement to a philological tradition that had occupied itself with tracing the root-words of a primitive tongue, generally thought to be primitive Hebrew. Moreover, in the use of the term *langue matrice* there was the clear implication that the inventor had succeeded where the sixteenth- and early seventeenth-century philologists had failed. However, Descartes was probably quite correct in assuming that such a claim was made for the *langue matrice* of the anonymous prospectus because it was said to be lacking in irregularities. That is, 'n'y ayant point en celle-cy [the grammar] d'irregularitez comme aux autres, il la prend pour leur primitive.'[26] For the assumption behind this and other similar claims seems to have been that the primitive tongue of mankind had been simple and regular in its flexional system and syntactical relations, that it had represented things directly and not letters, and that it had once been universally comprehensible. Inasmuch as the new language was held to possess certain of these particular virtues, it was considered reasonable to claim that it supplied a *langue matrice*.

A simplified, completely regular grammar was one of two characteristics that Descartes chose to emphasize in the new character – for though it was described throughout by Descartes as a language it was in fact simply a form of character-writing. As part of this simplified grammar there would be only one declension and one conjugation, while the inflexion of substantives and verbs would be effected simply and consistently by means of affixes. The second element of the proposed character stressed by Descartes was a dictionary showing the symbols that were assigned to words in different languages that have the same meaning. This Descartes explained as follows: Mettant en son dictionnaire un seul chifre, qui se raporte à *aymer, amare,* φιλεῖγ, et tous les synonimes, le livre qui sera écrit avec ces caractères pourra estre inteipreté par tous ceux qui auront ce dictionnaire.'[27]

Descartes's criticism of the proposed universal character bore upon its awkwardness and impracticability. First, he objected to the disagreeable combinations of sounds that would result from the juxtaposition of certain letters, and explained that many of the modifications that languages have undergone were unconsciously brought about by the desire to avoid such discordant sounds. Secondly, Descartes pointed out that the method of using the language meant either that the person concerned must possess a prodigious memory or that he would need to refer constantly to the accompanying dictionary. The disadvantages of such a method of procedure are self-evident and, as far as is known, this early sketch of a universal character never became known in any form other than that of this preliminary prospectus. If we are indeed to accept des Vallées provisionally as the most likely person to have composed this work, we may recall that Tallemant des Réaux in the *Historiettes* neatly summed up its fate: 'Le cardinal de Richelieu voulait pourtant qu'il [des Vallées] fît imprimer ce qu'il savait de cette langue matrice. "Mais vous me faites divulguer mon secret; donnez-moi donc de quoi vivre." Le cardinal le négligea, et le secret a été enterré avec des Vallées.'[28]

Equally secretive was another Frenchman, Jean Le Maire,[29] who is said to have invented a universal character by means of which, in Comenius's words (echoing a phrase from a letter of Mersenne), one would be able to 'converse not only with the inhabitants of every part of the world, but with the denizens, if there are any, of the moon not less.'[30] His secretiveness prompted Mersenne to write to Haack in 1639 that 'c'est peine perdue de penser tirer aucune chose de luy, il luy faut laisser suivre ses boutades et sa fantaisie,'[31] and the communicative Haack asked in exasperation in 1647, 'Quel but peut Monsieur le Maire avoir d'estre si chiche de ses inventions au bien public? À qui ou à quoi sert le talent dans un mouchoir?'[32]

Le Maire came to Paris from Toulouse in 1635. He became fairly well known in court and scholarly circles in the 1640s as the inventor of a musical instrument resembling a lute, called an *Almérie*[33] (an anagram of his own name), and of a new form of musical notation that was often discussed in Mersenne's correspondence with Haack, Doni,

Huyghens, Ban, and de Villiers.[34] Yet these were only two of Le Maire's numerous plans and inventions. Among his other ambitious schemes were ideas for joining the Mediterranean and the Atlantic by using the rivers Garonne and Aude (a scheme which was encouraged by Louis XIII),[35] a simplified arithmetic and algebra, an instrument for facilitating navigation, and a method for learning and translating languages rapidly and easily. In *De la perfection de l'homme* Charles Sorel relates how Le Maire had taught a child of eight or nine years old to write and translate Hebrew, Greek, and Latin on sight: 'Je l'ai veu en une celebre compagnie au milieu d'une grande bibliothèque, où l'on prenoit les livres au hasard, et l'on les ouvroit de mesme, pour luy en donner des passages à traduire ... Cela semblait pourtant merveilleux que cet enfant eust la connoissance de trois langues en un âge où à peine les autres peuvent sçavoir les rudimens de la langue latine seulement.'[36]

Although Descartes set Le Maire among the likely charlatans,[37] Mersenne seems to have esteemed his talents as an inventor quite highly, and he often refers to Le Maire's proposal for an 'alphabet' that would be intelligible to men of all nations. Although it is first mentioned in a letter to Pierre Gassendi in January 1636,[38] Le Maire's work in this field is said in the letter from Mersenne to Comenius of 22 November 1640, to which we have already referred, to date back to about 1620: 'quibus addit se a 20 annis alphabetum reperisse, quo absque ullo praevio interprete ad quoslibet mortales, puta Sinenses, Japonenses, imò et Lunares, si qui sint, sit quaecunque voluerit scripturus, ut et illi respondeant, quaecunque petierit ab illis, modo voluerint.'[39]

Although Mersenne uses the term *alphabet*, it is likely that Le Maire's idea was not simply a way of writing French, Chinese, Japanese, or any other language, but a universal character in which a set of invented symbols could be read off by each person in his own language. There seems no reason to believe, however, that Comenius was right in associating Le Maire with Mersenne in having laid the foundations for a universal language based upon the 'exact and perfect representation of things.'[40] If this were indeed the case, Mersenne would seem to be singularly ill-informed concerning the details of Le Maire's own project.

Finally, an early scheme of which high hopes were entertained in England in the early 1640s was that initiated and sponsored by Bishop William Bedell. This was to be executed by a Reverend Johnson, of whom Gilbert Burnet wrote:

> He was of a mean Education, yet he had very quick Parts, but they lay more to the Mechanical than to the Spiritual Architecture. For the Earl of *Strafford* used him for an Engineer, and gave him the management of some great Buildings that he was raising in the County of *Wicklo*. But the Bishop finding the Man had a very mercurial Wit, and a great capacity, he resolved to set him to work, so that he might not be wholly useless to the Church; and therefore he proposed to him the composing an Universal character, that might be equally well understood by all Nations ... Johnston [Johnson in all earlier references] undertook it readily, and the Bishop drew for him a Scheme of the whole Work, which he brought to such perfection, that, as my Author was informed, he put it under the Press, but the Rebellion prevented his finishing it.[41]

Reference is again made to Bedell and Johnson's project in Hartlib's *Ephemerides*. A note written in 1639 states that 'Johnson purposes to grave his characters next year 1640. He hase beene all this while too much taken up with my Lord deputy's businesses.'[42] But among the same papers a copy of a letter from a Mr Sumner to Sir Robert King, undated but clearly written some ten years later, tells the sad tale of what happened to Johnson's scheme during the Irish Rebellion: 'You know Sir that if this great Rebellion had beene delayed a while, he had put his Booke into the presse: which now I believe ye Fryars in Anthony have torne into pieces for heresy; And you know that hee had allmost all his copper-plates cutt and graven, and wee heare, that they have suffered Tinkers to stopp kettls with them.'[43] It is almost certainly Johnson's universal character that is referred to in the Mersenne-Haack correspondence when Haack wrote in a letter dated 24 May/3 June 1647 that 'we are still awaiting a gentleman from Ireland from whom we are told to expect great things, as he has brought to a conclusion so I am informed, the efforts of more than twenty years of a certain very skilful man of that kingdom (died 3 or 4 years ago) to write in a way that the message may be read at once in all languages known or understood.'[44]

Nothing appears to have come of the Irish churchman's project, in spite of Sumner's promise that he would gladly become 'a midwife, nurse and adopting father to Mr. Johnson's Universall Character,'[45] although a further entry in the *Ephemerides* suggests that a portion of the work was probably known in England in 1650. This particular entry offers the only known piece of criticism of the scheme, for a certain Dr Fuller is there described as having 'found fault with Johnson's Characters for making characters for all synonyms, and was of opinion that his later contrivances and labors were beyond the first thoughts of which this draught seemed to bee which his wife the widdow hath brought over.'[46] It would appear from this entry that a scheme that once aroused so much interest passed quickly into obscurity and that few traces of it remained to be judged even by Johnson's immediate successors in the field.

All the schemes considered so far are known to us only in the most vague and general way. It is nonetheless possible to recognize in them certain common attitudes and aspirations. First, it is clear that the term *universal character* or *escriture universelle* is no misnomer. For the primary aim behind all these early schemes was to provide a set of *written* symbols that could be read off in their own tongue by men who naturally spoke different languages. The important fact therefore was that the written symbols (whatever their form) would bypass speech-sounds by representing objects directly, after the fashion of arithmetical numbers, astrological signs, musical notes, Chinese characters, or cryptograms.

Yet, even at this early stage, general intelligibility was not the only aim, for simplicity, brevity, regularity, and clarity were seen to be important virtues that might perhaps be built into the new character, since only an invented character could be systematized in such a way as to avoid the irregularities and exceptions that are so common in existing languages. Unlikely though it may seem, then, what was stressed in these early rudimentary schemes was not the impoverishment of language but its improvement. Such a view of the superiority of the new character emerges most clearly in the work of Jean Douet, who maintained that on account of its easiness his character surpassed all other languages, which he described as being 'tellement difficilles qu'à peine l'une d'icelles seulement peut estre apprise parfaictement en une douzaine d'années, quelque dilligence que l'on y puisse apporter.'[47] One result of the ease with which the new character could be learned and remembered was, he maintained, that less time would be spent in learning words, leaving far more for the study of things.

But it was not only a question of saving time. The directness of the link between the symbol and the thing it represented was also admired for other less practical reasons. For, with the example of Chinese in the forefront of their minds, the early inventors of a universal character clearly found the idea of a single symbol for a single idea attractive because it brought the 'words' of the new character into closer and less equivocal contact with material reality. Moreover, the emphasis that was laid at the time upon simplicity, brevity, and regularity should not lead us to ignore entirely associations of a quite different order that probably remained present in the minds of the authors of the universal character and the public for which these projects were intended. For the claim to have invented what Douet called *figures mystiques* and des Vallées and the author of the anonymous prospectus termed a *langue matrice*, as well as being a useful means of attracting attention, linked these schemes with the quest for a primitive language of mankind that had once provided an insight into the nature of things and had bound humanity together by their understanding of notions common to them all.

The methods of construction that were followed in these early projects for a universal character are rather more difficult to determine, owing to the mystery with which they were surrounded. And although in the majority of cases it is possible to surmise what principles were being followed, it is far more profitable to look at the more explicit, earliest published schemes to see some of the methods that were then in use. For all the indications are that none of the projects from the 1620s to the 1640s went beyond these published proposals in ingenuity or sophistication. The only exceptions to this were the suggestions made by Descartes, Mersenne, and Comenius for a philosophical language that would correspond to the relations that exist between ideas. And so Comenius wrote in the *Via lucis* (1668) that men should devote themselves 'to the discovery not only of a language but of thought and, what is more, of the truth of things themselves at the same time.'[48] This far more interesting proposal is one that will be considered separately in the next chapter.

Writing of Chinese characters, Francis Bacon had commented upon the large number of signs that were necessary to such a language of real characters, observing that there would be 'I suppose as many as are radical words.'[49] The idea of basing a universal character upon a large number of root-signs representing radical words, and a smaller number of symbols standing for derivatives, was one that dominated the earliest published schemes and almost certainly lay behind several of the highly secretive proposals that have just been examined. In his interesting treatise on various ways of communicating privately, the *Mercury, or the Secret and Swift Messenger* (1641), John Wilkins put forward this suggestion, adding the recommendation that, since any list of radical words would inevitably be rather lengthy and cumbersome, Hebrew should be taken as the language upon which the universal character should be modelled, since that language was thought to consist of fewer radical words than any other. He also proposed that distinguishing marks might be added to the radical words to convey case, conjugation, tense, and so on. Wilkins is clearly not, however, convinced at this stage in his own thinking about the subject that this general procedure would provide the only, or even the best, system available, for in another chapter of the *Mercury* he goes on to discuss with equal seriousness the intriguing notion of a language of musical notes, along the lines suggested some three years earlier by Bishop Francis Godwin in *The Man in the Moone: or a Discourse of a Voyage thither by Domingo Gonsales, the Speedy Messenger*.[50] It would appear in fact that, realizing something of the difficulty of the task of representing all things by characters in such a way that the language did not become impossible to learn, remember, and use, Wilkins was open to any seemingly worthwhile suggestion.

It is worth noting in passing that Wilkins's ideas on a universal character showed no signs at this stage of having been influenced by the proposal found in the work of a number of Continental scholars for a philosophical language based upon the relations between ideas. The suggestion that Wilkins was inspired to compose the section of the *Mercury* concerned with a universal character as a consequence of a meeting with Comenius during the latter's visit to England in 1641 or in the light of ideas found in the *Via lucis* written in that same year[51] is not supported by the evidence available.[52]

First, Wilkins does not mention Comenius in the course of discussing a universal character. Next, Comenius arrived in England only on 21 September 1641[53] and composed the *Via lucis*, on his own statement,[54] *during* his stay in that country: that is between the end of September 1641 and April 1642. A copy of the manuscript, or a part of the manuscript, was then left in England on Comenius's departure for Sweden, in the care of Samuel Hartlib. It is therefore highly unlikely that Wilkins could have written in the chapter on universal language in time for the *Mercury* to be published in 1641, after seeing the manuscript of the *Via lucis* (which was probably not yet written anyway), or indeed after consulting at all with Comenius. Finally, there is no convincing evidence that Wilkins was a member of Hartlib's circle at this time. And even if he had met Comenius during his visit to England, Wilkins's work shows absolutely no signs of having been influenced by the latter's ideas on a philosophical language, always assuming that these were already fully formulated by that time, a fact which in itself is by no means certain.[55] It seems unlikely that Wilkins took the title of his book from a phrase of Comenius ('This Mercury, this messenger who must make his way among all nations alike'),[56] and much more likely that Comenius was thinking of Wilkins's own recently published treatise on communication when he came to discuss the universal character. Wilkins's title probably comes from Francis Godwin's *Nuncius inanimatus*, which Wilkins himself describes as the source of the *Mercury*.[57]

Wilkins's early treatise is very much a broad survey of the ideas on secret communication known in England at that time, and it reflects both contemporary curiosity concerning the question of a universal character and ignorance as to the exact manner in which such a character was best to be constructed. Most important of all perhaps was Wilkins's commendation of the invention to the attention of those 'who have both abilities and leisure for such kinds of Enquiries,'[58] among whom he himself was to figure most prominently in the course of the next few decades.

Francis Lodwick's *A Common Writing: Whereby Two, Although*

Not Understanding One the Others Language, yet by the Helpe thereof, May Communicate Their Minds One to Another (1647), published by Samuel Hartlib, furnishes one of the rare examples from this period of an actual scheme of real characters, worked out on a basis of root-signs and derivatives.[59] Even then, although the method to be followed is described, the character itself is not elaborated in full.

Lodwick described his common writing as

> rather a kind of hieroglyphical representation of words, by so many severall Characters, for each word a Character, and that not at *Random*, but as each word is either Radical, or derivative, the Radical, have their radicall Characters, the derivatives beare the Character of the Radix of their descent, with some differentall addition, whereby they may be differenced, from other derivatives, proceeding from the said Radix.[60]

The first signs in Lodwick's character are to be determined by the choice of certain radical words, which are then divided into root-words of action and non-action, the second group of which may then be subdivided into four groups: substantives, pronouns, adjectives, and a fourth group comprising adverbs, prepositions, interjections, and conjunctions. Each of these radical words is then allocated a radical character. Words closely related to these radicals may be formed from them by fixing upon and adding certain abbreviated signs, each of which will reveal that a particular character is being used in, as Lodwick put it, an analogical, synonymical, contradictional, or relatival manner. The various forms of a single root-sign will thus be indicated by other signs that are attached to it. For example, the root-sign for *to drink* is ∂. Derivatives are:

∂⌐ = *the drinker*
∂ᑭ = *drink*
∂ᖇ = *the drinking*
∂ᗺ = *the drunkard*.

This manner of relating words, (and it applies to associated, or analogical, ideas such as *to moisten*, *to wet*, and *to wash*, as well as to etymological derivatives) is clearly adopted by Lodwick as a means of combatting the enormous number of characters that would otherwise be needed in such a common writing. The various tenses catered for (only four in number in Lodwick's scheme) are to be rendered by a dot placed in different positions with respect to the initial root-signs. And, inspired by the example of the musical script, Lodwick carefully described, in the third part of the book, a way of writing the character between five lines, illustrating this by a detailed transcription of the opening verses of the Gospel according to St John (see plate 1).

Finally, a postscript explains the system according to which the necessary English-common writing 'lexicon' (which in the event never materialized) would be arranged. Working from English to the common writing, one would refer to an alphabetical list of English words bearing numbers, which were also assigned to characters with the same meaning as their English equivalents, listed alphabetically for the radicals, then in order of descent from the radix for derivatives.

The objection of complexity and clumsiness can, of course, quite legitimately be levelled at Lodwick's scheme, for, although he has reduced the number of characters by means of the system of derivations, it still remains enormously high. As a result, simply learning all the radicals would prove to be an impossible task, requiring an entire lifetime (much as was related of the Chinese characters), and references would constantly need to be made to the two parts of what would have to be a vast lexicon. Moreover, a glance back at the example of the derivatives of the root sign for *to drink* will indicate how difficult it could be to distinguish between one related 'word' and another – an objection that could justifiably be applied to most seventeenth-century scripts of universal characters.

Lodwick's *A Common Writing* (1647) was known to most of the English scholars interested in the universal character, and the fact that they continued with the search in itself shows that it was recognized as offering an inadequate solution. Lodwick himself went on to produce in 1652 a very much modified version of his common writing, and, after John Wilkins's death, he worked with a number of others[61] upon improving the latter's *Essay towards a Real Character and a Philosophical Language* (1668), acknowledging in this way, it would seem, the superiority of this more elaborate treatise over his own

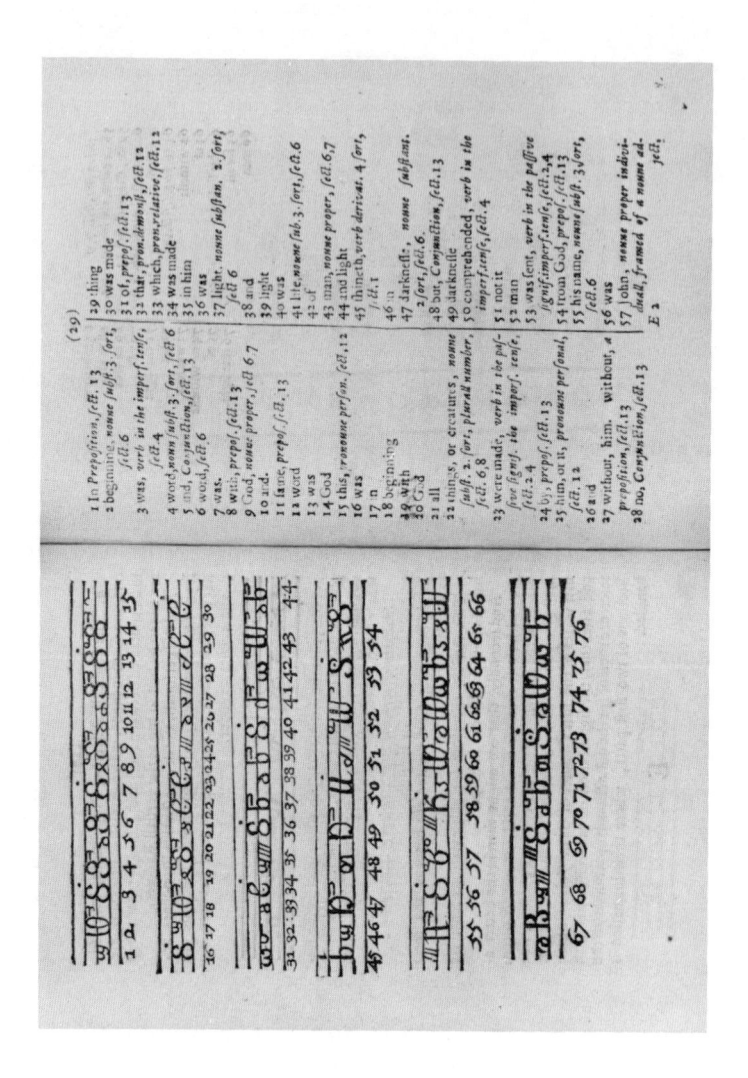

1 In Prepoſition, ſect. 13
2 beginning, nomen ſubſt. 3. ſort, ſect. 6
3 was, verb in the imperf. tenſe, ſect. 4
4 word, nomen ſubſt. 3. ſort, ſect. 6
5 and, Conjunction, ſect. 13
6 wood, ſect. 6
7 was.
8 with, prepoſ. ſect. 13
9 God, nomen proper, ſect. 6.7
10 and.
11 ſame, prepoſ. ſect. 13
12 word
13 was
14 God
15 this, pronomen perſon. ſect. 12
16 was
17 in
18 beginning
19 with
20 God
21 all
22 things, or creatures, nomen ſubſt. 2. ſort, plurall number, ſect. 6.8
23 were made, verb in the paſſive ſignif. the imperf. tenſe, ſect. 2.4
24 by, prepoſ. ſect. 13
25 him, or it, pronomen perſonal, ſect. 12
26 and
27 without, him, without, a Prepoſition, ſect. 13
28 no, Compoſition, ſect. 13
29 thing
30 was made
31 of, prepoſ. ſect. 12
32 that, pron. demonſt. ſect. 12
33 which, pron. relative, ſect. 12
34 was made
35 in him
36 was
37 light, nomen ſubſtant. 3. ſort, ſect. 6
38 and
39 light
40 was
41 life, nomen ſub. 3. ſort, ſect. 6
42 of
43 man, nomen proper, ſect. 6.7
44 and light
45 ſhineth, verb derivat. 4. ſort, ſect. 1
46 in
47 darkneſſe, nomen ſubſtant. 2. ſort, ſect. 6.
48 but, Conjunction, ſect. 13
49 darkneſſe
50 comprehended, verb in the imperf. tenſe, ſect. 4
51 not it
52 man
53 was ſent, verb in the paſſive ſignif. imperf. tenſe, ſect. 4
54 from God, prepoſ. ſect. 13
55 his name, nomen ſubſt. 3. ſort, ſect. 6
56 was
57 John, nomen proper individ, framed of a nomen ad. ſect.

Plate 1 Francis Lodwick *A Common Writing* London 1647
28–9: the Gospel according to St John, chapter 1,
in Lodwick's universal character
By courtesy of the British Library Board

earlier efforts. Lodwick played a significant part in the universal language movement in England, however, and the publication of his manuscript notes will show that he was an important figure in the history of seventeenth-century linguistics, comparable certainly with William Holder and John Wallis.[62]

The use of common reference numbers as a part of Lodwick's scheme of common writing leads us to consider briefly a system in which numbers themselves were used as the signs of the new character. Listing words alphabetically and attaching to each a number that is then given to words having the same meaning in other languages, is an obvious method, and it was proposed very early as the basis for a written universal character. In this system, for example, the words *homo, homme, hombre, man, Mann*, and so on, would all bear the same reference number. An Englishman reading this number written down by a Spaniard who had thought of the word *hombre*, would turn up the number in the numerical dictionary and find the corresponding word *man* in his own language. We should bear in mind, however, that the characteristic feature of this type of language was not so much the use of arithmetical numbers as the alphabetical listing of the words to which these numbers were applied.

Although languages based on this principle varied greatly in detail, they were fundamentally of the same type and were numerous throughout the seventeenth century. Kinder's universal character may well have been one of the first of its kind. Cave Beck published, both in English and in French, another scheme of this type entitled *The Universal Character* (1657). This was followed by Johann Joachim Becher's *Character pro notitia linguarum universali* (1661) published at Frankfurt, by Athanasius Kircher's *Polygraphia nova et universalis* (1663)[63], and by de Vienne Plancy's *écriture universelle* described in the *Extraordinaire du Mercure* (between 1681 and 1685). Written characters constructed around this simple idea of a common reference number were not, however, confined to the seventeenth century, although each 'inventor' up to the early nineteenth century in his turn expressed surprise that so simple a device had not been discovered much earlier!

An excellent example of this kind of universal character is Cave Beck's *Universal Character* (1657). J. Waite addressed the following inflated lines to Beck in an introductory poem to this work: 'Great *Bacon*'s Soul, my Friend, divides with thee, / He found the Plot and Thou the Husbandrie.' Beck made many of the usual claims for his universal character. Chiefly it was, he maintained, admirably simple and free from irregularities, and could therefore be learned very rapidly. An easy character that would guide us out of what its author called this labyrinth of languages, Beck's universal character had, he claimed, none of the complexities or confusions that were characteristic of other methods of 'symbolical' writing. Egyptian hieroglyphs, Beck pointed out with some wit, showed one picture to the eye and gave another, quite different meaning to it, so that 'they justifi'd the Painter who drew a misshapen Cock upon a Sign-board, and wrote under it, [*this is a Bull*].'[64] As for the Chinese character, used as a kind of general writing in the East, it had the inconvenience of having no proportion or method in the form of its signs, so that, Beck observed, 'an European with his one Eye (which they [i.e. the Chinese] afford him) would think they shut both theirs (they so much boast of) when they drew the shapes of those Characters.'[65]

The basis of Beck's universal character is the system of a numerical dictionary described above. Numerical figures have the advantage, Beck pointed out, that, being familiar as a result of being used in arithmetic and many kinds of secret writing, they will 'fright no Eye with an unusual shape.'[66] To the arithmetical numbers which represent words are added letters indicating tense, case, gender, and number. Nouns are known, for example, by the letters p, q, r, or x, set before the arithmetical figures. Similarly the vowels a, e, i, at the beginning of a syllable, followed by the consonants b, c, d, f, g, and l after them, convey the three persons of the pronouns and the six tenses of the verbs. Plurals are shown invariably by an s following the numbers. Yet Beck is not content that his character should be merely written, and he endeavours to make his numerical language pronounceable by using a simplified version of the English sounds *one*, *too*, *tre*, *for*, etc. In respect to the sounds of the language Beck asks us to note that 'this Character thus pronounced, will sound like Greek, having divers of its sweetest Cadencies, and is capable of Rhetorical, and Poetical figures.'[67] At the end of the book, Beck set out the fifth commandment in the written and spoken versions of the universal character. The opening line will give some idea of how the method he proposed would work, and how the character would both look and sound. 'Honour thy Father and thy Mother' is written: 'leb2314 p2477 and pf2477' and is spoken as follows: 'leb toreónfo, pee tofosénsen and pif tofosénsen.' By way of explanation, we may note that in the Lexicon *2314* is the verb *to honour*; *eb* is the second person singular of the verb, which preceded by the consonant *l* becomes the imperative; *2477* again is the number of the word *father* in a section of the Lexicon headed 'kindred'; *p* is the sign of the noun substantive personal male, *pf* is the noun substantive person female, hence *pf2477* means *mother*.

Throughout Beck's language the hold of the classical languages is apparent. He assumes that the syntax of the Romance languages is the only one possible, and there is no simplification of the classical system of tenses, moods, and cases. Instead of being full of the 'sweetest cadencies,' his language would in fact be awkward and ugly to pronounce, and also monotonously repetitive because of the use of the same numerals and the limited number of sounds described. More important still is the defect of clumsiness and inconvenience common to all schemes of this type, which demand either a prodigious memory or constant recourse to a dictionary – in the case of Beck's character, to a meagre and unadaptable one of four thousand English words. In this respect, Becher's similar system is an improvement upon Beck's in that he uses Latin as the basic language for the first lexicon, and allows for a vocabulary of ten thousand words.

Nonetheless, this defect, common to all the schemes based upon an alphabetical listing of words, clearly remained a crucial drawback, and, understandably, there was little enthusiasm in the seventeenth century for any of the would-be universal characters mentioned. For all the grammatical regularization and simplification in the world could not render acceptable a character that, although in principle perfectly feasible as a means of general communication, could scarcely be more difficult to learn, remember, and use. The obvious inadequacies of such a system,[68] combined with the keen desire to go beyond the fairly rudimentary aims of the authors of a common writing and bring language into a much closer relationship with 'real knowledge,' led a number of distinguished scholars both in England and on the Continent to envisage a quite different solution which was thought to have most important consequences for the progress of learning; namely, that a character and language might be framed, in Wilkins's words, to accord with the 'Nature of Things,' a suggestion that could still lead, as we shall see in a moment, to significant differences in conception and approach.

3/The philosophical language

DESCARTES AND MERSENNE

After criticizing the universal language prospectus forwarded to him by Mersenne in November 1629, Descartes proposed that, instead of the unsatisfactory system that he had found outlined there, a universal language might possibly be formulated along much more philosophical lines. Such a philosophical language, he recommended, would need to be based upon a strict analysis and an ordered classification of ideas; 'C'est à dire,' he wrote, 'établissant un ordre entre toutes les pensées qui peuvent entrer en l'esprit humain, de mesme qu'il y en un naturellement étably entre les nombres.'[1]

Complex ideas would need, in addition, to be analysed into their simple, clear, constituent elements, and the relations between these various elements would need to be firmly established. Descartes himself pointed out that the constitution of this language would depend for its success upon the progress, indeed upon the total establishment, of the 'true philosophy.'[2] 'Car,' he wrote,

> il est impossible autrement de denombrer toutes les pensées des hommes, et de les mettre par ordre, ny seulement de les distinguer en sorte qu'elles soient claires et simples, qui est à mon advis le plus grand secret qu'on puisse avoir pour acquerir la bonne science. Et si quelqu'un avait bien expliqué quelles sont les idées simples qui sont en l'imagination des hommes, desquelles se compose tout ce qu'ils

pensent, et que cela fust receu par tout le monde, j'oserais esperer ensuite une langue universelle fort aisée à aprendre, à prononcer, et à ecrire, et ce qui est le principal, qui aiderait au jugement, luy representant si distinctement toutes choses, qu'il luy serait presque impossible de se tromper.[3]

Descartes believed that in theory it was quite possible to make the detailed analyses of ideas that were essential to the development of the science upon which the new language would depend. To do this, however, would clearly mean realizing a philosophical achievement of the first order. He argued further that, even if this philosophical language were eventually to be constituted, it would never become generally accepted, since 'cela présupose de grans changemens en l'ordre des choses, et il faudrait que tout le monde ne fust qu'un paradis terrestre, ce qui n'est bon à proposer que dans le pays des romans.'[4]

Other thinkers after Descartes were not, however, prepared to accept this last judgment as invalidating the entire notion of a universal language based upon philosophical principles. Mersenne himself, after reading Descartes's views in the letter addressed to him, considered the question further, discussed it with a number of his correspondents,[5] and in the *Harmonie universelle* (1636) sketched the outline of a proposal for a universal language of his own. Although Mersenne's name has sometimes been coupled with that of Descartes as one of the earliest supporters of a type of philosophical language, this interesting aspect of his work has so far received relatively little attention. A major study of Mersenne's ideas in this field is, I understand, at present near completion in France,[6] and I should like to attempt only a brief preliminary examination of what is undoubtedly an extremely complex subject.

In the *Harmonie universelle*, Mersenne showed himself attracted to the idea that a primitive, *natural* language might be discovered that would signify immediately and without convention. He agreed that

si l'on pouvait inventer une langue dont les dictions eussent leur signification naturelle, de sorte que tous les hommes entendissent la pensee des autres à la seule prononciation sans en avoir appris la signification, comme ils entendent que l'on se réjoüit lorsque l'on rit, et que l'on est triste quand on pleure, cette langue serait la meilleure de toutes les possibles: car elle ferait la mesme impression sur tous les auditeurs, que feraient les pensees de l'esprit si elles se pouvaient immediatement communiquer entre les hommes comme entre les Anges.[7]

And yet Mersenne was forced to conclude that a language that signified naturally lay completely outside the bounds of possibility, for, as we have seen in an earlier chapter, he argued that all known languages signified as a result of convention alone. Even the language of Adam must have consisted of a collection of arbitrarily selected sounds that might equally well have been applied to any other objects than those to which they had been given. It was not to be expected that any artificial language would succeed in this respect where all instituted languages had so far failed. For Mersenne was firmly convinced that speech, as distinct from mere emotional utterance, was wholly dependent upon agreement between human beings,

> toutes les paroles estant indifferentes pour signifier tout ce que l'on veut, il n'y a que la seule volonté qui les puisse determiner à signifier une chose plutost qu'une autre. Quant aux differentes voix qui servent à expliquer les passions de l'ame, et les douleurs, elles sont aussi naturelles à l'homme qu'aux autres animaux: mais puisque les paroles sont artificielles, elles dépendent de l'imagination, et de la volonté d'un chacun.[8]

The only form of 'natural language' which Mersenne suggested might conceivably be formed with existing alphabetical letters would be onomatopoeic in type. The idea behind such a language was that certain letters would appear to be particularly suited to the expression of different kinds of things, feelings, or ideas. In Mersenne's view, for example, the vowels of the language could represent the following feelings or objects:

a and o = what is great and noble
    e = delicate, subtle things, apt for the representation of sadness and mourning

i = very thin, small things
o = the expression of great passion
u = dark, hidden things[9]

By the liberal use of quotations from classical poetry in which sensitive use is made of assonance and alliteration, Mersenne tried to demonstrate that what might be termed an 'analogical' language had, in fact, a certain empirical foundation.

Yet, interesting though this theory is in pointing to a possible onomatopoeic basis for existing languages (a theory which has, of course, been elaborated on a number of occasions since that time[10]), the construction on such principles of a complete language that would be immediately intelligible was a very different matter, and a much more dubious undertaking than the mere laying down of a few general sound-associations. And Mersenne recognized that only the merest skeleton of a language could be built on such vague lines as these. What he seems rather to have ignored was the fact that even in the examples that he quoted the element of agreement was already considerable. Such a language could therefore never signify without consent.

Mersenne was, however, far more enthusiastic about his proposals for an ideal 'combinatory' language, which he referred to on several occasions in the course of his correspondence and described at some length in the *Harmonie universelle*. In a letter to Nicholas Claude Fabri de Peiresc, for instance, to whom he dedicated a part of the work, Mersenne wrote most explicitly: 'Je me suis imaginé une sorte d'escripture et un certain idiome universel, qui vous pourrait servir ... en dressant un alphabet qui contient tous les idiomes possibles, et toutes les dictions qui peuvent servir à exprimer chasque chose en telle langue qu'on vouldra.'[11] Again, as in the reference to Le Maire already quoted, what Mersenne meant here by the word *alphabet* was clearly not what is commonly understood by the term, since this alphabet, we are told, was to consist of 'plus de millions de vocables qu'il n'y a de grains de sable dans toute la terre, quoyqu'il soit si ayse à apprendre et à retenir, que l'on n'a besoing d'aulcune memoire, porveu que l'on ayt un peu de jugement.'[12] Equally clearly, what Mersenne did intend was that the alphabet would provide an artificial written character that would be superior to the defective natural languages in the brevity and simplicity of its elements, in the comprehensiveness of its vocabulary, and in the ease with which it would be both learned and remembered. For Mersenne's initial supposition was that the best language that could possibly be constructed would be one in which a small number of basic elements would be combined in the clearest possible manner to cover as wide a range of ideas as could conceivably be required. Mersenne believed that the superiority of such a language was proved by the example of arithmetic, 'qui se sert seulement de 10 caracteres differens pour exprimer tout ce qui est dans sa puissance, et dans son estenduë,'[13] and by algebra.

The section of the *Harmonie universelle* that is devoted to the proposed 'idiome universel' makes it abundantly clear that Mersenne's ideas on that subject resulted directly from his interest in an *ars combinatoria*, which is known today primarily in its mathematical form as the permutation of numbers, but which, prior to the seventeenth century, had already had a long, interesting history in the course of which it had been put to rather different uses from those which Mersenne had in mind. This highly complex subject will be examined further shortly. For the moment I want to consider Mersenne's own suggestions in isolation from this earlier background.

In a preface to the *Harmonic universelle* the proposed universal language is expressly described by Mersenne as furnishing one of several possible applications of the tables of permutations.[14] So whatever elements Mersenne chose to use as the characters of his language, all were dependent upon the tables of mathematical permutations that he had been busy working out for many years. So, to take one example, if one wished to know how many possible 'words' (that is, in Mersenne's scheme, combinations of a given number of individual elements) one could form out of, let us suppose, six numbers, musical notes, or letters, one need only refer to the table of permutations of six that had been set out most fully in Mersenne's earlier work, *La Vérité des sciences*,[15] and was partially reproduced in the *Harmonie universelle*.[16]

The theory of permutations is a familiar enough feature of modern existence to require no detailed explanation. We may note, however, that from the basic notion of the combination of a given number of characters, Mersenne envisaged the provision of both a written character and a spoken language, rich enough to represent all the ideas that one might wish to communicate or use, while at the same time retaining the mathematical virtues of brevity and clarity. For by using all the possible combinations that exist, one would need, he pointed out, only a very small number of individual characters to provide a vocabulary of many thousands of 'words.'

The resulting language might be composed, Mersenne suggested, of almost any characters that one cared to invent. He was decidedly casual on this point, as he was with respect to the ways in which lines and dots should be used to indicate case, mood, or tense – clearly relatively straightforward problems, in his view, which he left for others to solve. In the first place, a language of musical notes could be constructed on this basis which could be used to discuss any subject with another person. Thinking back to the sixteenth-century treatises of secret-writing, it could serve, for instance, as a kind of secret language, 'car l'on peut discourir avec un autre en joüant de l'Orgue, de la Trompette, de la Viole, de la Fleute, du Luth et des autres instrumens, sans que nul puisse entendre le discours, que celuy qui sçait le secret, ce qui se peut pratiquer en plusieurs manieres.'[17] Or again, once the secret is shared, it could be used as a common means of communication between men who speak different languages, 'en exprimant tout ce que l'on voudra, tant en François, qu'en Hebrieu, en Grec, en Espagnol, en Italien, ou en autre sorte de langue, avec quatre Sons, ou mouvemens différents.'[18] Alternatively, the characters employed could consist of the arithmetical figures of the original tables; in this case, a numerical pasigraphy would result which could be read off by men of different nations, each in his own language.

Finally, Mersenne suggested the possibility that a spoken language, as well as a written character, might be constructed merely by the application of the same principles. For if one chose to compose a language using twenty-two letters of the alphabet as its characters, by referring to the table of the permutations of twenty-two one would discover that, with only three characters in each 'word,' a total vocabulary of more than eleven thousand distinct combinations became possible. Clearly a combination of all the letters of the alphabet, if unlimited, would easily provide a possible vocabulary of many millions. But of course, as Mersenne recognized, not all of these combinations could be pronounced; he therefore proposed several different ways in which by combining vowels and consonants in easily pronounceable juxtapositions many thousands of 'words' could be produced.[19] Nineteen consonants and ten vowels (all of which are named by Mersenne) would therefore suffice, he believed, to express everything that one could possibly wish to say.

There remained of course, the greatest problem of all, that is, exactly how the various combinations were to be disposed so as to represent objects and ideas. Most commonly, as we have seen in the preceding chapter, the distribution of vocabulary in the early schemes of the seventeenth century had been according to an alphabetical listing, a solution which Mersenne seems to have considered quite unworthy of his consideration. And, although he is far from explicit on this point, it is nonetheless clear that he had in mind a distribution based upon some kind of ordered classification of ideas. In the letter to Peiresc already quoted, for example, he wrote that his language had 'ceste proprieté que sa seule lecture peut tellement enseigner la philosophie accomodee à son ordre, qu'on ne peut l'oublier ou, si on l'oublie, qu'on peult la restablir sans l'ayde d'aulcun,'[20] a clear indication that he intended the language to depend upon a pre-established order that could be easily recalled and referred to whenever this proved necessary. Moreover, in one of the prefaces to the *Harmonie universelle*, Mersenne provided a brief example that also pointed in the direction of an ordered classification of ideas. Supposing, he wrote, that God, the independent and sovereign being, was thought of as the unit *one* and that the divine perfections were then assigned the numbers from two to ten, every person seeing one of these numbers would immediately understand in his own language the particular divine attribute that was being referred to.[21]

The exact system according to which all things are to be ordered is not, of course, elaborated by Mersenne, although it is touched upon briefly:

Si l'on prend la liberté de feindre une langue universelle composee de toutes les dictions possibles, dont les racines, ou les dictions radicales soient dans un assez grand nombre *pour fournir des noms differens à chaque proprieté de toutes les espèces, ou de tous les individus*; et que l'on suppose qu'Adam ... a eu la parfaite connaissance de toutes les sciences, et des proprietez de chaque chose, l'on peut s'imaginer qu'il a donné autant de noms à chaque espèce, par exemple à chaque animal, comme il y a reconnu de proprietez différentes.[22]

Although it was obvious to Mersenne that, at the creation, Adam could not possibly have invented so comprehensive and philosophically ordered a language, the idea that a language might conceivably be based upon a symbolization according to species and differences is here quite specifically proposed. Mersenne, one should add, does not go on to elaborate any tables of things classified according to this method. Furthermore, his reliance upon a system founded on the permutation of numbers would undoubtedly have involved him in a lengthy, cumbersome, and very complex method of determining precisely where a particular combination of symbols is located in the tables of this philosophical language. Nonetheless, the proposal for a classificatory language in which individual properties are to be represented by a separate symbol – a language in fact very similar in principle to the one sought after by Dalgarno, Wilkins, Lodwick, and others later in the century – is already outlined by Mersenne in 1636. For the French scholar the difficulty lay not in the simplification of grammar nor in the invention of a character but in the discovery of the actual order that exists between ideas. And, since this process seemed to him to demand little short of divine omniscience, Mersenne clearly regarded it as unlikely ever to be successfully accomplished: 'la table générale pourrait servir pour establir une langue universelle, qui serait la meilleure de toutes les possibles, si l'on sçavait l'ordre des idées que Dieu a de toutes choses.'[23] Although Mersenne finally casts doubt on the practicability of such a scheme, it is important to note that the emphasis here is squarely placed on the onerous task of the ordering of concepts.

THE UNIVERSAL CHARACTER AS A MIRROR OF REALITY

In the second half of the seventeenth century, there was, in the words of a modern scholar, 'a progress from the conviction that a satisfactory pattern for a new language can be taken from an old language [namely

Hebrew; i.e. a language with few radical words] to the belief that such a pattern must derive from a correct description of the order of reality.'[24] By the early 1650s in fact, many of the scholars who were interested in the possibility of seeking out a universal language had come to accept the view that the new language should consist of what were termed *technical words* constructed in such a way as to indicate unambiguously the various qualities of the objects they represented. By this date, Cyprian Kinner and William Petty were both engaged in the construction of a botanical character that would convey by means of its symbols certain properties of herbs and plants, while in 1650 Seth Ward was already seeking a way of extending this procedure to the symbolization of all knowledge.[25] Moreover, it was soon recognized that one of the major tasks confronting the philosopher-linguist was that of preparing tables, in which objects and ideas would be classified according to their distinctive features. John Wilkins expressed this idea most clearly in his *Essay towards a Real Character and a Philosophical Language* (1668), when he wrote:

> The principal design aimed at in these Tables, is to give a sufficient enumeration of all such things and notions, as are to have names assigned to them, and withall so to contrive these as to their order, that the place of everything may contribute to a description of the nature of it. Denoting both the *General* and the *Particular head* under which it is placed; and the *Common difference* whereby it is distinguished from other things of the same kind.[26]

In the *Ekskubalouron*, (1652), Sir Thomas Urquhart, a writer rarely quoted on this subject, suggested a particular form of subject grouping as the basis for the classification:

> As all things of a single compleat being, by *Aristotle* into ten Classes were divided; so may the words whereby those things are to be signified, be set apart in their several store-houses.
> Arts, Sciences, Mechanick Trades, notional Faculties, and whatever is excogitable by man, have their own method; by vertue whereof, the Learned of these latter times have orderly digested them: Yet hath none hitherto considered of a mark, whereby words

of the same Faculty, Art, Trade, or Science should be diagnosced from those of another by the very sound of the word at the first hearing.[27]

In the same year as the *Ekskubalouron*, Francis Lodwick proposed that a new language should be based upon the 'knowledge of things and their order in nature,'[28] while two years later an anonymous Spanish Jesuit published at Rome, the *Arithmeticus nomenclator mundi omnes nationes ad linguarum et sermonis imitatem invitans* (1654), a character based upon a series of rather sketchy philosophical tables.[29] In the mid-1650s, Wilkins was asked to compile certain 'Tables of Substance' for George Dalgarno's scheme, which was in the process of evolving from a kind of universal shorthand to the philosophical language that was to appear in 1661 as the *Ars signorum*.[30] And when, partly at Seth Ward's suggestion and partly as a consequence of his own interest and participation in Dalgarno's project, Wilkins started to prepare his own *Essay towards a Real Character and a Philosophical Language* (1668), it was with the aid of a willing band of specialist helpers, each of whom was to concentrate on the particular section of the important philosophical tables of which he had expert knowledge. The transition that took place in England in the middle years of the century was thus from a character which merely *represented* things and notions by agreement, to one which *mirrored* the whole of human knowledge by means of the combination of its elements. The precise innovations that characterized the new philosophical type of universal language were, first, the attribution of written symbols to the various individual properties of an object or an idea, so that a group of symbols together not only represented a particular thing but also, to some extent, defined it, and, secondly, the closely associated notion of grouping all the things that one wished to include in the vocabulary of the language according to their relations and differences.

A number of rather different explanations have been put forward to account for the appearance in England of the idea of a philosophical language as it has just been outlined. One suggestion is that English scholars came upon the idea, first, in Comenius's *Via lucis* (1668), and secondly, in a letter to Hartlib of Cyprian Kinner, a Silesian, who was also an associate of Comenius.[31] As I have argued in an earlier chapter,[32] the evidence for attributing this change in direction in universal-language planning in mid-seventeenth century England to the influence of Comenius's book is quite unconvincing. But is Kinner's letter to Hartlib any more likely to be the source for the idea of a universal character consisting of 'technical words' whose composition describes the order of reality?[33] Samuel Hartlib, in accordance both with current practice and his self-appointed role as a disseminator of knowledge, would almost certainly have passed on Kinner's proposals to his associates and friends. Yet the manner in which Hartlib alluded to Kinner in his *Ephemerides* suggests that he regarded the Silesian's letter as outlining a scheme that he saw as running parallel to the related activities of Petty and Ward, rather than providing the inspiration for the Englishmen's ideas.[34] Again, no definite source can be proved.

If the idea of a vocabulary of symbols denoting the properties of things and a language based on the classification of ideas did not apparently originate in the *Via lucis* or in Kinner's letter, how in fact did it arise?

First, we have noted that Mersenne had already anticipated the English language planners in his suggestions for a language based upon the ordering of concepts according to genus, species, and difference. And there is no doubt at all that there were many possible ways in which the French priest's discussion of the philosophical language could have reached the ears of Ward, Wilkins, Lodwick, Dalgarno, and even Sir Thomas Urquhart. Most directly, of course, this would be through the pages of the *Harmonie universelle* (1636), of which several copies were in the possession of English men of science, Digby and Cavendish most notably.[35] Possible links with the English proponents of a universal language may also be traced through a number of personal contacts, such as Mersenne's meetings and correspondence with Digby, his discussions with Petty while the latter was in Paris in the mid-1640s,[36] or his correspondence with Theodore Haack or Samuel Hartlib himself, a part of which has probably been lost.[37] However, none of the English language planners specifically acknowledged a debt to Mersenne for the idea of a philosophical language and the evidence in favour of such an influence remains purely circumstantial.

Both of the features of the philosophical language that we have mentioned may, however, as has already been suggested, have developed quite spontaneously out of a number of different preoccupations and interests of the age.[38] All the indications are indeed that, whatever individual debts there may have been, as, for instance, with John Wilkins who acknowledged his own debt to Seth Ward in the *Essay*, these two related notions grew so naturally out of ideas that were already familiar at that time that no single specific source is discernable.

In the first place, it needed no very great genius to recognize the convenience of a scientific nomenclature that would indicate briefly the chief properties of the things named, so that in the botanical and medical fields one would be able, as Hartlib put it, 'to know the virtues besides the names of all herbes and plants.'[39] Such an idea could have arisen in a number of different ways: as a consequence of dissatisfaction with the variable and often highly confusing terminology of the day; out of the alchemists' efforts to combine or modify substances, each of which was represented by a characteristic symbol;[40] possibly by analogy with the mathematicians' conjunction of different algebraic symbols; or, most probably perhaps, out of the Lullists' or the Cabalists' combining of symbols. An emblematic character such as Egyptian hieroglyphic writing, or, even more strikingly, Mexican picture-writing, also provided an example of a form of script in which certain specific characteristics of an object were represented.[41] Whatever the precise source of inspiration was, the project of forming a vocabulary of 'technical words' was already being attempted, as we have noted, both on the Continent and in England in the late 1640s. All that was required was to extend this idea to the whole of human knowledge, making it the basic principle governing the constitution of the philosophical language, a step which, according to a statement of Hartlib,[42] Seth Ward seems to have been the first to take in England, soon to be followed by Sir Thomas Urquhart,[43] Dalgarno, Lodwick, and Wilkins, among others.

The closely related notion of a classification of things into groups according to genus and species, within which they are distinguished by their more individual differences, is one which can be seen even more clearly to have evolved out of a number of seventeenth-century intellectual interests. In her discussion of this question, Vivian Salmon refers particularly to the grouping of words for ease in language learning by teachers of the classics, the systematization of knowledge practised by the Lullists and Cabalists, and the non-alphabetic symbolization of the shorthand writers and cryptographers.[44] The classification of words by the grammarians, and particularly the break-down and labelling of concepts by Lullists and Cabalists are worthy of rather more detailed consideration here.

The experience of earlier inventors of a common writing, together with a growing familiarity with Chinese character-writing, had tended to suggest that the principal difficulties in the way of realizing such a project were the vast numbers of signs that were required and the manner in which the words were to be distributed in the lexicon for ease of reference and recall. The solution was fairly obvious – a form of classification that would permit related concepts to be denoted by like symbols.[45] One may, in fact, recognize in Lodwick's first published scheme, *A Common Writing* (1647), an early effort to cope with the first problem by an extension of the notion of derivation to include words possessing a related meaning. Hence, as we have seen, words such as *to moisten*, *to wet*, and *to wash* were all allocated the same root-sign, which was then modified by the addition of a special distinguishing mark.

Not surprisingly, the grouping of related words was commonly favoured by English and Continental grammarians and teachers of language in late sixteenth and early seventeenth century, and this procedure was also adopted by Timothy Bright in the *Characterie*. Comenius followed this practice extensively in his reformed Latin text-books, in which both single words and whole phrases or sentences were placed into ordered groups, selected with a view to the resemblances and affiliations of the ideas that they contained. Apart from these textbooks, which were well-known in mid-seventeenth century England, several lexicons, organized according to generic criteria appeared in the early decades of the century. Holyband's *French Littelton* of 1609, for instance, had several sections in which the French words to be learned and their English equivalents were grouped under such headings as 'Of all the members of a mans bodie,' 'Of the kindred,' 'the dayes of the weeke,' and so on.[46] Moreover it seems clear that a number of grammarians may well have had in mind a mode of classification less general than the above, and more closely in accordance with the 'philosophia rerum.'[47] By this was probably meant a system in which the groupings would follow closely the relations observed between real objects and in which the internal order of ideas within the different groups would be carefully planned, again in an attempt to accord with the order of reality.

Once scholars had accepted this need for a classification of concepts before any real character could be successfully formulated, it was natural enough that they should seek a model in the long-established Aristotelian-Scholastic way of ordering knowledge in terms of a hierarchy of ideas, descending by way of various groupings from the most general heads to the most particular properties of things. For, although Aristotelian thought and its methods came under attack in the second half of the century, when scholars or scientists were dealing with the world of nature *in toto* (as distinct sometimes from the investigation of individual phenomena) the classificatory way of conceiving knowledge was still widely accepted and practised, even among leading scientists like John Ray and Francis Willoughby, who transformed the classified tables by close observation of nature into valuable aids to scientific progress. It is scarcely surprising, then, that the later seventeenth-century language planners should have chosen to group objects and ideas more or less according to Aristotelian categories.

However, the systematic classification of things to form a virtual encyclopaedia of knowledge, together with the symbolization of these ideas, cannot be satisfactorily explained without reference to the highly complex interplay of Lullist, Cabalist, and art-of-memory themes that have recently been studied by Paolo Rossi and Frances Yates, in the *Clavis universalis* and *The Art of Memory* respectively. Frances Yates wrote in the final chapter of her important book on memory treatises that the seventeenth-century efforts at constructing a universal language 'come straight out of the memory tradition with its search for signs and symbols to use as memory images.'[48] Although memory treatises were only one of the many influences that bore upon the development of the universal language movement, her judgment is sound and, drawing upon her account and that of Rossi,[49] we may explore briefly a few of the ways in which the universal language schemes may be related to this fascinating tradition.

In a general way, memory images may, first, be set alongside Egyptian hieroglyphs, Mexican picture-writing, and mathematical, musical, astrological, and alchemical symbols, as indicating both the force and the usefulness of a symbolic representation of ideas. But memory images had the special function of recalling things easily, and it was precisely this function that interested the universal language planners, who from the first recognized that mnemonic considerations were important to their chances of success.[50] For there was no point whatsoever in forming a universal character or language if it could not be easily learned and remembered, an objection that was levelled in fact against at least one of the earliest schemes of a common writing.[51]

To organize the 'words' of the new character into classified groups was, as we have seen, an obvious way of cutting down on the number of signs required; but it was also a possible way of resolving some of the difficulties encountered in remembering them. It seems likely that those language planners who first envisaged the ordering of ideas as a basic principle of language-building found their inspiration in the practice of the art-of-memory writers themselves, as well as in the subject-groupings of language teachers (itself, of course, a memory device). For it was an accepted part of the classical art of memory that places, *loci*, were chosen to which usually striking images, *imagines*, representing the things to be remembered, were assigned; because these places were situated in a known order with respect to each other, they permitted one to move freely and easily from one image to the next. Frances Yates pointed out that arrangement in order was one of the precepts of the classical art of memory, and was strongly insisted upon by Aristotle and Thomas Aquinas.[52] Further, she continued, 'in the memory text-books of Romberch and Rossellius a way is taught of arranging material in inclusive "common-places" within which are individual places,' adding that this has something in common with Ramus's insistence in his dialectical method on descending from 'generals' to 'specials.'[53] There are thus many apparent similarities between the classical art of memory, Ramus's notion of 'dialectical order,' and the ordered classifications of the projectors of a philosophical language, and it is worth looking for a moment at the universal language schemes for rather more precise evidence of the influence upon them of this type of memory treatise. In disposing the words of his proposed new language Sir Thomas Urquhart suggested a technique that was derived directly from the classical art of memory tradition. Urquhart first advised that words in our own language should be set apart in 'their several storehouses' (a significant memory term) according to the things to which they refer – terms of the 'Arts, Sciences, Mechanick Trades, [and] notional Faculties' were some of the groupings that he had in mind.[54] Next, Urquhart claimed to have been the first to suggest the allocation of a recognizable mark to words of the same Faculty, Art, Trade, or Science so that these words should be 'diagnosced,' as he put it, from those of another group by the very sound of the word at the first hearing. When he comes to discuss the scheme in greater detail, Urquhart's debt to the memory tradition emerges even more distinctly, for we are told that the structure of the new language depends, first of all, upon two hundred and fifty prime root-signs, from which, wrote Urquhart, in language directly recalling the Lullist and Renaissance image of the tree of knowledge, spring 'all its dependant boughs, sprigs, and ramelets.'[55] Secondly, the distribution of the words in the lexicon is organized

> into so many Cities, which are subdivided into streets, they againe into lanes, those into houses, these into stories; whereof each room standeth for a word; and all these so methodically, that who observeth my precepts thereanent, shall at the first hearing of a word, know to what City it belongeth, and consequently not be ignorant of some general signification thereof, till after a most exact prying into all its letters, finding the street, lane, house, story and room thereby denotated, he punctually hit upon the very proper thing it represents in its most special signification.[56]

The system described here is a common enough memory device. However it does not seem to me that it is simply borrowed for the purpose of setting terms in a particular order once the scheme has been formulated, but rather that the actual idea behind the distribution, and the suggestion of assigning a mark to words belonging to the same group, may have come to Urquhart as a direct result of considering a specific memory system.

Few of the seventeenth-century language planners reveal quite so clearly as Urquhart the influence that the memory treatises had upon their work. However, a number of schemes show signs of this influence in general in the principle of an ordered arrangement, the grouping by relations between things, and the movement from the general to the particular.[57] In addition to these important basic considerations, there are other similarities that suggest a keen awareness of memory problems on the part of a number of universal language builders.

Mersenne was most concerned in a letter to Peiresc to explain the mnemonic virtues of his proposed *idiome universel*, which, once constituted, would allow one to discover any term in the lexicon, and re-establish it in its former position, should one forget this. Mersenne claimed, moreover, that because of the ordered nature of the tables, the language required no natural memory on the part of the learner; in other words, the language in itself constituted an artificial memory system.[58] Cyprian Kinner similarly compared his scheme of a botanical character to a golden chain in which each link leads directly on to the next, so that by its use, 'anything (provided its beginnings were known) could be recollected and recited without break.'[59] Cave Beck wrote a letter 'Of Memory,' which is preserved among the papers of the Royal Society;[60] for another correspondent of Hartlib, John Beale, work on a memory system and preparation for a universal character seem to have been virtually synonymous.[61] George Dalgarno claimed that from the method followed in his *Ars signorum* (1661) 'can be discovered, a more easie way of the Art of Memory than any commonly known.'[62] But as DeMott and Rossi have clearly shown, it is John Wilkins above all who stresses the mnemonic value of the real character and philosophical language and who caters most carefully in his scheme for mnemonic aids that will assist in locating precisely a natural object in the philosophical tables. So, as DeMott has explained, the symbols of Wilkins's real character can be easily recalled by working from the genus downwards, and the place within the genus of, for instance, the salmon, can be understood by reference to the alphabetical progression of the character.[63] Other purely mnemonic features of Wilkins's work are the choice of a fixed number of species within each genus and of a determined number of plants under each difference, and the pairing of species and certain differences 'for the better helping of the Memory.'[64] Wilkins himself regarded the mnemonic aspect of his work as far from being the least important, and although it led sometimes to the imposition of an artificial order upon natural things to which one of Wilkins's collaborators, John Ray, in particular was averse,[65] it also meant that the *Essay* was praised by other contemporaries of Wilkins for its natural method and for the ease with which it could be learned and remembered.[66]

In addition to the memory treatises that developed out of a rhetorical tradition mention should be made of that extraordinarily complex great art of the thirteenth-century Spanish philosopher, Ramon Lull, and his Renaissance commentators and successors, which offers another kind of art of memory and far more besides. For in the *Ars brevis*, the *Ars inventiva*, and other works, Lull had attempted to describe a universal art that was intended to provide a key to an understanding of the entire universe, an art based essentially upon a combination of letters representing the divine attributes or perfections, which for Lull were the fundamental concepts to which all reality could and should be reduced. Lull offered by his Art a method for discovering the truth, for proving it to non-Christians, and for training men to recognize, love, and remember it. The *dignitates Dei*, or divine attributes, were present at every level of creation, and, since each of these nine attributes (together with other divine names) was assigned a letter which, for purposes of the art, became that attribute or name, it was necessary only to combine these letters according to certain well-defined goemetrical procedures at every step on the ladder of being in order to attain a profound understanding of reality. The Lullist art is therefore a logical art, a method for investigating the world at a physical as well as a metaphysical and spiritual level. For the mysterious depths of divine energy in creation are revealed to man by the practice of the art, which is itself the key to these mysteries.

The resemblances between Lullism and the spirit and methods of the Cabala are most striking, and in the Renaissance, as Frances Yates has shown, Lullism came in fact to be closely associated with Cabalism, for the first time perhaps in the work of Pico della Mirandola.[67] While it is not proposed to examine in detail the connections between Lullist and Cabalist thought here, we may recall that there is a similar use of letters and combinations of letters to reach divine truth. The *Sephiroth* consists of the divine emanations or attributes, ten in number, while the *Golem* is composed of the twenty-two letters of the Hebrew alphabet, which are themselves expressions of divine energy and power. The spirit that lay behind the Cabalist belief in the importance of names and letters, which is also very close to that of Lullism, is well captured by Gershom Scholem in his book *On the Kabbalah and Its Symbolism*, where he writes:

> The secret world of the godhead is a world of language, a world of divine names that unfold in accordance with a law of their own. The elements of the divine language appear as the letters of the Holy Scriptures. Letters and names are not only conventional means of communication. They are far more. Each one of them represents a concentration of energy and expresses a wealth of meaning which cannot be translated, or not fully at least, into human language.[68]

How aware were the seventeenth-century language planners of this tradition? The nature of the relationship between, on the one hand, schemes that have often been labelled 'scientific' and, on the other, a profoundly religious, even at times decidedly occult, art is, of course, of the greatest interest not only for an understanding of the language schemes themselves, but also as an illustration of how earlier ideas may undergo transformation in the course of a century. For behind this question there lies the much wider issue of the relationship of seventeenth-century scientific or mathematical method to earlier attempts to investigate and understand reality.

Although some of Ramon Lull's work remains unpublished even today, seventeenth-century scholars already had access to a considerable body of his writing, as well as to a number of Lullian commentaries and pseudo-Lullist works. Out of many editions one may mention the *Ars brevis*, published in 1578, the *De auditu kabbalistico* published in the same year, which was widely believed to be an authentic work by Lull, and the explanation of Lullist thought contained in de Lavinheta's *Opera omnia* published in 1612.[69]

Francis Bacon and Descartes both referred in major works to Lull's method, and, although Descartes, like Bacon, spoke of the art with contempt,[70] his proposal for an analysis of complex ideas into their simple constituent elements had something in common with that earlier, more occult art. Of the enthusiasts for a universal philosophical language, Mersenne shows himself in the *Harmonie universelle* to be familiar with the Lullist system of combinations and, in the course of explaining how one might order ideas and attach a number to each, he significantly chooses as his examples the name of God and the divine attributes to which the numbers one to ten are to be allocated.[71] Comenius, whose 'pansophic language' is described in the *Via lucis* (1668), followed very much in the steps of his teacher, Alsted, who had attempted a reconciliation of Lullism, Cabalism, Ramism, and Aristotelianism. Athanasius Kircher, the Jesuit author of the *Polygraphia nova et universalis* (1663) was both a Lullist and a Cabalist, and himself composed an *Ars magna sciendi*.[72] In England, Samuel Hartlib's papers contain several references to Lull's work,[73] as well as to schemes such as Bisterfeld's suggestion for a 'philosophical alphabet' which has many affinities with the Spanish philosopher's aims.[74] In the *Vindiciae academiarum*, Seth Ward, to whom, it is worth repeating, Wilkins said he owed the procedure that he adopted in his essay, referred to 'Lully, and others who have made Symbols of the Letters of the Alphabet,' a device that, Ward pointed out, had been applied to the 'nature of things' by the Pythagorean philosophers, the Cabalists, and the Combinatorian Jews.[75] The Aubrey-Paschall-Pigot correspondence, preserved in the Bodleian Library, Oxford, and in the archives of the Royal Society,[76] shows that this was far more than a casual reference on Ward's part and that a knowledge of the art of Lull was fundamental to his own plan for a philosophical language, which, in the event, differed from that followed by Wilkins in his essay. Finally, of course, the *Dissertatio de arte combinatoria* (1666) is sufficient indication of Leibniz's knowledge of Lullism and the Lullist tradition.[77] These few references, which could certainly be multiplied, are enough to show that the work of Lull, his imitators, and his commentators was consulted by several of the proponents of a philosophical language, and even explicitly linked with their own undertakings.[78]

But what signs are there that knowledge of Lullist and Cabalist methods and ways of thinking actually influenced the approach to language building of these scholars? First of all, the analysis and decomposition of natural things and complex notions into their particular attributes and the representation of these things and notions by combinations of letters or other symbols, both of which have sometimes been regarded as the specific discoveries of the planners of a philosophical language, had clearly long been familiar features of Lullist and Cabalist procedures. Lullism differed, of course, from a work like Wilkins's real character and philosophical language in that the art operated with a very small, fixed number of irreducible elements (the divine attributes) that were the product of an essentially theological view of reality, while, on the other hand, the philosophical language defined things by using a much wider range of properties derived from a more orthodox classification according to genus, species, and specific difference. It differed also in that Lullism was a far more mobile art, working by means of a series of combinations, read off from revolving circles, upon which were set out the letters of the 'alphabet' of the art, or otherwise formed by conjoining other letters that were linked by the shape of the triangle (the Trinity) or the square (probably the four elements).[79]

These considerations may appear somewhat remote from the philosophical languages of Dalgarno and Wilkins, which, although they use symbols to identify various properties of things, are closer in form to the more static Aristotelian-Scholastic compilations of knowledge than to the revolving circles of Lull. And yet in the early seventeenth century, Alsted had already attempted to graft the Lullist system of combining letters on to Aristotelian and medieval groupings of ideas which were to be systematically classified with the aim of establishing a single, unified body of knowledge.[80] This was not intended to be a collection of facts for their own sake, but a universal system by means of which one would arrive at an understanding of the principles underlying all reality. This emphasis upon encyclopaedism and a search for general principles led naturally enough to an enumeration of 'general terms' and to their symbolization by letters or other characters, much as had been done in Lull's great inventive art. The fusion of Lullism and encyclopaedism that characterizes the work of

Alsted anticipates the more extensive attribution of symbols to all the things that were set out in the philosophical tables of the later universal language schemes.

It had been a widely held Lullist belief that practice of the *ars inventiva* would lead inexorably to a deep understanding of the true nature of things, a belief which had much in common with the Cabalist view that the contemplation and combination of their sacred symbols illuminated the real essence of things. Primitive Hebrew letters, it will be recalled, were supposed to constitute the *lingua humana*, the first, truly universal language of mankind, which was spoken before the confusion of tongues at Babel and into which God had, as it were, written the meaning of his creation. Claims that the invented philosophical languages of the seventeenth century would also lead one into the 'nature of things' suggest a further possibility of influence, which was touched upon briefly in the opening chapter of this book[81] and which raises the whole question of the nature of the relationship between this phase of the universal language movement and the Lullist-Cabalist tradition.

On the whole, scholars have tended to divide themselves into two camps on this wider issue. On the one hand, there are those (Otto Funke, Richard Foster Jones, and, to some extent, Vivian Salmon)[82] who have concentrated upon the Baconian origins of the movement, stressing the strictly nominalist, materialistic way of looking at language and the scientific aims of the philosophical language planners. On the other hand, there are those (DeMott, Aarsleff, and Rossi)[83] who have focused attention more upon the links that these schemes have with the mystical ideas of Andreae, Alsted, and Boehme. These differences in view have arisen, partly at least, from the fact that the first group of scholars has been concerned in the main with the English language schemes, which were indeed generally regarded as likely to contribute to the progress of scientific knowledge, but which also draw from sources more occult than Bacon's *De augmentis scientiarum* that have often not been recognized. While these scholars have separated too sharply what they regarded as the 'scientific' from other currents of ideas, the second group has been too eager to absorb all the philosophical schemes into an occult tradition, without noting how occult ideas have been, in some cases, radically transformed in a different age and a different context, and without distinguishing sufficiently clearly between a writer like Comenius, who stands squarely in the mystical tradition, and Wilkins, whose ideas, perhaps in spite of appearances, were undoubtedly influenced by it.

My own view coincides more nearly with that expressed by Frances Yates in the final chapter of her book *The Art of Memory*, where she writes, 'The seventeenth-century universal language enthusiasts are translating into rational terms efforts such as those of Giordano Bruno to found universal memory systems on magic images which he thought of as directly in contact with reality.'[84] What is important in this statement is not the specific reference to Bruno – indeed I see no signs at all that it was Bruno's more magical version of the Lullist combinations in particular which influenced the universal language planners – but the view that certain ideas in the language schemes (and specifically the idea of a set of symbols standing in a direct relationship with reality) have been taken over from more occult works and *transformed* into something different. The detailed knowledge that we now possess of the origins and development of the universal language movement suggests that such a transformation of earlier, more occult ideas did, in fact, occur. It also tends to confirm the broader thesis of Frances Yates that what we are witnessing in the seventeenth century is the emergence from medieval and Renaissance methods and ways of thinking of what is generally thought of as a more rational, more 'scientific' view of reality and of a method for investigating and describing it that is more appropriate to that view.[85]

Seth Ward wrote in 1654 that a new language of real characters would enable one to convey something of the nature of things.[86] But, as we saw in our opening chapter, the meaning that he and his collaborator, John Wilkins, attributed to this word ('where every word were a definition' of the thing represented) was different from that lent to it by the occult philosophers. For the barely expressible revelations that were hoped for from the various forms of occult symbolism have been replaced by a far more rational enumeration of the properties of natural objects and ideas, or, as Wilkins expressed it quite explicitly in the *Essay*:

It were likewise desirable to a perfect definition of each species, that the *immediate form* which gives the particular essence to everything might be expressed; but this form being a thing which men do not know, it cannot be expected that it should be described. And therefore in the stead of it, there is reason why men should be content with such a description by *properties* and *circumstances*, as may be sufficient to determine the primary sense of the thing defined.[87]

And yet Ward's allusions to the practice of Lull, the Cabalists, and the Jewish mystical writers,[88] together with definite evidence from the unpublished Aubrey-Paschall-Pigot correspondence concerning Ward's special debt to Lull's method,[89] indicates that, although one should distinguish one use of the term *nature of things* from another, the two cannot be entirely divorced. And this example of an evolution from the occult to the more rational in the universal language schemes is neither the first nor the last.

Earlier, in France, Descartes's proposal for a universal language based upon the analysis of complex ideas into their simple elements, to each of which would be assigned a character, calls inevitably to mind the art of Ramon Lull, which was also a kind of geometrical logic.[90] But while Lull's system was determined by a set of given attributes and procedures (divinely revealed to its author, as Lull believed), the simple elements of Descartes's language had still to be discovered by the light of the human reason with its ability to distinguish between the clear and the distinct. More than twenty years before Izquierdo's *Pharus scientiarum* in 1659 and thirty years before Kircher's *Ars magna sciendi* in 1669, we see in Mersenne's work, and particularly in the *Harmonie universelle* (1636), how the symbolic meaning of Lull's letters has already come to be totally ignored, as Mersenne concentrates upon purely numerical combinations. Comenius, who put forward the idea of a language 'adapted to the exact and perfect representation of things'[91] in the *Via lucis* (1668) was much closer to the occult tradition than were the English language planners. Nonetheless, he clearly had in mind a method similar to that employed by Wilkins in his essay, when he wrote that the new language would be a hundred times more perfect than Latin 'in as much as it is ready to express all concepts and all things in their special characteristics: and a thousand times better fitted harmoniously to express the qualities of things,

[95]

Lexicon Latino-Philosophicum.

Abacus *fran.*
Abbas *kaf.*
Abdicare *sofkafisu,* trud *sofstem.*
Abdere *dit.*
Abire *bempnd.*
Abhinc *shub lol dan, bem lol dad*
Abhorrere *prebesu sumpron, trof*
Abjurare *scabe trimesu*
Ablactatio *saffus, sosinn*
abolere *sosjhanesu, grupesu, sosiavresu*
abominari *sumpronesu*
aboriri *pratesu sub danu*
abripere *dos don bemdep shekii*
abrogare *sosiavresu, sofkebesu*
abrumpere *domesu donesu*
absolvere *konshon sis*
abstemius *sosprasemp*
abstinere *trus preb tim sodesu*

absurditas *shib prem sostos*
abundantia *sumu stvdu*
abusus *shig*
abyssus *dadbaf*
academia *dadtem santem dadtis*
accendere *nnmesu, semesu nnm*
accidere *sakesu prk ded*
accingere *drod sitresu*
accipere *sprnb*
acclivitas *blnmu*
accolere *slid shumbem*
accommodare *stop sitresu*
acervus *drotor,* ——: *ind ex nnfind*
acetum *snm* vel *slem grnba*
acies *bnbu*
acqiescere *dram tup*
acquirere *stis spnm*
aculeus *sabdik*
acumen *bnbu primu*
additamentum *shunu drasa, tnno*
adeo *sum lolsns ses*

adjuro

Plate 2 George Dalgarno *Ars signorum* London 1661
95: first page of the Latin-universal character lexicon
By courtesy of the British Library Board

[118]

Primum Caput Genesios.

1. DAN sieru, Sava samefa Nam, ton Nom.
2. Ton nom avesa sof-shama ton drag, ton gromu avesa ben mem suf basu: ton uv suf Sava damesa ben mem suf nimmi.
3. Ton Sava tinesa, gomu aveso: ton gomu avesa.
4. Ton Sava muesa gomu suma: ton Sava dosesa gomu dos gromu.
5. Ton Sava tonesa gomu Dan-gomu, ton tonesa gromu Dan-gromu: ton shem-gomu ton sem-gomu avesa dan-ve vasi.
6. Ton Sava tinesa, dad-dreku aveso bred brepu suf nimmi: ton doleso nimmi dos nimmi.
7. Ton Sava samesa dad-dreku, ton dosesa nimmi bren dad-dreku dos nimmi ben dad-dreku: ton lel-sa avesa.
8. Ton Sava tonesa dad-dreku, Nam: ton shem-gomu ton sem-gomu avesa dan-vevsa.
9. Ton Sava tinesa, nimmi bren nam dekoso bred dadu suma, ton granar mesoso: ton lel-ses avesa.
10. Ton Sava tondsa granar Nom, ton tonesa deku

[119]

deku suf nimmi, IIss; ton Sava muesa lolar suma.
11. Ton Sava tinesa, nom gvpeso nab, neibeid gune rug, ton rag-sneig gune rag sos sugu lvla, rug suf lul tim bred lol ben nom: ton lel-ses avesa.
12. Ton nom gunesa nab, neibeid gune rug sos sugu lvla: ton sneig gune rag, rug suf lul tim bred lol, sos sugu lvla: ton Sava muesa lolar suma.
13. Ton shem-gomu ton sem-gomu avesa dan-ve vesa.
14. Ton Sava tinesa, gomu avesa bred dad-dreku suf Nam tham dolesu dan-gomu dos dan-gromu: ton lelli aveso sas dannu, ton vesti, ton dan-vusi.
15. Ton lelli aveso sas gomu bred dad-dreku suf nam, tham gonesu ben nom: ton lel-ses avesa.
16. Ton Sava samesa vn gommu suma, gomu sona sham sudesu dan-gomu, ton gomu shuna sham sudesu dan-gromu: ton samesa aisi.
17. Ton Sava dadesa lelli bred dad-dreku suf nam sham gonesu ben nom.
18. Ton tham sudesu dan-gomu, ton dan-gromu, ton dolesu gomu dos gromu: ton Sava muesa lolar suma.
19. Ton shem-gomu, ton sem-gomu avesa dan-ve vesa.
20. Ton Sava tinesa, nimmi sum-gunesu neir, ton neip pu ne bred dad-dreku suf nam ben nom.
21. Ton

I 4

Plate 3 George Dalgarno *Ars signorum* London 1661
118–9: first chapter of Genesis in Dalgarno's universal character
By courtesy of the British Library Board

since its individual names will be made to match the numbers, measurements, and weights of things themselves.'[92] Lullism was in fact (to adopt Frances Yates's term) being 'mathematicized'[93] in the course of the seventeenth century, a process which was to culminate in Leibniz's concept of a *characteristica universalis* as a logical method suitable for the solution of all problems. The abstract tendencies of Lullism have therefore come to be developed to the point where, in Leibniz, reasoning has become synonymous with calculating.

Part way along this line of development lie the rational universal languages of George Dalgarno (see plates 2 and 3) and John Wilkins (plates 4–6). Although these *a priori* language schemes may quite properly be termed philosophical languages, since they depend upon a classification of 'things and notions' according to their properties and their relations one with another, we should note that they are philosophical in a rather different manner from the language that was envisaged by Descartes and was more fully considered by Leibniz. The emphasis in Dalgarno's and Wilkins's philosophical languages is placed upon a description of the order of reality rather than upon mathematical analysis and decomposition. Wilkins's language in particular is much closer to the world of observation than to that of the more abstract combinations of mathematical symbols that Leibniz most often had in mind as constituting the elements of his *characteristica universalis*. General metaphysical relations form, of course, a part of Wilkins's scheme, but they are treated as being the most difficult to handle satisfactorily, for, as Wilkins wrote:

> The right ordering of these Transcendentals is a business of no small difficulty; because there is so little assistance or help to be had for it in the Common Systems, according to which this part of Philosophy (as it seems to me) is rendred the most rude and imperfect in the whole body of Sciences; as if the compilers of it had taken no other care for those General notions, which did not fall within the ordinary series of things, and were not explicable in other particular Sciences, but only to tumble them together in several confused heaps, which they stiled the Science of *Metaphysic*.[94]

In the main, Dalgarno's and Wilkins's languages define things (mainly

Chap. I. *Concerning a Real Character.*

Transcend.	General	~	Animals	Exanguious	⊥	Action	Spiritual
	Rel. mixed	v		Fish	T		Corporeal
	Rel. of Action	n		Bird	⊥		Motion
	Difcourfe	u		Beaft	T		Operation
	God	—	Parts	Peculiar	+		
	World	+		General	+	Relation	Oecon.
	Element	⊥	Quantity	Magnitude			Poffef.
	Stone	T		Space	T		Provif.
	Metal	+		Meafure	+		Civil
Herb confid. accord. to the	Leaf	⊥		Power Nat.	⊥		Judicial
	Flower	T	Quality	Habit	T		Military
	Seed-veffel	⊥		Manners	⊥		Naval
	Shrub	r		Quality fenfible	g		Eccelf.
	Tree	+		Difeafe	θ		

The Differences are to be affixed unto that end which is on the left fide of the Character, according to this order;

1 2 3 4 5 6 7 8 9

The Species should be affixed at the other end of the Character according to the like order.

1 2 3 4 5 6 7 8 9

And whereas feveral of the Species of Vegetables and Animals, do according to this prefent conftitution, amount to more than Nine, in fuch cafes the number of them is to be diftributed into two or three Nines, which may be diftinguifhed from one another by doubling the ftroke in fome one or more parts of the Character; as fuppofe after this manner, —⸺ —⸺. If the firft and moft fimple Character be made ufe of, the Species that are affixed to it, will belong to the firft combination of *Nine*; if the other, they will belong according to the order of them, unto the fecond Combination.

Thofe Radicals which are paired to others uppon account of *Oppofition*, may be expreffed by a Loop, or (o) at the left end of the Character, after this manner, ↼

Thofe that are paired upon the account of *Affinity*, are to be expreffed by the like Mark at the other end of the Character, thus, ⇀

The double Oppofites of *Excefs* or *Defect*, are to be defcribed by the Tranfcendental points, denoting *Excefs* or *Defect*, to be placed over the Character, as fhall be fhewed after.

Ddd 2 *Adje-*

CHAP. II.

Instances of this Real Character in the Lords Prayer and the Creed.

For the better explaining of what hath been before delivered concerning a Real Character, it will be necessary to give some Example and Instance of it, which I shall do in the *Lords Prayer* and the *Creed* : First setting each of them down after such a manner as they are ordinarily to be written. Then the Characters at a greater distance from one another, for the more convenient figuring and inter lining of them. And lastly, a Particular Explication of each Character out of the Philosphical Tables, with a Verbal Interpretation of them in the Margin.

The Lords Prayer.

[Real Character text]

1 2 3 4 5 6 7 8 9 10 11
Our Parent who art in Heaven, Thy Name be Hallowed, Thy
12 13 14 15 16 17 18 19 20 21 22 23 24 25 26
Kingdome come, Thy Will be done, so in Earth as in Heaven, Give
27 28 29 30 31 32 33 34 35 36 37 38 39 40 41 42 43
to us on this day our bread expedient and forgive us our trespasses as
44 45 46 47 48 49 50 51 52 53 54 55 56 57 58
we forgive them who trespass against us, and lead us not into
59 60 61 62 63 64 65 66 67 68 69 70
temptation, but deliver us from evil, for the Kingdome and the
71 72 73 74 75 76 77 78 79 80.
Power and the Glory is thine, for ever and ever, Amen. So be it.

Chap. III.   *Concerning a Real Character.*   415

That which at present seems most convenient to me, is this;

Transcend.	General	Ba	Animals	Exanguious	Za	Action	Spiritual	Ca
	Rel. mixed	Ba		Fish	Za		Corporeal	Ca
	Rel. of Action	Be		Bird	Ze		Motion	Ce
	Discourse	Bi		Beast	Zi		Operation	Ci
	God	Dα	Parts	Peculiar	Pα			
	World	Da		General	Pa		Oecon.	Co
	Element	De	Quantity	Magnitude	Pe	Relation	Possess.	Cy
	Stone	Di		Space	Pi		Provis.	Sα
	Metal	Do		Measure	Po		Civil	Sa
Herb consid. accord. to the	Leaf	Gα	Quality	Power Nat.	Tα		Judicial	Se
	Flower	Ga		Habit	Ta		Military	Si
	Seed-vessel	Ge		Manners	Te		Naval	So
	Shrub	Gi		Quality sensible	Ti		Ecclef.	Sy
	Tree	Go		Disease	To			

The *Differences* under each of these *Genus*'s, may be expressed by these Consonants ℸ B, D, G, P, T, C, Z, S, N.
in this order; ℒ 1 2 3 4 5 6 7. 8 9.

The *Species* may be expressed by putting one of the seven Vowels after the Consonant, for the Difference; to which may be added (to make up the number) two of the Dipthongs, according to this order
{ α, a, e, i, o, ȣ, y, yi, yȣ.
{ 1 2 3 4 5 6 7 8 9.

For instance, If (De) signifie *Element*, then (Deb) must signifie the first difference; which (according to the Tables) is *Fire*: and (Debα) will denote the first Species, which is *Flame*. (Det) will be the fifth difference under that Genus, which is, *Appearing Meteor*; (Detα) the first Species, viz. *Rainbow*; (Deta) the second, viz. *Halo.*

Thus, if (Ti) signifie the Genus of *Sensible Quality*, then (Tid) must denote the second difference, which comprehends Colours; and (Tida) must signifie the second Species under that difference, viz. *Redness*: (Tide) the third Species, which is *Greenness*, &c.

Thus likewise, if (Be) be put for the Genus of *Transcendental Relation of Action*, then (Bec) must denote the sixth difference, which is *Ition*; and (Becȣ) will signifie the sixth Species, which is *Following.*

As for those Species under Plants and Animals, which do exceed the number of Nine, they may be expressed by adding the Letters *L*, or *R*, after the first Consonant, to denote the second or third of such Combinations. Thus, if Gαde be *Tulip*, viz. the third Species in the first Nine, then Glαde must signifie *Ramson*, viz. the third in the second Nine, or the twelfth Species under that Difference. So if Zana be *Salmon*, viz. the second species in the first Nine, then Zlana must signifie *Gudgeon*, viz. the second in the second Nine; or the eleventh Species under that Difference.

It

material) by their general and individual properties, without attempting to penetrate far beneath the apparent order of reality. Theirs is a method for enumerating the known, rather than for investigating the unknown. Their analysis stops short, in other words, at relatively easily determinable characteristics. Above all, there is no effort to reduce complex ideas to a few philosophical simples, a procedure that Descartes probably had in mind when he first wrote to Mersenne concerning a philosophical character and language in 1629. It was essentially because of this difference in conception that Leibniz was later to assert that the schemes formulated by Dalgarno and Wilkins were not philosophical enough, and that Seth Ward, influenced by Lull's conception of the art as functioning with only a small number of general attributes, was to propose, after Wilkins's death, a plan that differed from the one followed in his former colleague's essay.[95]

Before 1650 approximately, the universal character had interested scholars for a variety of reasons that may be usefully summarized at this point. Most obviously, it offered a possible means of general communication between peoples of different nations and languages. Because it was invented by human art, it also seemed to promise a means of communication that would not be subject to the many defects of instituted languages, and, since it was simple, clear, and unequivocal, it could be learned, its supporters claimed, much more quickly than any foreign language, without taking up the time that should be devoted to 'real studies.' Finally, the real character was thought to be worthy of serious attention because its characters represented things simply and directly.

Many of these same virtues continued to be extolled by the language builders after the change in direction that has just been described. But other claims were also made that were new or that received fresh emphasis in an individual scheme. The latter is the case, for instance, with George Dalgarno, who stressed that his 'universal character and new Rational language' was superior to any known Brachigraphy (a common term used to indicate a shorthand system), and then added a further claim that was probably, up to that date at least, original to him: 'This Character shall be a ready way, and a singular means, to convey Knowledge to deaf and dumb people (which is a secret of learning heretofore not discovered) and it is conceived upon good ground that a deaf man might be taught to communicate in this Character, in the sixth part of the time that any other man could learn a foreign language.'[96]

More important, however, was the major claim that by adopting the new principle of symbolizing the properties of things and notions, the universal language builders were revealing the order of reality which was transcribed in the very combinations of its elements. And so the new language would, in Comenius's words, lead to the 'discovery not only of a language, but of thought, and, what is more, of the truth of things themselves at the same time.'[97] The consequences of formulating such a language appeared tremendously exciting to many of the scholars who took an interest in this question in the 1650s and 1660s. For it meant, first of all, that the earlier, relatively common claim that a real character would help to ease the critical situation caused by disputes over words was given added force. For the philosophical language would now be presenting to all men an 'exact and perfect representation of things,'[98] that is, a scientifically accurate description and definition of the world in which there would be no place for verbal ambiguities, irregularities, and disputes concerning words. So Dalgarno, looking back some twenty years after the publication of his *Ars signorum*, claimed that his character was designed 'not only to remedie the confusion of Languages, by giving a much more easie medium of communication then any yet known; but also to cure even Philosophy itself of the disease of Sophisms and Logomachies; as also to provide her with more wieldy and mannageable Instruments of operation, for defining, demonstrating etc.'[99] Similarly, John Wilkins maintained that his real character and philosophical language would

> likewise contribute much to the clearing of some of our Modern differences in *Religion*, by unmasking many wild errors, that shelter themselves under the disguise of affected phrases; which being Philosophically unfolded, and rendered according to the genuine and natural importance of Words, will appear to be inconsistencies and contradictions. And several of those pretended, mysterious, profound notions, expressed in great swelling words, whereby some men set up for reputation, being this way examined, will appear to be either nonsense, or very flat and jejune.[100]

Again, because of similarities in both idea and expression, we need to point out, by way of parenthesis, that in advocating the usefulness of his universal character for healing sectarian disputes, Wilkins was not necessarily inspired by either the writings or the precise aims of Comenius. For it was quite possible for Wilkins to express an idea that brought him close to Comenius's views, without wholeheartedly sharing the latter's pansophic ideals. Broadly speaking, I agree with Vivian Salmon's view that 'such a statement is exactly what might be expected from a supporter of the seventeenth-century movement, entirely unconnected with Comenius [not entirely, surely], for the simplification of prose style.'[101] But one needs to stress again, first, that the religious motive, though not identical with that of Comenius, was nonetheless a perfectly genuine one, and, secondly, that the proposal for a language that actually portrayed the world with some accuracy of detail introduced a new element into that movement.

The real character had been placed for some time by scholars among the *desiderata* of learning, largely as a consequence of Francis Bacon's discussion of the subject. However, once it was realized that a language might be framed that would present an ordered description of reality, such a project came to be regarded as of even greater importance to the advancement of knowledge. For, as we have mentioned earlier, scholars soon came to recognize that, if such a pattern were to be followed, learning and using the philosophical language would be the linguistic equivalent of learning and using real knowledge. It is clear from the *Essay* that it was for this reason above all that Wilkins considered his real character and philosophical language to be as much preferred to the work of dictionary-making, 'as *things* are better than *words*, as *real knowledge* is beyond *elegancy of speech*, as the *general good of mankind* is beyond that of any *particular Countrey* or *Nation*.'[102]

It is this particular aspect of the English philosophical languages of the 1660s that will be considered in the next few pages. And, since George Dalgarno's *Ars signorum* (1661) and John Wilkins's *Essay towards a Real Character and a Philosophical Language* (1668) are founded upon a similar classification of ideas according to genera, species, and specific differences, we shall look only at the *Essay*, partly because it was the more ambitious, complex, and successful of the two, and partly because it was around this particular universal language scheme that much of the interest and activity of the time was crystallized.[103]

JOHN WILKINS'S 'REAL CHARACTER AND PHILOSOPHICAL LANGUAGE'

John Wilkins (1614–72) was one of the founder-members of the Royal Society, its first secretary, and, prior to the publication of the essay, the author of a number of works of scientific vulgarization, among others the fascinating *Discovery of a World in the Moone* (published in 1638), as well as several treatises on prayer and on preaching.[104] Wilkins's interest in the possibility of providing a real character was long-standing, dating back, as has been seen, to his early work on communication, the *Mercury, or the Secret and Swift Messenger* (1641), in which a universal character was already praised as having much to contribute to the advancement of 'real learning.' When Seth Ward (1617–89) became Professor of Astronomy at Oxford in 1649 and entered himself as a Fellow-commoner at Wadham College, where Wilkins was warden, it was hardly surprising that the universal character became one of the subjects of their 'daily and intimate converse.'[105] According to Wilkins, Ward soon showed that he was something of an expert on this subject, and it was as a result of these conversations that the future Bishop of Chester came to appreciate that, to be of real use to mankind, the universal character would need to be founded not upon a 'Dictionary of words according to some particular language' but upon the 'nature of things' and the common notions that men possessed of them.[106]

The occasion to carry out the preparation of such a scheme was offered to Wilkins by the project of a universal character that was being undertaken from 1657 onwards by George Dalgarno. Wilkins offered to draw up for Dalgarno 'the Tables of *Substance*, or the species of *Natural Bodies*, reduced under their several Heads,' which were eventually refused by Dalgarno, who considered that the tables were 'of too great a Compass, conceiving that he could sufficiently provide for all the chief Radicals, in a much briefer and more easy way.'[107] Following this refusal, Wilkins continued to work along lines possibly mapped out with Ward and, having recognized the extreme difficulty and labour involved in enumerating and defining all things according to their relations in nature, he called upon the specialist help that was at hand among his colleagues and friends of the Royal Society group. So, in spite of having some serious reservations about the plan to which he was asked to conform,[108] John Ray was prevailed upon to draw up the tables of plants, Francis Willoughby gathered the material for the section on animals, Samuel Pepys helped with nautical terminology, and Dr William Lloyd, who was also entirely responsible for the dictionary of words that followed the essay proper, assisted Wilkins generally.

The essay itself is divided into four parts: firstly, the Prolegomena, which is devoted principally to criticisms of established languages; secondly, what Wilkins termed the Universal Philosophy, which consists of the tables of things and notions; thirdly, the philosophical, natural, or general grammar; and, fourthly, the real character and philosophical language itself. Of these four sections, the heart of Wilkins's scheme is the universal philosophy, which occupies over two hundred and fifty pages, that is over half of the book. Wilkins himself described this, the 'scientifical' part of the essay, as 'the great foundation of the thing here designed,'[109] and, in the 'Epistle Dedicatory to the Royal Society,' he showed how important he considered this classification to be for the progress of real knowledge. The tables, he explained, 'would very much promote and facilitate the knowledg of Nature, which is one great end of your Institution.'[110] These tables were so contrived that the place of everything in them would contribute to the 'description of the nature of it' and it was precisely because the language both enumerated and *defined* things that Wilkins's philosophical language was thought to have such an important part to play in the advancement of learning. Wilkins also claimed that, whether the real character and philosophical language was adopted for international usage or not,

> yet this I shall assert with greater confidence, That the reducing of all things and notions, to such kind of Tables, as are here proposed (were it as compleatly done as it might be) would prove the shortest and plainest way for the attainment of real Knowledge, that hath yet been offered to the World. And I shall add further, that these very

Tables (as now they are) do seem to me a much better and readier course, for the entring and training up of men in the knowledge of things, then any other way of Institution that I know of.[111]

Another hope of Wilkins was that the tables, as they were represented in the essay, or as they would be amended subsequently by the Royal Society, would provide an excellent method for ordering the Natural History collections which the society had set up shortly before.[112] In fact, we know that, even before the publication of the essay, Robert Hooke had begun to arrange what was called the Repository according to the various groupings established by Wilkins as part of what was clearly intended to be the most up-to-date and the most accurate classification of natural things ever attempted.[113]

In Wilkins's tables, objects and ideas are categorized, first of all, according to forty broadly based generic groups. These *genera* consist of 'transcendentals' (general, relation mixed, and relation of action), groupings according to divisions noted in the natural world (e.g. stone, metal, herb, shrub, tree, fish, bird, beast), and others related, for instance, by a common factor of quantity (magnitude, space, and measurement). However complex the scheme may tend to become in its subsequent development and execution, the method for applying a system of written symbols (the real character) and spoken sounds (the philosophical language) to these philosophical tables is basically very simple. Each *genus* has assigned to it a particular consonant and vowel and a corresponding written character-sign, and, since both character and language are intended to proceed methodically, each *genus* leads on to the next and is related to other associated *genera*. For instance, the sounds representing the *genera* that include all vegetative matter, herbs, shrubs, and trees, all have the initial letter G followed by either *a, e, i,* or *o*. Similarly, birds, beasts, and fishes all have the initial letter z followed by these same vowels in the same order.[114] Equally in the real character, herbs, shrubs, and trees again are represented by similar written symbols (⊢, ⊤, ⊣).[115] *Genera* are thus represented by a systematically organized, basic set of letters and characters.

Differences are next expressed by adding the consonants B, D, G, P, T, C, Z, S, N, to the letters of the *genera* in the philosophical language.

So, taking Emery's example,[116] *Di* is the basic generic sign for stone, to which, if one adds a B (*Dib*) marking the first difference of that *genus*, one refers to a stone classified according to the first difference, that is, a vulgar stone. Species are then denoted by adding one of a number of vowels and diphthongs. Thus *Diba* will identify the stone even more closely as a 'Rag,' that is, a coarse-textured, vulgar stone.

The real character proceeds in the same way by adding to the basic generic sign certain additional strokes which, when placed to the left-hand side of the character, denote one of nine differences, and when placed to its right-hand side indicate a particular species. In addition, a certain number of hooks and loops are added to the character to denote affinity or opposition, adjectival and adverbial forms, the active and the passive voice, the plural, and so on. Thus each variation in both sounds and written characters leads one to a more closely individualized object or idea. The process is an exceedingly cumbersome one, but it is rendered as methodical as possible by Wilkins, who was concerned, he informed the reader, to keep the words as brief as possible, to make them easy to learn, euphonic, and, at the same time, easily distinguishable one from another, a crucial problem that he is, of course, far from having solved.[117] It is, however, important to stress that the principal virtue of such a process of identification seemed at the time to be that a term (whether it be in the character or the language) both defined the object or idea it signified and established its relationship with other related or opposed things.

It would be quite absurd to attempt here any detailed critique of a language that by its very nature must reflect the scientific and linguistic errors or part-truths of the age. A few general remarks may, however, be of interest. Viewed from the vantage point of the twentieth century, Wilkins's (and even more so Dalgarno's) classifications are necessarily incomplete or imperfect: in view of the fact that their classes were but emended versions of the logical categories of Aristotle this could hardly be otherwise. Neither language, moreover, seems to be constructed in a way that would easily allow for the many changes in its symbols that would need to be made as scientific knowledge progressed and increased our understanding of the natural world. Indeed, a radical recasting of the whole system would have been required long ago. Moreover, the quest for comprehensiveness in the descriptions of objects in nature would certainly have rendered the language impossibly clumsy and wholly impracticable. Finally, one could hardly expect men to cope in everyday speech or even in general scholarly exchanges with the elaborate combinations of symbols or sounds that went to make up these philosophical languages. These few fundamental defects are, of course, much more serious than the linguistic oddities, which a modern philologist could undoubtedly correct. Nonetheless, although certain to fail as languages, these philosophical languages were not without interest and not wholly lacking in influence either.[118] Wilkins's *Essay* in particular has attracted the attention of many writers and thinkers since its publication, primarily on account of the impressive nature of his classification of ideas.

Wilkins showed himself to be well aware of the enormity of the task that confronted him in founding his real character and philosophical language upon an enumeration and definition of things. To complete such a task was, he recognized, work enough for a whole college of scholars or even for a whole age rather than for a single person.[119] Therefore, as we have seen, he enlisted help from specialists in the preparation of the essay; but also, recognizing that there were clearly defects in the work as it was published, he himself suggested that a number of the Fellows of the Royal Society should be appointed to consider the whole scheme and report on the amendments to it that they felt to be necessary. A fairly large committee was therefore appointed on 9 May 1668,[120] of which any three or more were to constitute a *quorum*. This committee included among its members Seth Ward, Robert Boyle, John Wallis, Christopher Wren, John Ray, and Robert Hooke, almost as distinguished a group of scientists as could have been assembled in England at that time.

Strangely enough, there is no record of any report having been received from this committee, and it has often been assumed for this reason that interest in Wilkins's efforts faded almost immediately among the members of the Royal Society group.[121] DeMott's examination of a few of John Ray's letters that deal with the essay,[122] in which there is considerable hostility to the whole notion of making a classification of natural things conform to a preconceived mnemonic system, has tended to foster this impression. However, the papers of John Aubrey preserved in the Bodleian Library, Oxford, and the archives of the Royal Society[123] allow one to see something of the fortunes of Wilkins's celebrated scheme and indicate quite clearly that this hostility was by no means as general as has been supposed. They show in fact that the hope of rendering Wilkins's essay of real use to scholars and to mankind as a whole had certainly not been abandoned following its author's death in 1672. And, although the subject is worthy of much fuller treatment than can be accorded to it here, a number of points can usefully be made.

John Aubrey wrote of Wilkins's real character and philosophical language: 'This last was his Darling, and nothing troubled him so much when he dyed, as that he had not compleated it; which will now in a yeare more be donne by the care and studies of Mr. Robert Hooke, of Gresham College; Mr. Andrew Paschall B.D. of Chedzoy in com. Somerset; Mr. Francis Lodwyck of London, merchant; Mr. John Ray R.S.S. of Essex and Mr. Thomas Pigott M.A. (Wadham College).'[124] Of the five names that Aubrey mentioned here, Paschall, Lodwick, and Pigot were by far the most active in discussing the essay and working towards a possible revision or recasting of it, with Aubrey and Hooke acting as intermediaries, almost as controllers, of an operation in which John Ray, it is clear, played virtually no part. Another person who, without figuring on the list given by Aubrey, had an important, if enigmatic, role to play in this affair was Wilkins's old friend and colleague, Seth Ward, who differed most radically from all the others in his views. Paschall and Lodwick both seem to have made something of a habit of corresponding in the character,[125] and Aubrey, Hooke, and Pigot, though understanding less readily, also occasionally used it in their letters.

Whatever reservations they had concerning the detailed formulation of Wilkins's essay, all the scholars referred to by Aubrey were fully convinced of the importance of the project in question for the progress of learning and for the benefit of mankind as a whole. Paschall described it as a 'great and most useful work,'[126] and although he conceded that it did not pretend to give a *perfect* definition of things, yet it was 'a most likely way (not to hinder but) to promote and improve the knowledge of things.'[127] For Thomas Pigot, the essay was 'a noble structure,'[128] while Robert Hooke, having written out in the character a description of a pocket-watch, published in the *Description of Helioscopes and Some Other Instruments*, wished that all things of that nature would be communicated in the same way, 'it being a Character and a Language so truly Philosophical, and so perfectly and thoroughly methodical, that there seemeth to be nothing wanting to make it have the utmost perfection, and highest Idea of any Character or Language imaginable, as well for Philosophical as for common and constant use.'[129] Even John Ray, who considered that no universal character could be invented that would satisfactorily represent the diversity of the natural world, conceded that 'as it is, it far excels any essay of that kind before published.'[130]

Several proposals made in the course of this correspondence aimed therefore at promoting knowledge of Wilkins's essay, either as it stood or with a few amendments; Hooke's description of the pocket-watch was but one of a series of efforts to publicize the real character. In 1678, Paschall thought of composing a book to describe it,[131] and two years later there was talk of publishing an appendix to the essay,[132] while a Latin version of the same work certainly existed in manuscript and a further French translation was planned.[133] Each of the scholars referred to, moreover, was expected to publicize it in his own part of the world, Aubrey in London, Pigot in Oxford, Lodwick in Holland, and a Danish admirer of Wilkins's work in Denmark.[134] Among other suggestions were a game by which 'a child about 10 years old, knowing no tongue but its mothers, hath in a short time with ease and pleasure master'd ye great difficulties of ye language, and will probably ere long have *a foundation for general learning, not to talk so much as to know*';[135] a series of 'maps' of various groups of plants, arranged according to tables revised from those of the essay, which could be hung up in greenhouses, and similar 'maps' of stones, metals, insects, fishes, birds, and beasts;[136] finally, a way of using the character as a kind of common-place method for remembering and learning what one observes and reads.[137]

Nonetheless, all of these efforts were somewhat undermined by the growing feeling that, impressive though Wilkins's essay undoubtedly was, it still needed to be substantially improved. Indeed one of the key questions that was discussed in these letters was whether the essay should be merely amended or radically altered. Paschall, who at first felt quite simply that it could be made easier to learn and to use, came to feel after much discussion that a rather more radical revision was necessary, a view that was shared to some extent by the other scholars involved. Paschall preferred, for instance, a script consisting of common letters to the very different character of lines, hooks, and loops that Wilkins had employed,[138] while Lodwick and Paschall both elaborated individual versions of a 'universal alphabet,' different again from that used by Wilkins.[139]

Wilkins himself had recognized that the philosophical tables constituted the heart of his work and it was to the structure of these tables that most attention was subsequently directed. That some kind of revision was necessary came to be generally accepted in the late 1670's and Paschall suggested to Aubrey that John Ray should be asked to draw up fresh tables of plants and animals for this 'new model,' but this time 'according to the nature of things and not with regard to a particular institution.'[140] As to the manner of organizing things in the tables, Paschall put forward a suggestion that seems to look forward to an eighteenth-century sensationalist approach to the question. For he envisaged that a philosophical language

> ought to proceed as our knowledge doth. As we begin to know a number of the common objects of sense, and their modes, and from this foundation, or rather centre go on to the accuracies in severall arts and sciences. So I judge we ought regularly to give marks or names, first to a competent number of such things and modes, and with them to deliver the way and manner of the language, as it were for common use; and then to do the like in the more exact and full accounts that are to be contrived for the severall parts into which the universall object of knowledge is to be distributed and divided.[141]

The issue that separated Paschall, Pigot, Lodwick, and probably Hooke, from Seth Ward was the central one of the number of generals and transcendentals that were required in such a project. For it soon became clear to the people involved that Ward had in mind a character radically different from that of Wilkins, one consisting of a small number of transcendentals (about a hundred according to Paschall)[142] to which *all* things and notions could be reduced. Although for some time he had difficulty in understanding the lines along which Ward was working, Paschall's doubts were resolved after reading, at Ward's suggestion, Lull's *Ars magna* and George Ritschel's *Contemplationes metaphysicae*.[143] Paschall, in fact, later drew a clear and very important distinction between the ideas of Wilkins and Ward, pointing out that, while the former envisaged a character for common use, Ward's scheme was intended rather for 'severe and strict reasoning.'[144] And so, taking his illustration from mathematics, he stated that, while Wilkins assigned separate marks, as it were, to every number to infinity, so that every species had its distinct name, Ward employed symbols that exhibited 'so much of the notion of a number as is common to all else.'[145] In other words, as in Lullism, all things and notions could be regarded as consisting of the diverse combinations of a given number of attributes, which could provide a universal key to the understanding of reality.[146]

The reception accorded to Ward's ideas among the Aubrey group of scholars was, on the whole, unfavourable, although criticism was usually tempered by the esteem in which Ward was held both as a person and as a scholar. Moreover, Paschall's letters reveal considerable respect for a plan aimed at producing a language for 'severe and strict reasoning.' Of all the critics, Pigot was the most hostile, arguing that Ward's scheme 'inclines too much to Lullius, whose radices of Bonitas, magnitudo, duratio, whose Trunchus, Branchae, Rami, folia, flores and fructus can never as I suppose make any one reap any fruit from his tree of knowledge.'[147] In a slightly earlier letter, Pigot had voiced a criticism that was recognized as being fundamental at the time; he pointed out that too small a number of transcendentals would lead to exceedingly lengthy definitions of things so that, as he wrote:

> I must to the learning of this language be forced to get by heart all these definitions, which are but single words perhaps in other tongues, but this would be a task by some hundred degrees harder than to learn the whole greek lexicon memoriter the compositions being longer by so many degrees in ye former and the contextures of ye simples exactly to be observed, what though they be agreable to right reason: it is probable I myself would not have drawn them up in the same manner so that I must be obliged to learn your compositions and definitions before I can make them my own.[148]

Since Seth Ward's papers have not been traced (if they have been preserved, which appears unlikely), we do not know how far he had proceeded with the formulation of such a character. What is obvious, though, is the interesting similarity between the ideas proposed by Ward and those being expressed by Leibniz at about the same time.

A BRIEF LOOK AT LEIBNIZ

A lengthy consideration of Leibniz's thought in this field clearly lies outside the limits imposed upon this study. Louis Couturat's vast work, La Logique de Leibniz, in fact has already dealt with this subject far more authoritatively and comprehensively than could be attempted here.[149] And yet, in order that later developments in this field may be understood, it is necessary to attempt a brief outline of Leibniz's most important suggestions.[150]

Leibniz's ideas concerning the formulation of a universal character arose first as a consequence of the work on permutation that he was engaged upon during his youth. This was published under the title Dissertatio de arte combinatoria (1666). In this work Leibniz suggested, as Descartes had done in 1629,[151] that all complex concepts might be resolved into the simple ideas of which they were composed. Couturat explained Leibniz's scheme in the following way:

> Dès lors, il suffirait de faire le dénombrement complet de ces idées simples, véritables éléments de toute pensée, et de les combiner ensemble pour obtenir progressivement toutes les idées complexes par un procédé infaillible. On constituerait ainsi l'Alphabet des pensées humaines, et toutes les notions dérivées ne seraient que des combinaisons des notions fondamentales, comme les mots et les phrases du discours ne sont que des combinaisons indéfiniment variées, des 25 lettres de l'alphabet.[152]

I shall do no more than mention here the links between Leibniz's discovery and the earlier proposals of Ramon Lull for an Ars magna, or those between the German philosopher's suggestion and the recent reformulation of the Lullist art by Athanasius Kircher in his Ars magna sciendi of 1665.[153] It is worth noting, however, that this latter work appeared shortly after the publication of Kircher's earlier effort at constructing a universal language, the *Polygraphia nova* (1663). Both of these books were known to Leibniz and, taken together, they may well have suggested to him the idea of applying the analysis and classification of concepts to the formulation of a universal character – a fusion of ideas that, oddly enough, Kircher himself does not seem to have made. If it were not Kircher's example alone that led Leibniz to conceive of this application of his logical invention, the idea certainly resulted from his knowledge of this and other contemporary efforts at universal language building. For at this period Leibniz knew the *Arithmeticus nomenclator* (1654) of the dumb Spanish priest, Becher's *Character pro notitia linguarum universali* (1661), and Kircher's *Polygraphia nova et universalis* from the discussion and extracts of all three that were printed in the *Technica curiosa* (1664) of Gaspar Schott.

The universal language that Leibniz had in mind at this period was to be formed by means of an analysis of complex concepts into their simplest constituent elements. To each single element or 'first idea' there would then be assigned an appropriate symbol, which would represent this idea alone. This would result, as Couturat pointed out, in the formation of 'une sorte d'alphabet idéographique, composé d'autant de symboles qu'il y a de concepts élémentaires ou catégories.'[154] In this way, every complex concept would be represented by a combination of signs each of which represented individually one of its simple constituent elements.

At this early stage in his thought (and again perhaps later in the *Nouveaux Essais sur l'entendement humain*),[155] Leibniz probably envisaged that the signs chosen for this task would, like picture-writing and hieroglyphics, bear a direct analogy with the ideas they represented. At different times, however, he appears to have considered various kinds of symbols, ranging from a *langage par images*,[156] a form of hieroglyphic writing, to primary numbers and their products, or to numbers expressed in terms of fractions. His views on the degree of convention that was required in such a universal character varied throughout his life.

Partly as a consequence of his study of the relatively elaborate English projects of George Dalgarno and John Wilkins, Leibniz went on to develop his own ideas very considerably, particularly in the early 1670s. Although the results of his acquaintance with the English universal language schemes were not wholly negative,[157] it does seem that they served mainly to emphasize for him the uniqueness and superiority of his own ideas. This superiority lay, he believed, in the fact that concepts were formed by combinations of signs representing their constituent ideas.

The provision of his own form of rational language depended, as we have seen, upon the complete analysis and reduction of concepts into their simple elements. 'Or,' writes Couturat, 'cela revenait à faire l'inventaire des connaissances humaines, et même comme l'analyse des concepts est en même temps l'analyse des vérités, à démontrer toutes les vérités connues en les ramenant à des principes simples et évidents, c'est-à-dire à édifier une Encyclopédie démonstrative.'[158] The encyclopaedia that Leibniz thought needed to be established would indicate both the ideas that go to make up our complex concepts and their relations with each other. The rational language also depended upon the invention of a sign-system which would express these combinations and relations in the most natural and appropriate manner possible. A considerable portion of Leibniz's time and energies was devoted to studying the various ways in which these two requirements could best be satisfied.

It is clear that Leibniz intended the *caractéristique universelle* to supply not only a clear, regular, unequivocal means of communicating between scholars, but also an instrument of reasoning that, if composed with the greatest care, would, he believed, lead inevitably to a certainty of conclusion comparable with that found in mathematical demonstrations. This rational language would then provide at the same time a calculus, or an algebra of thought, which would sustain the understanding even in its most complex metaphysical or moral reasoning. Leibniz wrote in 1677, 'Si nous l'avions telle que je la conçois, nous pourrions raisonner en métaphysique et en morale à peu près comme en Géometrie et en Analyse, parce que les Caractères fixeraient nos pensées trop vagues et trop volatiles en ces matières, où l'imagination ne nous aide point, si ce ne serait par le moyen de caractères.'[159] Leibniz aimed, in fact, to ensure by means of the universal character that reasoning would become a series of more or less mechanical operations, like calculating, as a result of which truths could be arrived at without any serious risk of errors arising. For, as Couturat has expressed it:

> Elle [la caractéristique universelle] n'aide pas seulement le raisonnement, elle le remplace. Elle dispense en effet l'esprit de penser les concepts qu'il manie, en substituant le calcul au raisonnement, le signe à la chose signifiée. On n'a plus à faire attention au contenu réel des idées et des propositions; il suffit de les combiner et de les transformer suivant des règles algébriques. La déduction se traduit ainsi par un jeu de symboles et de formules; et Leibniz ne craint pas de la réduire à un mécanisme purement formel.[160]

By providing a form of calculus, such as is used in mathematics, the universal character would thus lead to the termination of disputes, since disputants would need merely to combine symbols as they would do in the solution of an algrebraic equation, in order to arrive at evident, demonstrable conclusions.

It is primarily on account of this conception of the universal character as a calculus of reasoning and as an instrument of discovery that Leibniz may be distinguished from other late seventeenth-century universal language planners, and, of course, rightly regarded as an important precursor of twentieth-century symbolic logic.[161] It is for this reason too that Leibniz is of special interest here. For his suggestion that a universal language might be formed which would lead man inexorably to truth in metaphysical and moral, as well as in mathematical, reasoning, marked an important step in the development of the idea that this book has set out to trace. Leibniz's interest and reputation also lent considerable distinction to the search for a universal language,[162] and his example served to indicate certain lines along which his successors could proceed.

On the other hand, it is perhaps too easy, with the hindsight of twentieth-century developments in the field of symbolic logic, to overstate Leibniz's contribution to the universal language movement. We may note, for instance, that much of his writing on this subject was theoretical in nature. Moreover, a large part of the material referred to in the preceding pages was inaccessible to immediately succeeding generations, and became available to scholars only in the course of the past hundred years.[163] In addition, we shall find in France, during the second half of the eighteenth century, conclusions that, though closely resembling those of Leibniz, were arrived at by a rather different philosophical route.

4 / Ideal languages in the imaginary voyage[1]

In the once exceedingly popular imaginary voyages of the seventeenth and eighteenth centuries it was quite customary for the author to conduct the hero of his tale to some imaginary, or little-known, remote corner of the globe, or, alternatively, have him travel much further afield in the universe to discover an exotic, often utopian land on the sun, the moon, or one of the planets. Jacques Sadeur's destination, for instance, in Gabriel de Foigny's *La Terre australe connue* (1676) was the distant Austral continent, the existence of which was then suspected but not definitely known.[2] In the mid-eighteenth century, Nicholas Klimius and Peter Wilkins found worlds hidden deep down in the bowels of the earth,[3] while a century earlier Domingo Gonsales, Bishop Godwin's 'speedy messenger,'[4] had been accidentally carried off, as Cyrano de Bergerac was to be some twenty years later, to a world situated on the surface of the moon.[5]

But whether placed on earth or anywhere else in the universe, these imaginary lands were generally peopled by rational beings, who were there partly as a consequence of man's natural anthropomorphism – a world without intelligent beings would have seemed very dull indeed – and partly because they enabled the writer to effect a comparison, whether stated or implied, between the customs, dress, religion, and government of his imaginary people and those of the civilization that the hero had left behind him in Europe. European civilization often emerged badly tarnished from this comparison: inevitably so, since although some of the imaginary societies may have owed a lot to the accounts of authentic travellers, they also often represented the materialization of many of the writer's most cherished ideals, dreams, or fantasies. The portrayal of these societies moreover, introduced European readers to uncommon *mores*, and often to revolutionary new ideas and values that were to play a most important part in the breakdown of the old order and prepare and encourage that more open critique of established religion, society, and government which was to characterize the middle years of the eighteenth century.[6]

Since the beings who inhabited these worlds were usually capable of intelligent thought (though they were not always human in form), it was almost inevitable that the writer should feel the need to make them communicate with each other and, preferably for the interest of the tale, speak with the traveller too. And so they are often endowed with a language that is especially constructed by the author, who frequently quotes specimen words or phrases from it, or occasionally even provides a brief description of its grammatical structure.

The appearance in such stories of suitably exotic-sounding words is hardly surprising in view of the tradition within which these writers were working and their keen desire to pretend to authenticity. Reports from Jesuit missionaries in China, for instance, or from the Recollect Fathers working among the Huron Indians,[7] contained numerous allusions to the intriguing new languages that they had encountered there. Similarly, what may be termed language samples occurred in many of the accounts of authentic voyages written by sea-captains, merchants, or adventurers.[8] So the imaginary voyages, which were modelled partly on the reports of these real-life travellers, followed suit by including references to the languages that were supposed to be spoken in the land of the 'Australians,' the Severites, the subterraneans, or the lunarians.

Yet it was not only a wish to ape the accounts of authentic travellers that made these writers devise new languages for the 'noble savages, debonair giants, well policed myrmidons or hermaphrodite philosophers'[9] who lived in these 'lands of nowhere.' For many of them also took considerable delight in exercising their own linguistic knowledge and inventiveness.

In certain instances the aim of the author seems to have been merely to entertain himself and intrigue his reader by providing fanciful fragments of an enigmatic new language. No more could be claimed, for instance, for the anagram technique that Fontenelle used in the *Relation de l'isle de Bornéo* of 1684[10] or for Restif de la Bretonne's device of writing French backwards in *La Découverte australe* of 1781.[11]

Other writers, however, claimed rather more for their invented languages. Even some of those who composed only the briefest of fragments were not at all reluctant to congratulate themselves on their achievement. Sir Thomas More described the language of Utopia, for instance, as 'both copious in woordes, and also pleasaunte to the eare, and for the utteraunce of a mans minde verye perfecte and sure.'[12] Veiras's language of the Severites, or Sevarambi, is said to be the most agreeable in the world,[13] while the chief virtue of Tyssot de Patot's imaginary tongue is its great precision and regularity, for, in this language, 'ce qui est admirable, c'est qu'il n'y a aucune exception.'[14]

Most of these languages possess the additional advantage of being very simple to learn, a few weeks or months generally sufficing for this purpose, compared with the number of years which was then considered necessary to learn either a classical or a modern language. Gulliver learns the language of the Houyhnhnms so quickly that after about ten weeks he is able to understand most questions put to him and in three months can produce 'tolerable answers.'[15] And Gabriel de Foigny's traveller, Sadeur, requires only five months to acquire a fair knowledge of 'Australian,' even though we are assured that this language is so remarkable that 'on devient philosophe en apprenant les premiers éléments.'[16]

One should, of course, beware of taking all these claims too seriously, since, following the example of More's *Utopia*, it soon became traditional to endow a society that was itself often very much idealized with a language that not only differed from existing languages but was also superior to them. Nonetheless, a number of these writers at least were perfectly serious in the belief that they had gone some way towards constructing a language which, in certain, if not all, respects, represented a significant improvement on existing languages. As such, in spite of the fictional, even fanciful context, the more systematically conceived of these imaginary languages are as much a part of the search for an improved language as are the universal language schemes looked at in previous chapters. While attention must clearly be focused upon these more fully developed 'ideal' languages, it is also interesting to glance, if only briefly, at some of the slighter, often rather lighthearted language fragments, which offer many intriguing suggestions concerning the various possible methods of communication which were envisaged in the course of these two centuries.

Sir Thomas More has been described as the first pioneer to venture into the domain of imaginary languages.[17] Yet, although More himself provided a literal Latin translation of the passage of Utopian verse that was printed in the first edition of his famous book, it is only relatively recently that his imaginary language has given up the secrets of its morphology and syntax. By examining every word quoted with an eye to the analogies between this language and Greek and Persian, Émile Pons was able to suggest some of the principles according to which More's imaginary language was constructed,[18] adding thereby to the more humorous verbal contrivances that had already been elucidated by More's editors.[19] The details of his demonstration need hardly concern us here, but it is worth noting that in constructing the language More was following an *a posteriori* method that Rabelais and Swift were to adopt after him.

Proceeding as George Psalmanaazaar was to do later with his fake Formosan language, More wrote out the lines of verse not only in conventional letters but also in the symbols of the Utopian alphabet.[20] Again, the majority of the shapes of this alphabet appear to be derived from an existing language, in this case either directly or indirectly from Greek letters, though a Russian scholar has recently suggested that certain of them resemble quite closely the letters of the glagolitic alphabet in use among the southern Slavs.[21]

This alphabet and the fragment of the Utopian language that were printed in the 1516 edition appeared again in only one of the many subsequent editions and translations that were published up to the end of the last century. It is therefore probable that the quotation from the Utopian language was much less well known to More's seventeenth- and eighteenth-century successors than was the book itself.

Much better known to them, as to most modern readers, were the spirited jargons of Panurge which occur in the ninth chapter of *Pantagruel*.[22] In linguistic inventiveness Rabelais surpasses here the medieval *Farce de Pathelin* that the scene inevitably calls to mind. For, in addition to requests for food and drink made in German, Italian, English, Basque, Dutch, Spanish, Danish, Hebrew, and ancient Greek, Rabelais provides Panurge with three other imaginary *jargons*, or *baragouins de fantaisie*, as they are often called. The different 'flavour' of each of these languages (the language of the Antipodes, the *langage lanternois*, and the language of another Utopia, different from that of Sir Thomas More), may be savoured from a juxtaposition of the opening phrases of each fragment. The so-called *langage des Antipodes* begins exotically 'Al barildim gotfano dech min brin alabo dordin falbroth ringuan albaras';[23] the more heavily consonantal *langage lanternois*, 'Prug frest frins sorgdmand strochdt drhds pag brlelang Gravot chavygny pomardiere rusth pkalhdracg Deviniere pres Nays';[24] and, finally, the language of Utopia with its obvious erotic associations, 'Agonou dont oussys vou denaguez algarou, nou den farou zamist vou mariston ulbrou, fousquez vou brol tam bredaguez-moupreton den goul houst, etc.'[25]

Again, with the exception of certain parts of Rabelais's Utopian language, the meaning of most of these passages has been ingeniously worked out by the late Émile Pons, whose astute transcriptions need not be repeated here.[26] In general terms, however, we may note that Rabelais adopts a method of construction in which words and sounds are chosen partly by analogy with those of a variety of existing languages. This results in a language rich in half-hidden humorous associations (both of sound and sense), which, it has been suggested, influenced Swift much later when he came to endow the 'little people' of Lilliput with a language of their own. Indeed the example of Rabelais's imaginary languages, together with the air of general linguistic exuberance, vitality, and humour that is displayed in this chapter, offered a more appealing, as well as a better known, precedent to later writers than More's more stolid fragment had done. For by carrying over into prose fiction some of the spirit of verbal fantasy that characterized medieval drama, Rabelais was able to demonstrate both the immense variety and the comic possibilities of this type of imaginary language.

Joseph Hall's *Mundus alter et idem*, or *The Discovery of a New World or a Description of the South Indies*, written in the first decade of the seventeenth century, and translated into English by John

Healey,[27] is aimed specifically at satirizing occult, and particularly Paracelsist (i.e. alchemical), terminology, though it also contains numerous examples of humorous modifications of English terms, such as *Eat-allia* (otherwise called *Gluttonia*), *Drink-allia* (or *Quaffonia*), *Letcheritania* and *Shee-landt*, *Fooliana*, and so on. In an academy of Fooliana, the author tells us, 'they have devised a new language wherein they kept the misteries of their knowledge, onely to themselves: it is called the *Supermonicall* tongue,' to which a note adds the information, 'So do the Paracelsists call their balderdashe.'[28] The author, who adopted the pseudonym Mercurius Britannicus, was a churchman who later became the Bishop of Exeter, then of Norwich.

Another English Bishop, Francis Godwin, Bishop of Hereford, was the author of *The Man in the Moone, or A Discourse of a Voyage Thither by Domingo Gonsales, the Speedy Messenger*, in which an unusual and rather appealing musical language is spoken by the inhabitants of the lunar world. This early moon-voyage, interesting above all for its echoes of the new scientific discoveries of the early years of the century, was probably written in the late 1620s,[29] but was not published until 1638, five years after its author's death.

Domingo Gonsales, the Spanish hero, recounting his own story, tells how, while travelling back from the East Indies, he was taken ill on board ship, and put off to recover his health on the 'blessed Isle of S. Hellens' (i.e. St Helena).[30] Described here as a 'miracle of Nature' and 'the only paradice, I thinke, that the earth yeeldeth,' this island must indeed have appeared so to the Spanish, Portuguese, Dutch, and English sailors who were able to rest and obtain food and fresh water there after the long sail from the Indies. This section of Godwin's book, in fact, owes much to the narratives of travellers on the East Indies trade route, such as Sir Thomas Cavendish, James Lancaster, or the Dutch pilot, Van Linschoten.[31]

While on St Helena, Gonsales trains a number of unusually large birds, called Gansas, to fly harnessed to a trapeze-like flying machine, and to respond to the signal of a white sheet spread upon the ground. The flying machine is equipped with a sail, controlled by the traveller who is seated astride his trapeze, with his weight distributed evenly between the birds by a system of weights and pulleys. The birds take off, the craft rises into the air, and in this way flight is achieved.

The actual journey to the lunar world is undertaken, however, quite accidentally. While in flight, the birds, mistaking the white, snow-capped peak of El Pico – that is Pico de Teyde on the island of Teneriffe in the Canaries – for their sheet signal, head directly for the mountain's summit. By a coincidence they reach it at the precise moment at which they are due to migrate. The pilot is naturally amazed when the birds begin to fly directly upwards and away from the earth in the direction of the moon, to which, he concludes, certain migrating birds fly to spend the winter months. This idea appears less ridiculous if we bear in mind that bird migration remained something of a puzzle in the seventeenth century, various theories having been put forward to explain the phenomenon.[32] As well as the explanation that birds followed the sun in search of warmer climes, it had also been suggested that they passed the winter lying in clefts in rocks or rolled in clay at the bottom of a river, needing no air and living on body fat alone. Godwin's theory of migration to the moon in fact had several supporters in the seventeenth century, and was referred to later several times in poetry, among others by Dryden and Pope. The naturalist in John Gay's 'Shepherd's Week'

> ... sung where wood-cocks in the summer feed,
> And in what climates they renew their breed;
> Some think to northern coasts their flight they tend,
> Or to the Moon in midnight hours ascend.[33]

The lunar world to which the traveller is taken is described as a Utopian land where there is eternal spring, with no wind or rain, and where the temperature remains constantly agreeable; food grows plentifully there without the labour of man, and since no one eats anything harmful, doctors are not required. Disease is unknown among the lunar inhabitants, and injury can be cured simply by applying the juice of a special herb. There being no illness, death comes at the end of one's allotted span and is greeted with feasting and rejoicing rather than with sorrow and mourning. The community of lunarians is a highly moral one, for marriages are never broken there, since after marriage a man feels no desire for any other woman than his wife.

Among the many unusual features of this lunar civilization,

Domingo Gonsales finds that the lunarians speak a language that 'consisteth not so much of words and Letters, as of tunes and uncouth sounds, that no letters can expresse. For you have few wordes but they signifie divers and several things, and they are distinguished onely by their tunes that are as it were sung in the utterance of them, yea many wordes there are consisting of tunes onely, so as if they list they will utter their mindes by tunes without wordes.'[34]

It is highly probable that the general idea of a vocabulary composed partly of musical notes came from the reports of the Jesuit missionaries in the Far East concerning the 'tonal system' of the Chinese. And in a recent book Paul Cornelius has plausibly linked this language of 'tunes' with Godwin's likely reading of Father Ricci's diaries, published by Nicholas Trigault in 1615.[35] This link with Chinese characters is supported by the fact that, when Domingo Gonsales returns to earth and finds himself in China, he is spoken to by a Chinaman 'in a different language (which al the *Mandarines*, as I have since learned do use,) and that like that of the Lunars did consist much of tunes.'[36] Godwin, however, goes much further than the Chinese in proposing 'a language (and that easie soone to bee learned) as copious as any other in the world, consisting of tunes onely, whereof my friends may know more at leisure if it please them. This is a great Mystery and worthier the searching after then at first sight you would imagine.'[37] In fact, the author quotes two musical phrases in the text, the first meaning 'Glorie be to God alone' (i.e., *Gloria Deo soli*), the second being the Spaniard's own name, 'Gonzales.' From the reproduction of these phrases in McColley's modern reprint (in spite of several errors in the placing of the notes, some of which are indeed rather doubtful in the original 1638 edition),[38] one can see that Godwin's idea was simply to allocate to each letter of the Latin alphabet a place on the musical scale, so that words could be either written in musical script, sung, or played on a musical instrument. In spite of Godwin's claims, this musical 'language' is not then a language at all, but simply a cipher in which the letters of an existing language may be transcribed.

There is an important distinction to be made between a scheme of this nature, which presents merely an enigmatic way of writing Latin, and the would-be universal musical languages of the nineteenth century – Jean Frédéric Sudre's *Solrésol* of 1818 or Don Sinibaldo de Mas's

Idéographie of 1863. These latter languages, while based similarly on a system of musical notation, aimed nonetheless at representing ideas directly without recourse to the letters of existing languages.

The more precise origins of Godwin's idea are, in fact, almost certainly to be found, not merely in a general Chinese influence, but rather in a number of the sixteenth- and early seventeenth-century works on cryptography and signalling. The well-known French author, Blaise de Vigenère, wrote, for instance, that 'la musique même se peut déguiser en forme de chiffre; faisant servir les lignes et leurs entr'espaces de lettres, avec les notes brièves, semi-brièves et noires, selon qu'elles y seront situées; dont se peuvent former plusieurs alphabets à la discretion de chacun.'[39] The idea is further amplified and well illustrated (as it is in Godwin's own book) in Daniel Schwenter's *Steganologia et steganographica*, published around 1620,[40] and it is discussed even more fully by Gustav Selenus (a pseudonym for the Duke of Brunswick) in the *Cryptomenytices et cryptographiae* of 1624.[41] The suggestion of a musical cipher seems, indeed, to have been something of a commonplace in early books of cryptography and may well have been in others that I have not seen.[42] It would probably be most plausible to suppose that Godwin came across the idea in the pages of Joan Baptista Porta's *De furtivis literarum notis, vulgo de ziferis libri iv*, first published at Naples in 1563 but republished in 1606 under the title *De occultis literarum notis*. In this later edition of Porta's work, there appears in the new book 5 a chapter entitled 'Musicis notulis quomodo sine suspicione uti possimus,'[43] where Godwin could have read a description of a method of writing in musical notes similar to the one that he was to adopt. In view of Godwin's tremendous interest in the various possible ways of transmitting messages by means of codes and signals – he was himself the author of a treatise on this precise theme in the *Nuncius inanimatus* of 1629 – it would seem reasonable to conclude that Godwin would have been acquainted with at least some of these earlier works on the subject. This is made even more likely by the similarities that exist between the other methods of sending messages that are described in *The Man in the Moone* (birds, a tame fox, flashing lights, and dust and smoke signals) and those found in Porta's work on ciphers. It is true that in the *Nuncius inanimatus* Godwin cites only classical sources; nevertheless it remains highly unlikely that a person as well read as Godwin was in so many other fields should have been ignorant of the more modern works on a subject in which he was something of a specialist. His innovation was, then, not the idea of the musical code as such but the suggestion that it be used as a means of communicating knowledge rather than concealing it.

Godwin's proposal that a language might be formed by musical notes was taken up and discussed in a more serious context by John Wilkins in the *Mercury, or the Secret and Swift Messenger* (1641). A whole chapter of this book was devoted to a consideration of a possible musical language, Domingo Gonsales and *The Man in the Moone* being referred to specifically by name.[44] Here Wilkins described the musical language as it had been used by Godwin's lunarians, and presented his own emended (and more strictly accurate)[45] version of the phrase quoted by Godwin – *Gloria Deo soli* – commenting afterwards, 'I suppose that these letters and notes might be disposed to answer one another, with better advantage than here they are expressed. And this perhaps, would bee easie enough for those that are thoroughly versed in the grounds of Musicque, unto whose further enquiry, I doe here only propose this invention.'[46]

Wilkins went on, however, to stress how much more important such an invention might prove to be, if it were made to represent things and notions directly, linking this proposal with his discussion of the universal character:

> But now if these inarticulate sounds be contrived for the expression not of *words* and *letters*, but of *things* and *notions*, (as was before explained, concerning the universall Character) then might there be such a general language, as should be equally speakable, by all People and Nations; and so we might be restored from the second general curse, which is yet manifested, not in the confusion of *writing*, but also of *speech*.[47]

Wilkins left this possibility to be considered by someone better versed in music than himself. In fact, although this was almost certainly unknown to Wilkins at the time, Mersenne had, as we have noted in an earlier chapter, already proposed a similar idea, some five years before the publication of Wilkins's own book.

The limitations of the idea of a musical 'language' as it was found in

Godwin's tale apply *a fortiori* to Cyrano de Bergerac's repetition of the same idea in the *Histoire comique des états et empires de la lune*, published posthumously by Le Bret in 1657. For, although Cyrano borrowed the general idea of a language consisting of musical tones directly from the English moon-voyage, which was probably known to him through Baudoin's translation of 1648, he does not seem to have understood that the method used was that of a genuine cipher, and the examples quoted by Cyrano, unlike those of Godwin, followed no discernible cipher system. Nonetheless it is characteristic of Cyrano that he should have recognized the humorous possibilities of the suggestion that a theological disputation or a case at law might take the form of a melodious concert. The language, he wrote,

> n'est autre chose qu'une différence de tons non articulez, à peu près semblables à nostre musique quand on n'a pas adjousté des parolles; et certes c'est une invention tout ensemble bien utile et bien agréable, car quand ils sont las de parler, ou quand ilz desdaignent de prostituer leur gorge à cet usage, ilz prennent tantost un Luth, tantost un autre instrument dont ilz se servent aussy bien que de la voix à se communiquer leurs pensées: de sorte que quelquefois ilz se rencontreront jusques à quinze ou vingt de compagnie qui agiteront un point de Théologie, ou les difficultez d'un procès, par un concert le plus harmonieux dont on puisse chatoüiller l'oreille.[48]

The idea of people speaking a musical language is taken a stage further in the popular tale by the Norwegian, Ludvig Holberg, that was translated into English as *A Journey to the World Under-Ground by Nicholas Klimius*.[49] Here the travellers encounter a strange group of beings who not only speak like musical instruments but resemble them too, the only apparent difference being that they possess hands and arms to enable them to play with a bow on their own strings! Again a conversation, this time concerning the price of the ship's cargo that the instruments want to buy, sounds like a symphony, and a serious form of punishment for offenders consists in removing their bows for a period of time, thus depriving them of their power of speech.

Returning to Cyrano de Bergerac's tale, we find that the use of the musical language is restricted to an aristocratic elite, the populace speaking an entirely different language. Musical language is in fact an indication of nobility of birth in the lunar society, rather as long noses, aptly in view of the length of the author's own proboscis, are said by Cyrano to be a sign of superior intelligence.

The idea of two distinct languages spoken by different social groups was probably inspired by Cyrano's appreciation of the linguistic discrepancies that already existed in contemporary French society, and more particularly perhaps by the refinements of *précieux* terminology. It is worth noting, however, as Edward Seeber has pointed out,[50] that the idea of two languages spoken by different sections of a single community is not entirely fanciful, since the women of the warlike Carib tribe of South America and the West Indies were reputed to speak an entirely different language from their menfolk. Tradition had it that these islands, originally inhabited by a colony from Florida, were invaded by the Galibri tribe from South America; the Galibri killed all the men but preserved the women, who continued to speak in their native tongue.[51]

Instead of speaking in musical notes, the lower classes in Cyrano's lunar world express themselves by a wide repertoire of gestural signs:

> L'agitation, par example, d'un doigt, d'une main, d'une oreille, d'une lèvre, d'un bras, d'une jouë, feront, chacun en particulier, une oraison ou une période, avec tous ses membres; d'autres ne servent qu'à désigner des mots, comme un pli sur le front, les divers frisonnemens des muscles, les renversemens des mains, les battemens de pied, les contorsions de bras, de façon qu'alors qu'ilz parlent, avec la coustume qu'ilz ont prise d'aller tous nuds, leurs membres, accoutumez à gesticuler leurs conceptions, se remuent si dru qu'il ne semble pas d'un homme qui parle, mais d'un corps qui tremble.[52]

Although the idea of a language composed of facial expressions and movements of the limbs probably derived from an exaggeration of the flamboyant gestures used by the orator or actor, the humorous presentation suggests that Cyrano may well have had in mind Panurge's burlesque disputation with Thaumaste in Rabelais's *Pantagruel*.[53]

Naturally, signs offered the imaginary traveller, as they did his real-life counterpart, a most obvious way of establishing some elementary form of communication with creatures whose language he did not understand. And in innumerable stories of this type gestures are used in place of words until such time as the hero manages to acquire some knowledge at least of the language of the country. But in at least two tales in the eighteenth century, gesture is light-heartedly proposed as the actual language of the country in which the traveller finds himself. In the land of the 'man-lions' visited in Restif de la Bretonne's *La Découverte australe* the spoken language consists of no more than twenty or thirty words. The addition of a number of gestures, however, considerably widens its range of expression, making communication possible on everyday topics at least. Gestures alone stand in place of a number of adjectives: to say that someone is good, for example, the hand (or paw!) must be placed flat upon the heart, while to reverse the meaning the hand is moved away from the body.[54] Similarly, animals are assigned a language of gesture in Béthune's *Relation du monde de Mercure*, for 'au lieu de la voix que la nature leur a refusée, elle les a doués d'un langage muet, composé de mines, d'actions et de différentes postures qui ne sont guère moins intelligibles que la parole, et les peuples de Mercure les entendent mieux, que les habitants du sérail n'entendent les muets, dont le langage est fort clair à ceux qui y sont accoutumés.'[55] Relations between the animals of the planet and the Mercurians are most cordial, a reflection of a serious vein of speculation concerning a unifying language of nature that lies behind the suggestion of a common language of signs.

As we have seen earlier, the quotation of the occasional sentence, phrase, or single word of an invented exotic language soon came to be a conventional feature of the imaginary voyage. So much so that the anonymous author of *A Voyage to the World in the Centre of the Earth*, after quoting two sentences in the language of the subterranean country, trades wittily on an established tradition by begging the reader's pardon for inserting extracts from a language that is unknown to him: in future, he assures us, he will use plain English, 'without first repeating the Words used in the Country I was then in, and after that translating them, as is practised by many of our Historians, not even the famous Gulliver himself excepted, and I believe with no other view than to fill up a Page.'[56]

Although language fragments had of course appeared in imaginary voyages prior to the publication of *Gulliver's Travels* – Defoe's political poem written in the lunar language in *The Consolidator* is an excellent example[57] – it is clear that Swift influenced later writers just as much in this respect as he did in so many others. Lilliputian sentences, such as the surprised comment *Hekinah degul* (interpreted by Pons as 'hé, qu'il a grande la gueule'[58]) and the Houyhnhnms' horse-like terminology, confirmed a fashion which was to be followed by Desfontaines, Samuel Brunt, Ludvig Holberg,[59] and the anonymous authors of *The Voyages Travels and Wonderful Discoveries of Capt. John Holmesby*, *The Life and Adventures of Peter Wilkins*, or *A Voyage to the World in the Centre of the Earth*. Swift's techniques of language building have often been studied and I do not want to add further to this literature.[60] It is worth stressing, though, the remarkable diversity of the methods that Swift adopted: anagram, reversal, omission, substitution or transposition of letters, and other more complex devices, with these distortions all operating upon material borrowed from numerous languages. It is a mark of Swift's ingenuity and the complexity of his many linguistic innovations that the countless puzzles set in *Gulliver's Travels* continue to attract interpreters, who, hardly surprisingly, sometimes reach widely differing conclusions.

An earlier work than *Gulliver's Travels* that requires separate consideration is George Psalmanaazaar's *Historical and Geographical Description of Formosa* (1704).[61] The author of this book, which was published and often accepted at the time as an authentic account of Formosan life, was a young Frenchman whose real name remains unknown, but who called himself Psalmanaazaar, after Shalmaneser, the King of Assyria in the Second Book of Kings. In the course of his youth, Psalmanaazaar deceived countless English notables and scholars into believing that he was a native of the island of Formosa, wrote his historical and geographical description of his 'native island,' and even went so far as to teach a language invented by himself to certain 'gentlemen at Oxford,' who believed that they were learning a true Oriental language.[62]

Following the example set in accounts of authentic travellers, a whole chapter of Psalmanaazaar's book is devoted to a description of the 'Formosan' language. This is, we learn, basically a purer form of

Japanese, but with two principal differences, first, a more guttural form of pronunciation and, secondly, a system of tenses based partly upon the rising and falling of the voice. Thus, the perfect tense differs from the present only in that the same word is pronounced with a rising intonation; the future uses the same word again but this time with 'a falling of the voice.' Few indications as to the detailed grammar of the language are given. Psalmanaazaar merely indicates that 'Japanese-Formosan' has three genders (all inanimate creatures being neuter), which are indicated by the article only (*oy*, *ey*, *ay*) and which become one and the same in the plural (*os*). The self-styled Formosan went on to cover himself to some extent, in the event of close examination of his language, by stating:

> Since I do not intend to write a Grammar of the Language but only to give some Idea of it, it may be sufficient to add this general Observation, That it is very easy, sounds musically and is very copious. If any one shall ask from what Language it is derived? I answer, That I know of no other Language, except that of *Japan*, that has any great affinity with it, but I find many Words in it which seem to be deriv'd from several other Languages, only changing either the signification or termination.[63]

Although there is no grammar, Psalmanaazaar does provide a list of the most common Formosan words,[64] for example the word for King is *Bagalo*, from which, by a change in ending, is formed *Bagalendro*, which means Vice-Roy; the Formosan for a man is *Banajo*, from which, by a transposition of letters and a change in ending, is derived *bajane*, meaning woman; from *bot*, meaning a son, is derived by a different ending *boti*, a daughter. Indeed, although Psalmanaazaar claimed that the language was essentially simple, he took great care to make it sufficiently irregular not to appear too obviously fabricated. His reference to the large number of words in Formosan derived from other languages allowed him to borrow indiscriminately, then modify recognizable words, attributing to each a meaning quite different from the original.

In addition to the word-list (and the numerous nouns scattered throughout the book) Psalmanaazaar also sets out in detail the Formo-

The Formosan Alphabet

Name		Power		Figure			Name
Am	A	a	ao	ıX	I	I	ɹI
Mem	M	m	m	⌐	⌐	⌐	ɹ⌐
Nen	N	ñ	n	u	ŭ	U	ŭɛU
Taph	T	th	t	ō	ƀ	O	xı O
Lamdo	L	ll	l	ɼ	ғ	Г	ɔɹΓ
Samdo	S	ch	ș	与	ⴺ	与	ɔɔ与
Vomera	V	w	u	Δ	Δ	Δ	ıρɛɔΔ
Bagdo	B	b	b	/	√	/	ɔɔɹ/
Hamno	H	kh	h	ꓶ	ꓶ	ꓶ	ɔuɹꓶ
Pedlo	P	pp	p	ᴛ	ᴛ	△	ɔɔᴄ△
Kaphi	K	k	x	Ý	Ý	Ⴘ	ɒxı Ⴘ
Omda	O	θ	ω	Ͻ	Ͻ	Ǝ	⌐ɔɹ Ǝ
Itda	I	y	i	o	□	▯	ɯɔ▯
Xatara	X	xh	x	⸮	⸮	⸮	ıǫꝸı⸮
Dam	D	th	d	⊃	⊃	⊃	ɹı⊃
Zamphi	Z	tf	z	Ƅ	Ƅ	Ƅ	ɒxɹı Ƅ
Epfi	E	ε	η	Ƈ	E	Ƈ	ɒƅı Ƈ
Fandem	F	ph	f	X	X	X	ɹυı X
Raw	R	rh	r	ꝗ	ꝗ	ꝗ	ΔI ꝗ
Gomera	G	g	j	ꝿ	ꝿ	ꝿ	Iρɛɔꝿ

T. Slater fec.

Plate 7 George Psalmanaazaar
An Historical and Geographical Description of Formosa London 1704
facing 267: the Formosan alphabet
By courtesy of the British Library Board

san alphabet (see plate 7) and follows this with his version of the Lord's Prayer, the Creed, and the Ten Commandments. The plate illustrating the alphabet shows twenty letters, clearly set out in a deliberately haphazard order.[65] Compared with English there is no *e*, *j*, *g*, *y*, *u*, or *w* (*v*, *vomera*, is presented as a combination of three letters, *u*, *w*, and *v*). An attempt is then made to represent the way in which these sounds were pronounced, in a column headed 'power', followed by a representation of the written character itself. In this one notes the way in which Psalmanaazaar has made the writing go from right to left in accordance with Oriental habit and how the majority of the alphabetical figures are variants of geometrical shapes, the square, rectangle, triangle, and circle. Finally, again shirking the issue and preserving the mystery of his language, Psalmanaazaar informs the reader that 'there are many Particular Rules, as to the use of these Letters, which it would be endless as well as useless here to set down, and therefore I shall only add the names of some things that are most common and subjoin to them the Lord's Prayer, the Creed, and ten Commandments in that Language, to give the Reader some Idea of it.'[66] The Lord's Prayer in Psalmanaazaar's fake Formosan language reads as follows (with an interlinear translation added):

Amy Pornio dan chin Ornio viey, Gnayjorhe sai Lory,
Our Father which art in Heaven, Hallowed be Thy Name,

Eyfodere Sai Bagalin,
Thy Kingdom come.

Jorhe sai domion apo chin Ornio, kay chin Badi eyen,
Thy will be done in earth, As it is in heaven.

Amy khatsada nadakchion toye ant nadayi,
Give us this day our daily bread.

kay Radonaye aut amy Sochin, apo ant radonem amy Sochiakhin,
And forgive us our trespasses, As we forgive them that trespass against us.

bagne ant kau chin malaboski, ali abinaye ant tuen Broskaey,
And lead us not into temptation. But deliver us from evil:

kens sai vie Bagalin, kay Fary, kay Barhaniaan, chinania sendabey.
For Thine is the kingdom, The power, and the glory,
For ever and ever.

Amien.
Amen.[67]

This example suggests a language that has closer affinities with the *a posteriori* constructs of More, Rabelais, and later, Swift, than with the universal language schemes of the previous century, although the emphasis upon the ease with which it can be learned and the careful elaboration of a character based upon lines and marks indicates a possible knowledge of some of the earlier schemes of a real character, if not a philosophical language.

Turning finally to the lengthier descriptions of invented languages that occupied a chapter of Foigny's *La Terre australe connue* (1676), Veiras's *Histoire des Sévarambes* (1677–9) and Simon Tyssot de Patot's *Voyages et avantures de Jaques Massé* (1710) respectively, we shall look at the basic principles on which these languages were formulated and their relation to the shifting concept of the 'perfect language' and to earlier schemes of a universal language. Such an enquiry shows not only that these writers shared certain common attitudes and aspirations with the universal language planners, but that they also owed something either to specific schemes of universal language, or, more frequently, to ideas for which the universal language planners had been directly responsible.[68] This contradicts the commonly held view that these ideal languages are the product of the imagination alone (together with a few borrowings from little-known existing languages),[69] and suggests that they owe just as much to contemporary preoccupations as the exotic description of unknown or little-known lands owes to authentic accounts of travellers, missionaries, and merchants.

There is no uniformity in the ideal languages of Veiras, Foigny, and Tyssot de Patot. To the best of our knowledge, Veiras and Foigny were unknown to each other; the fact that their books were written at approximately the same date excludes any likelihood of influence by either upon the other.[70] On the other hand, since the *Voyages et avantures de Jaques Massé* appeared more than thirty years after the *Histoire des Sévarambes* and *La Terre australe connue*, the earlier works were almost certainly known to Tyssot de Patot. However, apart from providing the latter with the model of a digressionary chapter, written in the form of a miniature grammar, they appear to have had little or no influence in determining the precise characteristics which his language possessed. In fact all three writers seem to have had different aims and to have varied in the sources from which they drew their inspiration and example.

The supreme virtue of the *langue australienne* imagined by Gabriel de Foigny is, we are told, that 'on devient philosophe, en apprenant les premiers éléments, et qu'on ne peut nommer aucune chose en ce pays qu'on n'explique sa nature en même temps.'[71] Since the knowledge contained in the words is thought to be all-important, the emphasis is placed exclusively upon meaning; questions of harmony and euphony are entirely ignored, and combinations of meaningful, yet to Western ears jarring, symbols, such as *llga*, or *mmdu*, commonly occur. Everything is sacrificed to providing a symbolism that might allow the easiest possible access to the objects or ideas signified.

The language represents, however, much more than a post-Comenian attempt to introduce the young to knowledge more rapidly and more directly. For Foigny claims that his new language provides *itself* an important key to knowledge: its words will convey by means of their internal composition something of the nature of the objects signified: 'Ils forment si parfaitement leurs noms: qu'en les entendant, on conçoit aussitôt l'explication et la définition de ce qu'ils nomment.'[72]

The language is constructed by a combination of five vowels, each of which represents one of five elements – fire, air, salt, water, and earth – with a number of consonants larger than any European language possesses. Each consonant is intended to represent a particular quality:

Le B signifie clair; le C chaud; l'X froid; L humide; F sec; S blanc; N noir; T vert; D désagréable; P doux; Q plaisant; R amer; M souhaitable; G mauvais; Z haut; H bas; I consonne rouge; A joint avec I, paisible. Aussitôt qu'ils prononcent un mot, ils connaissent la nature de ce qu'il signifie: comme pour dire une pomme douce et désirable, ils écrivent 'Ipm', un fruit mauvais et désagréable 'Igd'.[73]

The effect of combining these letters to form words is therefore that of giving a very rudimentary description of the thing represented. So, in Foigny's words, 'Quand on enseigne un enfant on lui explique la signification de tous les éléments; et quand il les joint ensemble, il apprend à même temps l'essence et la nature des choses qu'il profère.'[74]

The terminology that is used by Foigny might suggest that this is yet another example of the long-established quest for a natural language that would signify without convention and hence be understood by all, conveying by means of its natural sounds the original, divinely revealed truth of all created things. Yet to 'l'essence et la nature des choses' must be assigned a new, more precise meaning. The aim is no longer to discover through a revelationary language the true meaning of the world, but rather to reproduce in the form of language an image or a description of objects as they are already known to man.

Thus by framing his language so as to present a description of the basic composition and important qualities of material objects, Foigny is clearly falling closely into line with a procedure widely accepted some twenty years earlier by the universal language planners. For after 1650, as we have noted, Hebrew was largely abandoned as the model upon which an artificial language based upon root-signs might be constructed, and description by individual qualities, as well as philosophical classification, became a part of language-building.

The similarity in the theory upon which Foigny and the English language planners in particular constructed their ideal languages might suggest that Foigny had direct knowledge of the schemes of Wilkins and Ward, Lodwick, and Dalgarno. It is unnecessary, however, to suppose that there were any direct links between Gabriel de Foigny and the English universal language builders. As far as is known, Foigny never visited England.[75] Nor is there any more precise evidence, apart from the common principle of composition and similarity in terminology that we have described, to suggest that he might have been directly influenced by the English schemes. Indeed, the complete absence of philosophical tables, combined with a naïve reliance upon a combination of five elements to describe the fundamental composition of all material objects, suggests the contrary. Nonetheless, one cannot entirely exclude the possibility that Foigny was acquainted with a work such as Dalgarno's *Ars signorum* (1661), perhaps the scheme most readily available, since it was written in Latin. More important is the fact that, by 1676, the suggestion for a language that would convey the 'essence and nature of things' was so common both on the Continent and in England that no specific source need be looked for. Thus, Comenius's *Via lucis* (1668) with its proposal that 'everything in our new language must be adapted to the exact and perfect representation of things,' Leibniz's *Dissertatio de arte combinatoria* (1666), Gaspar Schott's discussion of a number of schemes in the *Technica curiosa* (1664), and even Mersenne's or Descartes's early references to the idea, may have provided Foigny with the principle upon which his *langue australienne* was to be constructed.

Like the majority of the universal languages published between 1650 and 1668, Foigny's ideal tongue has a written character quite distinct in form from conventional alphabetical symbols. This written character, affirms Foigny, is even more admirable than the spoken language:

> Ils n'ont que des points pour expliquer leurs voyelles, et ces points ne se distinguent que par leur situation. Ils ont cinq places, la supérieure signifie l'A, la suivante l'E etc. ... et bien qu'il nous semble que la distinction en soit assez difficile: l'habitude qu'ils en ont la leur rend très-commune. Ils ont trente-six consonnes dont vingt-quatre sont très remarquables: ce sont de petits traits qui environnent les points et qui signifient par la place qu'ils occupent.[76]

A number of the earlier schemes for a universal writing had similarly adopted a character consisting of lines and dots, a continuation, we have seen, of the practice of the sixteenth-century cryptographers. Of these schemes for a universal character, Johann Joachim Becher's *Character pro notitia linguarum universali* (1661) is perhaps the work most likely to have inspired Foigny's own proposal, though again no single specific source need be sought. In Becher's written character, the place of the word (or, in this case, its dictionary number) is denoted by a certain arbitrary geometrical shape surrounded by a series of lines and dots. As in the written character of the 'Australiens,' variation in meaning arises from the position of these lines and dots in relation to the basic shape selected.

We may conclude that, if Gabriel de Foigny's knowledge of specific schemes of universal language appears to have been limited to the better-known of the Continental schemes, the rudimentary nature of the execution of his language should not obscure the fact that in the theory of language-building Foigny was relatively well-versed and up-to-date. For it was the aim both of Foigny and the seventeenth-century universal language builders to ensure that language fulfilled a function more exalted than merely aiding the memory, or serving as an imperfect instrument for the communication of ideas. Language in the newly constructed tongue would become knowledge itself; the process of obtaining knowledge about the world would be simultaneous with that of learning the language. It is therefore in the manner in which Foigny attempts to bridge the gap between word and object that he approaches most nearly the universal language planners of the two previous decades.

The biography of Denis Veiras d'Alais, author of the *Histoire des Sévarambes* (1677–9) might lead one to suppose that he would have been better acquainted than his contemporary, Foigny, with the movement which reached its climax in England with the publication of John Wilkins's *Essay towards a Real Character and Philosophical Language* (1668). It is known, for instance, that, apart from a diplomatic visit to the Continent, Veiras resided in England in the service of the Duke of Buckingham, probably from 1665 until 1674, years which witnessed the most intense activity in the field of universal language planning in England.[77] It is most unlikely that Veiras could have remained in the entourage of the Duke of Buckingham without learning something at least about a subject that had become a common after-dinner topic of conversation among the learned.

Like the *langue australienne*, though in a totally different manner, the ideal language of Veiras represents a revolt against the arbitrary formation and signification of ethnic languages. Yet, unlike Foigny, Veiras is intensely concerned with the euphonious quality of his language, and, more important still, with the congruity of sound and meaning. Hence the language is based not upon a descriptive, but upon an onomatopoeic, principle, according to which a given meaning is assigned to a combination of sounds because they appear to convey something of the nature of the object or idea represented. In this way each combination of sounds has its own particular 'character': 'Les uns ont un air de dignité et de gravité; les autres sont doux et mignons. Il y

en a qui servent à exprimer les choses basses et méprisables et d'autres les grandes et relevées, selon leur position, leur arrangement, et leur quantité.'[78] Thus, whenever a harsh ending is given to a word, it is used to convey a quality of harshness in the thing signified. It will be noted that Veiras, like Foigny and the *a priori* language builders, aims at producing words that will tell more of the *nature* of things. Veiras differs from other language planners in refusing to acknowledge the necessary arbitrariness of existing human speech-sounds, and in attempting to construct his language along lines consciously rejected by many of his predecessors. In his *Essay*, we may recall, Bishop Wilkins had divided all characters into those which signify either naturally or by institution:

> Natural characters are either the Pictures of things or some other Symbolical Representations of them, the framing and applying of which, though it were in some degree feasible as to the general kinds of things; yet in most of the particular species, it would be very difficult, and in some perhaps impossible. It were exceedingly desirable that the Names of things might consist of such sounds, as should bear some Analogy to their Natures; and the Figure or Character of these Names should bear some proper resemblance to these sounds that men might easily guess at the sense or meaning of any name or word, upon the first hearing or sight of it. But how this can be done in all the particular species of things, I understand not; and therefore shall take it for granted that this character must be by institution.[79]

Carried to its logical conclusion, the ideal language of Veiras might be thought to be the natural language that Mersenne had discussed in the *Harmonie universelle* and had ultimately rejected as impossible: 'Une langue dont les dictions eussent leur signification dans la nature, de sorte que tous les hommes entendissent la pensée des autres à la seule prononciation sans en avoir appris la signification, comme ils entendent que l'on se réjouit lorsque l'on rit et que l'on est triste quand on pleure ...'[80]

Nowhere in the *Histoire des Sévarambes*, however, does Veiras claim that his new language might be entirely understood in the same

way as these natural cries of joy or grief, and he appears to recognize some of the limits foreseen by both Wilkins and Mersenne. If the basic principle of Veiras's language is to be found in a recognition of a possible 'natural' congruity of word and object in 'all the particular species of things,'[81] for him also institution must finally predominate; hence, the language must be learned, although many sounds may be understood or guessed at without any previous knowledge of their meaning.

Although Mersenne had rejected a language that might signify in an entirely natural, non-instituted manner, he had put forward in the *Harmonie universelle* an alternative mode of language-building, which was the same as that found in *Histoire des Sévarambes* and may have provided Veiras with the basic principle upon which he was to construct his own scheme.[82] The same idea is also put forward in Comenius's *Linguarum methodus novissima*.[83] There is no documentary evidence that Veiras knew either this work or the *Harmonie universelle*; the resemblances are, however, so close that a debt to one or other seems more than likely.

The language of Veiras was supposedly formed by the ruler of the Severambians, Sévarias, who, foreseeing that by his laws he would render the manner of his people gentle and regular, imagined that they would require a language of like qualities. Sévarias therefore took the existing language of the land, that of the Stroukarambians, tempered the roughness of many of its terms, removed any superfluities, and added terms invented in imitation of all other languages he knew. The language that resulted consisted of forty distinct sounds, of which ten were vowels and thirty consonants. But Veiras, like Sir Thomas Urquhart in the *Ekskubalouron* (1652), aimed as much at comprehensiveness as at regularity and simplicity. Hence, to the forty sounds already mentioned he added thirty diphthongs and triphthongs to produce an even greater variety of sounds; moreover, he employed marks for tones and inflexions of the voice, as well as providing three characters (acute, grave, and circumflex) to denote the quality of each vowel.

In order to express so many sounds in writing, Veiras invented a universal alphabet. During the years in which he was in England, there was much discussion of the alphabet found in Wilkins's *Essay*, and of another universal alphabet invented by Francis Lodwick. Although not presented at a meeting of the Royal Society, nor recorded in the *Philosophical Transactions* until 1686,[84] this alphabet had been in manuscript circulation at least as early as 1673.[85] A comparison of Lodwick's universal alphabet with that of Veiras reveals a number of similarities. For example, both claim that children, being accustomed to pronouncing the wide range of sounds contained in their alphabets, can learn to speak other languages with the greatest accuracy and ease. Although the number of vowels and consonants that they require differs, Veiras follows Lodwick in his division of consonants into two major groups, Primitives and Derivatives, and in his use of subdivisions to show the derivation of letters from the same organ of speech. There are, moreover, a number of resemblances of detail that suggest that Veiras had scrutinized Lodwick's universal alphabet before incorporating into his language those features that fitted in best with his own intentions.

Finally, we may merely note here, since the question has been more fully explored by Paul Cornelius, that in the pages of the *Histoire des Sévarambes* devoted to language Veiras, who in 1681 was to become the author of a *Grammaire méthodique*, was clearly expressing his interest in a rationalized grammar, encouraged probably by the *Grammaire générale et raisonnée* of Port Royal, published in 1660.[86]

The chief interest of Veiras's ideal language clearly lies, however, less in its detailed formulation than in the basic onomatopoeic principle by which meaning is assigned to words. For the language of the Severambians represents an effort to contrive a closer relationship between language and the material world that is quite different in manner from the approach of Foigny and the earlier English planners, and distinct again from the traditional search for a *langue matrice*, the primitive catholic tongue of mankind, revealed by God to Adam, but lost to man at Babel.

Writing several decades after Foigny and Veiras, Simon Tyssot de Patot, himself a teacher of mathematics at the École Illustre of Amsterdam, reverted, in the section of the *Voyages et avantures de Jaques Massé* (1710) devoted to the strange new language, to a mathematical ideal of precision, regularity, and simplicity. By this time the interest of scholars in questions of universal language building was no longer as

Ideal languages in the imaginary voyage 137

intense as it had been in 1668. Moreover, Tyssot de Patot is able to use ideas from the earlier *voyages imaginaires* and from schemes of universal language, ignoring what perhaps already appeared to him to be unattainable philosophical ideals. Here, language is reduced to what appeared to be its barest essentials: the letters of the alphabet are twenty in number, composed of seven vowels and thirteen consonants; only three tenses are provided in the indicative of each verb: 'Le Présent, le Parfait indéfini ou Composé, et le Futur: qu'ils n'ont point d'Impératif: que dans leur Subjonctif il ne se trouve que l'Imparfait et le plus que parfait premier: avec l'Infinitif et le Participe. Ils n'ont aussi que trois Personnes pour le Pluriel et Singulier tout ensemble.'[87]

Finally, declension is made simple and regular: for example, *brol* means a sheep, and *brolu* a ewe. Comparable changes in termination occur logically and consistently in the case of every substantive. Conjugation is effected in the same manner, a separate letter being added on all occasions to designate the person, number, and tense of the verb.

It seems probable that, in both the basic conception and the detailed formulation of his language, Tyssot de Patot owed almost everything to an earlier specimen of a universal language written in Latin by Father Philippe Labbé.[88] This language was basically a simplified and regularized form of Latin. The personal pronoun *ego* is represented, for example, by the letter *a*; for the plural *nos*, *s* is added, forming *as*; similarly, *e*, which represents *tu* adds *s*, becoming *es* in the plural. Tense is indicated by the insertion of a consonant into the verb. The temporal system thus reads as follows: present, *amo*; imperfect, *ambo*; perfect, *amto*; pluperfect, *amro*; future, *amso*.

Tyssot de Patot differs from Foigny and Veiras in making no effort to bridge the gap between word and thing. Like Labbé, he aimed solely at producing a language that would be easier to learn and simpler to use than any existing language. The regular languages that resulted from these aims were thus the simplest, and yet perhaps the most feasible, of all the early schemes of universal language.

Just as much of the exotic material of the imaginary voyages was borrowed from earlier or contemporary accounts of authentic travels around the world,[89] so the ideal languages that are described by Veiras, Foigny, and Tyssot de Patot have their origins in the preoccupations with universal language that reached their peak in the middle decades of the seventeenth century. Analysis reveals then, I think, a view of these ideal languages which conforms more closely with the customary mode of composition of these armchair travellers and founders of imaginary utopian states.

In their knowledge of precise schemes of universal language, Veiras, Foigny, and Tyssot de Patot are no more than interested amateurs; moreover, the views they expressed in their tales were frequently naïve, even for their own age. Yet their curiosity was acute and wide-ranging, and their linguistic inventiveness was at times impressive, even though the lines into which it was channelled were quite unoriginal. These ideal languages reflect, moreover, in a clear (because simple) manner some of the variety of ways in which seventeenth-century scholars aimed to construct a perfect *lingua mundi*.

5 / The eighteenth century: origins of language, general grammar, and a universal language

Although it was Leibniz who was responsible for the most profound thinking on the universal language question, interest in the subject in the 1680s was not entirely dead in England and in France. The discussions of Paschall, Pigot, Aubrey, and Ward continued into the middle years of the decade,[1] and, while Ward was working on a radically different scheme from that of Wilkins, the Philosphical Society of Oxford expressed interest in the project of John Keogh, about which so far little is known.[2] The Royal Society of London heard Francis Lodwick's 'Essay towards a Universal Alphabet and a Universal Primer,' (1686) a work that, as has been noted, had been circulating in manuscript form for some time before it was printed in the *Philosophical Transactions*. Meanwhile, in France little of any importance seems to have appeared since the early ideas of Mersenne and Descartes concerning a philosophical language. De Vienne Plancy's extremely superficial proposals, described in the *Extraordinaire du Mercure* from 1681 to 1685, merely resulted in the resurrection of a certain amount of information relative to earlier schemes, most of which had by that time been almost entirely forgotten.

In the first few decades of the eighteenth century, interest in the construction of an artificial universal language (both as an international and as a philosophical language) appears to have flagged considerably, and only the occasional, unexciting language scheme was produced at that time.[3] This decline in interest may partly be explained by the obvious impracticability as a working language of a vast scheme such as had been elaborated by Wilkins and his associates. There had also been a considerable lack of agreement concerning the ways in which Wilkins's *Essay* could be either improved or recast, and, since there had been no general diffusion or use of the character itself, hardly surprisingly the death of the principal enthusiasts for a philosophical language[4] led to an almost complete neglect of Wilkins's efforts.[5]

Another quite different factor probably also diverted attention from the search for an *artificial* universal language. This was the rise of French to the position of the virtually international language of Europe.

The diffusion of the French language in the final decades of the seventeenth century and its use by many nations as an auxiliary language during the eighteenth century has already been very fully discussed and documented, and numerous examples spring immediately to mind.[6] Already by the end of the seventeenth century, for example, French had replaced Latin as the diplomatic language of Europe. The French language was also most frequently used in treaties, even when neither party was French, as with the treaty of Nijmegen between Spain and the Netherlands. By the middle of the eighteenth century, French was spoken in most of the court and diplomatic circles of Europe: in Russia, Germany, Austria, England, Poland, Norway, Denmark, Hungary, and Rumania.

But its use was not confined to diplomatic and court circles. Many French schools had been established all over the Continent of Europe; an international press that used French as its linguistic medium had grown up, particularly in the Netherlands and England, owing largely to the arrival of Huguenot refugees; and a large number of books produced in other vernaculars were now republished in French in order to reach a wider public. The Royal Academy of Berlin, on its foundation in 1700, adopted French as its official language, while, later in the century, the Imperial Academy of St Petersburg used both French and Latin, as did the Royal Academy of Turin. This virtual universality prompted the Academy of Berlin – somewhat belatedly – to set as the subject of a prize essay in 1782 the question: 'Qu'est-ce qui a fait de la langue française la langue universelle de l'Europe?'[7] The memoirs of that academy for the years 1782 to 1784 contain several minor communications devoted to this subject, before the prize was awarded in

1784 jointly to the well-known dissertation of le Comte de Rivarol and the lesser-known one of Jean Christophe Schwab.[8]

A language situation of this kind is, of course, an extremely precarious one, since its continuation hinges upon the voluntary acceptance and use by scholars, diplomats, and courtiers of a language other than their own. This acceptance of French by men from other countries was likely to be adversely affected by the Europeans' growing pride in their own vernaculars, prompted by the achievements of writers working in these vernaculars, as well as by inevitable social, economic, and political factors.[9]

Yet, as we have seen, the new universal language schemes offered more than a mere means of communication, and Leibniz's ideas concerning a universal characteristic based upon a combination of simple ideas were not forgotten. This was particularly the case in the early 1760s and 1770s in Germany, and to a lesser extent in Italy, when a number of scholars consciously attempted to follow in Leibniz's footsteps. Among these were Jean Henri Lambert, whose *Neues Organon*, published in 1764, represented an attempt to apply mathematical analysis and symbolization to logic, and one of his correspondents, Godefroi Plouquet, who became Professor of Metaphysics and Logic at Tubingen in 1750, and published in 1763 a *Methodus calculandi in logicis*. In this work syllogisms were designated by geometrical shapes, and were expressed in terms of mathematical formulae. Mention should also be made of Richeri's 'Algebrae Philosophicae in usum artis inveniendi,' published in the *Miscellanea Taurinensia* for the years 1760 and 1761.[10] The universal language scheme of the Hungarian, Georgius Kalmar, of which there were three versions (one in Latin published at Berlin in 1772, a second in Italian published at Rome in 1773, and a third in German published at Vienna in 1774), is expressly linked, as Madeleine David has pointed out, with Leibniz's hopes for the realization of a universal character.[11] The Italian version contains numerous references to Descartes, Mersenne, Leibniz, Wilkins, Dalgarno, and Kircher, as well as extracts from letters and manuscripts of Lambert that describe and praise Kalmar's efforts as furthering Leibniz's own researches.

Although these particular schemes lie outside the scope of this study, it is important to note that it is now recognized that the resurgence of interest in the construction of a universal character and language that would be a form of algebra of thought owed much to the printing of texts of Leibniz in which he dealt with the feasibility and importance of such a character.[12] The influence on French thinkers of Leibniz's ideas in this field is a large subject, about which one or two tentative suggestions will be made later. For the moment, I want to look at a single French work from the 1770s, which, although it does not lack interest in itself, has been selected primarily because it illustrates in a very clear way how two further contemporary preoccupations were related to a renewal of interest in these problems.

Dieudonné Thiébault, the author of the work in question, was a former Jesuit who, after the disbandment of the Order in 1762 and their expulsion from France in 1764, was offered by Frederick II the chair of general grammar at the École militaire in Berlin, on the recommendation of the Abbé d'Olivet, d'Alembert, and Cerutti. While in Berlin, Thiébault became an active member of the Royal Academy, contributing a number of memoirs to its proceedings, among which we may note in particular, some 'Observations générales sur la grammaire et les langues' (1776).[13]

In this memoir, the first question considered by Thiébault was 'Pourrait-on établir une langue universelle qui fût de quelque utilité?' In reply, Thiébault argued, contradicting Herder,[14] that a universal language would indeed be of immense usefulness to mankind, since, he wrote, echoing many of the seventeenth century universal language enthusiasts, 'si l'on consacre toutes ses facultés et tout son temps à l'étude des mots, que deviendra l'étude bien plus essentielle des choses? Une langue universelle serait donc un trésor inappréciable pour tous les peuples.'[15] Thiébault's recommendations concerning the method that might be employed in the construction of the universal language may be considered, first, as they relate to the provision of a suitable nomenclature, and, secondly, as they concern the grammar of the language.

The nomenclature of the new language could be formed, Thiébault suggested, by choosing a few hundred root-words, usually monosyllables, possessing a single, constant meaning. From these radicals all other terms could then be derived by following a uniform manner of procedure. Once this was done, Thiébault postulated, it would be necessary only to know by heart the original radical words and the system of derivation, in order to understand the whole language without difficulty.

Thiébault's rather vague proposals for a language established upon a nucleus of primitive root-words seem to echo, of course, the early, elementary seventeenth-century theory of universal language building. Yet, in fact, it is very different from this, for his suggestion must be seen in relation to the wide-spread contemporary interest in the problems of the origins of language, and, more particularly, in the light of specific speculations as to the nature and composition of the primitive language from which, it was believed, all existing forms of speech had developed.

The question of the origins of language was a source of great fascination to many eighteenth-century thinkers. Although the theory of a divine origin for language continued to have its adherents, the sensationalist solution, which was often put forward cautiously as a mere hypothesis, was a more typical outcome of the spirit of eighteenth-century critical enquiry. The Bible has explained to us how language was formed: let us then try to imagine how it might have been formed naturally, if it had not been divinely revealed to man. Such was the argument used, for example, by the Abbé Condillac in the *Essai sur l'origine des connaissances humaines* in 1746.[16] Condillac then went on to elaborate a theory which regarded articulate speech as developing out of the contact that had already been established between individuals by the use of primitive gestures, movements of the face, and spontaneous cries of emotion. This first form of conventional primitive language Condillac believed to have been constituted chiefly on a basis of analogy and imitation; the first actual words were therefore onomatopoeic in form.[17]

To Charles de Brosses, whose *Traité de la formation méchanique des langues* appeared in 1765, this primitive language was rigorously determined by man's physical organization and by the sensations that he receives from external objects, that is from nature herself. And so, he wrote, there exists 'une langue primitive, organique, physique et nécessaire, commune à tous le genre humain, qu'aucun peuple au monde ne connaît ni ne pratique dans sa première simplicité, que tous les hommes parlent néanmoins, et qui fait le premier fond du langage de tous les pays; fond que l'appareil immense des accessoires dont il est chargé laisse à peine appercevoir.'[18] Languages as we know them all derive, therefore, de Brosses believed, from a common stock of necessary root-words; they form, as it were, an extension of this primitive language:

> extension établie par un système de dérivation suivi pas à pas, d'analogies en analogies, par une infinité de routes directes, obliques, transversales, dont la quantité innombrable, les variétés prodigieuses et les étranges divergences constituent la grande diversité apparente qu'on trouve entre tous les langages; que néanmoins toutes les routes malgré la diversité de leur tendance apparente ramène toujours enfin, en revenant sur ses pas, au point commun dont elles se sont si fort écartées.[19]

Although de Brosses expressly rejected the possibility of instituting an artificial universal language, he conceded nonetheless that the root-signs that he was to go on to describe in the *Traité* in fact laid the foundations of such a language. So he wrote that he was not to be concerned there

> à fabriquer par art une langue factice, qui, par l'usage universel qu'on en pourrait faire, tant verbalement que par écrit, tiendrait, dans le commerce et dans les connaissances de toutes les nations, le même lieu que l'algèbre tient dans les sciences numérales, projet qu'on ne peut espérer de faire jamais adopter aux hommes dans la pratique. On se borne à montrer ici que ce fond de langage universel existe en effet.[20]

De Brosses's researches into the composition of this language of primitive root-words played an important part in the formation of Thiébault's proposals for a universal language. 'Le savant et ingénieux auteur du *Traité de la Formation mécanique des langues*,' wrote Thiébault, 'a dressé et détaillé le plan d'un *Archéologue* ou d'un *Dictionnaire* qui sous un petit nombre de racines primitives, nous donnerait la nomenclature universelle de toutes les langues Européennes et orientales.'[21]

This plan, Thiébault continued, served to draw attention to a number of truths closely related to the formulation of a universal language. It showed, first, he surmised, that all languages may be reduced to a very small number of common root-words (under four hundred in all, according to de Brosses); that all these roots consist of monosyllables of one, two, or three letters; that each of them possesses a single, constant meaning; that this meaning is the foundation-stone, the common centre of our ideas; that the consonants represent the important parts of these roots, vowels being there merely to facilitate their pronunciation; that words in various languages are formed from these roots in a much simpler and more restricted order of progression than has hitherto been thought to be the case; and finally, that derivation is normally carried out in a regular, uniform manner.

The relation between these particular thoughts of Thiébault, prompted by a study of de Brosses's treatise, and his recommendations concerning a universal language based upon a nomenclature of root-signs is too obvious to require much further emphasis. For, concerning the composition of the basic nomenclature itself, Thiébault was able merely to refer to de Brosses's work: 'Quant au tableau des racines, nous n'en parlons point; on peut le tirer de l'ouvrage de Mr de Brosses et de quelques autres auteurs: on pourrait même le former d'une manière arbitraire, et sur l'inspection seule d'un alphabet complet.'[22]

De Brosses was not the only scholar at this period to attempt a reconstruction of the primitive language. Court de Gébelin's *Histoire naturelle de la parole* was important also.[23] For one of Court de Gébelin's confessed aims in this work was to demonstrate 'l'analogie de toutes les langues, à les réduire toutes à une seule, à une langue primitive et donnée par la Nature, dans laquelle les hommes aient toujours été et seront toujours obligés de puiser leurs mots.'[24] Part of Court de Gébelin's work therefore consisted in establishing a *Dictionnaire primitif*, which, it was intended, would provide the roots of all the languages which have developed from it.

There seems little doubt that interest in the formulation of a universal language was greatly stimulated by these researches into the nature of the primitive language, approached, it should be emphasised, not by a study of Ancient Hebrew letters but by an examination of the organs of speech that make the sounds and their relations with natural things.

Thiébault was not alone in perceiving the relevance of this activity to the provision of a basic nomenclature for such a language. For example, in a note following and commenting upon the article of Faiguet on a *langue nouvelle*, Nicholas Beauzée wrote in the *Encyclopédie méthodique*:

> Il ne s'agissait point ici, pour proposer une *Langue* universelle dont on pût agréer le projet, de simplifier les règles de la Grammaire, comme l'auteur semble se l'être uniquement proposé: il fallait au contraire ajouter, à la Grammaire, des règles générales de formation, par lesquelles on pût déduire d'un petit nombre de racines toute la nomenclature de la *Langue*; car c'est la nomenclature, et surtout les irrégularités de la nomenclature, qui rendent longue et épineuse l'étude des Langues.[25]

Similarly, it was because its foundations lay in a nomenclature of natural, and in this case gestural, root-signs that the Abbé de l'Épée could claim in 1776 that his language of methodical signs would provide a universal language as well as an excellent method of instructing the deaf.[26] In this way, although no specific universal language scheme based upon such a system of root-signs appears to have been produced at this time, attention was directed to the provision of a basic nomenclature, which would be arrived at by the 'Etymologist's' art, and upon which a universal language might one day be constructed.

The second part of Thiébault's recommendations concerned the grammatical relations of the proposed universal language. A brief examination of these will once again serve as an introduction to a movement that in the late eighteenth century becomes of particular significance to our theme.

Thiébault suggested first that the grammatical relations of the new language should be highly simplified and regularized: there would, for example, be only one declension for nouns and another for adjectives, while all verbs would be conjugated in a uniform manner. Yet Thiébault had in mind more than the mere removal of superfluity. For the grammar of the new language would provide, he wrote, 'en même temps le meilleur livre de Logique et de Métaphysique; parce que les mots y auraient entr'eux une marche constante et fixe, toujours analogue à la marche des idées et de leurs combinaisons.'[27]

Thiébault's conception of an ideal grammar is clearly that of the eighteenth-century general grammarian, who regarded his task as one of discovering the universal principles of human thought that lie behind the apparent profusion of existing grammatical forms.[28] For, as Nicholas Beauzée expressed it: 'Il doit donc y avoir des principes fondamentaux communs à toutes les langues, dont la vérité indestructible est antérieure à toutes les conventions arbitraires ou fortuites qui ont donné naissance aux différens idiomes qui divisent le genre humain.'[29] Belief in the existence of universal principles which the *grammairien-philosophe* might discover by the careful study of a number of languages arose naturally out of the view that the human reason was one. There was, according to James Harris, 'ONE TRUTH like one Sun that has enlightened human Intelligence through every age, and saved it from the darkness both of Sophistry and Error.'[30] And so, as the Abbé Pluche wrote in *La Mécanique des langues et l'art de les enseigner*, 'Comme le travail de la pensée est le même partout, il y a même ressemblance dans l'emploi de la parole dont tous les peuples se servent pour représenter ce qui fait le fond de leurs jugements et de leurs affections.'[31]

It is important to stress not only the universality of these principles but also their correspondence with the principles according to which we combine our ideas. General grammar was thus closely akin to logic. Gunvor Sahlin wrote of the early *Grammaire générale et raisonnée* of Lancelot and Arnauld, published in 1660:

> La Grammaire dans le sens de Port-Royal n'est pas une collection de règles pour apprendre à bien parler, elle est plutôt un raisonnement sur ces règles destiné à les fonder en raison et à établir une correspondance parfaite entre les catégories grammaticales et les catégories logiques. La grammaire générale résulte d'une confrontation de la grammaire avec la philosophie; surtout avec la logique.[32]

Although by no means a new phenomenon, general grammars proliferated in the second half of the eighteenth century throughout Europe.[33] Towards the end of the century the tendency to regard general grammar and logic as but two differing ways of dealing with the same subject became even more pronounced. Thiébault, for example, in his *Grammaire philosophique*, published in 1802, saw metaphysics, logic, and grammar as 'toujours une science en elle-même, quoi qu'on puisse ainsi la diriger vers des buts différents.'[34] And Destutt de Tracy wrote concerning the new science of *idéologie*:

> Cette science peut s'appeler *Idéologie*, si l'on ne fait attention qu'au sujet; *Grammaire générale*, si l'on n'a égard qu'au moyen; et *Logique*, si l'on ne considère que le but. Quelque nom qu'on lui donne, elle renferme nécessairement ces trois parties; car on ne peut en traiter une raisonnablement sans traiter les deux autres. *Idéologie* me paraît le terme générique, parce que la science des idées renferme celle de leur expression et celle de leur combinaison.[35]

During the 1790s, indeed, general grammar pushed traditional studies out of the schools, and many chairs of general grammar were introduced into the Écoles centrales. There is evidence of a concern at the time to provide a course that would be 'le complément et le couronnement du cours de langues anciennes, et l'introduction aux cours de belles-lettres, d'histoire et de législation.'[36] For it was intended that the course in general grammar in the Écoles centrales should, in fact, be a course in the new science of the study of the human understanding.

Even within this much wider framework, however, one of the principal concerns of the general grammarian remained the discovery and investigation of those universal principles that they believed join our ideas to each other – principles that were at once logical and grammatical. Since general grammarians, by the very nature of their task, were constantly being made aware of the divergencies found between the grammatical principles of existing languages, it is scarcely surprising that many of them should have conceived of a new, ideal language in which the grammar would reflect accurately the relations between ideas. So of those scholars who, in the late eighteenth century, either actually proposed the formulation of an ideal and universal language, or considered with some seriousness the possibility of its institution, many were also directly involved in the writing or teaching of general grammar. Nicholas Beauzée, for example, clearly considered that in order to succeed in the construction of an ideal language it was necessary to follow the principles of general grammar. For he objected that Faiguet, author of the article on the *langue nouvelle* 'n'avait pas assez aprofondi les principes de la Grammaire générale, pour proposer un plan digne d'être adopté.'[37]

In the memoir with which our discussion of this question began, Thiébault similarly suggested that the syntactical rules of the new language would need to be modelled upon contemporary general grammars.[38] And twenty years later the same writer in his *De l'enseignement dans les écoles centrales* placed a universal language among those topics commended to the attention of the general grammarian. Among other scholars who took a keen interest in the subject during the 1790s figure the names of Garat, Destutt de Tracy, Sicard, and Baradère, all of whom, like Thiébault, taught or wrote about general grammar.

The brief and far from comprehensive analysis undertaken in this chapter is intended to provide little more than a backcloth against which the intense interest in universal language building of the 1790s may be better understood. Research still needs to be done on the slightly earlier period. Nonetheless it is clear that from about 1760 onwards there was a renewed interest throughout Europe in the possibility of constructing a universal language and in the methods that should be followed in order to succeed in this aim. Undoubtedly some of this interest resulted from the publication of a number of previously unpublished writings of Leibniz. Our enquiry suggests, however, that the search for a universal language received a powerful stimulus from contemporary investigations into the nature of a primitive language from which all existing languages were thought to have been derived, and from the growing popularity and importance of the general grammar movement. The first, it was hoped, might lead to the provision of a basic nomenclature for the new language, and the second, to a grammar that would indicate clearly a set of universal relations between ideas.

6/Pasigraphy in the 1790s

Although the possibility of inventing a universal language based on a universal nomenclature and a general grammar was being discussed with some enthusiasm during the preceding two decades, it was in the 1790s in particular that the subject came to be the focal point for an important discussion concerning the whole question of linguistic reform and its influence on the progress of knowledge. In considering a phase in the history of thought that has been almost entirely ignored and yet is perhaps more interesting than any so far discussed, we shall look, first, in this chapter, at the main schemes of universal writing or language that were proposed in France in the 1790s, for it was around these proposals that some of the discussion revolved.[1]

Delormel's *Projet d'une langue universelle présenté à la convention nationale* (1795) is the scheme most frequently mentioned from this period by writers on the universal language movement, though the work represented nothing new in language planning.[2] Introducing his classificatory language, the author defined his aim as that of forming a very simple language that would be free from exceptions and in which the letters would be organized, like numbers, in series. Following a regular system it would, he believed, be extraordinarily simple to learn and use. Classification of substantives by genera and species, a system that Wilkins and Dalgarno had employed in the seventeenth century, was again adopted by Delormel, who thus provided himself with a number of syllables that formed the radical signs of his language. From these radicals, he went on to form derivatives (which, in his case, were verbs, adverbs, and adjectives) by placing one, two, or more letters between these syllables.

Explaining the system, the critic of the English *Monthly Review* wrote sceptically: 'Changes on words are to be rung with all the regularity of a multiplication-table. z is to indicate animal substance, т vegetable matter, and N artificial productions; so that every word may be analysed into its constituent ideas, with nearly as little trouble as we guess an aenigma. In all matters pertaining to religion, a G is to occur; and in all matters pertaining to government, a к.'[3] Thus, the writer continued wittily 'the mighty difference between a theist, a jew, and a christian, is to be expressed by the syllables ga, ge, gi; and the common quality of royalists and republicans is to be expressed by ko, ku.'[4] Instead of an unfamiliar script of lines and dots, such as had been used many times in the seventeenth century, Delormel preferred to use the letters of an improved alphabet from which he had discarded those (like c), which, in French at least, represent several sounds. Although the alphabet that he adopted had the virtue of regularity, it had many faults. For example, ten vowels were decided upon merely to conform to a preconceived decimal system, and no indication was given as to how four of these vowels, composed of two characters, were to be pronounced. Delormel's scheme was in fact so unimpressive that it inspired the contemporary view that 'the chief use of these systems, in the present state of science, is to excite the attention to the remediable defects of living language; and to direct the spirit of improvement towards those changes, which may approximate the art of communicating ideas to the regular method and rapid progress in which they are essentially generated.'[5] A later survey of universal language works, while describing this (quite wrongly, of course) as 'le premier projet sérieux,' judged it even more severely, stating that 'si l'idée fondamentale est bonne ... s'il se recommande par son caractère analytique, sa méthode sériaire et son essai de classification des connaissances humaines, le plan en est très défectueux et l'exécution détestable.'[6]

The scheme of a universal language composed during his youth by the distinguished scientist André-Marie Ampère is known almost entirely from occasional references in his early correspondence,[7] for, as far as I have been able to ascertain, there is no longer any trace of the grammar and dictionary of the new language that was said to have been seen (and heard) by his friends.[8] From the little information that is available, however, one may surmise that, in spite of his later work in that field, Ampère's scheme was not based upon any system of classification, but rather built up in an *a posteriori* manner from a detailed analysis of the vocabulary and grammar of a large number of languages. It probably represented something of a compromise between simplicity and comprehensiveness, analogous perhaps in this respect with the language described by Veiras in the *Histoire des Sévarambes* (1677–9). For Launay tells in his study of Ampère that his language had at first no fewer than eighty-two tenses, some of which he managed to avoid by the use of adjectives that conveyed some of the past, present, or future tenses that he had imagined: 'Les divers temps étaient eux-mêmes obtenus par une simple terminaison: *at* au présent, *it* au passé, *et* au futur. Par exemple, le radical *liber* impliquant l'idée de liberté, on avait: *liberat*, qui est libre; *liberit*, qui a été libre; *liberet*, qui sera libre.'[9]

Far more interesting and relevant to our theme was the preliminary draft and sample of an ideal 'philosophical' language composed by Condorcet probably between October 1793 and April 1794, which has not been printed in published versions of the *Esquisse d'un tableau historique des progrès de l'esprit humain*, in which it was originally intended to figure as the '4 ième fragment, xe époque.'[10] Considering the rather specialized nature of the manuscript this omission is understandable enough.

Condorcet clearly believed that it was feasible that one might formulate a kind of algebraic notation that would embrace the whole of human knowledge. The published version of the *Esquisse* in fact reveals quite clearly that he had in mind a universal language that would bring to the whole of human knowledge a precision and a certainty akin to that of mathematics, so that the search for truth would become relatively easy and error almost impossible.[11] The close similarity of these ideas with those of Leibniz is obvious, and it is interesting to note that part of the manuscript is devoted to an attempt to represent by means of symbols the operations of the intellect. However, it is significant that the manuscript is broken off and left unfinished at precisely the point where Condorcet is about to pass on to a consideration of the metaphysical sciences, linguistics, ethics, and politics. At the end of the manuscript, Condorcet himself pointed out that there was a great difference between these 'sciences' and the mathematical ones that he had considered earlier.

Dans celles-ci, l'objet de la science est en général déterminé, connu, et, même dans celles qui procèdent par des opérations intellectuelles, qui, par une suite de ces opérations, se créent de nouveaux objets, ces objets sont déterminés au moment même où l'esprit les a produits.

Au contraire, dans celle dont nous allons parler, ce sont les objets eux-mêmes qu'il s'agit d'abord de faire connaître. Il est nécessaire de former, de trouver les premières combinaisons d'idées, et de chercher à les désigner.[12]

The manuscript scheme confirms, therefore, the objections foreseen by the same writer in the published text, where he wrote: 'l'obstacle le plus réel qui l'empêcherait de l'étendre à d'autres [objets], serait la nécessité un peu humiliante de reconnaître combien peu nous avons d'idées précises, de notions bien déterminées, bien convenues entre les esprits.'[13] Thus, Condorcet faltered in the event, as he was certain to do and as Leibniz had done before him, because of the difficulty of ascertaining what constitutes the simple ideas and in what manner these are combined.

Although several other schemes of universal language were to appear in the course of the 1790s,[14] none aroused more than a fraction of the interest that greeted the *Pasigraphie* (1797) of Joseph de Maimieux (see plate 8).[15] The announcement of the work appeared in 1795, and before its eventual publication, after a delay of two years, de Maimieux claimed that he had received almost six thousand letters from scholars, teachers, and businessmen from all parts of Europe expressing hopes that the work would be brought to a successful conclusion.[16] An article published in 1795 in the *Magasin encyclopédique*,[17] having offered a brief history of the search for a universal language, pointed out that 'les auteurs pasigraphes, [i.e. de Maimieux and Sicard] dans leur prospectus paraissent comme certains d'un plein succès. Ils peuvent donc se promettre, comme le premier auteur de l'alphabet, de rendre à

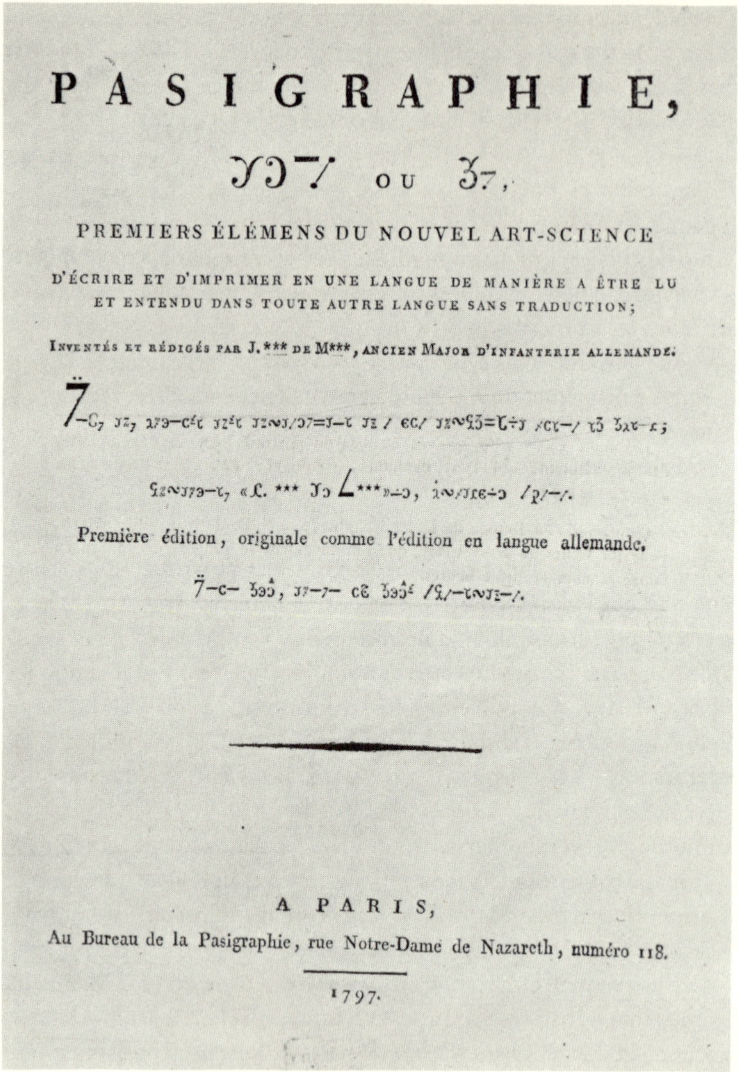

PASIGRAPHIE,

ꙮ ou ꙮ,

PREMIERS ÉLÉMENS DU NOUVEL ART-SCIENCE

D'ÉCRIRE ET D'IMPRIMER EN UNE LANGUE DE MANIÈRE A ÊTRE LU ET ENTENDU DANS TOUTE AUTRE LANGUE SANS TRADUCTION;

INVENTÉS ET RÉDIGÉS PAR J.*** DE M***, ANCIEN MAJOR D'INFANTERIE ALLEMANDE.

Première édition, originale comme l'édition en langue allemande.

A PARIS,
Au Bureau de la Pasigraphie, rue Notre-Dame de Nazareth, numéro 118.

1797.

Plate 8 Joseph de Maimieux
Pasigraphie, ou premiers élémens du nouvel art-science Paris 1797:
title page

jamais leurs noms immortels, en formant entre les hommes de nouveaux liens; en créant entre nos semblables de nouveaux moyens d'une communication facile de secours, de lumières et d'instructions réciproques.'[18]

The work finally appeared in September 1797 in both French and German editions, and its appearance aroused further interest throughout Europe, but particularly in France. The invention was praised, for example, by Goupil-Préfelne as being of as great importance to humanity as the invention of printing.[19] It was presented to Napoleon who is said to have admired it considerably,[20] and from 1797 onwards the new language was demonstrated several times in public, most successfully perhaps at the Lycée des arts in 1798 by a young pupil of de Maimieux.[21] Moreover, we may note that the *pasigraphie* went a stage further than any would-be universal language up to that time, by actually being taught, first by de Maimieux himself at the Bureau de la pasigraphie in Paris, then by a number of other teachers both in France and in Germany. In 1800 the *Décade philosophique* was able to report that it was being taught in a state-school at the École centrale of the Basses-Pyrénées at Pau, by the teacher of general grammar, Baradère, and 'quique moins publiquement, à Toulouse et dans quelques autres villes de France mais surtout en Allemagne.'[22]

As a consequence of the interest aroused by his pasigraphy, de Maimieux met with a certain amount of personal, if short-lived, success.[23] The work was submitted in 1798 to the second class of the Institut national for its approval, and it is for this reason above all that it merits attention. For it served not only to inspire memoirs on pasigraphy from Joseph Marie de Gérando, Destutt de Tracy, and Pierre-Louis Roederer,[24] but also formed the basis for a theoretical, and at times profound, discussion of universal language that was to continue for several years to be 'une des constantes préoccupations de la section de philosophie.'[25] For this reason, it is worth looking briefly at the structure of de Maimieux's system of universal writing.

As the name of the scheme indicates, it was intended as a means of communicating by writing rather than by speech, although de Maimieux later went on to form a spoken version of the pasigraphy, entitled a 'pasilalie.' The elements that go to make up the universal character are of three kinds. First, only twelve separate characters are used,[26] but these are combined in various ways; secondly, there are twelve general rules that admit of no exceptions and that the author claimed might be learned in a matter of a few hours' study; thirdly, the accentuation and punctuation already in use in Europe are to be retained. The twelve characters are combined to form three types of words, consisting of three, four and five characters respectively: 'Connective and expletive particles of frequent recurrence are to be of the first class; objects and ideas daily noticed in society, of the second; and terms of art, science, and recondite inquiry, of the third.'[27]

Since the number of basic characters is strictly reduced and yet it is claimed that together they form a complete image of thought, the manner of their combination is clearly all-important. The individual characters are thus to be combined in what is termed pasigraphical order. 'Par l'ordre pasigraphique,' writes de Maimieux

> on entend ici une classification de pur sens-commun, où l'intelligence éclairée par l'analogie, l'attention économisée le plus possible, et la mémoire aidée de tous les moyens de rappel, vont ensemble, ou du genre à l'espèce et de l'espèce à l'individu, ou du simple au composé, ou du plus connu au moins connu, selon que les rapports les plus frappans des idées entre'elles permettent l'une ou l'autre de ces marches.[28]

The order of the characters as they are written will lead the pasigrapher to a tripartite table, or map of thought, in which objects, ideas, feelings, and grammatical relations are all assigned to their particular place (or 'latitude' and 'longitude') by one of the above methods of procedure.[29] Each word thus has its own fixed, invariable position, in one of three tables termed the *Indicule* (in which are listed only words of three characters) (see plate 9), the *Petit Nomenclateur* (words of four characters), and the *Grand Nomenclateur*[30] (words of five characters). And so it will be seen that 'le principal fondement de l'art pasigraphique est dans le moyen si simple de substituer le signe de la place des mots aux syllabes dont toutes les langues composent leurs mots.'[31] However, in the case of the planned pasigraphy, 'la place du mot pasigraphé demeurant la même pour tous les peuples, ceux-ci s'entendront nécessairement, puisque les signes de la place du mot devenus le corps du mot, seront les mêmes, de quelques lettres que le mot placé dans la ligne soit formé, si d'ailleurs la méthode est réduite à douze règles qui n'éprouvent aucune exception.'[32]

It will be noted that, as in the earlier philosophical languages of Dalgarno and Wilkins, each character of a word serves, in effect, as a guide to discovering the location of the word and thereby its meaning in one or other of the tables. In the case of a word of three characters, for example, the first character indicates the column in which the particular word will be discovered, the second the sub-division of this column, and the third the line of the *Indicule*. Similarly, in the case of words of four and five characters, references are given to the *classe* in the *Grand Nomenclateur*, and to the *cadre*, the *colonne*, the *tranche*, and the *ligne* of either the *Petit* or *Grand Nomenclateur*. 'L'ordre pasigraphique,' writes de Maimieux, 'est donc un ordre naturel, où la place du mot en fixe la signification et concourt à déterminer celle des mots voisins, où la suite des caractères ramène l'idée, tandis que la gradation des idées ramène aussi sûrement les caractères.'[33]

Of the detailed formulation of the pasigraphy it is worth noting only that de Maimieux reduced the number of verbs to three, these being *devenir*, *être*, and *cesser d'être*; that the gender and number of substantives are indicated not by any special part of speech or by wordending, but by dots or signs; that there are special signs to represent prepositional forms; and lastly, that there exist modificatory signs which, placed before a given word and separated from it by an apostrophe, modify its meaning. Thus the sign Z ⟩ preceded by the modificatory sign ♃ (becoming ♃ Z ⟩) changes the meaning of the first sign from *God* to the *action de devenir ou de faire que ce dont on parle devienne ce que dit le mot*. The modified word would then signify in English *deifying*, and in French *déification*.

A brief résumé such as this can describe only the mere skeleton of the scheme of universal writing. Some of the pasigraphy's major defects will, however, immediately become apparent. It will be noted, for instance, that the unusual characters employed resemble each other much too closely, making the recognition and distinction of individual differences very difficult. The effect of the modificatory signs would be confusing, and to recognize all the pasigraphical signs immediately would take many years of sustained practice. As in the case of the early

(4)

1er CADRE. INDICULE DE MOTS SERVANT DE LIEN OU DE COMPLÉMENT

Ire COLONNE. Matière, Positions et Modifications.	IIe COLONNE. Végétaux.	IIIe COLONNE. Animaux.
—	∞	£
— Haut, en haut.	A fleur, - de terre.	Avant terme, à terme.
∞ Au haut, par en haut.	Au bord, sur le bord.	A plat, à plat ventre.
£ Bas, en bas.	En terre, en pleine terre.	Sur le dos, à la renverse.
Ϋ Au bas, par en bas.	Au fond, à fond, du fond.	A terre, par terre.
Ϲ Du haut en bas.	A l'abri, à couvert.	En rond, à croupetons.
Є Du bas en haut.	Au vent, à l'air, en plein -.	A rebrousse poil.
— Sur, dessus.	Vers, sur (direction).	Terre à terre.
∞ Au dessus, par dessus.	Près, proche, de près.	Pas à pas, pied à pied.
£ Sous, dessous.	Joint, contre, à bout portant.	A 2 -, à 3 -, à 4 pattes.
Ϋ Au dessous, par dessous.	Ras, au ras, rez, - de chaussée.	A clochepied, clopin, clopant.
Ϲ Entre, parmi.	A, après (adhérence).	A tire d'aile, d'une aile.
Є Sens dessus dessous.	De proche en proche.	En haleine, hors d'haleine.
— Devant, sur le devant.	Le long, en long, au long.	Avant, en avant.
∞ Au devant, par devant.	En large, au large, à l'aise.	Loin, de loin, à perte de vue.
£ Derrière, sur le derrière.	A l'étroit, en pointe.	Après, à la suite.
Ϋ Au derrière, par derrière.	Autour, aux environs.	A la file, à la queue.
Ϲ A rebours, au rebours.	Vis-à-vis, à l'opposite.	A la trace, à la piste.
Є Sens devant derrière.	A travers, au -, outre.	A l'affût, aux aguets.
— Au commencement [1].	A côté, de côté.	En tapinois, en cachette.
∞ Au milieu, au centre.	En deçà, de ce côté, - ci.	A la dérobée, à la sourdine.
£ Au bout, à la fin.	Au-delà, de ce côté, - là.	A la ronde, en tournoyant.
Ϋ En tout sens, pêle-mêle.	A droite, vers la -, sur la -.	D'un saut, d'emblée.
Ϲ A la fois, d'un coup, d'un seul -.	A gauche, vers la -, sur la -.	En arrêt, en défaut.
Є Tout à coup, coup sur coup.	De tout côté, de toute part.	A reculons, de retour.
— En quantité, en nombre.	Droit, en droite ligne.	A la nage, à vau-l'eau, à gué.
∞ A verse, à flots.	De biais, de guingois.	En l'air, au haut des airs.
£ Par torrent, en masse.	De travers, en travers.	A la volée, à vol d'oiseau.
Ϋ D'une seule pièce.	Au revers, à l'envers.	Par sauts, - bonds, - saccades.
Ϲ En totalité, en tout.	En croix, en zig-zag.	Ventre-à-terre, à corps perdu.
Є De fond en comble.	De part en -, d'outre en - [2].	Aux abois, à bout.
— Peu à peu, par degrés.	Brin à -, feuille à feuille.	A jeun, sur les dents.
∞ Tour à tour, tantôt.	Grain à grain.	Contre, sur, sus.
£ Bout à bout.	En abondance, à foison.	En chaleur, en rut.
Ϋ Goutte à goutte.	A tout rompre.	A coup, d'un coup (de).
Ϲ Couche à couche.	A temps, à point.	A belles dents, d'une bouchée.
Є En morceaux, en poudre.	De garde, en réserve.	En pièces, en lambeaux.

(5)

DE SENS ENTRE LES AUTRES PARTIES DU DISCOURS. Ier CADRE.

IVe COLONNE. HOMME PHYSIQUE.	Ve COLONNE. HOMME, SENSIBLE ET INTELLIGENT.	VIe COLONNE. HOMME PIEUX ET SOCIAL.
ᴛ	ᴄ	ᴇ
Debout, droit, sur pied. A tâtons, en bronchant. A tort et à travers [3]. A part, en particulier. Sans, à défaut, manque. A l'abandon, à dire.	Ah! ahi! oh! hem! Eh! eh bien! hoho! holà! O! quoi! las! hélas! Bah! bz, fi, ouf! Certes, comment? peste! Qu'est-ce?mal-peste!morbleu!	Plaise -, s'il plaît à Dieu. Dieu veuille, Dieu aidant. Au nom, - de Dieu. Dieu garde,-préserve,-sauve. A la bonne heure. Ainsi soit-il, patience.
En présence, face à face. Tête à tête, à la tête. De front, de face. De compagnie, côte à côte. Avec, ensemble. Par bande, en foule.	De gré, volontiers. De cœur, de bon cœur. Malgré, en dépit. A contre-cœur, à regret. Au gré (de), à volonté. Comme, de même, en guise.	De -, en bonne foi. De -, en bonne part. De -, en bonne grace. De grace, en grace. Daignez, s'il vous plaît. Graces, grand-merci.
Sur le séant, en (son) séant. A genoux, à deux genoux. A pied, à toutes jambes. A cheval, à toute bride. A crud, à poil, en selle. En croupe, en trousse.	Et, aussi, et cetera. Ou, ou bien, soit [6]. Concernant, touchant. A propos, quant (à). Mal à propos, à tort. A contre-sens, par -.	Bonjour, bon matin. Bon soir, bonne nuit. A vos souhaits, à (la) santé. Au plaisir, à l'honneur. A revoir, au retour. Adieu, portez-vous bien.
A pleine main, à poignée. D'un tour de main. A tour -, à revers de bras. A bras tendus, - ouverts. De force, de vive force. En eau, en nage [4].	Pour, afin, pourquoi. A cause, attendu, vu. Par, parce que, puisque. D'autant, - plus, - moins. Quoique [7], loin (de, que). Excepté, hormis, sauf.	De la part, de part. A l'occasion, au sujet. Par rapport, eu égard, à l'-. A titre, en qualité. A juste titre, à bon droit. Pour, en faveur, envers.
Prêt (à), à même (de). Après (à), en train (de). Au dépourvu, en sursaut. En butte, à la merci. En proie, à quia. A l'extrémité, sans retour.	Si, sinon, au cas. Mais, d'ailleurs. A la vérité, au reste. Car, cependant, pourtant. Néanmoins, nonobstant. En vain, vainement.	De manière, de façon. En sorte, de sorte. En -, par considération. A condition, à la charge. En forme, pour la forme. Sous prétexte (de, que).
Bien, mieux, au mieux. Tant mieux, pour le mieux. De mieux en mieux. Mal, au pis, au pis-aller. Tant pis, pour le pis. Dommage, de mal en pis [5].	Oui, soit, d'accord, tope. Exprès, à dessein. Au vu, au su, de bon. Non, - pas, - point. En conséquence, donc. Encore, enfin, à la fin.	De peur, de crainte. Au risque, en danger. Malheur (à)! contre. Gare, au secours, au feu. Pardon! merci! trève! quartier! Tout beau, paix, silence.

IIe Partie.   B

Plate 9 (above and opposite) Joseph de Maimieux
Pasigraphie, ou premiers élémens du nouvel art-science Paris 1797
4–5: index of link words and phrases
By courtesy of Glasgow University Library

seventeenth-century schemes of common writing, until this stage was reached, the 'pasigrapher' would have to use the tables to locate the meaning of every word. De Maimieux disregards, moreover, the important fact that in conventional spoken languages a sound (or a composite group of sounds) is more readily associated with an object or idea than is a collection of symbols each of which must individually be the object of an equal amount of the pasigrapher's undivided attention. An even more fundamental criticism could be levelled at the varying methods of procedure that are used in the compilation of the metaphysical tables, or *Grand Nomenclateur*. For in this respect and a number of others, de Maimieux's scheme lacks the methodical planning of Wilkin's *Essay*, which in many ways it resembles.[34]

7 / Signs and thought

The causes of the remarkable increase of interest in universal language that occurred in the 1790s are various, and have to be sought both in the immediate preoccupations and aspirations of the age, and in certain important philosophical problems that came very much to the fore at this time.

First, and most obviously, the hope that a new rational language would heal the long-standing divisions between men of different nations and creeds remained an important motive behind the activities of the latest proponents of an ideal artificial language. This motive took on a form, however, that clearly reflected fervent Republican aspirations. For, judging from statements made in the introductions to these would-be universal languages, and from contemporary speeches and articles, it would appear that such schemes proliferated particularly at this time in France, partly at least from a desire to extend to the whole world the hard-won principles of *liberté, égalité, fraternité*: the rights that had been proclaimed to be not merely the rights of the Frenchman, but the Rights of Man. Hence, although the diffusion of the French language was still gratefully acknowledged, many men believed that, national pride being what it is, no single language could ever succeed completely in breaking down the formidable barrier that was presented to the brotherhood of man by the confusion of tongues. Thus what a century before had been regarded as a potentially powerful instrument for carrying the word of God to all nations and uniting men in Christian harmony was now seen as likely to contribute to the diffu-

sion of Republican ideals. In his *Projet d'une langue universelle* (1795) Jean Delormel wrote, 'si le Gouvernement fait entrer dans l'instruction l'étude de cette langue, elle sera avant six mois, sans qu'il soit nécessaire d'y employer chaque jour beaucoup de tems, déjà bien utile pour les communications, propre à disséminer les principes de l'égalité, et fera honneur partout dans le monde à la République."[1] Several years later, in 1798, Joseph Dominique Garat, a member of the second class of the Institut national and an esteemed thinker and teacher at the École normale, made an eloquent speech to the Conseil des anciens, in the course of which, while eulogizing the new *pasigraphie* of Joseph de Maimieux, he maintained that those who loved liberty and looked for revolutions that would lead to the institution of reason and wisdom in the country would recognize the importance of an invention that would extend the concepts of the revolution throughout the world, while avoiding 'les malheurs et les horreurs qui en paraissent inséparables, et qu'elles ne produisent cependant que lorsqu'elles sont combattues d'une part et dirigées de l'autre par les affreuses passions que nourrit et qu'enflamme l'ignorance.'[2] Pasigraphy is portrayed here as an instrument of peaceful revolution as well as a weapon of moderation to be used against ignorance and passion. In a course given earlier at the École normale, the same philosopher had stated with admirable, though as yet unfounded, optimism:

> Si jamais, comme nous en avons formé déjà le voeu et l'éspérance, l'Europe est établie en républiques, il ne faut pas douter que ces républiques ne forment un jour un congrès de philosphes, chargés de l'institution de cette langue, qui serait pour toutes les nations, la source de tant de lumières, de tant de vertus, de tant de richesses, de tant de prospérités nouvelles.[3]

The desire to extend the ideals of the Republic to the rest of the world may therefore be said to have provided part of the inspiration that lay behind a number of the French ideal language schemes of the 1790s, though one suspects, of course, in a number of cases that the usefulness of the new language in this respect was pressed by its authors only after it had been constructed. For it was clearly expedient that language builders like Delormel should point out the political significance of their linguistic invention.

Secondly, interest in providing a newly planned, rational language is scarcely surprising at a period when men were widely engaged in a highly progressive, anti-traditional, rational organization of human affairs. Examples of this kind of reform and reconstruction are numerous, and may be borrowed from the fields of education, administration, and science.

The institution in October 1794 of the École normale in Paris, the establishment throughout France of Écoles centrales in 1795, and the foundation of the Institut national towards the end of the same year, all point to a keen desire to form a distinctively national and co-ordinated educational system.[4] A fresh start was to be made in education with a new approach, the most distinguished scientists and scholars as its teachers, a new method (that of analysis), and aims fully in tune with the rational, forward-looking outlook of the age. Similarly, after the Revolution, France was divided into uniform administrative divisions; she was endowed with a unified coinage and system of taxation, and the revolutionary year III saw the first elaborations of what was later to become the Code civil.[5] In science, the creation of the Institut national and the growth of political unity made possible the standardization of weights and measures and the adoption of the metric and decimal systems.[6] This general climate of rationalization, replanning, and reconstruction – much of it aimed fairly successfully at facilitating the advance of knowledge and trade – was clearly favourable to both the formulation and reception of a new, rationally planned language.

Yet these factors, important though they are in certain respects, do not satisfactorily explain why the universal language question should have become one of the main interests of that somewhat heterogeneous group of French thinkers who are commonly termed *Idéologues*.[7] This name was applied at the opening of the nineteenth century to all those thinkers who investigated what Destutt de Tracy had first called the science of *Idéologie*, or the analysis of sensations and ideas.[8] F. Picavet in his weighty study *Les Idéologues* included among them philosophers, scientists, economists, historians, and critics; all those, he wrote, 'qui acceptent le mot nouveau et la science qu'il désigne, tous ceux qui continuent les traditions philosophiques du XVIIIe siècle.'[9] We shall be concerned here, in the main, only with those philosophers who were members of the second class of the Institut national (often called the Académie des sciences morales et politiques), until this class was disbanded by Napoleon in 1803, or who gathered together as a group in the salon of Mme Helvétius at Auteuil, or later at the rue du Bac.[10] Of the Idéologues who were keenly interested in questions of language, the most distinguished were Destutt de Tracy, de Gérando, Garat, Lancelin, Prévost, Laromiguière, and finally Maine de Biran, who, although he could scarcely be described with any accuracy as an Idéologue even in his early years as a philosopher, nonetheless had close associations with the group and shared many of their interests, if not all of their conclusions.

The nineteenth-century historian of the second class of the Institut, J. Simon, wrote of the interest of the Idéologues in the universal language question, 'cette prétendue science [la pasigraphie] inventée par M. de Maismieux était, avec la question de l'origine des idées, une des constantes préoccupations de la section de philosophie,' and he continued: 'La pasigraphie semblait à la plupart des philosophes une découverte de premier ordre. C'etait un des côtés de la fameuse question des signes, si populaire à la fin du XVIIIe siècle et dans les premières années de celui-ci.'[11]

Although Simon was almost entirely mistaken in his view of the Idéologues' attitude to the new pasigraphy of de Maimieux, his assessment of their general interest in the universal language question was accurate enough. And in order to understand the real importance of the subject to the Idéologues, one needs to view their interest in terms of the wider controversy concerning the influence that the signs of language had on thought, which flared up most strongly in the closing decades of the eighteenth century.

Deriving originally from Francis Bacon's statement that errors may creep into the understanding through the misuse of words, the notion that language exercised a considerable influence on the processes of thought, and was to a considerable extent responsible for either the clarity or the obscurity of our ideas, was elaborated at length by John Locke in his famous *Essay Concerning Human Understanding*.[12] The Abbé Condillac, in the *Essai sur l'origine des connaissance humaines* published in 1746, lent even greater importance to the signs of language, making them responsible not only for the more or less precise recollection and communication of ideas, but also for the very presence in the mind of many of our complex or abstract ideas.

Largely as a result of Locke's and Condillac's writings, the important question as to the degree of influence that language exercised on the understanding was already being widely discussed in philosophical circles by the middle decades of the eighteenth century. In 1760, for example, Charles Bonnet discussed the general effects of language on our ideas in the *Essai analytique sur les facultés de l'âme*, and in Turgot's fragment, *Réflexions sur les langues*, we read the following concise description of the role of signs in the development of ideas:

> On a vu que les signes de nos idées inventés pour les communiquer aux autres, servaient encore à nous en assurer la possession, et à en augmenter le nombre; que les signes et les idées formaient comme deux ordres relatifs de choses qui se suivaient dans leurs progrès avec une dépendance mutuelle, qui marchaient en quelque sorte sur deux lignes parallèles, ayant les mêmes inflexions, les mêmes détours, et s'appuyant perpétuellement l'un sur l'autre; enfin, qu'il était impossible de connaître bien l'un sans les connaître tous deux – nos idées abstraites n'ayant point un modèle existant hors de nous, et n'étant que des signes de nos idées collectives, tous les raisonnemens des philosophes ne seront que de perpétuelles équivoques, si par une juste analyse on ne marque avec précision quelles sont les idées qui entrent dans la composition de ces idées abstraites et surtout à quel point elles sont déterminées.'[13]

Less typical of the thought of those writers who, broadly speaking, followed Condillac on this question, were Maupertuis's *Réflexions philosophiques sur l'origine des langues et la signification des mots*[14] where Condillac's philosophy of language received a somewhat unexpected twist in the direction of an early kind of linguistic relativism.[15]

In Germany, at approximately the same period, the problem of the reciprocal influence of language and reason was also being discussed at some length. It was set as an essay subject, for example, by the Royal Academy of Berlin in 1759, the prize being awarded to J.D. Michaelis, professor of philosophy at Gottingen.[16] J.G. Sulzer's 'Observations sur l'influence réciproque de la raison sur le langage et du langage sur la raison' also appeared in the *Histoire de l'académie royale des sciences et belles-lettres de Berlin* for 1767.

Yet, in spite of so prolonged a discussion, it was above all during the 1790s that the subject came to be most hotly debated. For at this time Condillac's views on the role of language in the development of thought were considered with an enthusiasm that, before the late eighteenth century, had been reserved only for the most vital metaphysical questions. Indeed, in the eyes of the philosophers of the Institut, the problem of signs and thought was of much greater significance to the future of mankind than any of those questions that they would have felt one was stigmatizing by describing them as 'metaphysical.' A closer look at Condillac's reasoning and conclusions will show why this was so.

Like Locke, Condillac accepted, of course, that since we are in a state of sin we can possess no innate ideas, and based his philosophy on the old stoic maxim that *nihil est in intellectu quod non prius fuerit in sensu*. Knowledge, which comes to us by way of the senses, requires, however, the analysis or decomposition of what is presented to the senses. And so, as H.B. Acton has explained:

> If someone were taken at night into a castle which overlooked an extensive landscape, and if, in the morning, a window were opened and immediately closed again, the visitor would *see* the whole landscape, that is to say it would affect his sense of sight, but he would not be able to *observe* it or to describe it to others. If he is to get *knowledge* of the landscape, the window must be kept open long enough for him to attend first to one part then another. What is simultaneously presented to the sense of sight must be successively attended to and thus *decomposed* into its elements. Sight is only transformed into knowledge and observation when the parts that have been distinguished from one another are recomposed so as to be apprehended in the relations they actually have with one another. Condillac uses the word 'analysis' for this decomposition and recomposition, and it is his view that it is by means of analysis that human knowledge is gained and advanced.'[17]

The process of analysis, of distinguishing and comparing the various elements of experience permits the development of elementary forms of thought and the more elaborate processes of reasoning (*réflexion* and *raisonnement*). However, Condillac argued, analysing ideas is virtually possible only by means of signs. For, although he conceded that the existence of the faculties of mind, which he regarded, incidentally, merely as transformations of sensation, would allow some elementary combination and comparison of perceptions, from which a few more complex notions might be formed, nonetheless these ideas or images, produced in the mind as a result of the impressions made by external objects upon the senses, would arrive simultaneously and in a state of disorder. Hence, without signs, these impressions could not be apprehended, distinguished from one another, fixed in the mind, and then expressed successively. For, 'décomposer une pensée, comme une sensation,' wrote Condillac, 'ou se représenter successivement les parties dont elle est composée, c'est la même chose; et, par conséquent, l'art de décomposer nos pensées n'est que l'art de rendre successives les idées et les opérations qui sont simultanées.'[18] Artificial signs, in particular, are thus necessary in order that we should be able to 'fix' the relations between the various elements of our perception, of which we should otherwise be only very dimly aware. And so, wrote Condillac, 'ayant, par vous-même, la faculté d'apercevoir un rapport, vous devez à l'usage des signes artificiels, la faculté de l'affirmer ou de pouvoir faire une proposition.'[19]

Signs, and in particular the signs of language, the most elaborate of all sign-systems, are therefore, Condillac concluded, in themselves methods of analysis. 'Car, si nous ne connaissons les choses qu'autant que nous les analysons, c'est une conséquence, que nous ne les connaissions qu'autant que nous nous représentons successivement les qualités, qui leur appartiennent. Or c'est ce que nous ne pouvons faire qu'avec des signes choisis et employés avec art.'[20]

Moreover, Condillac went on, we should follow in our analyses an order that nature had already followed in endowing us with the raw material of our ideas. Since this was, he believed, the natural order, it would also be that best suited for the mind to comprehend the relations between the qualities of external objects and of ideas. It seemed to Condillac to follow from this that languages, being, as he had shown, analytical methods, would fulfil their function more or less well inasmuch as they adhered to this natural order of the generation of ideas. As a result, if the language were to follow this method only imperfectly, 'la pensée ne se débrouillerait qu'imparfaitement; les idées s'offriraient confusément et sans ordre à celui qui voudrait parler; et il ne pourrait se faire entendre qu'autant qu'on le devinerait.'[21]

Unfortunately, Condillac discovered that languages were in fact exceedingly defective as methods of analysis. For, although, as man's needs have increased, languages have developed greatly in complexity, as methods of analysing our experience and ideas, they have not evolved as far as the philosopher would wish. Condillac indeed conjectures that in this respect earlier forms of articulate speech were superior to the languages of more advanced civilizations, since 'la génération des idées et des facultés de l'âme devait être sensible dans ces langues, où la première acception d'un mot était connue, et où l'analogie donnait toutes les autres.'[22]

As languages have become more elaborate and richer in terms, they have also tended to become less effective as methods of analysis, incorporating words that reveal less clearly the true resemblances or analogies that exist between ideas, hence confusing, in the philosopher's view, our understanding of the natural world. Man has distinguished less sharply between his ideas; he has also admitted into his language words of foreign origin, which have greatly confused the original analogies between signs that once corresponded closely to the analogies that exist between ideas. As a result, Condillac maintained, our modern languages have become confused and confusing, a mere hotchpotch of words applied quite indiscriminately to ideas, without regard to their origin or their true relations. These languages, he wrote, 'confondent tout: l'analogie ne peut plus faire apercevoir, dans les différentes acceptions des mots, l'origine et la génération des connaissances: nous ne savons plus mettre de la précision dans nos discours, nous n'y songeons pas: nous faisons des questions au hasard, nous y répondons de même: nous abusons continuellement des mots et il n'y a point d'opinions extravagantes qui ne trouvent des partisans.'[23]

Such defective instruments of analysis, Condillac realized, could clearly do most harm in philosophy and in the sciences. He held metaphysicians most to blame for allowing their language to reach such a state of utter disorder and chaos: 'Subtils, singuliers, visionnaires, inintelligibles souvent ils semblaient craindre de n'être pas assez obscurs, et ils affectaient de couvrir d'un voile leurs connais-

sances vraies ou prétendues. Aussi la langue de la philosophie n'a-t-elle été qu'un jargon pendant plusieurs siècles.'[24]

Having inherited from Bacon and particularly from Locke an acute awareness of the errors that can creep into the understanding as a result of these defects in languages, Condillac concluded in *La Logique* that these errors result from the habit we have fallen into of using words without having determined their real meaning, without even having felt the need to do this.[25] And so, he went on, we think that we are acquiring knowledge, while in fact we are merely learning words that are meaningless in any real sense.

Condillac did not believe, however, that definition could provide any truly satisfactory solution to this problem, since 'elle ne fait que me montrer une chose que je connais et dont l'analyse peut seule me découvrir les propriétés.'[26] Therefore, only analysis can guide us to a truer understanding of things. For all ideas, he went on to explain, are either simple or complex. If they are simple, they cannot be defined, but analysis will reveal the sensory data from which they are derived and show how they came to us. If they are complex, analysis is once again of greater value than definition, since by this means alone can one distinguish clearly between the partial ideas of which each complex notion is composed.[27]

The nomenclatures of the various sciences of the day Condillac regarded in no more favourable light than he did that of metaphysics. He asserted indeed that, with the exception of algebra and certain parts of the terminology of physics and chemistry,[28] the languages of science were as thoroughly riddled with defects as that employed by metaphysicians: 'On les parle tout aussi souvent sans rien dire: souvent encore on ne les parle que pour dire des absurdités; et, en général, il ne paraît pas qu'on les parle avec le dessein de se faire entendre.'[29]

The exception of algebra was, however, an important one. For here, Condillac believed, was the example of a method of analysis that corresponded perfectly to the analogies that exist between the ideas treated in mathematics. 'L'algèbre est une langue bien faite,' wrote Condillac, 'et c'est la seule: rien n'y paraît arbitraire. L'analogie qui n'échappe jamais, conduit sensiblement d'expression en expression. L'usage ici n'a aucune autorité. Il ne s'agit pas de parler comme les autres, il faut parler d'après la plus grande analogie pour arriver à la

plus grande précision.'[30] It was almost entirely as a consequence of the success of its language *as an analytical method* that mathematics was a truly demonstrable science. It seemed to Condillac to follow that all that had to be done to attain in the other sciences a degree of certainty comparable to that found in mathematics was to refashion their languages until they too became perfect in their analogies. Hence, in *La Logique*, Condillac wrote:

> S'il y a donc des sciences peu exactes, ce n'est pas parce que on n'y parle pas algèbre, c'est parce que les langues en sont mal faites, qu'on ne s'en aperçoit pas, ou que, si l'on s'en doute, on les refait plus mal encore. Faut-il s'étonner qu'on ne sache pas raisonner quand la langue des sciences n'est qu'un jargon composé de beaucoup trop de mots, dont les uns sont des mots vulgaires qui n'ont pas de sens déterminé, et les autres des mots étrangers ou barbares qu'on entend mal? Toutes les sciences seraient exactes, si nous savions parler la langue de chacune.[31]

And, in his later works, *La Logique* and *La Langue des calculs*, the latter published posthumously in 1798, Condillac formulated the extreme view that 'une science bien traitée n'est qu'une langue bien faite.'[32] From this it appeared to follow that if languages were 'portées à la plus grande perfection, les sciences parfaitement analysées seraient parfaitement connues de ceux qui en parleraient bien les langues.'[33] Thus the reconstruction of language emerged from Condillac's reasoning as one of the most far-reaching of all reforms, which, if properly conducted, could lead inevitably to certainty in the conclusions of the chemist, the physicist, the moralist, and the metaphysician alike.

Yet Condillac did not leave the subject with mere vague admonitions as to the need and the value of a reform of language. His whole critique of existing languages was guided by the ideal of a philosophical language, the characteristics of which derived from his theory of knowledge. Against this ethnic languages and scripts could be measured and (with the exception of the specialized script used in algebra – a sign-system that Condillac believed already approached perfection in this respect) found sadly wanting. The ideal language that he had in mind would be strict, exact, and simple in its analyses, that is to say, ideas would be clearly distinguished from each other and seen in relation to their origins in sensation and to analogous ideas. Words would then be assigned to these ideas in such a way as to indicate by means of the analogies between their signs how one idea leads on to and may be contained in another. For Condillac makes it clear that he regards analogy as the most desirable quality of an ideal analytical language. Hence he wrote, 'Si nous parlons pour nous faire entendre, nous devons préférer le langage qui montre comment nous passons d'une idée à une idée: car une langue bien faite devrait être comme un tableau mouvant dans lequel on verrait le développement successif de toutes nos connaissances.'[34] The ideal language, Condillac hoped, would therefore lead its user by a series of careful analogies, corresponding to the natural analogies existing between ideas, back to the sensations from which all our more complex ideas were derived. It would therefore contain within its own sign-system a résumé of both the derivation and the filiation of our ideas.

This view of the philosophical language clearly has close affinities with that of Wilkins and Dalgarno, and, above all, with that of Leibniz. It differed essentially from the latter, of course, in that the structure of the language is determined by Condillac's own epistemology, simple sensations taking the place of the 'simple ideas' of Descartes and Leibniz as the irreducible factors into which complex ideas may be analysed.

Condillac is, however, even closer to Leibniz in his later works in regarding the operations of metaphysical reasoning as following certain rigid mechanical rules and in seeing them as more or less identical with the operations involved in solving mathematical problems by equation. For he claimed that, as in algebraic analysis, there were two processes involved in metaphysical analysis:

> Par le premier on établit l'état de la question, c'est-à-dire, en d'autres termes, qu'on raisonne sur les conditions, qu'on n'en oublie aucune, et qu'on les traduit dans l'expression la plus simple; par le second, on va de proposition identique en proposition identique jusqu'à la conclusion qui résout la question, ce qui est encore, en d'autres termes, aller d'équation identique en équation identique jusqu'à l'équation finale.[35]

From this he concluded that metaphysical and mathematical analysis were precisely the same, the only difference between them being that

> par la nature des idées, ou plutôt par la nature de nos langues qui, sur toute autre chose que les nombres, ne nous donnent que des notions mal déterminées, l'analyse est infiniment plus difficile en métaphysique qu'en mathématique. Mais, enfin dans l'une et l'autre science, on fait la même chose toutes les fois qu'on analyse, si l'on analyse bien.[36]

The question as to whether Condillac's later writings were influenced by a reading of Leibniz clearly requires too extended a discussion to be dealt with here. Georges Le Roy, the modern editor of Condillac's *Œuvres philosophiques*, regards these resemblances as purely fortuitous.[37] De Gérando, in the *Histoire comparée des systèmes de philosophie* was less sure, and quoted a remarkable passage from Leibniz's *Considérations sur la culture et la perfection de la langue allemande* of which, he suggested, *La Logique* and *La Langue des calculs* seemed to some extent to be the natural development.[38] Purely on a basis of the similarity of their ideas, I tend to agree with de Gérando that such an influence was highly likely, though the problem still has to be properly solved.

Condillac's conclusions, whether influenced or not by the ideas of Leibniz, clearly seemed of the utmost importance for the future advancement of knowledge. For, if his assessment of the role played by language in thought were accurate, and if all existing languages were in fact, as he believed, imperfect, it appeared at least that by concentrating upon perfecting his language man might ultimately bring to all fields of knowledge the certainty that had hitherto characterized mathematics alone. The perfecting of language could, then, be regarded as a major step in the direction of human perfectibility.

There is no doubt that in the 1790s these implications of Condillac's thought were recognized by the Idéologues. His writings were of course well known to these thinkers: so well known, indeed, that it became common practice for nineteenth-century historians of philosophy to regard the Idéologues as nothing but zealous disciples of Condillac. Moreover, a number of factors combined to concentrate attention in the 1790s upon this aspect of Condillac's thought.

First was the fact that the closing decades of the eighteenth century witnessed a growing concern at the inadequacies of the nomenclatures of a number of sciences. For this Condillac can be held only in small part responsible. For, to take but one example, attempts at reforming the archaic and highly misleading nomenclature of experimental chemistry had already been made by Macquer, Guyton de Morveau, and Bergman some years before the appearance of Condillac's *La Logique* in 1781.[39]

However, Condillac's views on language reform were often quoted after that date and were referred to specifically by Lavoisier in the paper 'Mémoire sur la nécessité de réformer et de perfectionner la nomenclature chimique,' which was given at a public meeting of the Académie des Sciences on 18 April 1787, and which, together with other papers by de Morveau and Fourcroy, marked a most significant breakthrough for the new chemistry.[40]

This example is an important one. It served to draw attention, for instance, to the highly defective nomenclatures of other sciences.[41] Yet, more important to our theme, the progress that was made in the new chemistry after the adoption of the reformed nomenclature was commonly invoked in the 1790s to substantiate Condillac's claim that the advancement of knowledge and the perfecting of a science depended upon a complete overhaul, and perhaps a total reconstruction of language. Thus it was partly owing to the outstanding advances in chemistry during the 1780s that interest was focused upon the full implications of Condillac's proposals for language reform and for the formulation of an ideal analytical language.

Secondly, in the 1790s a first complete edition of Condillac's writings was being prepared and was finally published in 1798 in twenty-three volumes. Included in this edition for the first time was *La Langue des calculs*, to which we have referred for some of Condillac's more extreme statements concerning a mathematically precise, analytical language. This work was certainly well known to the leading Idéologues prior to its publication, since among those responsible for preparing the edition was Pierre Laromiguière, an associate member of the second class of the Institut, an *habitué* of the salon of Madame Helvétius at Auteuil, and a close acquaintance of Destutt de Tracy, Cabanis, Sièyes, Garat, Daunou, and others.[42] In the editors' note that followed the unfinished study, *La Langue des calculs*, it was pointed out that Condillac had himself considered it as but a prelude to a work of much vaster proportions in which he would attempt a radical reconstruction of metaphysical and ethical, as well as scientific, terminology. The note indicates quite clearly that the direction, scope, and importance of Condillac's thought was appreciated at this period, and it is worth quoting almost in full. 'Ce qu'il [Condillac] avait principalement en vue,' wrote the editors,

> ce qui avait été le but constant des recherches d'une vie employée toute entière à perfectionner la raison, c'était de débrouiller le chaos où les abus et les vices du langage ont plongé les sciences morales et métaphysiques. Les jargons inintelligibles qu'elles parlent trop souvent auraient été convertis en autant de belles langues que tout le monde aurait apprises facilement, parce que tout le monde les aurait entendues; et dans ces langues on eût vu les idées qui paraissent les plus inaccessibles à l'esprit humain, sortir d'elles-mêmes et sans efforts des notions les plus communes.
>
> Qu'on ne croie pas que c'est une conjecture que nous hasardons; ce que Condillac avait communiqué de son projet à quelques amis, ce qu'il fait dans sa logique, le degré étonnant de simplicité auquel sur la fin des ses jours il avait porté son esprit, enfin ce qu'il annonce dans l'introduction de l'ouvrage qu'on vient de lire, *les mathématiques, dont je traiterai, sont dans cet ouvrage un objet subordonné à un objet bien plus grand*; tout nous donne la conviction la plus entière qu'il ne se serait pas borné à perfectionner une langue qui, tout admirable qu'elle est, ne sera jamais parlée que d'un petit nombre d'hommes.'[43]

Condillac's conclusion that creating a science – be it mathematical, physical, moral, or metaphysical – consisted in little more than constructing a well-made language was thus clearly of great importance and could scarcely be ignored by subsequent thinkers.

With a view to examining this question more closely, therefore, the second class of the Institut national focused attention in the year v upon the problems of perfecting language by setting the following general subject for a prize essay competition: 'Déterminer l'influence des signes sur la formation des idées.'[44] This important contest – the first to be announced since the class was established on the 29th of brumaire, year IV, (20 November 1795) – was won by the contribution of Joseph-Marie de Gérando. His essay was published in a much amplified form in 1800, under the title *Des signes et de l'art de penser considérés dans leurs rapports mutuels*. The runner-up was Pierre Prévost, professor of philosophy at Geneva, with a much shorter work, also published at Paris in the same year, under the title *Des signes envisagés relativement à leur influence sur la formation des idées*. As a result of the success of their work both de Gérando and Prévost soon became associate members of the second class in the section 'Analyse des sensations et des idées.'[45] Also specially commended by the class was the contribution of P.-F. Lancelin, an 'Ingénieur-Constructeur de la Marine Française,' which appeared in three parts, published between 1801 and 1803, under the title *Introduction à l'analyse des sciences, ou de la génération, des fondemens, et des instrumens de nos connaissances*, a work which has come to be known to literary scholars because of its influence upon Stendhal.[46] Probably superior to all of these, however, stylistically as well as philosophically, were 'les notes qui doivent servir pour un mémoire sur l'influence des signes,' prepared apparently with this competition in mind, but never, in fact, submitted, or even completed, by Maine de Biran. These notes, to which we shall refer in the course of this and the next chapter, remained in manuscript form until they were published by Pierre Tisserand in the *Œuvres de Maine de Biran* in 1920.[47]

To judge merely from the title of the essay that was set by the second class, it might appear that the enquiry was intended to be of a purely speculative or historical nature. However, if one looks rather more closely at the detailed terms of the announcement, it is clear that such an intention was far from the minds of those members of the Institut who had formulated the subject. For the attention of the contestants is directed immediately to the practical implications of the question that they are asked to investigate. They are reminded that too few of that select group of philosophers, who in the past have concerned themselves with the study of the human understanding have ever considered how its force might be increased or its energies better directed. 'Cependant,' the announcement continues, 'à la voix de quelques hommes de génie, on a senti depuis quelques années, qu'il fallait abandonner la recherche des premières causes, et porter enfin l'attention sur *les moyens de perfectionner l'entendement.*'[48]

It has been suggested, the announcement goes on, that the human mind owes the tremendous progress that it has already made over the ages chiefly to the fact that man alone has the use of the signs of language. For, 'malgré l'autorité de quelques grands hommes qui les [les signes] avaient regardés comme des entraves à la justesse et à la rapidité de nos conceptions, on osa avancer qu'un homme séparé du commerce de ses semblables aurait encore besoin de signes pour combiner ses idées.'[49] Moreover, the claim has been made that signs are necessary in order that we should possess any ideas at all, so that we owe the existence of even those ideas that spring directly from the sensations to our capacity to employ signs. Yet, it is pointed out, 'si une certaine influence des signes sur la formation des idées est une chose incontestable et avouée de tout le monde, il n'en est pas de même du degré de cette influence. Ici les esprits se divisent; et ce que les uns regardent comme des démonstrations évidentes, les autres le traitent de paradoxes absurdes.'[50] The first question contestants are asked to consider is, therefore, whether it is true that sensations can be transformed into ideas only by means of signs. What in appearance is a purely academic issue becomes quite different when it is considered in relation to the questions that follow:

2 / L'art de penser serait-il parfait, si l'art des signes était porté à sa perfection?
3 / Dans les sciences où la vérité est reçue sans contestation, n'est-ce pas à la perfection des signes qu'on en est redevable?
4 / Dans celles qui fournissent un aliment éternel aux disputes, le partage des opinions n'est-il pas un effet nécessaire de l'inexactitude des signes?
5 / Y'a-t-il quelque moyen de corriger les signes mal faits, et de rendre toutes les sciences également susceptibles de démonstration?[51]

The initial directions and the detailed questions of the announcement thus show that members of the second class, a large number of whom were leading Idéologues, not only wished to encourage an examination of the part that signs have played in the formation and development of our ideas, but also wanted the contestants to consider the possibility of reforming and even attaining perfection in our language and to assess the impact that a perfected or improved sign-system would have on the subsequent development of the human mind.[52] As a result, it is within the framework of this contest that we find an extended discussion of an ideal philosophical language, considered not for its own sake but because it was hoped that such a language would lead to a corresponding improvement, if not to a complete 'perfectionnement,' of the understanding. However, it should be noted that, although the terms of the announcement indicate that the Idéologues recognized the possible implications for the future of human progress contained in the reform of signs, the fact that it was considered necessary to re-examine these questions at all, after the work of Condillac, suggests that there was already some measure of doubt as to the validity of at least certain of the latter's conclusions.

There was, in particular, considerable reluctance in the second half of the 1790s to accept the view that the simplest and earliest of our ideas depend for their existence upon the presence of signs. It was sometimes pointed out that Condillac had himself never made this particular claim for signs.[53] Pierre Cabanis, a leading Idéologue, physiologist, and member of the second class, was himself partly responsible for encouraging such an extreme view and was blamed by Maine de Biran for over-estimating the role of signs.[54] In a mémoire entitled 'Considérations générales sur l'étude de l'homme et sur les rapports de son organisation physique avec ses facultés intellectuelles et morales,'[55] which was read to the second class in 1795 and formed a part of the important *Rapports du physique et du moral de l'homme* published in 1802, Cabanis wrote:

> On ne distingue les sensations, qu'en leur attachant des signes qui les représentent et les caractérisent: on ne les compare, qu'en représentant et caractérisant également par des signes, ou leurs rapports, ou leurs différences. Voilà ce qui fait dire à Condillac qu'on ne pense point sans le secours des langues, et que les langues sont des méthodes analytiques: mais il faut ici, donner au mot *langue*, le sens le plus étendu. Pour que la proposition de Condillac soit parfaitement juste, ce mot doit exprimer le système méthodique des signes par lesquels on fixe ses propres sensations ... On peut penser, sans se servir d'aucun idiome connu ...

Mais, je le répète, sans *signes* il n'existe ni pensée, ni peut-être même, à proprement parler, de véritable sensation, c'est-à-dire, de sensation nettement aperçue et distinguée de toute autre.[56]

For Cabanis, therefore, man becomes truly aware of his sensations only when he 'fixes' them in his mind by the use of signs. Garat, in his course entitled 'Analyse de l'entendement,' also adopted this view of the necessity of signs in order that thought should be possible. For, 'puisque ce n'est qu'avec des *signes* qu'on peut faire ces divisions et ces *liaisons*, ces *additions* et ces *contradictions*; il est évident que pour penser, il faut des signes, c'est à dire des langues.'[57] It was probably as a result of extreme views such as this and of internal disagreements on the issue that the second class of the Institut felt that some more extended discussion of this aspect of the topic was called for.

Although the question of the exact degree and nature of the influence that signs exercise in the earliest stages of acquiring knowledge would be important for a consideration of the various philosophers' views upon the essential activity or passivity of man (that is to say, his ability to control his attention and direct it to the various disparate elements of his experience), it may be dealt with here fairly briefly.[58] For the question is clearly extremely complex, and, as de Gérando and Maine de Biran both recognized, a solution must hinge partly on the meaning that was given to the terms *idée* and *signe*.[59] These two thinkers in particular were far from blind to the philosophical niceties of the problem.

On this point, Destutt de Tracy argued that if we were to accept as 'ideas' the most simple perceptions and consider 'thought' as having perceptions, that is, making 'to think' virtually synonymous with 'to feel,' we must acknowledge ourselves capable of having ideas and of combining them in thought without the aid of signs. How far we could progress in our thinking remained, however, a matter for dispute. Hence, de Tracy concluded that the question was insoluble in its detail.

Nonetheless, there was more or less general agreement among these various thinkers that simple ideas, formed as a result of the contact of our sense-organs with the outside world, needed no help from signs in order to be present in the understanding. Prévost, Lancelin, and Destutt de Tracy all believed that to maintain the opposite view would be absurd. De Gérando claimed that, since the mind was itself able to focus attention upon one part of a landscape rather than upon another, it was unnecessary to suppose that signs were needed to distinguish between the various elements of a complex whole.

When we turn to consider the Idéologues' views upon the precise role played by signs in the development of ideas rather than in their earliest formation, we see that they also tend to differ among themselves in points of detail rather than in fundamentals, and on the whole tend to clarify rather than contradict Condillac. For Destutt de Tracy, for instance signs are necessary for us to be able to compare and contrast ou simple ideas, and decompose our complex ones. He therefore concluded, as did Condillac, that languages are 'analytical methods' upon which we are dependent for building up knowledge and which guide our mind in its calculations. 'Mais, suivant moi,' he wrote,

> Condillac aurait dû énoncer différemment sa découverte, et dire que tout signe est l'expression du résultat d'un calcul exécuté, ou, si l'on veut, d'une analyse faite, et qu'il fixe et constate ce résultat; en sorte qu'une langue est réellement une collection de formules trouvées, qui ensuite facilitent et simplifient merveilleusement les calculs ou analyses qu'on veut faire ultérieurement.[60]

De Gérando, who gave a most detailed account of the role of signs in the development of our thought and in their influence upon the operations of our faculties, also regarded the signs of language as essential to the formation of abstract ideas and adds, 'L'influence des signes du langage, détermine en nous le réveil et le développement de la faculté de réflexion, et avec elle, l'essor de l'esprit philosophique.'[61]

Only Maine de Biran differed radically from the Idéologues in that he considered that man possesses *naturally* that power to distinguish between his perceptions and compare them with each other that constitutes the *faculté d'abstraire*. It is this power, Maine de Biran believed, and not the ability to use signs, that makes man an *être raisonnable* and distinguishes him from the animals. Language is created as a result of the operation of this faculty to abstract, rather than that the faculty itself owes its existence to the presence of signs. Yet even Maine de

Biran did not ultimately reject the importance of signs for the development of knowledge, but deferred the point at which signs begin to be of use. Most of the Idéologues, for example, would have accepted unhesitatingly the following statement made by him concerning the effect of signs, though they would have felt that it accorded to them perhaps too little importance. 'Cependant,' he wrote,

> ces premières idées abstraites sont fugitives; séparées de l'objet réel d'où elles ont été tirées, elles n'ont plus d'existence. L'entendement ne peut en tirer aucun secours: l'imagination ne saurait les réveiller puisqu'elle ne rappelle que l'objet de la sensation totale de la même manière dont il frappe les sens. Comment fixera-t-on cet être de raison, cette abstraction fugitive? Il faut la revêtir d'un signe, et dès ce moment, elle acquiert de la réalité. L'entendement en dispose, la rappelle à son gré, et donne à son ouvrage la même réalité qu'aux œuvres de la nature.'[62]

More typical of Idéologue thought on the role of signs in the development of knowledge are the views of Pierre Laromiguière as expressed in his inaugural lecture given at the Faculty of Letters in Paris in 1811. Laromiguière stated there that 'celui-là seul possédera tout le secret des signes, à qui les langues offriront, à la fois, des moyens de communication pour la pensée, des formules pour retenir des idées prêtes à nous échapper, et des méthodes propres à *faire naître* des idées nouvelles.'[63] Our earliest analyses, argued Laromiguière, resulted from the confrontation of our sense-organs and the physical world: in this way we obtain a number of elementary ideas, to which are added others arrived at by the use of a *langage d'action*. But it is only with the birth and development of the artificial signs of spoken (and later written) language that the human mind becomes, as it were, master of its own perceptions. 'Dès lors,' he continued, 'les idées les plus circonscrites s'étendent, se généralisent; les plus éloignées se rapprochent; les plus fugitives se fixent: l'esprit en dispose à son gré; il les étudie à loisir; il les choisit, les ordonne; et des rapports nouveaux apparaissent en foule, environnés d'une vive clarté.'[64]

While conceding that thought of a somewhat confused and primitive kind was possible without signs, Laromiguière stressed that the human mind owed its ability to reason (*l'art de penser*) entirely to the development of language. And so, just as it is sure that languages do not create thought, so, argued Laromiguière, is it incontrovertible that the signs of language are necessary in order that it should be analysed and developed. Languages are not only, therefore, 'means of analysis':

> Elles sont des *méthodes analytiques* : vérité fondamentale, qui donne la possibilité d'apprécier la bonté relative de toutes les langues, et de discerner, soit parmi les langues qui appartiennent aux différens peuples, soit parmi les langues propres aux différens écrivains chez un même peuple, soit encore parmi les langues diverses que le génie a créées pour l'avancement des sciences, celles qui, décomposant la pensée dans l'ordre le mieux approprié à la nature de l'entendement, pourraient donner à ses facultés une facilité inattendue et des forces incalculables.[65]

To sum up, our brief account of the Idéologues' views on the role of signs in thought reveals that, although they considered signs unnecessary in the early formation of ideas, they recognized the need for signs and, in particular, the signs of language in order to analyse our sense impressions, to compare and combine our perceptions, and to develop a body of ideas not limited to mere physical notions. In this aspect of their thought, therefore, the Idéologues differed only slightly from Condillac.

Also like Condillac, they were greatly concerned at the obvious inadequacies of all existing languages to fulfil properly the functions that we have described above. For example, Destutt de Tracy, in the 'Mémoire sur la faculté de penser,' wrote of the ancient languages that they are 'moins assujetties à un système méthodique qu'aux caprices d'un usage aveugle et fortuit. Quant à nos langues modernes, composées des débris de cinq ou six idiomes différens, et formées, pour ainsi dire, de toutes pièces, elles sont de vrais tas de décombres, où il ne commence à règner un peu d'ordre que depuis qu'ils ont été maniés et arrangés par des hommes subtils ou ingénieux et savans dans tous les genres.'[66] The Idéologues were thoroughly versed in Locke's analysis of the imperfections of language and, if they did not themselves dwell upon these imperfections, this was because Locke had already devoted considerable attention to them. In de Gérando's own words, Locke and Leibniz 'nous apprirent combien le raisonnement devenait incertain et défectueux dans un langage sujet à mille équivoques, et de quel nuage épais l'abus des mots couvrait pour nous le sentier qui conduit à la vérité.'[67] They had learned also from Condillac that, as languages developed in order to express more complex or abstract ideas, they lost their original virtues of accurate analysis and careful analogy.

Their preoccupation with general grammar also convinced the Idéologues of the extreme inadequacies of existing languages. General grammar formed, we have seen, along with the science of *Idéologie* and logic, what they regarded as a complete course in the philosophy of language. Concerned as they were with the 'science' rather than the 'art' of grammar, that is with the rational, hence, universal principles that they believed lay at the root of all languages, rather than with the rules of any particular one, the imperfections of all the languages that were known to them became only too obvious. As Destutt de Tracy wrote: 'Il est impossible de s'occuper un moment de la Grammaire générale sans être frappé des vices de tous nos langages et des inconvéniens de leur multiplicité.'[68]

In view of this background, it was clearly tempting for the rest of the Idéologues to agree with Cabanis, who maintained that 'ce sont donc l'exactitude et le bon emploi des mots ou plus généralement des signes, qu'il faut considérer comme le *criterium* de la vérité: c'est à leur caractère vague, à la manière incertaine et confuse dont on les emploie, qu'il faut attribuer les notions imparfaites, les préjugés, les erreurs et toutes les habitudes vicieuses de l'esprit.'[69]

Language, wrote Lancelin, is the work of many architects and, as such, is full of inexactitudes. 'Les langues parvenues à ce point de désordre et de confusion,' he went on, 'ne sont plus que des méthodes analytiques extrêmement imparfaites, et si l'on veut en tirer tout le parti possible, il faut absolument les *reconstruire*.'[70] And, of course, a radical reconstruction of language, which at its most drastic would mean building a completely new, truly analytical language, seemed to some to be the logical solution to this problem. However, it is from this point onwards that the Idéologues' views diverge most sharply from those of Condillac and that many of his conclusions are most convincingly challenged. It is with their views on the construction of a perfectly methodical, analytical language that we shall be concerned in the following chapter.

8 / The Idéologues and the perfect language

The notion of a perfected language had a considerable and, as we have seen, an understandable appeal for many of the French Idéologues. A number of them, indeed, seem to have accepted wholeheartedly Condillac's view that the institution of such a language would lead to the perfecting of the various sciences. In this way the provision of an ideal philosophical language would prove to be one of the most important contributions that could ever be made to human advancement. Garat, who seems more than any of them to have fallen victim, at first, to the extravagant claims of the pasigraphists of the age, saw no reason at all why, when philosophy had already advanced so far, a perfect, analytical language should be at all difficult to construct.[1] And Condorcet, while admitting the sad truth that few of our ideas are clear and precise in their meaning, nonetheless appears to have envisaged an epoch when, once this difficulty could be resolved, the conclusions of all the sciences would approach the certainty already found in mathematics. Lancelin foresaw many likely obstacles: the objections of governments reluctant to allow so much prejudice and error to be cleared away, the general remoulding of all our knowledge that would need to be effected, and the fact that, since science itself was always advancing, it would be necessary to make constant changes in the terminology of any such new language. Nonetheless Lancelin still appeared to regard the institution of an ideal, analytical, and universal language as well within the bounds of possibility, even if the enormous amount of co-operation required at national and international levels made the realization of such a project appear highly unlikely.

It is worth recalling in addition that a commission composed of Fleurieu, Destutt de Tracy, Roederer, and Le Breton was specially set up by the second class of the Institut to determine how far one could hope for success in this matter,[2] and that, some ten years after Destutt de Tracy had placed an ideal, universal language 'dans le même cas que le mouvement perpétuel,'[3] Laromiguière still looked forward to the development of gesture as just such a language. Moreover, even Destutt de Tracy and Joseph Marie de Gérando, who eventually were to be among the most determined in their rejection of the proposal as chimerical,[4] were clearly fascinated by the idea and went so far as to elaborate what they felt the qualities of such a language ought to be.

Nonetheless, in spite of the enthusiasm of a number of Idéologues for the idea of a new, perfectly analytical language, it is not possible, as I have already suggested, to accept the judgment of J. Simon, the nineteenth-century historian of the Institut national, that 'la pasigraphie semblait à la plupart des philosophes une découverte de premier ordre.'[5] For, against the hopes of Garat, Condorcet, Lancelin, and Laromiguière must be set Destutt de Tracy's later statements in the *Elémens d'idéologie* and his more or less official, highly damning pronouncement that 'la pasigraphie est une conception vicieuse dans son principe, qui ne produira jamais un résultat utile, et à laquelle on ne se serait pas attaché, si l'on s'en était fait une idée bien nette.'[6] Taken together with the more detailed criticisms made by de Gérando in the work that won the contest on 'signs and thought' instigated and adjudicated by the second class of the Institut, and with the notes prepared for this contest by the young Maine de Biran, these statements of Destutt de Tracy point to an attitude that is quite the opposite to that imputed to the Idéologues as a group by Simon.

It soon becomes clear, in fact, that no generalization can adequately cover the attitude of the Idéologues to the question of a perfect analytical language. The truth would seem to be that, although a number of them remained faithful to the conclusions of Condillac, others, like Destutt de Tracy, evolved in the direction of a much more sophisticated appreciation of the richness and diverse functions of language, and of the complex nature of the problems involved in the formulation of an ideal, philosophical language. This evolution was brought about, I believe, largely as a consequence of the Institut's enquiry upon signs and thought, in the context of which a number of crucial questions were posed concerning the feasibility and value of a perfected sign-system.

It might seem that, even if Condillac's claims were only partially justified, the benefits to science and the value to philosophers of a regular, precise language, in which the composition and derivation of our ideas and their relations with each other could be reflected with some accuracy, would be so great that its desirability lay beyond question. And yet, although the Idéologues recognised the need for and the advantages of an improved sign-system, a number of them saw that the very philosophical composition and the adoption of a newly constructed analytical language, as it had been envisaged by Condillac, posed a number of problems that would greatly detract from its usefulness.

First, a language that was constructed explicitly to suit the needs of science and philosophy would, they believed, be used only by scientists and philosophers. Hence, the construction and adoption of an analytical language would serve to widen still further the gap between a scholarly minority and the rest of the population. De Gérando and Destutt de Tracy, both adopting here the educational outlook of Helvétius, regarded the future progress of humanity as partly dependent on the wider dissemination of knowledge and considered language not only as a way of communication, but also as a means of instruction. 'La langue,' wrote de Gérando, 'ne doit point être seulement pour les savans un moyen de communiquer entre eux, elle doit être aussi un moyen d'instruire ceux qui ignorent, de les appeler à la jouissance de la vérité.'[7] To institute a philosophical language distinct from everyday language might well therefore hold back, rather than advance, knowledge, and so ultimately prove actively harmful to the future development of mankind. In Destutt de Tracy's words: 'Par toutes ces raisons, je crois que l'utilité d'une langue universelle purement savante, est plus que compensée par ses inconvéniens, partout où elle n'est pas la langue usuelle; et que son effet inévitable, en supposant qu'elle ne rallentisse pas le progrès des lumières, est de les concentrer et de les réduire à un foyer unique, ce qui est une autre manière de leur nuire extrêmement.'[8]

The second major objection that was made against the institution of a strictly analytical language concerned its effect on literature. For the new language would be at once severe, regular, methodical, punctilious in its accuracy, and strict in its analyses: such a language, Lancelin argued, would scarcely be suitable for use in literature and particularly in poetry: 'Cette langue, n'étant point faite pour flatter l'oreille et remuer l'imagination par des compositions brillantes, originales, mais pour décrire soigneusement tous les objets, et analyser avec précision les idées de tout genre, aurait une marche sévère, méthodique et uniforme, qui la rendrait peu propre aux productions poétiques et littéraires.'[9] To Lancelin this seemed to be a relatively minor inconvenience, for he wrote, 'Le monde fabuleux et chimérique est le domaine de l'imagination et de la poésie; l'univers réel est celui de l'intelligence pure, des expériences et de l'analyse.'[10]

But there were those among the Idéologues who did not distinguish as sharply as Lancelin did between the respective spheres of literature and science. While recognizing that the needs of the poet and the philosopher differed, de Gérando saw literature and science as closely linked the one to the other. To separate them entirely would, he believed, be harmful to both: 'Nos langues étant destinées à-la-fois à un double usage, devant servir d'instrument aux littérateurs comme aux philosophes, obéissent aux uns comme aux autres, s'accommodent à leurs divers besoins, et ne peuvent sacrifier à la perfection philosophique, le pouvoir qu'elles exercent sur l'imagination des hommes.'[11] Moreover, Cabanis added to the qualities of clarity, precision, natural filiation of ideas, and ease of comprehension that he expected to find in the perfect language some of the very characteristics that Lancelin had excluded from it. 'Enfin,' he wrote, 'cette peinture parlée de nos sensations, ou plutôt des idées qu'elles font naître en nous, doit être capable de rendre par l'harmonie, la couleur, l'élégance, la force et la vivacité de l'expression, les différens caractères de ces mêmes idées: elle doit pouvoir en suivre tous les mouvemens, en faire sentir toutes les nuances, et s'adresser avec le même succès, à la raison, à l'imagination et à la sensibilité.'[12] Similarly, Destutt de Tracy, in spite of some harsh remarks he made on the subject of metaphor while discussing our liking for symbols and emblems,[13] took a rather different view when he came to describe the qualities of a comprehensive, 'perfect' language. This should, he stated, be sonorous, harmonious and picturesque, 'favorable à la poésie, à la musique, à l'éloquence, et [il faudrait] qu'elle se prêtât à tous les besoins de l'homme, et encore à tous ses plaisirs.'[14] It was therefore recognized that unless a language could be formed that was satisfying at once to the philosopher, the scientist, and the poet, the consequences of trying to introduce one suited only to the needs of the philosopher and scientist would be unfortunate for philosophy, science and literature.

The Idéologues concentrated the greater part of their attention, however, on two crucial questions: first, whether a perfect language as they envisaged it was, in fact, feasible at all; and secondly, whether, if it were, it would have all or any of the remarkably beneficial effects upon the progress of human knowledge that Condillac had claimed would result from its adoption.

Concerning the feasibility of constructing a philosophical language, the principal difficulty, Destutt de Tracy wrote in the 'Réflexions sur les projets de pasigraphie,' did not lie in inventing combinations of syllables or written symbols. The problem was rather the same one that Wilkins, Dalgarno, and Leibniz had already encountered, namely that of classifying the ideas that make up human knowledge and of organizing according to their true relations the vast number of derivations, modifications, and combinations of these ideas.[15] Even someone like Lancelin, who felt that, given sufficient goodwill, co-operation, and desire for agreement on the part of governments and scholars, the construction of such a language was indeed possible, admitted the necessity for 'une nouvelle analyse ou une refonte générale de presque toutes nos connaissances.'[16] To this end, Lancelin recommended as the basis for the philosophical language the compilation of an analytical dictionary, in which the order and structure of the words would reveal the various ideas of which each term was composed. And so he looked forward to the foundation of a union of scholars which would produce 'ce dictionnaire unique, qui devra présenter l'analyse de tous les corps naturels, celle de toutes les idées complexes et abstraites; la fixation ou détermination du nombre et de la qualité des idées élémentaires qu'on sera généralement convenu d'y faire entrer.'[17] What to Lancelin appeared only just feasible, though eminently desirable, seemed to Destutt de Tracy, de Gérando, and Maine de Biran totally impossible. A number of interesting reasons were put forward as a justification for this view.

First, it was argued that scholars in many fields could never be expected to reach agreement on the elementary ideas to be included in the dictionary, nor on the manner in which these ideas would be combined to form more complex or abstract concepts. For, how, asked de Gérando, could one hope for general agreement on the relations of ideas as a whole when scholars differed so radically in their views concerning the ideas signified by the various terms of a particular science?

> Ces philosophes eux-mêmes se diviseraient à leur tour [wrote de Gérando] en une foule de partis qui ne pourraient s'entendre entre eux. Car, une langue philosophique serait fondée sur une classification universelle des idées; mais si on n'est point d'accord sur la classification particulière d'une science, comment s'accordera-t-on sur la classification générale? La diversité des opinions dans chaque science, entraînerait autant de disputes sur la langue philosophique de cette science.[18]

There was, however, a second objection to the construction of a rigorous, analytical language and, because this objection arose out of the imperfect nature of our ideas themselves, it appeared quite insuperable to all three of the philosophers that we have mentioned. For, in order that a philosophical language could be constructed that would possess the virtues of the language of mathematics, it was important that all elementary ideas could be represented, as in mathematics, by a symbol or group of symbols, and that all complex or abstract ideas could be decomposed into their separate elements, which could then be combined in a regular, uniform manner. In other words, it was important that there should be no essential difference between the ideas treated in mathematics and those found in the physical, moral, and political sciences.

However, both de Gérando and Maine de Biran emphasized the uniqueness of the ideas of mathematics. In the introduction to *Des signes et de l'art de penser*, de Gérando, for example, completely rejected the view expressed by Condillac in *La Langue des calculs* that 'les mathématiques n'ont sur le reste des sciences d'autre privilège, que de posséder une langue meilleure, et qu'on procurerait à celles-ci une égale simplicité et une égale certitude, si on savait leur donner des signes semblables.'[19] Later in the book, de Gérando pointed out two major errors in Condillac's thought on this point. First, he argued that Condillac was wrong in his view that, if the analogies between the signs used in calculus were to be removed, our ideas of number would differ in no important respect from other ideas we possess. For he maintained that they would retain a great advantage, since they were essentially different by nature. As ideas of 'simple modes' they were characterized by an identity among the elements of which they were composed that could never be found in ideas or 'mixed modes,' in which the various elements differed in kind. From these differences de Gérando could therefore draw the following conclusions:

> ... que la réforme désirée ne peut s'appliquer aussi heureusement à la langue de toutes les sciences; que le degré de simplicité et d'analogie que nous pouvons donner à nos signes, dépend essentiellement de la nature des idées qu'ils expriment; que la Métaphysique est de toutes les sciences celle qui se prête le moins à recevoir une langue bien faite; que les Mathématiques, au contraire, ont à cet égard un privilège unique, et que toute idée d'appliquer aux sciences mixtes les expressions numériques, ou les procédés de l'algèbre, ne saurait être qu'une chimère.[20]

Thus, in de Gérando's view, any would-be 'perfect' philosophical language that failed to take account of these radical differences in the nature of our ideas was doomed to failure.

Maine de Biran made a similar point concerning the difference between those ideas found in mathematics and those found in other sciences. These other categories of ideas were divided by Maine de Biran into two groups: first, *les idées de corps*, occurring in the sciences that depend upon observation and experiment, and secondly, *les idées morales*. As for the first group of ideas, Maine de Biran argued that, because the signs we use correspond closely to the discovered qualities of external reality, it is easy to employ signs that will represent more or less precisely the present state of our knowledge of physical objects. He pointed out, however, that 'l'étendue de cette signification ou le nombre d'idées simples que l'on y fait entrer doit aller toujours croissant à mesure que les expériences et les observations se multiplieront.'[21] Hence, any language that included, as it must unless it were to be restricted to a specific field of knowledge, *les idées de corps*

could not be based on a rigid, immutable system, but must be subject to constant modification.

It was to *les idées morales*, however, that Maine de Biran devoted the major part of his attention, for these he regarded as differing most fundamentally from the ideas of mathematical sciences, and as being the least susceptible of rigorous 'decomposition.' Such a procedure indeed, he claimed, was quite incompatible with the very nature of moral ideas. For, although a certain regularity could perhaps be introduced into the relations between signs and ideas, how, he asked, could a precise meaning be given to ideas that vary from individual to individual according to habit, milieu, temperament, and upbringing, and that represent for the same person different things according to changes in inclination, age, and circumstance? In the sphere of moral ideas, since these ideas are formed by the mind without reference to external models, the individual has the power to allocate to his ideas almost any meaning that he might wish. Hence, wrote Maine de Biran, with a feeling for the diversity and essential fluidity of meaning richer than anything so far encountered in this study,

> comment ferez-vous entendre à un homme souvent intéressé par ses passions à attacher telle idée à tel signe, que sa liaison d'idées est fausse. L'avare se dit économe, le prodigue libéral, l'homme froid et dur se croît raisonnable. Les hommes ont évidemment dans leurs idées complexes des éléments autres que ceux qui sont donnés par la saine raison et la vraie philosophie, cependant si vous vous en tenez aux mots, ils ont autant de droit à appeler l'avarice, économie, que vous à la qualifier à votre manière, et cela, faute de modèles existants. Donc il faut remonter plus haut que les signes artificiels pour rectifier les idées morales.[22]

Words representing moral concepts cannot, then, be reduced to cold, emotionless symbols that may be rigorously defined or analysed into their constituent ideas. Terms such as *kindness*, *virtue*, and *pity* are, to use Maine de Biran's term, 'simple ideas of the heart' just as colours, smells, and sounds are 'simple ideas of the mind': they may not therefore be analysed further. Moreover, such moral concepts are formed by the mind only on the basis of a wide range of highly

individualized experience: 'De là il suit que les signes de ces idées morales, quelque exacts, quelque précis qu'on les suppose dans la tête des inventeurs et dans les moyens mêmes qu'ils peuvent employer pour nous les transmettre, ne peuvent acquérir la même signification, la même étendue que dans l'esprit de ceux qui auront senti, vécu, éprouvé comme eux.'[23] Moral terms may thus be regarded not so much as expressing intellectual concepts but rather as representing personal feelings. And so, even though, when I use a term like *pity*, we may agree on the ideas that such a term should contain, I can never be sure that I am being completely understood when I use this word. Of the word *justice*, for instance, de Biran wrote: 'Tous les hommes peuvent acquérir les mêmes idées de propriété, de bien, etc, mais le sentiment lui-même ne peut être dans tous, en sorte que réellement, il n'y a point de moyens artificiels de rendre la signification de ce mot uniforme, en sorte qu'on soit assuré qu'il est employé dans le même sens précis par ceux qui l'emploient dans le discours, comme le mot *triangle*. C'est cependant ce qu'il faudrait pour que la morale fût susceptible de *démonstration*.'[24]

Destutt de Tracy was also convinced, but for somewhat different reasons, that it was impossible to give any exact, determined meaning to the greater number of our ideas. We see, he said, that 'l'incertitude de la valeur des signes de nos idées est inhérente, non pas à la nature des signes, mais à celle de nos facultés intellectuelles; et qu'il est impossible que le même signe ait exactement la même valeur pour tous ceux qui l'emploient, et même pour chacun d'eux, dans les différens momens où il l'emploie.'[25] Describing the way in which changes in meaning are bound to arise, Destutt de Tracy wrote that man first experiences sensations, then 'il se fait des signes de ce qu'il sent; il ne peut penser qu'avec ces signes; et il ne peut éviter de mettre sous chacun de ces signes, tantôt plus d'idées, tantôt moins, sans s'en appercevoir. Il est donc impossible qu'aucun de ces signes ait une signification complètement déterminée et fixe; et qu'aucune collection de signes, aucun langage, nous conduise avec pleine assurance dans tous nos raisonnemens.'[26] For these reasons, he concluded, we must reject the idea of ever attaining to a wholly perfect, precise analytical language.

Two serious objections to the proposal of constructing a perfect language emerge, then, from the discussion of de Gérando, Destutt de Tracy, and Maine de Biran and reflect back on the desires of the seventeenth century and of Leibniz and Condillac for a philosophical, universal language which would enable one to combine ideas in much the same way as one combines numbers. First, the fact that the mathematical sciences alone work with identical elements means that a rigorous, precise analytical language resembling that found in mathematics would be impossible to attain, other sciences not being equally susceptible of demonstration. Secondly, such a language would be rendered unattainable by the essential fluidity of language – a fluidity that was indeed necessary in order that it should reflect the discoveries of science or the shifts or variations in our own moral concepts. To try therefore to decompose and 'fix' language by any process of rigorous analysis would be to attempt to remove its most valuable asset. This important conclusion is expressed in a splendidly eloquent passage by Maine de Biran:

> Hélas, lorsque tout est dans un flux perpétuel autour de nous, lorsque nous-mêmes entrainés par le courant, ne sommes pas deux instants de suite, absolument les mêmes, lorsque nos idées changent et varient comme les dispositions physiques de nos sens et dans les différents individus comme les tempéraments; peut-on espérer de donner de la fixité aux signes représentatifs des choses, dont la plupart sont variables par elles-mêmes, et dont les autres, inconnues sous plusieurs rapports, doivent nous montrer un jour d'autres propriétés?[27]

Of all the thinkers concerned at this period with the question of an ideal philosophical language, de Gérando wrote at the greatest length and with, at many points, considerable wisdom. To demonstrate further the impossibility of formulating a philosophical language that might justly be regarded as 'perfect,' de Gérando aimed to show the several contradictions that the project itself contained. With this in view, he first defined what the aims of such a language should be and what he required from it in order to consider it perfect.

A philosophical language was intended, he claimed, to convey accurately the meaning of ideas. Hence we should either find in the sign a perfect representation of the idea or, in order to understand it, we should only need to take account of a few easy, completely unequivocal, and invariable conventions. Secondly, the language should aid the human reason in its comparison of ideas: the analogies between the signs we use ought, therefore, in such an ideal language to correspond very closely to those that exist between ideas. Thirdly, in order to extend and hasten the operations of the mind, the philosophical language should be essentially simple in construction: that is, it should require few first conventions, and each sign should be brief and easy to understand. Fourthly, since the language has as one of its objects the avoidance of misunderstanding, all its signs should be readily distinguishable from each other. And finally, though simple in construction, it should still have a sufficient number of signs to give a distinct name to each individual idea.

Having set out what seemed to him to be the essential characteristics of a perfect philosophical language, de Gérando was then able to examine four different systems of language building, and show how in one or more of these respects all of them were found wanting. Since many of the languages that have been discussed in the course of this study follow one or other of these methods of language building, his criticisms form an interesting commentary on these efforts that remains, on the whole, perfectly valid today.

The first system examined by de Gérando is a character based on a direct imitation of ideas by means of pictograms, hieroglyphics, or descriptive gestures. According to this method, he pointed out, the symbol that is chosen to represent the object or ideas must be selected from among a number of possible characteristics, and, in the case of an abstract notion, a physical idea with which it has close associations must be chosen so that it can be represented by means of a picture or gesture:

> En un mot, la règle constante de ce système serait de chercher dans une idée complexe quelque caractère dominant ou principal qui fût susceptible d'être extérieurement décrit, ou qui pût du moins avoir quelque ressemblance avec un objet sensible, et de rapporter une

idée abstraite à son origine sensible, en choisissant parmi les faisceaux sensibles, dont elle aurait pu être déduite, celui qui en serait plus voisin, et qui serait plus naturellement lié avec elle.[28]

Judged by the standards that he had already set up for a perfect language – impossible standards, it is true, but it should be remembered that it was his aim to show exactly how impossible the notion of a perfect language was – what may be termed the 'hieroglyphic' system falls far short on each of the requirements of the philosophical language. Such a language, argued de Gérando, would be a constant source of misunderstanding, since it would represent only a very small number of the external characteristics of physical objects, it would lack simplicity, and it would also need to be elaborately metaphorical in order to convey any abstract ideas at all. For instance, as he had suggested earlier, sensations such as the smell or the colour of a rose would need to be indicated by the picture of a rose placed by the side of an eye or a nose; ideas such as friendship would require a symbol representing two men extending their hands towards each other; and metaphysical notions such as necessity or duration would be represented by the figure of a chain and a clock respectively. Such a metaphorical and pictorial language could lead only too easily to misinterpretation.

De Gérando's point is not, of course, that such a language could not be formed or that it could not indeed be used with a fair degree of success (he quoted Egyptian hieroglyphics and Mexican picture-writing to show that this was clearly possible) but rather that the number of conventions that needed to be made in such an imitative language in order to make it unequivocal were so great that it would quickly become exceedingly difficult to learn. Alternatively, if, for the sake of simplicity, the number of characters were to be restricted, the chances of misunderstanding and inexactitude would become even greater. These criticisms apply, of course, both to a written language of simplified pictures, such as Leibniz had at one time considered,[29] and to a gestural language such as de l'Épée and Sicard had developed as a way of instructing the deaf.

The second system examined by de Gérando was one which most philosophers of the sensationalist school would certainly have chosen as most likely to lead to the provision of an ideal philosophical language, since it aimed by its very formation and structure to trace the whole outline of the progress of man's ideas from the earliest sensations to his most complex or abstract notions. Although such a system would undoubtedly have been the one adopted by Condillac if he had gone on to elaborate a philosophical language, I know of no actual scheme constructed according to such a sensationalist pattern. The root-signs of this language would, de Gérando stated, be found in those ideas that derived immediately from sensation; ideally, other signs would then be formed by combining those root-signs in various ways according to an order corresponding to that found in the natural generation of ideas. Two particular defects of this system were recognized in the 1790s. First, although Destutt de Tracy himself regarded this language as theoretically the most perfect, he pointed out that it could never be constructed in practice, primarily because formulating a language in which the derivation and filiation of all our ideas are shown would demand completeness of knowledge. Hence, the discovery of all the elements that go to make up complex or abstract ideas and the relations between ideas is described by Destutt de Tracy as 'la partie la plus impossible du projet impossible, dont nous nous amusons actuellement à tracer le plan.'[30] Similarly for de Gérando, the construction of such a language could be possible only after the whole history of the generation of ideas had been described, a task which, he admitted, was far from having been accomplished.

Even if we could be sure of the exact order in which our ideas were formed in nature, a second defect of this system, according to de Gérando, would be its very complexity. For, even assuming that, by a few conventions, the number of root-signs representing simple sense impressions could be kept relatively small, each class of increasingly complex ideas would add further complexity to an already overcomplicated system. Writing about the class of abstract ideas, for example, de Gérando complained:

> Comme il est fort peu de notions abstraites qui ne résultent seulement que du rapprochement de trois ou quatre objets ... il faudrait donc, pour l'expression de la plupart des idées de cette classe, un assez grand assemblage de signes élémentaires, et comme ces signes

élémentaires eux-mêmes, destinés à représenter des objets sensibles, seraient déjà très-complexes, ainsi que nous venons de le voir, nous manquerions aussi, dans la nomenclature des idées abstraites, à cette simplicité qui devait être une loi essentielle de notre système.[31]

And so, he concluded, 'En s'attachant à l'ordre qui résulte de la génération de nos idées, on ne peut donc, sous aucun rapport, espérer de concilier dans la formation de la langue qui en résulterait, les conditions dont nous avions reconnu la nécessité.'[32]

The third system that de Gérando considered is based on the same principle of describing the constitution of our ideas, their derivation, and their filiations. In this case, however, the order to be followed in combining ideas would be what de Gérando termed *l'ordre métaphysique* instead of, as in the previous system, *l'ordre naturel*.

Pour bien concevoir ce que j'entends par la génération métaphysique de nos idées, [he wrote] il faut remarquer que chaque objet particulier, devenu pour notre esprit le sujet d'un certain nombre de comparaisons, se décompose en autant de notions abstraites que nous trouvons en lui de caractères généraux et spécifiques. Ces comparaisons successives nous conduisent, enfin, à certaines notions tellement générales, qu'elles sont pour nous le dernier terme de l'abstraction, et que nous les considérons comme simples, parce que nous n'appercevons plus aucun terme de comparaison qui puisse servir à nous faire décomposer encore.[33]

Thus, according to this reasoning, there would be no object that could not be considered as formed by the combination of a certain number of abstract, simple ideas or, alternatively, no abstract, simple ideas which might not be considered as the primitive elements forming a particular notion:

Si donc on parvenait à découvrir quel est le nombre précis de ces idées abstraites et simples, qui sont pour nous le dernier terme de la décomposition, si l'on pouvait observer comment ces idées premières s'associent, se combinent, se modifient, pour engendrer toutes les idées particulières ; si enfin, on attachait un signe radical et

The Idéologues and the perfect language 197

élémentaire à chacune de ces idées fondamentales, il ne resterait plus qu'à réunir ces signes d'une manière parallèle et correspondante à la combinaison de ces idées, pour avoir autant de signes analogues qui représenteraient exactement les idées des objets particuliers qu'on chercherait à exprimer.[34]

De Gérando appears to have been a little more favourably disposed towards this method of approach (favoured, of course, also by Descartes, Leibniz, and Ward) than the last system, though he seems to have been aware also of the enormity of the task that this system set for the language-builder, requiring as its starting point certainty in those ideas that are most difficult to determine. It would also have the same defect of complexity from which the previous system was seen to suffer. As a result, like the earlier schemes examined by him, a language constructed in this 'metaphysical' way would not satisfy the requirements of the perfect language either. However, he concluded with a positive suggestion:

Il n'y aurait donc que deux manières de faire servir la génération métaphysique des idées à fonder un système de signes méthodiques; ce serait d'employer ces signes, comme une langue, dans le cas ou l'on n'aurait à traiter que des questions très-abstraites: car alors il serait possible de leur conserver une simplicité suffisante; ou bien encore de s'en servir pour composer des formules qu'on placerait dans un dictionnaire, à côté des mots de nos langues, pour en expliquer la valeur, et qui pourraient au besoin leur être substituées dans les opérations de l'analyse métaphysique.[35]

Both of the systems we have just described were based upon the classification of ideas, which up to this time had been distributed according to genera, species, and specific differences. De Gérando quoted as a fourth system a rather different form of distribution, based on division rather than classification, in which the relationship between ideas would be one of part to whole, rather than individual to genus. The division he envisaged would consist of a number of groups of ideas, beginning with the general properties of matter and the sciences that deal with these properties, and coming down finally to a study of man in his physical organization, his senses, his feelings, the operations of his mind, and his relations with other men, and with nature:

> Lorsque, par une suite de divisions subordonnées les unes aux autres, on serait parvenu à marquer la place de toutes les idées, à tracer, dans tous les sens, les lignes de démarcation qui devraient les distinguer entre elles, on choisirait un certain nombre de signes simples qui servit à marquer l'ordre des différentes divisions. Pour exprimer une idée quelconque, on n'aurait plus besoin que de réunir les signes propres à annoncer le rang que cette idée occuperait, soit dans la première division, soit dans les diverses séries des sous-divisions.[36]

There was, of course, nothing new about a classification of this nature: de Gérando's version differs only in points of detail from that mapped out by Francis Bacon or followed by the *Encyclopédie*. The fifth part of Descartes's *Discours de la méthode*, in which the philosopher describes the outline of the treatise *De mundo*, also bears close resemblance to de Gérando's plan. What was new was the attempt to apply the encyclopedist method of classification by division to the construction of a philosophical language.

Whatever the limited uses of such a system were to be in the future, de Gérando recognized three chief disadvantages in the construction of a complete philosophical language on these principles. First, the earliest divisions would either be arbitrary or made for convenience only: these divisions would therefore not correspond to philosophically valid distinctions between the properties of ideas. Secondly, even the best divisions would reveal nothing about the nature or the constitution of our ideas. 'Ils ressembleraient,' he wrote, 'aux degrés de longitude et de latitude, qui font connaître la situation d'un pays, d'une ville, mais qui ne font point connaître la nature du sol, la population, la richesse et les autres circonstances locales.'[37] De Gérando's terminology is here probably more than a little determined by his acquaintance with Joseph de Maimieux's scheme of a 'geographical' *pasigraphie*, which he regarded with no particular favour. Finally, as he explained, complexity was again a major stumbling-block to the usefulness of such a system.

For in order to arrive at any one single idea in the field of political science, for example, at least five signs would be required to locate the group of ideas in which this particular one was to be found. Supposing that political science as a whole contained only twelve hundred ideas in all, at least a further six signs, making eleven in all, would be needed to locate (not even to describe) a single idea. Any artificial attempt to simplify the system, combining numbers up to ten so as to form different combinations, would, he believed, be quite inadmissible in the perfect language, since the 'natural' division of ideas would then be distorted and destroyed.

As a consequence of his examination of these four systems, de Gérando was able to conclude most convincingly that none of them would satisfy the requirements of a perfect philosophical language. And since, he maintained, all possible methods of formulating such a language followed one of these systems, or were, in fact, a mixture of several, 'on se trouverait donc toujours dans l'impossibilité de concilier à-la-fois toutes les conditions nécessaires, et on n'arriverait jamais à obtenir un ensemble de signes *parfaitement philosophiques.*'[38]

When de Gérando turned to consider the different attempts that had been made in the past to create a philosophical language and make reasoning into a kind of calculus, he discovered that most of them had been vitiated by their adherence to a scholastic system, so that 'leurs auteurs, quoique doués souvent d'une prodigieuse érudition, et d'une grande persévérance, n'étaient point éclairés d'une assez saine logique pour découvrir les véritables traces de la génération des idées.'[39] Of those that appeared to have some merit, he chose to examine the *Essay towards a Real Character and a Philosophical Language* (1668) of John Wilkins, and the contemporary *Pasigraphie* (1797) of Joseph de Maimieux, a work that he had already discussed in memoirs read to the second class of the Institut national.

It was upon Wilkins's system for the classification of ideas that de Gérando concentrated his attention. Having described at some length the distribution of ideas in Wilkins's language into genera, differences, and species, he pointed out that distinctions there resulted from several different rules of procedure: sometimes Wilkins had moved from the whole to the part, sometimes from the general to the particular. Distinctions were founded at times on a relationship of place, while at others they were based on operations of the mind, and on the manner of the formation of ideas. Further, Wilkins's *Essay* was constructed by a mixture of the two last systems that he had described, that is, sometimes by classification and sometimes by division. Not only did Wilkins's language possess the defects of both systems but it added to these the additional inconvenience of lacking any one uniform method to organize its distribution of ideas.

One further grave inconvenience indicated by de Gérando was that, since the *philosophie universelle* (that is the composition, order, and filiation of ideas) was first established in an instituted, and therefore imperfect, language, the defects inherent in that language would inevitably be transferred to the new language. For 'il faudrait donc supposer que nos langues fussent déjà bien faites elles-mêmes, leurs acceptions bien déterminées; s'il en était ainsi, le besoin d'une langue philosophique ne serait plus aussi pressant. S'il n'en est pas ainsi, l'incertitude propre à nos langues se communiquera à la langue méthodique elle-même.'[40]

Of the various detailed defects mentioned by de Gérando, the most important related to the actual classification of ideas in Wilkins's language. There were, for instance, he claimed, far too many genera (forty), while on the other hand the number of sub-divisions (differences and species) was far too limited. The result of this imperfect distribution was to make the signs of the new language deceive the user into making unnatural, arbitrary, and therefore false distinctions between ideas. Yet, in spite of these numerous defects, it is clear that de Gérando still believed Wilkins's real character and philosophical language to be the most ambitious and impressive of all the attempts so far made to construct a truly philosophical language: 'Au reste, on trouvera, dans cet ouvrage de Wilkins, des recherches très-précieuses sur l'origine et les révolutions des divers idiômes, des observations très-sages sur les vices de nos langues, sur la grammaire, et quelquefois même des analyses très-judicieuses sur la métaphysique de nos idées.'[41] For this reason, the very ways in which the language failed are useful to de Gérando's general line of argument.

Turning from this seventeenth-century scheme to the contemporary *Pasigraphie* of Joseph de Maimieux, a work which, as we have already seen, aroused tremendous interest and considerable enthusiasm in the 1790s, de Gérando introduced it in the following way:

> Qu'on imagine le nombre des genres de Wilkins réduit à 12 au lieu de 40, et le nombre des diverses sous-divisions, variable chez Wilkins, porté quelquefois par lui jusqu'à 9, fixé constamment. Qu'on suppose ensuite que les signes des genres servent aussi aux diverses sous-divisions, et même aux modifications grammaticales, de telle manière que l'ordre et le rang qu'ils occupent dans le mot, suffisent pour indiquer leurs diverses fonctions; on aura l'idée fondamentale de la *Pasigraphie*, dont le caractère propre est de puiser dans 12 signes différemment combinés, le moyen de représenter toutes les idées possibles.[42]

Compared with Wilkins's scheme, the *pasigraphie* possessed the apparent virtues of a greater philosophical simplicity and a smaller number of root-signs, used for different purposes, as well as the very real virtue of grammatical regularity. The first virtues were apparent ones only, however, because, by seeking a greater simplicity in the distribution of ideas and in the signs by which these ideas were represented, de Maimieux was imposing his own purely arbitrary order upon ideas, thereby greatly facilitating misunderstanding in the use of the signs. Although de Maimieux had claimed that his classification was never intended to be perfectly philosophical, he had not seen, went on de Gérando, that 'en abandonnant les rigoureux principes d'une classification philosophique, il renonçait au plus précieux avantage de sa méthode, et qu'il opposait lui-même à son admission l'obstacle le plus redoutable.'[43] Thus, although the *pasigraphie* could not be regarded as a true philosophical language, its system of construction was such that it would have been of real use to mankind only if it had been perfectly philosophical.

De Gérando's examination and detailed criticism of what seemed to be the most valuable attempts made up to that time to form a philosophical language, taken along with his demonstration of the inadequacies of all possible systems of philosophical language building, and with Destutt de Tracy's reflexions on the subject, constitute, of course, a formidable indictment of the quest for an ideal philosophical and universal language. Absolute perfection, they had shown, was no more attainable in language than it was in other fields. For man certainly lacked the completeness of knowledge that would enable him to analyse ideas and distribute them according to their true relations with each other. Indeed, it was argued, by their very nature a large number of our ideas could never be given any single, fixed meaning. Finally, as de Gérando demonstrated, the concept of a perfect language contained within itself contradictions that made the prospect of its successful formulation appear utterly fanciful.[44]

A further important question arising out of Condillac's thought was fully considered by the Idéologues and was included among those put to contestants in the enquiry upon signs and thought. If, it was asked, it were possible for the art of signs to be brought to a state of perfection, would this in fact (as Condillac had, on the whole, imagined) necessarily mean that a corresponding perfection would be brought to every field of human knowledge?

The answers given to this question differed considerably, and it is on this issue more than any other that many of the Idéologues modify, or even directly contradict, Condillac's conclusions. For, even among those like Garat, Condorcet, Laromiguière, and Lancelin who were closest to Condillac's position, it would be possible to point to divergencies of opinion that tended to reduce the element of over-simplification that was characteristic of a number of their predecessor's statements.[45]

For Destutt de Tracy, de Gérando, and Maine de Biran, however, there were a number of excellent reasons why perfecting the language that we use would certainly not result in the perfecting of thought. In their view, perfecting the signs used in a science was but one step, albeit an important one, in the probably endless, and not at all predictable, progress of human knowledge.[46] They felt that the examples that had most frequently led to the acceptance of Condillac's belief that perfecting signs would also perfect thought either were misleading or had been misinterpreted.

That mathematics owed its success entirely to the perfection of its language was not accepted because, as we have seen, the uniformity of its ideas appeared of even greater importance than the perfection of its signs. And, referring to the example of chemistry, de Gérando conceded that the new nomenclature that had been adopted by Lavoisier and his associates was 'la plus parfaite dont l'histoire des sciences ait jamais fourni le modèle.'[47] Yet he believed (rightly, of course) that this nomenclature could not be considered absolutely perfect, nor did he think that it could be held entirely responsible for the rapid progress that had been made in this science during the 1780s, since 'les belles expériences de Lavoisier étaient nécessaires pour préparer les réformes de la nomenclature.'[48] Both of these much-quoted examples, therefore, demonstrated for de Gérando almost the opposite of what Condillac had believed. Perfection in language appeared as the consequence, rather than the cause, of perfection of knowledge. And so de Gérando wrote in answer to Condillac: 'Il ne faut pas dire qu'*une science* n'est qu'*une langue*; mais bien que la science se peint dans la langue. La perfection de la langue ne produit pas celle de la science, mais elle en résulte et y ajoute le dernier trait.'[49] This was a view also shared by Destutt de Tracy: 'Nous voyons bien en masse que les connaissances et les langues marchent toujours de front, que le niveau se rétablit à chaque instant entre l'idée et le signe, et que par conséquent la langue la plus perfectionnée est toujours celle employée par les hommes les plus éclairés; et si elle n'est pas plus parfaite, c'est parce que leurs idées ne sont pas plus avancées.'[50]

The successful institution of a new, methodical nomenclature in the experimental sciences depended, argued de Gérando, upon two important factors. Such a nomenclature could be formed only if, first, as a result of experiment the science had already reached an advanced stage, and secondly, the 'facts' of that science lent themselves to this type of methodical treatment, which was not always the case. Thus he was led to conclude that 'pour instituer une langue parfaitement méthodique, il faudrait que la science elle-même se trouvât déjà portée à son plus haut degré de perfection ... Tant qu'on appercevra quelque analyse que les expériences déjà faites n'ont point encore exécutée, que les instrumens existans ne suffisent point à obtenir, on laissera malgré soi une imperfection dans son langage.'[51] Yet, even if these conditions could be fulfilled and a perfect nomenclature were to be introduced, the science would remain far from perfect, since, as de Gérando wrote in the conclusion to his study, 'les préjugés de l'habitude, l'aveuglement des passions, les illusions de l'imagination, les distractions de l'esprit, exercent des effets beaucoup plus sensibles sur les sciences des faits, et c'est au concours de ces causes diverses, bien plus qu'au vice du langage, qu'il faut rapporter les erreurs dont elles deviennent l'occasion.'[52] The perfection of an experimental science depended, then, on factors other than the reform of its nomenclature. It depended, for example, among other things, upon the greatest of care being taken to observe accurately, upon the ability to conceive of new experiments, and also upon the talent to use well the data obtained from them.

Condillac's view that perfecting a language would lead to perfection in knowledge was not, however, confined to what de Gérando called 'les sciences des faits': it extended also to the attainment of perfection in the moral and metaphysical sciences. For, according to this view, reasoning operated in all the sciences in the same way. Thus the procedure followed in resolving an ethical, a metaphysical, or a mathematical problem was one and the same. Condillac argued in much the same way as Leibniz: reasoning was a calculus; propositions, judgments, and equations did not differ in form; words or symbols were employed as they were in algebraic formulae to discover hitherto unknown, but now fully demonstrable, truths.

Criticism of these points by the Idéologues was lengthy, detailed, and fundamental. Reducing it to its essentials, however, we see first that the diverse nature of the ideas used in what de Gérando called the 'sciences mixtes' prevented reasoning in these sciences from being treated in the form of the calculus. Thus, with such mixed elements, reasoning in metaphysics and ethics could never be fully demonstrable. Secondly, as we have already seen, Maine de Biran objected that terms representing moral concepts could not be rigorously decomposed, since the meaning of these terms varied greatly from individual to individual, and from one time to another, according to the experience of the user of language. Finally, de Gérando pointed out that the common belief that *le perfectionnement des signes* would prevent all dispute was plainly absurd, since the verbal dispute was often merely an echo of a much more radical conflict between ideas.[53]

The criticisms offered by de Gérando, Destutt de Tracy, and Maine de Biran thus pointed to a number of formidable, indeed insurmount-

The Idéologues and the perfect language 205

able, obstacles to the realization of Condillac's dream. They did not, however, undermine the argument that languages stood badly in need of reform. For these thinkers Condillac's error lay not in recognizing the importance of language-reform for the progress of human knowledge, but in greatly over-simplifying the problem. And so, while a number of the Idéologues saw that the benefits to be derived from an improved sign-system had been grossly overstated, all of them remained extremely sensitive to the need to ameliorate language. And since an artificially constructed, wholly perfect philosophical language was recognized as an impossibility, reform could only by effected in existing languages.

An examination of the whole program of language-reform recommended by these thinkers would take us beyond the bounds of this enquiry. One or two points may, however, be mentioned here, as being relevant. First, reform of the specialized terminology of a number of sciences was acknowledged as an important requirement. This was not because this reform would in itself bring about the progress of that science, but because progress would not then be held back by a grossly ill-formed and inadequate system of terms. Yet, as de Gérando insisted, this reform, in order to be effective, needed to take account of the varying objects treated in the different sciences. Thus, in anatomy, for example, it would not prove possible to form words according to the system adopted in chemistry. A second warning came from Cabanis. One of the worst nomenclatures of contemporary medicine was, he maintained, myology (or the science of muscles). Yet its worst defects were not that it contained words whose origins were unknown to most students of anatomy, nor that it failed to help the memory, but rather that in the formulation of its terminology it aimed to do precisely what a universal language such as that of Wilkins had attempted to do, that is to represent the properties of its objects. 'Un mot, je le répète,' wrote Cabanis, 'n'est point une description; il ne doit pas même être une définition: il lui suffit de désigner clairement et sans équivoque, l'objet qu'il rappelle. Décrire cet objet, faire connaître ses qualités ou ses fonctions, n'est pas le nommer: c'est faire son histoire; c'est exprimer quels sont les éléments dont il se compose; c'est retracer son analyse, et en offrir les résultats.'[54]

Reform in the language used in the non-experimental sciences and

in our daily thinking was also thought desirable. And it is of interest to note here how much the suggestions concerning the pattern that this reform should take owed to the ideal of a rational language, as the negative conclusions reached on the feasibility of a perfect language influenced these positive recommendations for reform. So, although one cannot entirely remould existing languages, wrote Destutt de Tracy,

> on peut travailler sans relâche, 1/ à perfectionner leur prononciation et leur orthographe, et à rapprocher l'une de l'autre; 2/ à rendre leurs constructions et leur syntaxe conformes à la marche naturelle des idées dans les déductions; 3/ à bannir des écrits et des discours la timidité et la fausse finesse, qui portent à n'exprimer sa pensée qu'à demi, et à détourner les mots de leur vraie signification; 4/ à augmenter la pente de ces langues à se donner ou à adopter les mots dont elles ont besoin; 5/ à former de bonnes nomenclatures méthodiques dans toutes les sciences qui sont assez avancées pour en être susceptibles; 6/ enfin à rectifier les idées par l'acquisition de vérités nouvelles, surtout en idéologie; car c'est là, comme nous l'avons vu, le moyen le plus puissant pour perfectionner le langage, et *vice versa*.[55]

Yet legislation was regarded as a totally ineffective way of improving language. Maine de Biran, for instance, repeated Locke's statement that even Augustus could not by decree have altered the meaning of a single word. Pierre Prévost restricted the changes that could be made in language to the modification of word-endings, on the grounds that no philosopher can abolish a badly constructed sign once it has been established by usage, even less replace it by one that is better formulated. For, he concluded, 'l'usage est le maître des langues; il faut toujours le consulter.'[56] And although the Idéologues did not adopt the fierce linguistic individualism that is to be found in Locke's writing, they were still very aware of the difficulties that lay in the path of those who wished to reform language. For,

> les réformes possibles en elles-mêmes éprouveraient de très grands obstacles dans l'exécution, soit parce qu'elles auraient à lutter contre

les prétentions des faux savans, les préjugés de certains esprits, les habitudes de la foule; soit aussi parce que nos langues étant destinées à-la-fois à un double usage, devant servir d'instrument aux littérateurs comme aux philosophes ... ne peuvent sacrifier à la perfection philosophique, le pouvoir qu'elles exercent sur l'imagination des hommes.[57]

Since a perfect language was an unattainable ideal, and since the task of reforming existing languages would be both difficult and slow, there remained the less dramatic possibility of making much better use of the words that we have. For a number of the Idéologues were highly conscious of the change that language could undergo in the hands of the writer, philosopher, or scientist of genius. Lancelin, for example, wrote optimistically:

Sans vouloir percer dans un avenir objet des vœux et des espérances du philosophe, de ses craintes, on peut se consoler en songeant au grand nombre de savans distingués et à la multitude des bons esprits maintenant occupés à perfectionner les méthodes d'instruction, les élémens des sciences, et par suite ceux du langage; malgré les défauts des langues actuelles, le génie peut en tirer un assez grand parti, en les pliant à l'analyse; il peut insensiblement les adoucir, les corriger, et parvenir à la longue à effacer ce qu'elles ont de vicieux, et c'est en produisant beaucoup de bons écrits en tout genre, qu'il en viendra à bout.[58]

Finally, after quoting Leibniz's remarks on the perfection of language, de Gérando claimed that by using a conventional language in their own way, rather than each using a radically different one, a poet and a philosopher could provide three important advantages that could be found in no philosophical language,

je veux dire celui de soutenir l'empire de la vérité de tous les charmes de l'élocution, et d'associer ainsi les effets de la persuasion à ceux des démonstrations rigoureuses; celui d'éclairer les abstractions par un heureux choix de métaphores, et d'appeler les comparaisons au secours des définitions méthodiques; enfin, celui de pouvoir, à notre gré, ou simplifier l'expression de la pensée, ou lui donner un développement plus étendu, de pouvoir lui faire prendre les formes les plus convenables à la nature du sujet et à la disposition des esprits.[59]

We have moved a long way from Condillac's rather simplistic view that reform of the language used in a science necessarily meant perfecting the science itself. Perfection, if it could be reached at all in human affairs, was not so easily attained. And, although one finds among the Idéologues an intense concern with the influence that the clarity or vagueness of words has on our thinking, this is accompanied by a more sophisticated appreciation of the fact that the reform of signs represents only one out of the many possible factors that contribute towards the search for truth and certainty in human reasoning. One finds also in their work the seeds of a much richer and more modern view of language than the Idéologues have commonly been credited with. Of course, several of the philosophers whose views have been quoted (particularly de Gérando and Maine de Biran) were later to move even further away from Condillac's philosophical position. Nonetheless, both de Gérando and Maine de Biran were highly esteemed by other Idéologues, and their refusal to accept Condillac's conclusions in this particular field was shared by Destutt de Tracy, a philosopher commonly regarded as a stalwart Idéologue. The question of an ideal universal and philosophical language thus seems to have led several leading Idéologues to confront an issue that, in spite of Condillac's own confident assertions, clearly needed further consideration. This subject seems, in fact, to have contributed substantially to the swing away from Condillac's general philosophical outlook that becomes more marked in Maine de Biran's later writings.

Although the *a priori* constructed language did not entirely disappear from the scene in the nineteenth century, largely as a result of the criticisms levelled at such schemes by the Idéologues it became increasingly difficult to regard such artificial ideal languages as capable of supplying both an international auxiliary language and an improved instrument of thought. And so those who were seeking to construct a language for international usage tended to turn increasingly to the non-philosphical, *a posteriori* method of language building which so many of the modern inventors of would-be universal languages have followed, leaving philosophers and logicians to realize in certain limited fields the dream of Leibniz and Condillac for a language in which reasoning should become synonymous with calculation.

Appendix A
Gesture as a form of universal language[1]

The idea that someone unable to speak or understand another person's language might nonetheless communicate with him by the use of gesture is one that has occurred frequently from classical times to the present day. Personal experience has usually been enough to show that gestures may sometimes succeed in circumstances where words have failed. On the other hand, one has only to think of the misunderstandings and frustrations that can result from efforts to express by means of gesture anything in the least complex or abstract to realize very clearly the limitations of this mode of communication.

It is scarcely surprising, then, that those scholars who have acclaimed the language of gesture and commended it to mankind as the only truly universal language should have drawn their inspiration less from their own (or someone else's) direct experience than from the more highly developed forms of gesture used by the mime artist, the orator, or the deaf man. Lucian recounted, for example, in the dialogue *Of Pantomime*, how a Prince of Pontus, when promised a gift by Nero, requested that he should be granted the services of a well-known mimer, who could replace the various interpreters that he needed to employ in order to communicate with the notables of neighbouring lands.[2] At the beginning of the seventeenth century, Giovanni Bonifacio, in *L'Arte de' cenni*, revealed the astonishingly wide range of ideas that could be expressed by the orator's gestures, and suggested that these gestures could in fact provide a highly efficient form of universal language. As recently as 1953, indeed, Sir Richard Paget proposed that a sign-language 'might be taught as a form of play to all children, to develop their powers of observation and expression. If this were done in all countries by means of instructional films, there would be a very simple international language by which the different races of mankind, including the deaf, might understand one another.'[3]

Students of the universal language movement have concentrated their attention upon schemes of universal writing,[4] and, as far as I have been able to ascertain, have ignored the interesting suggestion that gesture might provide such a language. It is clearly impossible to trace in detail the entire history of this particular idea. I intend therefore simply to examine its emergence in the seventeenth century, and to show particularly how, in the seventeenth and eighteenth centuries, it was related to the development of gesture as a method of teaching the deaf.

The notion that gesture could provide an admirable universal language for mankind was inspired primarily, it would seem, by the remarkable variety and expressiveness of the gestures taught and used in Renaissance rhetoric. For, although there were many possible sources of inspiration (mime and the dance, secret sign-languages, the manual alphabets of certain religious communities, and even early reports of the use of signs among the American Indians)[5] it is in two of the best-known manuals of rhetoric published in the first half of the seventeenth century – Bonifacio's *L'Arte de' cenni* and John Bulwer's *Chirologia, or The Naturall Language of the Hand* – that we find the idea most clearly expressed. Referring to the barriers to understanding that have been raised between peoples by the diversity of tongues, Bonifacio wrote:

> E veramente il nostro parlare è tanto vario, e diverso, e tante sorti di linguaggi si ritrovano al mondo, che con grande incommodo spesse volte non intendiamo la favella de' nostri vicini, non che degli stranieri, e de' lontani, il che è avenuto perche tralasciando gli huomini questa visibile natural favella sono andati inventando varii artificiosi modi di favellare, che se il nostro parlare fosse naturale, tutti gli huomini con un solo idioma parlerebbono.[6]

Hence, he suggested, a language of gesture made up of that vast repertoire of rhetorical signs used by the orator could, if universally adopted, break down the barriers raised at Babel. For the English physician, John Bulwer, also, the hand 'speakes all languages, and as *universall character of Reason* is generally understood and knowne by all Nations, among the formall differences of their Tongue. And being the onely speech that is naturall to Man, it may well be called the *Tongue and Generall Language of Humane Nature*, which, without teaching, men in all regions of the habitable world doe at the first sight most easily understand.'[7] Gestural signs, moreover, Bulwer maintained, were infinitely superior to spoken words: they were, for instance, more striking in effect and speedier in execution (see plate 10). More important than this, however, was, he believed, the fact that the language of signs differed from all spoken tongues in being a natural language. It could therefore be universally understood without being learned or translated. The language of gesture appeared to Bulwer as the natural language of the beasts, of Adam, and of mankind as a whole. It was that primitive tongue that 'had the happinesse to escape the curse at the confusion of Babel: so it hath since been sanctified and made a holy language by the expressions of our Saviours *Hands*.'[8] For this reason above all, Bulwer believed that gesture was the language that should be adopted by mankind as a common tongue.

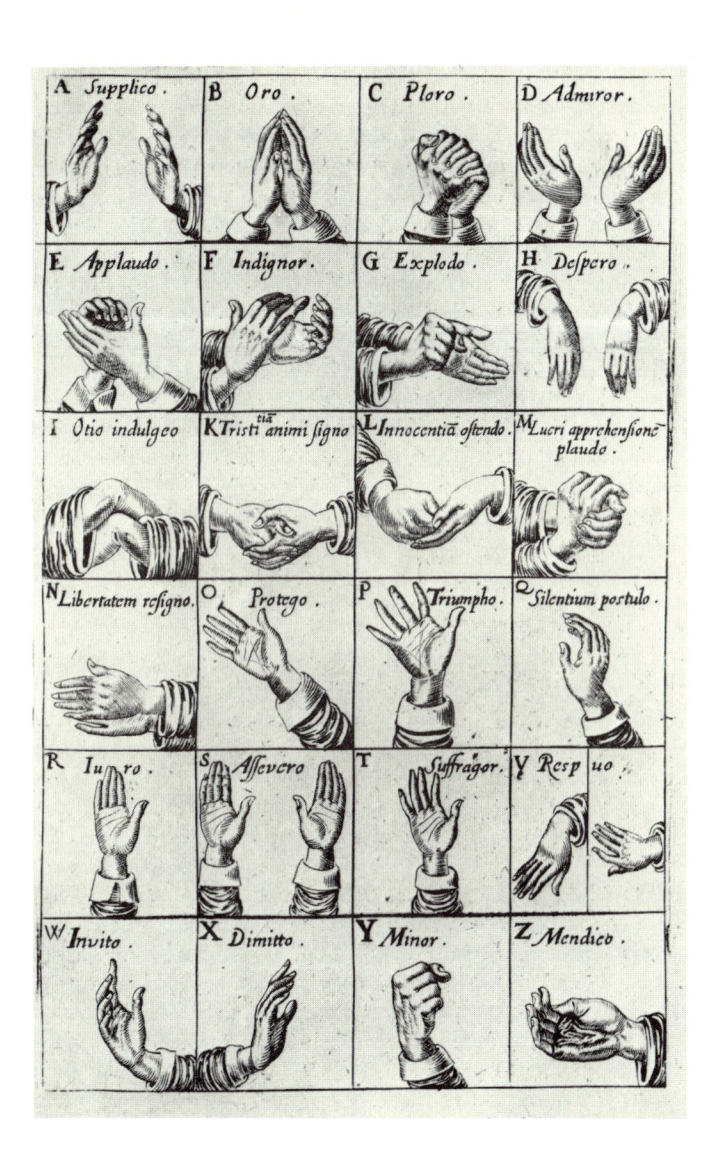

Plate 10 John Bulwer
Chirologia, or The Naturall Language of the Hand London 1644
151: gestural signs and their meaning
By courtesy of the Bodleian Library, Oxford

The example of the deaf and dumb confirmed Bulwer in his belief that the hand could serve as an excellent substitute for the tongue, as well as act as an accompaniment to it. He had been much impressed, he wrote, by 'that wonder of necessity that Nature worketh in men that are born deafe and dumbe; who can argue and dispute rhetorically by signes, and with a kind of mute and logistique eloquence overcome their amaz'd opponents; wherein some are so ready and excellent, they seem to want nothing to have their meanings perfectly understood.'[9] And so, after attempting to adapt the manual signs of the orator for use among the deaf, he concluded in a later work that such an adaptation was totally unnecessary, since they already possessed their own perfectly adequate system of signs. He went on indeed to reassure the deaf:

Though you cannot express your mindes in those verball contrivances of man's invention; yet you want not speech, who have your whole Body; for a Tongue, having a language more naturall and significant which is common to you with us, to wit gesture, the generall and universall language of Humane nature, which when we would have our Speech to have life and efficacy we joyne in commission with our wordes, and when we should speak with more store and gravity, we renounce words and use Nods and other Natural signs alone.[10]

The example of the deaf man's signs was thus already of some importance in the seventeenth century (and, we shall see, was to become more important still in the late eighteenth century). It is worth considering for a moment what the status of this form of gesture had been up to that time.

Throughout the Middle Ages, it had been widely believed that the deaf and dumb were quite incapable of benefiting from instruction of any kind.[11] Hence few men were bold or foolish enough to attempt what appeared to be an impossible task. Dumbness was considered more or less synonymous with deafness. The deaf were dumb, it was thought, not because they were unable to hear speech-sounds, but because they were afflicted with a disease that affected their organs of speech as well as their organs of hearing. And they could not be taught, partly because knowledge was acquired largely through conventional language, but also because, in many cases, the deaf and dumb appeared closer to the brutes in intelligence than they did to 'normal' (i.e. speaking) human beings. As a result of this attitude, the earliest reports that deaf-mutes had been taught to understand what was spoken or written down and to utter intelligible speech-sounds were treated as ill-founded rumours, as miracle-cures (since deafness and dumbness, being divinely inflicted, could only be cured by divine intervention), or as clear proof that the deaf person concerned could not truly have been deaf and dumb at all.

Yet, although the deaf had been regarded for many centuries as incapable of speech, it had long been known that they could communicate, to some extent at least, with those around them by means of a number of chiefly manual gestures that were simple and easy to understand. Plato, for example, in the *Cratylus* referred to those significant movements of the head, hand, and body that were made by the dumb, and Saint Augustine in the *De quantitate anima* spoke of a deaf person who could understand others and express himself by means of gestures.[12] One recalls also the burlesque use to which gestures were put by Panurge in Rabelais's *Pantagruel*.[13] Finally, Descartes mentioned in the fifth part of the *Discours de la méthode* that 'les hommes qui, étant nés sourds et muets, sont privés des organes qui servent aux autres pour parler, autant ou plus que les bêtes, ont coûtume d'inventer d'eux-mêmes, quelques signes, par lesquels ils se font entendre à ceux qui, étant ordinairement avec eux, ont loisir d'apprendre leur langue.'[14]

Gestural signs were indispensable to the deaf person, since they allowed him to communicate his physical needs and basic desires to other members of the family group. Equally, of course, the usefulness of these signs was recognized by those upon whom the welfare of the deaf-mute depended, and so a gestural language of a kind existed and was able to evolve naturally within the deaf person's family.

Yet gesture appeared suitable for communication at a primitive level only, and when there was development, it occurred, as it were, in isolation. For outside the family circle, signs appeared strange and clumsy to use; often stigmatized by association with an apparent idiocy, they were (and still are, of course) socially unacceptable. Moreover, since there was no institution or stable community to perpetuate any newly invented signs, there could be little general development of the language: frequently, the afflicted family would build up its own conventional signs only for them to be lost on the deaf person's death. The static nature of medieval family life also prevented any more extensive form of development from taking place. More important still was the fact that signs could not compensate for hearing in matters of religion. Indeed, the deaf were regarded throughout the Middle Ages as cut off from the word of God, since 'faith cometh by hearing, and hearing by the word of God.'[15] A typical view of gesture, written in fact by a practising teacher of the deaf at the end of the seventeenth century, but representing an attitude that had prevailed for many centuries before, was expressed by Johann Conrad Amman: 'How lame and defective is that Speech, which is performed by Signs and Gestures? How little are they capable to receive of those things which concern their eternal Salvation.'[16]

The discovery in the late sixteenth and early seventeenth centuries that deaf-mutes could be taught to associate the written characters of conventional language or the movements of the lips, tongue, and throat directly with objects and ideas, and that they could learn to produce recognizable speech-sounds meant that for over a century the teaching of the deaf, when it occurred at all, was to become equated with the teaching of conventional speech. So much was this so that success was judged at first, not by any assessment of the intellectual progress in general of a deaf pupil, but by the ease with which he could read the motions of speech on the face, and by the fidelity with which he could reproduce conventional speech-sounds.[17]

In spite of this emphasis upon normal speech, the language of gesture inevitably played an important part in the methods of almost all the early teachers of the deaf. In the sixteenth century, the Spanish monk, Pedro Ponce de Leon, though aiming ultimately at teaching his pupils to speak, apparently retained the signs that they had built up together for use whenever writing was at all inconvenient.[18] John Wallis, the first successful English teacher of the deaf, recognized the need for gesture as a means of bridging the gap which exists at first between teacher and pupil:

> It will be convenient all along to have Pen, Ink, and Paper ready at hand, to write down in Words what you signify to him [the deaf pupil] by Signes: and cause Him to Write ... what he signifies by Signes. Which way (of signifying their mind by Signes) Deaf persons are often very good at. And we must endeavour to learn Their language (if I may so call it) in order to teach them Ours: By shewing, what *Words* answer to their Signes.'[19]

For these early teachers of the deaf, however, the language of gesture had no importance *per se*: it represented nothing more than a convenient, though essential, step towards communicating by the more normal methods of speech and writing. Hence the idea that the gestures of the deaf man should be adopted universally by those who were able to speak would probably have appeared to them more than a little absurd. Yet, as we have seen, there were those who put forward this idea in all seriousness.

It should now be apparent that this divergence of views on the status of gesture up to the end of the seventeenth century may be reduced to disagreement on two fundamental but related issues. First, whether the signs of the untutored deaf signified naturally, by institution, or by a mixture of both; and secondly, whether the language of gesture was by its very nature restricted to the communication of a few limited, concrete ideas.

Some twenty years before Bulwer's *Chirologia*, in the first book devoted specifically to the problem of teaching the deaf, Juan Pablo Bonet had drawn attention to the unique position of gesture as a natural language.[20] Thus, the main recommendation of the manual alphabet that he described was, he claimed, that it had close affinities with this natural language of action. It was, he wrote, 'so well adapted to nature that it would seem as if this artificial language had been derived from the language of nature, or that from this, since visible actions are nature's language. And this is supported by the fact that if deaf-mutes meet, though they have never seen one another before, they understand each other by the use of the same signs.'[21]

Although Bonet noted that, since gestures signified naturally, they could be easily understood by all deaf persons, he did not go on, like Bulwer, to suggest that gesture might be adopted by everyone as a universal language. Probably Bonet would not have agreed with Bulwer's view that gesture could convey everything that the spoken word could express. For Bulwer appears to have believed that the natural signs of the deaf man needed no improvement in order to convey a wide range of ideas; rather, they would lose much of their clarity and universal intelligibility if tampered with in an unnecessary attempt to improve them. And so he wrote, addressing the deaf, 'This language you speak so purely that I who was the first that made it my Darling Study to interpret the naturall richnesse of your discoursing gestures ... am fully satisfied that you want nothing to be perfectly understood, your mother tongue administering sufficient utterance upon all occasions.'[22]

Yet to the majority of seventeenth-century teachers and writers on the teaching of the deaf, gesture (except in its most rudimentary form) required agreement just as much as the spoken languages did: hence the frequent emphasis upon the fact that the language of the deaf must be learned. Similarly those theorists such as Francis Bacon and John Wilkins who discussed the question of signs regarded only those spontaneous and expressive gestures that convey emotions of joy, anger, and fear as signifying without agreement.[23] The gestures of the deaf and dumb were placed among those non-emblematic signs requiring convention. Viewed in this light, gesture seemed in no way unique. And, while eminently useful as a preliminary stage in teaching the deaf to speak, read, and write conventional language, as an independent medium of communication, it appeared much too limited in range and too clumsy in use to be suitable for more general adoption.

In spite of Diderot's concentration upon the gestures of the deaf and dumb in the *Lettre sur les sourds et muets*, published in 1751,[24] in which the deaf-man became (as he did for Condillac) an important object of philosophical investigation, it was not until the final quarter of the eighteenth century that any significant change in attitude towards gesture became possible, and that, largely as a result of the Abbé de l'Épée's work in developing a system of what he described as 'des signes méthodiques,' the idea that gesture might supply a universal language became worthy of more serious consideration.[25] The claim of universality is expressed quite clearly in the title of the Abbé de l'Épée's first book on the teaching of the deaf, *Institution des sourds et muets, par la voie des signes méthodiques; ouvrage qui contient le projet d'une langue universelle, par l'entremise des signes naturels, assujettis à une méthode* (1776), published in Paris. The grounds on which the Abbé's claims were based are described at greater length in the work itself:

> On a souvent désiré une Langue universelle, avec le secours de laquelle les hommes de toutes les nations pourraient s'entendre les uns les autres. Il me

semble qu'il y a longtemps qu'elle existe, et qu'elle est entendue partout. Cela n'est pas étonnant: c'est une langue naturelle. Je parle de la langue des signes. Mais elle n'a point été jusqu'à présent d'un grand usage, parce qu'on l'a toujours retenue dans son état brut, sans la perfectionner, en l'astreignant à des règles.[26]

The language eulogized here was, of course, evolved originally purely as an instrument for teaching the deaf. Here de l'Épée's originality was to think in terms of the deaf pupil's over-all intellectual development rather than concentrate his entire attention upon teaching conventional speech-sounds. In close association with his pupils, therefore, he evolved a language of manual signs that consisted of gestures used naturally and spontaneously by the deaf, together with others developed from these natural signs or agreed upon by teacher and pupil. In this way he was able to build up a highly developed language of methodical signs that was part natural and part conventional. He thus clearly considered the mixture of nature and convention as one of the greatest virtues of his system of 'methodical signs.' Consequently his claim that they would provide an excellent universal language hinged largely upon this dual nature. For it was, de l'Épée stressed, at the same time a natural and a highly developed language.

Those writers in the seventeenth century who had made a claim for the universality of gesture had done so, we may recall, because they considered it to be the one natural language that was readily understood without previous knowledge. In the same way, since de l'Épée retained natural signs as the basis upon which he constructed his improved sign-system, he believed that he could still claim that it was a natural language. At the same time, because the language had been subjected to strict methodization and development, the improved language of gesture could more properly and advantageously be compared with existing spoken languages.

The success of de l'Épée's sign language, both as a medium of communication with the deaf and as a potential universal language, clearly depended upon the method by means of which the 'natural' language was to be improved. The first and most obvious problem de l'Épée encountered in developing the language of gesture was that of representing abstract ideas in terms of physical movements. For, if the language were to be enlarged by the more or less haphazard invention of a large number of arbitrary signs, it would quickly become too complex to be easily learned or recalled. The solution that de l'Épée found to this problem was to analyse all complex and abstract ideas into simpler and more concrete parts, which might then be expressed in terms of physical gestures.[27] In this way, he believed, all ideas might be conveyed by means of various combinations of gestural root-signs, all of which would, he maintained, still retain a natural analogy with the object or idea they represented. For

c'est la réunion de ces différens signes, toujours analogues à la Nature en première ou seconde instance, et découverts l'un après l'autre, en consultant cette même Nature, à proportion que le besoin l'exigeait, qui a formé notre méthode complette, sans avoir exigé d'autre travail de notre part, que l'application de quelques momens à chaque opération particulière. Avec des signes purement arbitraires, nous n'aurions jamais pu nous faire entendre; d'ailleurs, nos Sourds et Muets ne les auraient pas retenus, et nous nous y serions trompés nous-mêmes à chaque instant. Il n'en est pas de même de la Nature, on ne l'oublie point, et il est impossible de s'y méprendre.[28]

Analysis was thus the keystone of de l'Épée's method of development. It would, he claimed, simplify the language so much that it would possess the simplicity of arithmetical symbols rather than the complexity of the written Chinese characters: 'La différence qu'il y a entre nos signes et les caractères Chinois c'est que ceux-ci n'ont pas de liaison naturelle avec les choses qu'ils doivent signifier; nos signes, au contraire, sont toujours pris dans la nature, ou en la saisissant à la volée quand elle se présente d'elle-même, en y ramenant par le secours de l'analyse.'[29] Analysis would also remove, he claimed, all vagueness and lack of precision from the representation of ideas and even from the ideas themselves. For this reason, also, the language of gesture could be regarded as superior to existing languages. It was this apparent virtue of the language of signs that was most forcibly to strike Condillac, whose own earlier emphasis upon analysis may well have been influential in determining de l'Épée's approach.[30]

In certain respects de l'Épée's sign-language may be regarded as the visual equivalent of some of the earlier projects and schemes of a written universal language and it is of course, possible that the teacher of the deaf was acquainted with a number of these universal language schemes. In the emphasis that is placed upon keeping a natural analogy between an object or idea and the sign that represents it, the language of gesture may best be compared with those 'emblematic symbols' that Leibniz at one period considered would constitute the best possible universal character. Similarly, the root-signs into which de l'Épée analysed complex ideas may be regarded as equivalent to the 'simple elements' of the ideal philosophical language also envisaged by Leibniz. Here the resemblances end. For the root-signs of the gestural language are obtained by analysing abstract ideas into elements that have affinities with material things and that may therefore be rendered in terms of physical movements. De l'Épée's analytical method accords therefore in this respect with the sensationalist tendencies of French thought, taking man back in his analysis to the sensations that lay behind his abstract reasoning, hence ultimately back to the corporeal reality that prompted these sensations.

The analysis is also turned, we should note, to a practical rather than to a philosophical end. An example will perhaps make this clearer. The words *I believe* are expressed in de l'Épée's sign language by means of four elements, each of which is represented by an appropriate gesture. These elements are: first, *I say yes with my mind*; secondly, *I say yes with my heart*; thirdly, *I say yes with my mouth*; and finally, *I have not seen and I still cannot see with my eyes*. The example serves to demonstrate how much the signs representing abstract ideas depend upon analogies with material things and situations. It shows also that, although the root-signs are simple enough when used separately, the combinations required to express one abstract idea can become unduly lengthy and complicated.

Considered as a medium for instructing the deaf, de l'Épée's language of signs had tremendous success in the years following the publication of the *Institution des sourds et muets* in 1776. So much so that by the middle of the next decade, as a result of the success of his public demonstrations, the interest of royalty and scholars, and the continuation of his work in other countries by teachers first instructed by himself, the Abbé de l'Épée had seen his teaching techniques widely adopted throughout Europe. Yet the freely acknowledged success of his methodical signs as a means of educating the deaf did not mean that his secondary claim that the signs should be adopted universally by speaking human beings was considered with equal seriousness. Indeed, it is clear that this aspect of his writing met with little support. Contemporary accounts of the Abbé's work, for example, and *comptes rendus* of his books often either confine their attention to a mere reiteration of the author's claim, or simply do not refer to it at all.

It was, of course, quite possible to ignore de l'Épée's claim in this way, since its validity was quite extraneous to the merits of the sign language as an instrument for the instruction of the deaf. Moreover, if it had been taken seriously, problems would clearly have arisen of an order quite different from those he had already surmounted in the course of his practical teaching. Many of these problems the Abbé did not foresee or failed to recognize as problems at all.

After de l'Épée's death in 1789, his claim that methodical signs offered the best form of universal language was taken up and repeated by his former pupil, the Abbé Roch-Ambroise Cucurron de Sicard, who assumed the direction of what was two years later to become the Institution nationale des sourds et muets. Realizing, however, that if such a language were to stand any chance at all of being universally adopted, these gestural signs would need to be recorded, Sicard set to work to provide a 'dictionary of signs.' This dictionary appeared in 1808 under the title *Théorie des signes pour l'instruction des sourds-muets*, and consisted of descriptions of the gestures used by the deaf person and his teacher instead of the words of conventional speech. Sicard did not arrange the descriptions according to the alphabetical order of these words, but classified them in families.

Je divisais [he wrote] tous les mots qui devaient en former la nomenclature en autant de parties qu'on reconnaît d'éléments distincts dans le discours ; je divisais ensuite les mots, et chaque espèce de mots en autant de familles dont chaque primitif était de chef ; enfin je suivais l'ordre dans lequel tous les mots, s'ils eussent été inventés, auraient été classés. La première série était celle des objets physiques, la seconde, celle des adjectifs, la troisième, celle des noms abstractifs etc. Chaque nom, chaque adjectif, chaque verbe, outre la définition que j'en donnais était accompagné d'une exposition courte du nombre et de la forme des signes qu'il fallait faire pour chaque mot. Cette marche étant parfaitement analytique, était la seule qui pouvait remplir mon but.[31]

The dictionary thus provided a classified series of descriptions of gestures, covering a wider range of ideas than those of the Abbé de l'Épée, and including also signs to convey grammatical relations. It was this improved language of gesture, Sicard claimed in the *Cours d'instruction d'un sourd-muet de naissance* and again in the dictionary of signs itself, that was the work philosophers had waited so long for, 'qui pourra réaliser les espoirs de ceux qui désirent, depuis longtemps, un moyen général de communication, indépendant de toute langue articulée ; dont le savant *Leibnitz* avait conçu le projet si hardi.'[32]

Sicard's claim was voiced, we may recall, at a time when the question of an artificial universal language had become once again one of the chief interests of leading French thinkers, and Sicard himself had been an ardent supporter of de Maimieux's *pasigraphie*. The deaf also had by this time become a favourite object of study for philosophers of the *école sensualiste*, who, with the example of Diderot and Condillac before them, were anxious to learn all they could from the deaf man about the development of man's various faculties and the generation of his ideas.[33] In view of these interests, it is scarcely surprising that Sicard's suggestion should have received rather more serious consideration than the same idea had done when it had been voiced earlier by the Abbé de l'Épée. However, of those philosophers who considered the possibility of gesture supplying the universal language, only Pierre Laromiguière recommended it wholeheartedly as an admirable solution to the problem of Babel. Thus, concerning the possibility of inventing a universal language, he wrote, in language reminiscent of the Abbé de l'Épée, to whose work he later referred:

Savans, ignorans, tout le monde la comprend, tout le monde la parle. Que l'un de nous soit transporté aux extrémités du globe, au milieu d'une horde sauvage : croyez-vous qu'il ne saura pas exprimer les besoins les plus pressans de la vie? Croyez-vous qu'il se méprenne sur les signes d'un refus barbare, ou d'une intention généreuse et compatissante? Il ne s'agit donc pas d'inventer une langue nouvelle, de la faire : elle existe : c'est la nature qui l'a faite.[34]

De Gérando also approached the *signes méthodiques* of Sicard with considerable enthusiasm for the idea that they offered a practicable solution to the problem presented by the confusion of tongues:

> C'est là que nous venons chercher avec empressement, avec avidité, cette langue appelée *naturelle* ; cette langue annoncée comme si féconde, si belle, si expressive, si fidèle, si exacte ; cette langue destinée à devenir la langue universelle, ou plutôt qui déjà en possède par elle-même le privilège ; cette langue, objet perpétuel de l'enthousiasme de l'Abbé de l'Épée et de ses disciples.[35]

After examining closely the signs worked out by de l'Épée and further developed by Sicard, de Gérando was, however, forced to conclude that the language possessed a number of serious defects that made it quite unsuitable for universal adoption. Since many of de Gérando's criticisms still apply today, it is perhaps worth concluding this brief study by repeating the principal objections, which he first voiced in his prize-winning *Des signes et de l'art de penser*, and later developed in a special study of the education of the deaf.

The descriptions of signs in Sicard's dictionary were, de Gérando believed, too complex to be adopted universally. They were, he wrote,

> souvent ingénieuses, souvent claires, plus ou moins exactes, mais des descriptions qui sont généralement d'une extrême étendue, composées d'un grand nombre de détails, qui doivent à ces détails même ce qu'elles ont de fidèle et de pittoresque, qui exigent une pantomime presque toujours fort développée, et qui demandent un temps assez long pour être fidèlement exécutées ; nous y trouvons, en un mot, une suite d'explications, à l'aide de tableaux sensibles, exprimés par une longue suite de gestes.[36]

In use, these highly complex successions of signs tended to be abbreviated. However, in this way, as they became more and more laconic, de Gérando argued, they lost whatever analogies with material objects they had ever possessed. Moreover, in order to convey abstractions, metaphor had to be used in a confusing and unphilosophical manner: 'C'est ainsi que, par une dégradation continue et insensible, le langage mimique, d'un tableau vivant, animé, complet dont il se composait à l'origine, se transforme en une analogie successivement plus imparfaite, plus vague, pour se terminer enfin dans une pure convention.'[37] Thus, though not without its virtues, the language that Laromiguière considered universally intelligible because natural turned out to be necessarily the product of agreement.[38] Two final objections were made by de Gérando, both of which argued against the universal adoption of an already highly imperfect language. First, he pointed out that there existed no form of script in which gestural signs could be written down.[39] Secondly, he recognized most perceptively that there was no reason why signs that were interpreted in one way in one country should not, owing to varying social habits, be understood to mean something quite different in another.

De Gérando's rejection of gesture as a universal language did not, of course, prevent other teachers of the deaf like Bébian, author of the *Mimographie* published in Paris in 1825, or J. Rambosson, in the *Langue universelle, langage mimique, mimé et écrit*, published in Paris in 1853, from continuing to press de l'Épée and Sicard's claim. Nor is the idea quite dead today. And, although it is theoretically quite feasible, it seems even less likely that man, accustomed to communicating by the spoken word, will revert to a silent form of communication, that that all men will agree to adopt the same written language – an agreement that itself seems unlikely ever to be reached.

Appendix B
Checklist of schemes of universal writing and language in the seventeenth and eighteenth centuries

1627
JEAN DOUET
Proposition présentée au roy, d'une escriture universelle, admirable pour ses effects tres-utile et necessaire à tous les hommes de la terre Paris 1627

1628
PHILIP KINDER
Letter on 'The Universall Character' to Mr W. Beveridge, Bodleian Library, Oxford, Ashmolean Ms 788, 51

M. DE LA CHAMPAGNOLLE
Reference in above letter of Kinder and in Hartlib papers, Lord Delamere's collection in Sheffield University Library, Hartlib's *Ephemerides*

1629
AUTHOR UNKNOWN [des Vallées?]
Prospectus sent by Mersenne to Descartes. Discussion by Descartes in *Correspondance du P. Marin Mersenne* 2: 323–9; letter dated 20 November 1629

1633
REV JOHNS[T]ON
See *The Life of William Bedell, D.D. Bishop of Kilmore in Ireland by G.B.* [G. Burnet] London 1685, 79; other references in the Hartlib papers in Sheffield University Library

1636
MARIN MERSENNE
Harmonie universelle Paris 1636 and *Correspondance du P. Marin Mersenne* 5: 136–40, 6: 4–6, 9: 42, 10: 265

1636
JEAN LE MAIRE
See *Correspondance du P. Marin Mersenne* 6: 27, 10: 264–5

1641
JOHN WILKINS
Mercury, or The Secret and Swift Messenger: Shewing, How a Man May with Privacy and Speed Communicate His Thoughts to a Friend at Any Distance London 1641, chapters 13 and 18

1644
JOHN BULWER
Chirologia, or The Naturall Language of the Hand, Composed of the Speaking Motions, and Discoursing Gestures thereof, Whereunto Is Added Chironomia, or the Art of Manuall Rhetoricke by J.B. Gent, Philochirosophus 2 parts, London 1644

1647
FRANCIS LODWICK
A Common Writing: Whereby Two, Although Not Understanding One the Others Language, Yet by the Helpe thereof, May Communicate Their Minds One to Another London 1647; facsimile reprint, Menston 1969, *English Linguistics 1500–1800* no 147

1647
CYPRIAN KINNER
Ms letter in Hartlib papers, Lord Delamere's collection in Sheffield University Library; see B. DeMott, 'The Sources and Development of John Wilkins' Philosophical Language' *Journal of English and Germanic Philology* 57, 1958: 1–13

c 1650
BLAISE PASCAL?
'Explication d'un système alphabet universel attribué au célèbre Pascal' Bibliothèque d'Avignon, Ms 1030 (this is an eighteenth-century Ms and the attribution is far from certain); quoted in *Correspondance du P. Marin Mersenne* 10: 274

1652
FRANCIS LODWICK
The Groundwork or Foundation Laid (or So Intended) for the Framing of a New Perfect Language and an Universall or Common Writing London 1652

1652
SIR THOMAS URQUHART [Christianus Presbyteromastix]
Ekskubalouron, or The Discovery of a Most Exquisite Jewel London 1652

1653
SIR THOMAS URQUHART
Logopandecteision, or An Introduction to the Universal Language London 1653, reprinted in the *Works of Sir Thomas Urquhart* Edinburgh 1834; facsimile reprint, Menston 1970, *English Linguistics 1500–1800* no 239

1654
ANONYMOUS SPANIARD CALLED EL MUDO [known to be the Jesuit father Pedro Bermudo]
Arithmeticus nomenclator mundi omnes nationes ad linguarum et sermonis imitatem invitans Rome 1654, no copy traced; for extract see Schott, *Technica curiosa*

1657
CAVE BECK
The Universal Character, by Which All the Nations in the World May Understand One Another's Conceptions, Reading out of One Common Writing Their Own Mother Tongues London 1657; also in French *Le Charactere universel ...* London 1657

1657
GEORGE DALGARNO
Tables of the universal character (prospectus and correspondence), British Museum, add. Ms 4377 and Harleian Ms 6941

1661
JOHANN JOACHIM BECHER
Character pro notitia linguarum universali inventum steganographicum hactenus inauditum Frankfurt 1661; modern reprint *Zur mechanischen Sprachübersetzung: Ein Programmierungsversuch aus dem Jahre 1661* Stuttgart 1962

1661
GEORGE DALGARNO
Ars signorum, vulgo character universali et lingua philosophica London 1661; facsimile reprint, Menston 1968, *English Linguistics 1500–1800* no 116

c 1661
SIR ISAAC NEWTON
'An Universall Language' in Ms; for reprint and discussion see R.W. Elliott 'Isaac Newton's "Of an Universall Language"' *The Modern Language Review* 52, 1957

1663
PHILIPPE LABBÉ
Grammatica linguae universalis missionum et commerciorum, simplicissimae, brevissimae facillimae ... 3rd edition, Paris 1663 [date of 1st edition not known]

1663
PHILIPPE LABBÉ
Grammaire de la langue universelle des missions et du commerce ... *avec un essay du dictionnaire* 2nd edition, Paris n.d.

1663
ATHANASIUS KIRCHER
Polygraphia nova et universalis ex combinatoria arte detecta Rome 1663

1664
GASPAR SCHOTT
Technica curiosa, sive, mirabilia artis libris XII comprehensa Nuremberg 1664, book 7, 483 ff; prints extracts from the *Arithmeticus nomenclator* and other schemes

1665–6
JOHANN AMOS COMENIUS [KOMENSKÝ]
Panglottia and *Novae linguae harmonicae tentamen primum* in Mss of August Hermann Francke Library in Halle; see V.T. Miškovská's articles 'La Panglottie de J.A. Komenský' *Philologica Pragensia* 2, 1959 and 'Comenius on Lexical Symbolism in an Artificial Language' *Philosophy* 37, 1962

1666
GOTTFRIED LEIBNIZ
Dissertatio de arte combinatoria Leipzig 1666

1668
JOHANN AMOS COMENIUS [KOMENSKÝ]
Via lucis written in 1641 and published at Amsterdam in 1668; English translation by E.T. Campagnac *The Way of Light* Liverpool 1938

1668
JOHN WILKINS
An Essay towards a Real Character and a Philosophical Language London 1668; facsimile reprint, Menston 1968, *English Linguistics 1500–1800* no 119

1669–c 1683
Plans for revision of Wilkins's *Essay* by Lodwick, Paschall, Pigot, Aubrey, Hooke; scheme of Seth Ward for a philosophical character based upon a smaller number of transcendentals: Bodleian Library, Oxford, Aubrey Ms 13 and Royal Society Archives, misc. letters, P1, 53–60

1676
JOHANN C. STURM
Collegium, experimentale sive curiosum ... 1 'Specimens edens novi artificii' Nuremberg 1676

1676
[GABRIEL DE FOIGNY]
La Terre australe connue Vannes 1676

1677–9
[DENIS VEIRAS D'ALAIS]
Histoire des Sévarambes Paris, part 1, 1677, 2 vols; part 2, 1678–9, 3 vols

1681
DE VIENNE PLANCY
'L'ouverture de l'écriture universelle' *Extraordinaire du Mercure* 14, 1681; other articles by De Vienne Plancy on a universal writing are in the *Extraordinaire du Mercure* 19, 1682; 30, 1685; 31, 1685

1681
JOACHIM FRISICHIUS
Ludovicée Thorn 1681, not traced

1685
JOHN KEOGH
See R.T. Gunther *Early Science in Oxford* 12: *Dr. Plot and the Correspondence of the Philosophical Society of Oxford* Oxford 1939: 181

1686
FRANCIS LODWICK
'An Essay towards a Universal Alphabet and a Universal Primer' *Philosophical Transactions of the Royal Society* 26 June 1686, 16: 126 ff; see also British Museum, Sloane Ms 932

1704
GEORGE PSALMANAAZAAR
An Historical and Geographical Description of Formosa London 1704

1710
[SIMON TYSSOT DE PATOT]
Voyages et avantures de Jaques Massé Bordeaux 1710

1720
ANONYMOUS
'Dialogue sur un caractère universel qui serait commun à toutes les langues de l'Europe' *Journal littéraire de l'année 1720* 2: 181

1723
DAVID SOLBRIG
'De scripturae oecumenicae, quam omnes gentes absque notitia linguarum legant et intelligant, methodo facili et expedita' *Miscellanea Berolinensia* Berlin 1723, 2 and 3

1765
J. FAIGUET
'Langue nouvelle' *Encyclopédie ou dictionnaire raisonné des sciences, des arts et des métiers par une société de gens de lettres* 9 Paris 1765

1769
ROW[LAND] JONES
The Philosophy of Words, in Two Dialogues between the Author and Crito ... and a Plan for a Universal Philosophical Language London 1769

1772
GEORGIUS KALMAR
Praecepta grammatica atque specimina linguae philosophicae sive universalis, ad omnevitae genus adcommodatae Berlin and Leipzig 1772

1773
GEORGIUS KALMAR
Precetti di grammatica per la lingua filosofica, o sia, universale, propria per ogni genere di vita Rome 1773

1774
GEORGIUS KALMAR
Grammaticalische Regeln zur philosophischen oder allgemeinen Sprache Wien 1774

1774
FRANCESCO SOAVE
Riflessioni intorno all'instituzione d'una lingua universale Rome 1774

1776
DIEUDONNÉ THIÉBAULT
'Observations générales sur la grammaire et les langues: première question, pourrait-on établir une langue universelle qui fût de quelque utilité?'
Nouveaux Mémoires de l'académie royale des sciences et belles-lettres de Berlin 1774 Berlin 1776

1776
CHARLES MICHEL DE L'ÉPÉE
Institution des sourds et muets, par la voie des signes méthodiques: ouvrage qui contient le projet d'une langue universelle, par l'entremise des signes naturels, assujettis à une méthode Paris 1776

1779
C.G. BERGER
Plan zu einer überaus leichten unterrichtenden und allgemeinen Rede- und Schrift-Sprache für alle Nationen Berlin 1779; see report by Beguelin in *Nouveaux Mémoires de l'académie royale des sciences et belles-lettres de Berlin* Berlin 1780

1783
J. WILLIAMS
Thoughts on the Origin and on the Most Rational and Natural Method of Teaching the Languages: With Some Observations on the Necessity of One Universal Language for All Works of Science London 1783

1793-4
ANTOINE-NICHOLAS DE CONDORCET
Ms of the Institut de France, carton 885c; see Gilles Gaston Granger 'Langue universelle et formalisation des sciences: un fragment inédit de Condorcet' *Revue d'histoire des sciences et leurs applications* 7, 1954: 197 ff

1795
JEAN DELORMEL
Projet d'une langue universelle présenté à la convention nationale Paris 1795

1795-6
ANDRÉ-MARIE AMPÈRE
Project described in the *Correspondance du Grand Ampère publiée par L. de Launay* 3 vols, Paris 1936-43, 1

1796
THOMAS NORTHMORE
A Triplet of Inventions, Consisting of a Nocturnal or Diurnal Telegraph, a

Proposal for an Universal Character, and a Scheme for Facilitating the Progress of Science, Exemplified in the Osteological Part of Anatomy Exeter 1796

1796
JAMES ANDERSON
'On an Universal Character' *Memoirs of the Literary and Philosophical Society of Manchester* 5, Manchester 1798

1797
JOSEPH DE MAIMIEUX
Pasigraphie, ou premiers élémens du nouvel art-science d'écrire et d'imprimer en une langue de manière à être lu et entendu dans toute autre langue sans traduction Paris 1797; also in German, Paris 1797

1797
C.H. WOLKE
Erklärung, wie die wechselseitige Gedankenmittheilung aller kulti-virten Völker des Erdkreises oder die Pasigraphie möglich und ausüblich sey, ohne Erlernung einer neuen besondern oder einer allgemeinen Wortschrift oder Zeichensprache Dessau 1797

1798
WILLIAM BROWN
'Hints on the Establishment of an Universal Written Character in a Letter to the Rev. Dr. John Kemp' *Memoirs of the Literary and Philosophical Society of Manchester* 5, Manchester 1798

1799
JOHANN SEVERIN VATER
Pasigraphie und Antipasigraphie Weissensfels and Leipzig 1799

1800
J.M. DANTAS PEREIRA
Memoria sobre hum projecto de Pasigraphia composta, e dedicata a o Serenissimo Senhor Infante D. Pedro Carlos Lisbon 1800

1800
ZALKIND HOURWITZ
Polygraphie, ou l'art de correspondre à l'aide d'un dictionnaire dans toutes les langues Paris an IX

1801
P.R.F. BUTET
Abrégé d'un cours complet de lexicographie Paris an IX

1802
JOSEPH DE MAIMIEUX
Épître familière au sens-commun, sur la Pasigraphie et Pasilalie Paris an x

1808
JOSEPH DE MAIMIEUX
Carte générale pasigraphique Paris 1808

Notes

INTRODUCTION

1 See, for instance, Burney *Les Langues internationales*; Clark *International Language*; Durrant *The Language Problem*; Guérard *A Short History*; Monnerot-Dumaine *Précis d'interlinguistique*; Pei *One Language*. Couturat and Leau *Histoire de la langue universelle* still provides the fullest account of the early language schemes.
2 *The Tongues of Men* 71
3 Since I completed this book, Vivian Salmon has published her own study of Francis Lodwick's linguistic writings which includes an important survey of universal language thinking in the seventeenth century: *The Works of Francis Lodwick: A Study of His Writings in the Intellectual Context of the Seventeenth Century*, London 1972. We should also note two unpublished theses in this field: first, a Columbia University Master's thesis by Lillian Goodhart, 'The Universal Character: Projects for a Universal Language Developed during the Seventeenth and Early Eighteenth Centuries: A Study of the Background of Swift's Satire on Language in the Voyage to Laputa,' 1952, a study which, unfortunately, I came across very late in my own researches, and, secondly, Margaret M.C. McIntosh's 'The Phonetic and Linguistic Theory of the Royal Society School,' Oxford University B.Litt. thesis 1956.
4 But see Acton 'The Philosophy of Language.'

CHAPTER I

1 In 'Problems of Language-Teaching' 13, Vivian Salmon refers to some of the difficulties that Englishmen encountered in Europe in communicating in spoken Latin.

2 *On Education* 91–2
3 Quoted in Brunot *Histoire de la langue française* 2: 66
4 Boyle *Works* 1: 22
5 *Mercury* (1641) 110
6 Douet *Proposition* (1627) 5
7 *The Life of William Bedell* 78
8 For a discussion of Johnson's project, see below, pp. 53–4
9 *The Way of Light* 'Dedication' 8
10 Ibid 188
11 See below, pp. 56–7
12 See in particular the recent book by Margery Purver, *The Royal Society* part 2, chapters 2 and 3, but also Turnbull 'Samuel Hartlib's Influence.'
13 *Grammaire* [1663] 'Avertissement'
14 *Ars signorum* 'Letter of Recommendation'
15 'The Epistle Dedicatory'
16 In arguing against Comenius's influence on the English language planners in 'Language-Planning in Seventeenth-Century England' Vivian Salmon underestimates in my view this religious motivation.
17 *Harmonie universelle* (1636) 'Livre premier de la voix' proposition 47: 65
18 The question of a *lingua humana* is more fully discussed in the opening chapter of Cornelius *Languages in ... Imaginary Voyages.*
19 See also Kircher *Reductio linguarum ad unam.*
20 'Leibniz on Locke on Language'
21 See Ward [and Wilkins] *Vindiciae academiarum* 22–3 and Wilkins *Essay* (1668) 2, 5, and 9.
22 *Academiarum examen* 26
23 *Vindiciae academiarum* 5
24 Ibid 22
25 See DeMott 'Comenius and the Real Character.'
26 This view is expressed by Jones in 'Science and Language' 327.
27 *Clavis universalis* 213
28 Bacon *Philosophical Works* 121
29 Ibid 122
30 *De prima scribendi origine* 61
31 Ibid
32 *Essay* (1668) 20
33 *Débat sur les écritures* chapters 1 and 2
34 *Traicté des chiffres* 10
35 See Salmon 'Language-Planning' 384.
36 *Mercury* 105
37 *Proposition* 7–8
38 J. Gruterus *Inscriptiones antiquae totius orbis romani, in corpus absolutissimum redactae ... accedunt notae veterum romanorum A. Seneca ac Tironis*, Heidelberg 1602–3

39 For a discussion of these Roman shorthand notes see Pitman *A History of Shorthand*.
40 J. Douet *Mémoires*, Paris 1641, second factum 2, quoted in David *Débat sur les écritures* 36
41 *Characterie* 'Epistle Dedicatorie.' The relationship between Bright's 'Characterie' and sixteenth-century cryptographies is reinforced by the existence of another treatise in manuscript, dated 1587, and entitled 'De clandestino scripto methodica tractatio a Timotheo Brighto Cantabrigiensi ex libro Johannis Baptistae de furtivis literarum notis.'
42 John Locke *Some Thoughts Concerning Education* edited by E. Daniel, London 1880, 282–3
43 Samuel Hartlib papers in Sheffield University Library, bundle 18, letter dated 23 November 1640 (in fact 16 November). These letters are part of a collection of nineteen letters from Mersenne to Theodore Haack, nine of which are additional to those found among the Pell papers in the British Museum, Birch Add. Ms 4279. The letters found in Sheffield were communicated by the author to Bernard Rochot, the late editor of the Mersenne correspondence, and have now appeared separately as a group in an appendix to vol 11 of that work. (For this letter, see Mersenne *Correspondance* 11: 419–24.)
44 Comenius commented on this English habit of taking down sermons in shorthand 'using symbols to signify whole words' (quoted in Young *Comenius in England* 65).
45 Salmon 'Language-Planning' 387 and 'Evolution'
46 *Characterie* 'Epistle Dedicatorie'
47 Samuel Hartlib's unpublished *Ephemerides* in Sheffield University Library, Professor G.H. Turnbull's transcript, 1640 D-E 3. All references to this work are made by kind permission of the late Professor Turnbull's widow.
48 In a letter to Hartlib dated 9 January 1657 (Hartlib papers, Sheffield University Library, bundle 31), John Beale wrote 'And I verily beleeve, that a progresse in variety of attempts for the advancement of short-writing will in the end bring forth an universall character.' See also letter of 3 November 1657, bundle 52.
49 Salmon 'Evolution'
50 Ibid 355
51 See Keynes *Dr. Timothie Bright* 36. See also entry under Bright in the *Catalogue of the Books in the Cathedral Library of Salisbury*.
52 *Works* 1: 22
53 British Museum, Birch Ms 4377, f 143
54 Oughtred *Key of the Mathematics* 'To the Reader.' Oughtred's symbols are listed in Cajori 'List of Oughtred's Mathematical Symbols.'
55 See Cajori *William Oughtred* 58–60 and the preface to *Key of the Mathematics*, where Oughtred wrote 'I was unwillingly drawn, at this

my declined age, to appear unto the world in such a kinde of subject. But occasion was administered by one Mr. *Seth Ward*, a young man excellently accomplished with all parts of polite Literature, then Fellow of Sydney College in *Cambridge*, who tooke the pains to seek me out and by a gentle violence induced me to publish my former Tractate in a manner new moulded and perfected.'

56 *Vindiciae academiarum* 21
57 Iversen *The Myth of Egypt*
58 Ibid 16. See also Iversen's article 'Hieroglyphic Studies' and L. Dieckmann 'Renaissance Hieroglyphics.'
59 *Proposition* 6–7
60 Letter on 'The Universall Character,' Bodleian Library, Oxford, Ashmolean Ms 788, f 51. See below, pp. 47–8.
61 *Universal Character* (1657) 'To the Reader'
62 *Seconde Centurie des questions traitées ez conferences du Bureau d'Adresse, depuis le 3. jour de novembre 1634 jusques à l'11 fevrier 1636*, Paris 1636, 382
63 *Universal Character* (1657) 'To the Reader'
64 *La Science universelle* 4: 124
65 Gaspar da Cruz *Tractado em que se cõtam muito por estēco as cousas da China, cõ suas particolaridades, e assi do reyno dormuz cõposto por el R. padre frey Gaspar da Cruz da orde de Sam Domingos*, Evora 1569
66 Ibid in Boxer *South China* 161. The introduction to this edition is very useful for a knowledge of early works on China. See also the introduction to Gallagher *China in the Sixteenth Century* xvii–xxii; Appleton *A Cycle of Cathay*; Pinot *La Chine*; and, above all, Lach *Asia*, vol 1 *The Century of Discovery* and the same author's *China in the Eyes of Europe*.
67 *Historia ... del gran Reyno de la China*
68 Author of an unpublished 'Relacion de las cosas de China que propriamente se llama Taybin' written in 1575 or 1576. This text is translated from the Manila Ms in Boxer *South China*.
69 See Streit *Bibliotheca missionum* 4: 531–3.
70 Father Nicholas Lombard, in a letter printed in the *Nouveaux advis du Royaume de la Chine, du Jappon et de l'Etat du Roy de Mogor* ... Paris 1604, compared the Chinese character-writing with 'la langue de la Cour de Rome, qui est entendue par tous les quartiers de l'Italie' (20).
71 Trigault's book went through eleven editions between 1615 and 1625. See Streit *Bibliotheca missionum* 5: 716–17.
72 In Bacon's *De augmentis scientiarum* of 1605, Hugo's *De prima scribendi origine* of 1617, and Vossius's *De arte grammatica* of 1630.
73 *Mercury* (1641) 106–7
74 See, among others, M. Mersenne *Questions inouies ou récréations des sçavants*, Paris 1634, 117; Beck *Universal Character* (1657) 'To the

Reader'; B. Walton *Biblia sacra polyglotta*, London 1657, Prolegomena 2: 10.
75 *Extraordinaire du Mercure*, April 1681, 14: 338
76 Webster *Academiarum examen* 25
77 *Philosophical Works* 121
78 Hugo *De prima scribendi origine* 61
79 *Extraordinaire du Mercure*, April 1681, 14: 338–9
80 *Seconde Centurie des questions traitées ez conferences du Bureau d'Adresse* 382–3
81 *Essay* 451
82 Ibid 452. Fréret pronounced the same judgment on Chinese characters much later in the *Mémoires de l'académie des inscriptions et belles-lettres*, Paris 1729, 609 ff. Warburton's reply to Fréret is of some interest: 'To know whether the ancient Chinese characters were founded on philosophic relations does not depend on their having a true system of physics and metaphysics but on their having a system simple, whether true or false, to which to adapt these characters' (*Divine Legation of Moses*, London 1758, 4: 87).
83 A French translation of the *Institutio religionis christianae* of Calvin was published in 1541 and provoked replies in that language. See Brunot *Histoire de la langue française* 2: 14–15. Luther's German version of the Bible appeared in 1522, and the French translation by Lefèvre d'Étaples in 1523.
84 For a more detailed discussion of the development of French see Brunot *Histoire de la langue française* 2: 1–91.
85 See Migliorini *Lingua e Cultura* 135–58.
86 Hartlib papers, Sheffield University Library, letter dated 23 November 1640 (in fact 16 November). See Mersenne *Correspondance* 11: 420.
87 An interesting article on 'Travel as Education' by G.B. Parks will be found in Jones et al. *The Seventeenth Century* 264 ff.
88 *Correspondance* 11: 420
89 *Didactica magna*, quoted in the abridged translation of Keatinge *Comenius* 171–2
90 The *Porta linguarum trilinguis reserata et aperta* of 1631, the *Linguarum methodus novissima* of 1649, and the *Orbis sensualium pictus* of 1659 were all written in order to make of Latin a medium through which knowledge of the world could be most effectively imparted to the young.
91 See *The Way of Light* 180–2.
92 Ibid 183
93 Ibid, 'Dedication' 8
94 *Essay* 443
95 Ibid 448
96 *The Reformed School* 47

97 Ibid
98 *Ekskubalouron* (1652) 19
99 *Academiarum examen* 21
100 Ibid 22. See also J.H. [i.e. John Hall] *An Humble Motion to the Parliament of England concerning the Advancement of Learning and Reformation of the Universities*, London 1649, where we read that 'many men that could count their languages by their Fingers, might possibly be of no more use among mankinde, than so many Apes or Magpies. But such whose minds were strengthened with realities, were onely men, and indeed so much men, as they were masters of the true use of reason and how to guide it' (34).
101 *Advice of W.P.* 5
102 See Watson *Beginnings ... of Modern Subjects* chapter 6, and Jones *Ancients and Moderns*.
103 Dury *The Reformed School* 49
104 Several of the features described above were to characterize the dissenting academies that sprang up in England after the Restoration. See Parker *Dissenting Academies*.
105 *Philosophical Works* aphorism 59, 269. For a discussion of Bacon's views on language see Anderson *Philosophy of Francis Bacon* 102–4.
106 *Clavis universalis* 204–6
107 Jones 'Science and Language' 320. See *The Petty Papers* 1: 149–66 and the *Petty-Southwell Correspondence* 186–8. In November 1687, Petty wrote that the aim of the 'Dictionary of Sensible Words' was 'to translate all words used in Argument and Important matters into words that are *Signa Rerum* and *Motuum*' *Petty-Southwell Correspondence* 324.
108 *Works* 4: 365
109 *Ekskubalouron* (1652) 11
110 *Essay* 17
111 Ibid 17–18
112 See *Essay* 450–2. Wilkins, we may note, did not read Chinese character-writing himself and depended upon the books on China by Trigault, Semmedo, and Spizel (see *Essay* 450 and 452), as well as upon a manuscript of the Lord's Prayer and a Catechism in Chinese lent to him by Francis Lodwick, the author of *A Common Writing*, another project of a universal character.
113 *Essay* 19
114 Descartes's letter is printed in the *Œuvres complètes* 1: 76, and in Mersenne *Correspondance* 2: 323–8.
115 *Harmonie universelle* (1636) 'Livre premier de la voix' proposition 12, 12
116 Ibid, proposition 47, 65
117 *The Way of Light* 185
118 *Leviathan* 13

119 Ibid 15
120 Ibid
121 See *The Petty Papers* 1: 150–1, and Boyle *Works* 4: 358 ff.
122 *History of the Royal Society* 113. Different views of the influence of science and anti-Ciceronianism respectively on English prose style are put by Jones in 'Science and Language' and by Williamson in *The Senecan Amble*.
123 *Philosophical Works* aphorism 59, 269
124 *Universal Character* (1657) 'To the Reader'
125 *Grammaire* [1663]
126 E. Ashmole [James Hasolle] 'Prolegomena' to his translation of Arthur Dee *Fasciculus Chemicus or Chymical Collections*, London 1650
127 *Academiarum examen* 24
128 'Science versus Mnemonics'
129 British Museum Add. Ms 4377, f 143
130 *The Way of Light* 186
131 Essay 'Epistle Dedicatory'

CHAPTER II

1 See, for example, Couturat and Leau *Histoire de la langue universelle*; Guérard *A Short History*; Cohen 'On the Project of a Universal Character.'
2 'Language-Planning' 370. See also Mersenne *Correspondance* 2: 328–9.
3 *De prima scribendi origine* 60
4 Ibid
5 The reluctance of Jean Le Maire to publish the secret of his scheme was attributed by Charles Sorel to financial ambition: 'Il [le secret] n'a point esté publié par son Autheur, à cause qu'il demandoit cinquante escholiers qui luy donnassent chacun mille francs, ou un petit nombre qui luy fist pareille somme pour sa recompense' (*De la perfection de l'homme* quoted in Mersenne *Correspondance* 10: 271). It seems likely that Champagnolle and Douet withheld publication for similar reasons. An entry in Samuel Hartlib's *Ephemerides* in Sheffield University Library, 1650 C-D1 (Professor Turnbull's transcript), reports that 'Champagnolla gave orders that if his heires could not receive a competent reward for the worke of characters which hee left in their hands they should burn it.'
6 David *Débat sur les écritures* 36
7 Douet *Proposition* (1627). Until Madeleine David mentioned this scheme in *Débat sur les écritures* (36–7), the only reference I had seen to it was in Labbé *Grammatica* (1663), where the author wrote 'nec non cum Intel-

ligentiis, ut titulus praefert, Ioannis de Villiers Parisiis anno 1587 excusis, vel cum libello de charactere Universali Ioannis Doüet in eadem urbe anno 1627 publicato' (5).

8 Bodleian Library, Ashmolean Ms 788, f 51–2. The letter is headed 'The Universal Character' and a reply from Beveridge accompanying it is dated 14 January 1628. This William Beveridge was the father of Dr William Beveridge, the Bishop of St Asaph.

9 The Hartlib papers even reveal how Hartlib, Petty, and Ward learned of the existence of Champagnolle's work. Entry 1650 B-C3 relates: 'Champagnolla's widow lives in Fench street and is one of the patients of Dr. Gurdain. Sir W. Boswell affirmes to have his art but bound up to secrecy as long as hee lived, the whole direction being contained in halfe a sheet on both sides, which now hee may lawfully publish.' Gurdain, who was himself Hartlib's informant, then approached the widow and son who claimed that the sheet Sir William Boswell had was no use without the books, which had 'beene sealed up these 7 years' (1650 B-C4). This suggests 1643 as the date of Champagnolle's death. An entry in the journal for 1635 (C-D16) speaks of Champagnolle being 'yet in London perfecting his Characteres Reales.'

10 Hartlib papers *Ephemerides* 1650 F-G8
11 Salmon 'Evolution' 358. The references are to page 21 of the *Vindiciae academiarum* and to Hartlib's *Ephemerides* 1639 B-C8 and 1650 F-G8.
12 Bodleian Library, Ashmolean Ms 788, f 51
13 Ibid
14 Ibid
15 Mersenne *Correspondance* 2: 323–8
16 Ibid 329
17 Sorel *De la perfection de l'homme* 346
18 Tallemant des Réaux *Historiettes* 1: 259–65
19 Mersenne *Correspondance* 4: 332 and 5: 140
20 See *Nouvelle Biographie générale* vol 23, Paris 1858 'Claude Hardy' 370–1.
21 Cohen 'On the Project of a Universal Character' 52
22 My own conclusions agree entirely with those of the late M. Rochot, to whom I am grateful for his kindness in sending me the page-proofs devoted to this question prior to their publication in Mersenne *Correspondance* 10: 271–3. See note on line 26 of letter 945, Mersenne to Comenius, 22 November 1640.
23 Tallemant des Réaux *Historiettes* 66, quoted in Mersenne *Correspondance* 2: 329. Sorel also uses the term *langue matrice* with respect to des Vallées (*De la perfection de l'homme* 346–8). See Mersenne *Correspondance* 10: 271–2. The link that Tallemant des Réaux established between de Muys and des Vallées, and the possible one between the

latter and Gabriel Sionita, give added strength to the attribution of the prospectus to des Vallées. For we should note that it was Sionita who was to be consulted about the interpretation of an Arab music manuscript after 'l'homme de la langue universelle,' who was, quite wrongly I am sure, thought by Cornélis de Waard to be Claude Hardy.

24 Mersenne *Correspondance* 2: 324 ('cognita hac lingua caeteras omnes, ut ejus dialectos, cognoscere')
25 *La Science universelle* 4: 32
26 Mersenne *Correspondance* 2: 324
27 Ibid 325
28 Tallemant des Réaux *Historiettes* 66, quoted in Mersenne *Correspondance* 2: 329
29 See *Nouvelle Biographie générale* vol 30, Paris 1862, 'Le Maire' 599.
30 *The Way of Light* 191
31 Mersenne *Correspondance* 9: 42
32 Bibliothèque nationale Ms, N.A.F. 6206, f 167. See Brown *Scientific Organisations* 268–70.
33 See in particular Mersenne *Correspondance* 9: 16 and 42–3; the *Almérie* is referred to on many other occasions in the Mersenne correspondence.
34 See Cohen 'Jean Le Maire' and Knowlson 'Jean Le Maire.'
35 A document among the Hartlib papers in Sheffield University Library (bundle 18) is a copy of the *lettres patentes* to Le Maire from Louis XIII. A reference in the *Ephemerides* notes that 'Hack hase gotten Jean de Mair's patent of all his undertakings' (1639 E-F7). See for a list of references to Le Maire's scheme Mersenne *Correspondance* 10: 264, n 5.
36 *De la perfection de l'homme* 346–8
37 Mersenne *Correspondance* 8: 209
38 Ibid 6: 4
39 Ibid 10: 265. For a similarly extended use of the word *alphabet* see below, p. 68.
40 *The Way of Light* 191
41 *The Life of William Bedell* 78–9
42 Hartlib papers *Ephemerides* 1639 J-J7
43 Hartlib papers, bundle 47, 6
44 Bibliothèque nationale Ms, N.A.F. 6206, f 89
45 Hartlib papers, bundle 47, 6. See also Sloane Ms 427, f 85. An entry in Hartlib's *Ephemerides* for 1649 (1649 A-B8) reads 'Such an occasion [i.e. for advancing learning] is in Sumner's offers for bringing over Johnson's real char[acters]. See his letter and Bond's paper.' I have not found any trace of Bond's paper among the Hartlib manuscripts.
46 Hartlib papers *Ephemerides* 1650 K-L1
47 *Proposition* 9
48 *The Way of Light* 187

49 *Philosophical Works* 121
50 For a fuller discussion of this suggestion, see below pp. 119–23. It is worth noting the following passage from the *Parthenia* of 1613: 'Musick (like that miraculous tongue of th'Apostles) having but one and ye same Character is alike knowne to all the sundry nations of ye world.'
51 This suggestion is put forward by DeMott in 'Comenius and the Real Character' 1071–2.
52 I summarize here arguments that are marshalled most convincingly in Salmon 'Language-Planning' 378–9.
53 See Young *Comenius in England* 52, and Turnbull *Hartlib, Dury and Comenius* 354.
54 See Young *Comenius in England* 52–3, and Comenius *The Way of Light* 'Dedication' 3.
55 As Vivian Salmon suggests ('Language-Planning' 379), the section on a 'Pansophic language' might well have been added or altered in 1668, at the time when the Dedication to the *Via lucis* was certainly written.
56 *The Way of Light* 180
57 'That which first occasioned this Discourse,' wrote Wilkins in the *Mercury*, 'was the reading of a little Pamphlet, stiled *Nuncius inanimatus*' (quoted in Salmon 'Language-Planning' 396). Godwin's 'little Pamphlet' was published in 1629.
58 *Mercury* 110
59 For information concerning Lodwick, a Dutch merchant who later became a Fellow of the Royal Society, see Abercrombie 'Forgotten Phoneticians.' See also n 62 below.
60 *A Common Writing* 'To the Reader'
61 See *Aubrey's Brief Lives* 320.
62 These have now been published in Salmon *The Works of Francis Lodwick*, London 1972.
63 McCracken 'Athanasius Kircher's Universal Polygraphy'
64 *Universal Character* 'To the Reader'
65 Ibid
66 Ibid
67 Ibid 33
68 John Wilkins wrote in the *Essay* (1668) that in all the attempts to construct a universal character that he had either seen or heard of 'the Authors of them did generally mistake in their first foundations; whilst they did propose to themselves the framing of such a *Character*, from a *Dictionary of Words*, according to some particular Language, without reference to the *nature of things* and that common Notion of them wherein Mankind does agree, which must chiefly be respected, before any attempt of this nature could signifie anything, as to the main end of it' ('To the Reader').

CHAPTER III

1 Mersenne *Correspondance* 2: 327
2 Leibniz was later to dispute the fact that the completion of the 'true philosophy' was necessary for the invention of a universal language. See Couturat *La Logique de Leibniz* 57.
3 Mersenne *Correspondance* 2: 328
4 Ibid
5 See, for example, Mersenne *Correspondance* 5: 135–8, 6: 4, 9: 300–2, 10: 265.
6 This study has been undertaken by E. Coumet, with the support of the Centre national de la recherche scientifique.
7 *Harmonie universelle* (1636) 'Livre premier de la voix' proposition 47, 65
8 Ibid, proposition 11, 12
9 Ibid, proposition 50, 75–7
10 See also Miškovskà 'Panglottie'; de Brosses *Traité*. Mersenne's suggestion also compares interestingly with some twentieth-century theories on the origins of language; for example Paget *Human Speech* and Jespersen *Language*.
11 Mersenne *Correspondance* 5: 136–7
12 Ibid
13 *Harmonie universelle* 'Livre premier de la voix' proposition 49, 75. See also ibid proposition 11, 12 and proposition 47, 65.
14 Ibid 'Traitez de la voix et des chants' 'Préface au lecteur'
15 See *La Vérité des sciences* 3: 527–50, and for further references Mersenne *Correspondance* 5: 138–9.
16 *Harmonie universelle* 'Livre second des chants' 107–53
17 *Harmonie universelle* 'Livre premier de la nature et des proprietez du son' proposition 22, 39. For discussion of the idea of a musical language as it occurs in Francis Godwin's *The Man in the Moone*, in Cyrano de Bergerac, and in early treatises of cryptography, see below, pp. 119–23.
18 Ibid 40
19 For details of the ways envisaged by Mersenne of combining vowels and consonants see *Harmonie universelle* 'Livre premier de la voix' proposition 47, 66–7.
20 Mersenne *Correspondance* 5: 136
21 *Harmonie universelle* 'Traitez de la voix et des chants' 'Préface au lecteur.' The choice of example is significant in view of the earlier Lullist and Cabalist use of symbols to denote the divine attributes.
22 Ibid 'Livre premier de la voix' proposition 49, 73–4 (italics mine)
23 Ibid, proposition 12, 13
24 DeMott 'Sources' 2

25 For Kinner's letter on this subject, see ibid 11–13. See also Salmon 'Language-Planning' 391–2.
26 *Essay* 289
27 *Ekskubalouron* (1652) 9
28 *Groundwork* (1652) 10
29 A copy of the original of this work has not so far been traced. However, a lengthy extract is included in Schott *Technica curiosa* 'Mirabilia graphica' 478 ff. In the *Catalogo razonado de obras anónimas y seudónimas de autores de la Compañia de Jesús pertenecientes a la antigua asistencia de España, publicado por el P. Jose Eugenio Uriarte, S.J.*, Madrid 1904, 1: 49–50, the *Arithmeticus Nomenclator* is attributed to El P. Pedro Bermudo. See for fuller discussion Ceñal 'Un anonimo español.'
30 Salmon 'Evolution' discusses this development very fully.
31 DeMott 'Comenius and the Real Character'
32 See above, pp. 56–7.
33 See Salmon 'Language-Planning'
34 Ibid 391
35 Mersenne himself is the source of this information. In a letter to Comenius dated 22 November 1640, he draws Comenius's attention to his own attempts to construct a new language, referring explicitly to the *Harmonie universelle*, which anyone in England, he claimed, could get for Comenius, since three or four copies were already in that country. One, Mersenne went on, he had himself sent to Cavendish, and another (the one, incidentally, that is now in the Réserve of the Bibliothèque nationale in Paris) belonged to Sir Kenhelm Digby, who was a friend of Mersenne. See Mersenne *Correspondance* 10: 267. If Comenius indeed managed to obtain a copy of the *Harmonie universelle*, this raises the possibility that Mersenne influenced Comenius directly in his ideas on a philosophical language. This question is discussed, though necessarily inconclusively, in Hendrich 'Mersenne.'
36 Petty wrote to John Pell (author of the *Idea of mathematicks*, a work which impressed Mersenne greatly), thanking him for his introduction to Hobbes, who had put him in touch with Sir Charles Cavendish and Father Mersenne. See Vaughan *Protectorate* 2: 367–8, letter dated 8 November 1645.
37 Even with the addition of the letters from Mersenne to Haack in Lord Delamere's collection of Hartlib's papers (Sheffield University Library, bundle 18) it is unlikely that the entire correspondence has been preserved. Hartlib corresponded with Mersenne directly in the late 1640s (Hartlib papers, bundle 18, letter dated 25 June 1648) and, as Boyle's reference to a *resumption* of his former correspondence suggests, he may already have done so at an earlier date. See Turnbull 'Samuel Hartlib's Influence' 105–6.

Notes to pages 76–80

38 Salmon 'Language-Planning' 380–5
39 *Ephemerides*, an entry for 1650 quoted by Salmon ibid 391
40 See, for instance, Taylor *The Alchemists* 53–4, where reference is made to the various combinations of symbols that express the modifications of gold.
41 For a well-known account of Mexican picture-writing see Acosta *Naturall and Morall Historie*.
42 Hartlib papers *Ephemerides* 1650 (quoted by Salmon 'Language-Planning' 391)
43 The link between Urquhart's scheme and the earlier work on a botanical character is suggested by a statement in the *Ekskubalauron* (1652) that 'words expressive of herbs, represent unto us with what degree of cold, moisture, heat, or driness they are qualified; together with some other property distinguishing them from other herbs' (34).
44 'Language-Planning'
45 Ibid 380
46 C. Holyband *The French Littelton*, introduction by M.St Clare Byrne, Cambridge 1953
47 Salmon 'Language-Planning' 382, quotes what Thomas Hayne wrote of the philologist Henry Jacobs of Merton: 'ipse profitetur se methodo sua et hactenus intentata, per certas proprietatum classes subordinatim velle istas disponere, donec in paucissimis desinant Principiis: ut haec verborum Philosophia exacte imitetur illam rerum' (*Linguarum cognatio*, London 1639, 65). In Hartlib's papers there are references to the related scheme of indexing words and ideas of a certain Harrison: 'Harrison intends for every booke and an index of propositions, so contracted as hee hase invented. Then of all those indexes one universal index. Two things especially are his owne in that invention, 1/ the compendiousness of quoting or allegations by ciphers the like never has been knowen ... ' (Hartlib papers *Ephemerides* 1640 F-G3, which contain many other references to the same scheme).
48 *The Art of Memory* 378
49 *Clavis universalis*. See particularly chapters 2, 5, 6, and 7.
50 In the earliest schemes of Douet, Kinder, Champagnolle, and Le Maire, stress was laid upon the ease with which the invented characters could be learned.
51 Mersenne *Correspondance* 2: 326
52 *The Art of Memory* 233. My whole discussion of the memory treatises owes much to this book, and I should like to acknowledge a great debt to Miss Yates for clarifying some points that were doubtful in my own mind prior to its publication.
53 Ibid
54 *Ekskubalauron* (1652) 9

55 Ibid 29
56 Ibid
57 Most notably, of course, the *Ars signorum* (1661) of George Dalgarno and the *Essay towards a Real Character and a Philosophical Language* (1668) of John Wilkins
58 Mersenne *Correspondance* 5: 136
59 Kinner's letter to Hartlib, 27 June 1647. See DeMott 'Science versus Mnemonics' 7.
60 Royal Society Classified Papers, 16, no 2
61 Hartlib papers, Sheffield University Library, bundle 71. See also letters of Beale to Hartlib, bundles 31 and 52.
62 Dalgarno, printed prospectus, *News to the Whole World, of the Discovery of an Universal Character, and a New Rational Language*, British Museum, Add. Ms 4377 (Birch), f 143
63 'Sources' 2
64 *Essay* (1668) 22. Wilkins went on: 'Those things which naturally have *Opposites*, are joyned with them, according to such Opposition, whether *Single* or *Double*. Those things that have no Opposites, are paired together with respect to some *Affinity* which they have one to another.'
65 See DeMott 'Science versus Mnemonics.'
66 Ms letter from Thomas Pigot to John Aubrey, 5 February 1676/7, Bodleian Library, Aubrey Ms 13, f 16: 'The Essay makes about 3000 radicalls but these so stated by exact definitions so disposed in termes by a naturall method that they may be more easily learned than a thousand other words and I verily believe the world never yet produced a greater help to understanding or memory than those termes. His signs are so few and methodized that I dare undertake a man of ordinary capacity shall be able to analyse them in an hour.'
67 *The Art of Memory* 187–91
68 *Kabbalah* 36
69 For more detailed information on the diffusion of Lullism, see Rossi *Clavis universalis* 41–80. This whole tradition is dealt with much more fully in Rossi's book than it is here.
70 Descartes *Discours de la méthode* 17
71 *Harmonie universelle* (1636) 'Traitez de la Voix et des Chants' 'Préface au lecteur'
72 Amsterdam 1669
73 As well as several other treatises of logic, there is a logic-book, entitled *Revolutionum alphabetariarum artis brevis Raymundi Lully expositio*, among the Hartlib papers in Sheffield University Library, bundle 24.
74 See Salmon 'Language-Planning' 393 and, on Bisterfeld, Rossi *Clavis universalis* 197–200.
75 *Vindiciae academiarum* 19, 21–2

76 Bodleian Library 25287, Aubrey Ms 13, and Royal Society Ms P1, 53–60
77 First published in 1666, entitled *Ars combinatoria*, this dissertation begins with a Lullist circular figure; reference is made directly to Lull and to Leibniz's contemporary, Kircher. See Leibniz *Opera philosophica* 6–7. On Leibniz's relations with the thought of Lull, see Carreras y Artau *De Ramón Lull*.
78 I suspect that the role of intermediary between a Lullist system of combinations of symbols and the universal language planners may well have been played by the Abbot of Spanheim, Trithemius (Tritheim), whose *Steganographia* and *Polygraphia* were referred to several times in the early part of the century, for example in Wilkins *Mercury* (1641) and in Mersenne *Correspondance* 10: 42.
79 See Yates *The Art of Memory* chapter 8, 173–98 and the same writer's 'Art of Ramon Lull.'
80 See Rossi *Clavis universalis* 179–84.
81 See above, pp. 9–15.
82 Funke *Zum Weltsprachenproblem*; Jones *The Seventeenth Century*; Salmon 'Language-Planning'
83 DeMott 'Comenius and the Real Character,' 'Science versus Mnemonics,' 'Sources'; Aarsleff 'Leibniz on Locke on Language'; Rossi *Clavis universalis*
84 *The Art of Memory* 378
85 Ibid, chapter 17, 'The Art of Memory and the Growth of Scientific Method'
86 *Vindiciae academiarum* 22
87 *Essay* (1668) 289
88 *Vindiciae academiarum* 19
89 Letters from Andrew Paschall to John Aubrey show that Ward referred to Lull's *Ars magna* and George Ritschel's *Contemplationes metaphysicae* of 1648 when he wished to suggest the lines along which he himself was thinking (Aubrey Ms 13, Bodleian Library).
90 Yates *The Art of Memory* 375
91 *The Way of Light* 191
92 Ibid 191–2
93 *The Art of Memory* 375, 379
94 *Essay* (1668) 24
95 See Bodleian Library, Aubrey Ms 13.
96 G. Dalgarno *News to the Whole World, of the Discovery of an Universal Character, and a New Rational Language*, British Museum, Add. Ms 4377 (Birch). Work on the *Ars signorum* led Dalgarno to consider methods of communicating with the deaf.
97 *The Way of Light* 187
98 Ibid 191

99 *Didascalocophus*, introduction
100 *Essay* 'Epistle Dedicatory'
101 'Language-Planning' 378
102 *Essay* 'Epistle Dedicatory'
103 Dalgarno's and Wilkins's languages have both been discussed at length elsewhere: see, on Dalgarno, Funke *Zum Weltsprachenproblem* and Salmon 'Evolution'; and, on Wilkins, Andrade 'Real Character'; Emery 'John Wilkins' Universal Language' and Cornelius *Languages in ... Imaginary Voyages* chapter 4.
104 I have not yet seen the new biography of John Wilkins that came to my attention very recently: Barbara Shapiro *John Wilkins 1614–1672: An Intellectual Biography*, Berkeley and Los Angeles 1969.
105 Wilkins *Essay* 'Epistle Dedicatory'
106 Ibid
107 Ibid
108 These reservations are discussed in DeMott 'Science versus Mnemonics.'
109 *Essay* 'Introduction' 1
110 Ibid 'Epistle Dedicatory'
111 Ibid
112 'The ranging of these things into such an order as the Society shall approve, would afford a very good method for your Repository, both for the *disposal* of what you have already, and the supplying of what you want' *Essay* 'Epistle Dedicatory'
113 See Sprat *History of the Royal Society* 251: 'This Repository he [Robert Hooke] has begun to reduce under its several heads, according to the exact Method of the Ranks of all the *Species of Nature*, which has been compos'd by Dr. *Wilkins*, and will shortly be published in his *Universal Language*.' See also Robert Hooke's suggestions for reforming Natural Philosophy and for a philosophical algebra in *The Posthumous Works of Robert Hooke*, published by R. Waller, London 1705, and Hesse 'Hooke's Philosophical Algebra.'
114 *Essay* 415
115 Ibid 387
116 Emery 'John Wilkins' Universal Language' 181
117 See *Essay* 414.
118 The opinions of various later thinkers on Wilkins's real character and philosophical language are discussed in Emery 'John Wilkins' Universal Language.'
119 Comenius made the same point in the *Via lucis* (1668): 'Second, must no one individual person attempt to think it [the universal language] out; this duty we must leave to the College of Wise Men. Otherwise it might come about that several quick-witted men, spurred by their desire for so charming a thing, might attempt it, and then it could not but turn out that

a variety of opinions would be held by different men upon this or that matter' (*The Way of Light* 219–20).
120 See Birch *History of the Royal Society* 283.
121 For example, Andrade 'Real Character' 9
122 'Science versus Mnemonics'
123 See Powell *John Aubrey* 171, 193. In spite of Andrade's difficulty in tracing the contemporary history of Wilkins's *Essay*, these letters were in the Bodleian Library and the Royal Society papers at the time, and they are used here for the first time. They are also referred to in Salmon *The Works of Francis Lodwick: A Study of His Writings in the Intellectual Context of the Seventeenth Century*, London 1972.
124 *Aubrey's Brief Lives* 320
125 See various letters in the Bodleian collection of Aubrey papers, Bodleian 25287, Aubrey Ms 13 (e.g. f 15, f 18, f 135–6).
126 Bodleian Library, Aubrey Ms 13, f 3, f 13
127 Ibid, f 2
128 Ibid, f 16: this letter, dated 5 February 1676/7, is wrongly classified as being from Paschall; it is, in fact, a letter from Thomas Pigot in Oxford, which has been sent on by Aubrey to Paschall.
129 *Description* 30
130 Bodleian Library, Aubrey Ms 13, f 170, letter from Ray to Aubrey dated 8 May 1678
131 Ibid, f 32–3
132 Ibid, f 39–40
133 Ibid, f 87. See also ibid, John Ray's letters, f 169, f 170, f 181.
134 Ibid, f 15: an interesting letter written half in Wilkins's real character, and clearly a reply to a letter from Aubrey also written in the real character.
135 Royal Society Ms 3133, P1, 55
136 Bodleian Library, Aubrey Ms 13, f 31
137 Royal Society Ms 3133, P1, 55
138 See Bodleian Library, Aubrey Ms 13, f 28 and f 31.
139 Ibid, f 38, f 56, and f 57: the Aubrey letters contain sufficient material to enable a comparison to be made at some future date between these three different versions.
140 Ibid, f 34
141 Ibid, f 30
142 See Royal Society Ms 3134, P1, 57.
143 This latter work, which Ward acknowledged to be responsible for leading him to the same conclusions as Lull's *Ars magna*, was published in 1648 at Oxford. See Young *A Bohemian Philosopher*. Young thought that the only copy of this work in England was in the Bodleian Library, Oxford, but we should note another, which was Seth Ward's own, in the Library of Salisbury Cathedral (H.2.17).

144 Royal Society Ms 3134, P1, 57
145 Ibid
146 We may note other works in the Lullist tradition in Salisbury Cathedral Library that were almost certainly part of the Ward bequest: Lavinheta's *Opera omnia* of 1612, Trithemius's *Steganographia* of 1606, and Kircher's *Ars magna sciendi* of 1669, as well as several works of Lull himself that were published in the seventeenth century. See Salisbury Cathedral *Catalogue* under Lullius. Ward also probably possessed Mersenne's *La Vérité des sciences* of 1625 and the mathematical works of Hérigone and Harriot, among others.
147 Bodleian Library, Aubrey Ms 13, f 113–4
148 Ibid, f 16
149 See Couturat *La Logique de Leibniz*, particularly chapters 2, 3, 4, and 5, and notes 2, 3, and 4. See also Lewis *Symbolic Logic*; Stebbing *A Modern Introduction to Logic*; Cohen 'On the Project of a Universal Character'; Kauppi *Leibnizsche Logik*; David 'Leibniz et le "Tableau de Cébès,"' and Kneale *The Development of Logic*. This list has been confined to those books and articles that I have found most valuable on this topic. A fuller bibliography will be found in Kauppi *Leibnizsche Logik* 168–72.
150 In this outline, I lean very much upon Couturat's account, in which much of the documentation was published for the first time.
151 Although Descartes's letter of November 1629 to Mersenne had appeared in the Clerselier edition of 1657 (1: 111) it is not likely, writes Couturat (*La Logique de Leibniz* 57), that Leibniz knew the letter at this time, though he certainly knew of Decartes's ideas at a later date, when he commented that though the institution of the universal language depended upon the true Philosophy, it did not depend upon its completion and perfection. Rather would it develop and be perfected along with the science of which it was the instrument. Couturat continues: 'Quoi qu'il en soit, et malgré l'analogie du projet de Leibniz avec celui qu'esquissait Descartes, il ne paraît pas qu'il en soit dérivé; il semble plutôt que les deux philosophes se soient rencontrés, et cet accord n'en est que plus remarquable.' (50) If both philosophers' ideas are considered as developments of a Lullist method, their general agreement is, I think, less remarkable.
152 *La Logique de Leibniz* 35
153 These relations have been most fully discussed by Rossi *Clavis universalis* and Carreras y Artau *De Ramón Lull*.
154 *La Logique de Leibniz* 54–5
155 Although written at the beginning of the eighteenth century, this work was not published until it appeared in 1765 in the *Œuvres philosophiques*.
156 See David 'Leibniz et le "Tableau de Cébès"' and for other forms of symbolism suggested by Leibniz, see Couturat *La Logique de Leibniz* 106–14.

157 For example, Leibniz took from Dalgarno his method of transposing numbers into sounds; see Couturat *La Logique de Leibniz* 62–3.
158 Ibid 79
159 Lettre à Galloys from *Die philosophischen Schriften von G.W. Leibniz* edited by C.J. Gerhardt, 7 vols, Berlin 1875–90, 7: 21, quoted in *La Logique de Leibniz* 92
160 Ibid 101
161 This point is underlined by Cohen 'On the Project of a Universal Character' 50.
162 References to Leibniz's interest in the provision of a universal language by eighteenth-century language builders are, as would be expected, very frequent indeed.
163 In particular, material brought to light by Couturat in *La Logique de Leibniz* and *Opuscules et fragments inédits de Leibniz*, Paris 1903.

CHAPTER IV

1 This chapter owes much to the work of previous scholars in the field, and particularly to articles by Émile Pons and Edward Seeber referred to below. Cornelius *Languages in ... Imaginary Voyages* also discusses some of these same tales, and where I have adopted ideas from this book acknowledgment is duly made. However, the section of the chapter devoted to the languages of Veiras, Foigny, and Tyssot de Patot, in which I reach similar conclusions to Cornelius, appeared in the *Journal of the History of Ideas* 24 in 1963 – i.e. two years before the publication of the latter's book, which was apparently being prepared at the same time as my own article. I am grateful to the editorial board of the *Journal of the History of Ideas* for permission to reproduce this article here in an extended and modified form.
2 Gabriel de Foigny's book is better known by the title of its second edition: *Les avantures de Jacques Sadeur dans la découverte et le voiage de la terre australe*, Paris 1692. Before 1676 there had been considerable speculation concerning the existence of this southern continent. Jean Mocquet spoke of it as a 'Paradis terrestre,' and Thévenot, the French geographer, requested Louis XIV in 1663 to send an expedition to discover and chart it. See G. Chinard *L'Amérique et le rêve exotique dans la littérature française au XVIIe et au XVIIIe siècle*, Paris 1913.
3 In *A Journey to the World Under-Ground by Nicholas Klimius*, London 1742, of Baron Ludvig Holberg, published first in Latin in the preceding year, entitled *Nicolai Klimii iter subterraneum*, and Robert Paltock's *Life and Adventures of Peter Wilkins, a Cornishman, Relating his Shipwreck near the South Pole, His Wonderful Passage thro' a Subterraneous Cavern into a Kind of New World*, London 1751

4 *The Man in the Moone*
5 *Histoire comique*
6 See Paul Hazard *La crise de la conscience européenne, 1680–1715*, Paris 1935.
7 Numerous examples could be quoted. Two will perhaps suffice: Trigault *De Christiana expeditione* and Gabriel Sagard Théodat *Le Grand Voyage du pays des Hurons ... avec un dictionnaire de la langue Huronne*, Paris 1632.
8 The best-known of these collections were, of course, Hakluyt *Principal Navigations* and *Purchas his Pilgrimes*.
9 Translation of a statement by Émile Pons in 'Les Langues imaginaires ... Thomas Morus' 589
10 Fontenelle changes Rome to Mreo, Genève to Eenegu, and Soline (Jerusalem) to Mliseo. See Seeber 'Ideal Languages' 593.
11 In the third volume of *La Découverte australe, ou le dédale français*, Paris 1781, the Mégapatagons speak a language which will appear, we are told, 'un peu raboteuse à la première lecture; mais je suis sûr,' hints Restif de la Bretonne, 'qu'on la trouvera bientôt aussi douce, aussi claire, aussi facile à entendre que le français' (445). In case any of his readers are so obtuse as not to have understood, he explains later what his 'secret' is (478).
12 *Utopia* 184
13 *Histoire des Sévarambes* (1677–9) 3: 318
14 *Voyages* (1710) 122
15 Swift *Prose Works* 11: 219
16 *La Terre australe connue* (1676) 170
17 Pons 'Les Langues imaginaires ... Thomas Morus' 592. In Davis 'Bishop Godwin's "Lunatique Language"' 298–9 there are a number of references to strange, made-up languages in medieval drama that were previously unknown to me; see K. Young *The Drama of the Medieval Church*, Oxford 1933, 2:70.
18 'Les Langues imaginaires ... Thomas Morus'
19 See the introduction to J.H. Lupton's edition of the *Utopia*, where the name of Anemolius, a poet-laureate, is derived from the Greek for 'windy' or 'braggart,' *Syphogranti* is shown to be a comic rendering of 'steward' (at the Inns of Court), derived from 'Sty-ward' or keeper of a pig-sty, and *Tranibori* is presented as the 'Benchers' of the Inns, which can be read as 'bench-eaters.'
20 See ibid, facing xciv.
21 M.P. Alexéev 'Les Sources slaves de l'Utopie de Thomas More,' in *Sur l'histoire de la littérature anglaise: études, essais, et recherches*, Moscow-Leningrad 1960, 40–134. This work is known to me only through a summary entitled 'Nouvelles Lumières sur l'*Utopie* de Thomas More' in the *Bibliothèque d'humanisme et renaissance* 24, 1962: 481–2.
22 *Pantagruel* 45–51

23 Ibid 46–7
24 Ibid 48
25 Ibid 50
26 'Les Langues imaginaires ... les "jargons" de Panurge'
27 *The Discovery of a New World (Mundus Alter et Idem) Written Originally in Latin by Joseph Hall, c. 1605: Englished by John Healey, c. 1609* edited by H. Brown, Cambridge, Mass. 1937
28 Ibid 88
29 This question is discussed at length in McColley 'The Date of ... Domingo Gonsales.' According to McColley, the tale was composed unquestionably after 1615 and probably during the years 1627–8. In 'Bishop Francis Godwin' 47 and 51 Merchant suggests from internal evidence that it was first written in 1603–6 and then reworked in 1629–30.
30 *The Man in the Moone* 7
31 See Knowlson 'Note on Bishop Godwin'
32 I am indebted for details on the theory of birds migrating to the moon to T. Harrison 'Birds in the Moon' *Isis* 45, 1954: 323–30. Professor F.M.M. Mieklejohn kindly drew my attention to this article. See also Richard Garnett 'Defoe and the Swallows' *Times Literary Supplement* 13 February 1969.
33 Quoted in Harrison 'Birds in the Moon' 329
34 *The Man in the Moone* 35–6. My discussion of Godwin's musical 'language' follows closely that of my 'Note on Bishop Godwin' referred to above. This was written at the same time as, and quite independently of, Davies 'Bishop Godwin's "Lunatique Language."' Our conclusions on the sources of Godwin's idea are virtually identical. For a fuller discussion of Chinese 'tones' and the detailed composition of Godwin's cypher, see Davies's excellent article.
35 See Cornelius *Languages in ... Imaginary Voyages* 51.
36 *The Man in the Moone* 47
37 Ibid 36
38 The 1657 second edition contains even more errors: clearly its publisher did not understand at all the principles on which Godwin's cypher was based.
39 *Traicté des chiffres* 278
40 *Steganologia* 302–3
41 *Cryptomenytices* 311, 321–6
42 A shorthand writer, John Willis, wrote in *Art of Stenographie* chapter 1, note f that 'by this means may any thing be signified in the night season, by lifting up of Torches; and in the day time, by holding up of Hattes, or such like; or neere at hand by the Fingers. Concerning the Stratagem writeth Whitehorne in his Fireworks; and Baptista Porta de furt. lit. notis. Letters also may be signified by tolling Belles, by shooting of Gunnes: or neere at hand, by any Instrument of musique.'

43 *De occultis literarum notis* book 5, 335–7
44 *Mercury* 142. Chapter 18 is entitled 'Concerning a Language that May Consist Only of Tunes and Musical Notes, without Any Articulate Sound.'
45 For a fuller discussion of the differences between Wilkins's and Godwin's versions see Davies 'Bishop Godwin's "Lunatique Language"' 309–11. Note that Wilkins's decipherment has recently been challenged by J. Bersagel in *Music and Letters* 44, 1968: 195.
46 *Mercury* 143. P. Thicknesse, the eighteenth-century musical amateur, took up Wilkins's challenge in *A Treatise on the Art of Decyphering, and of Writing in Cypher* of 1772. See Davies 'The History of a Cipher' *Music and Letters* 48: 1967.
47 *Mercury* 143
48 *Œuvres libertines* 1: 38–9
49 See Cornelius *Languages in ... Imaginary Voyages* 151–7
50 Seeber 'Ideal Languages' 591
51 To substantiate his suggestion, Seeber quotes Jacques Bernard's remark in 1708 (*Nouvelles de la république des lettres* of 1708, 331) on the two separate languages. It seems likely in fact that this item of information was known some time before that date. James Burnet [Lord Monboddo] refers in *Origin and Progress* 1: 337–8 to such an account in Father Raymond Breton's *Dictionnaire caribe-français*, Auxerre 1665, and to a similar account given by a certain Davies in the reign of Elizabeth. I have not so far traced this latter account.
52 *Œuvres libertines* 1: 39
53 *Pantagruel* 101–6
54 *La Découverte australe*, Paris 1781, 2: 398–9
55 [Béthune] *Relation du monde de Mercure* in *Voyages imaginaires, songes, visions et romans cabalistiques* edited by C.C.T. Garnier, Amsterdam 1787, 16: 203
56 *A Voyage to the World in the Centre of the Earth*, London 1755, 20
57 *The Consolidator* 306–7
58 'Rabelais et Swift'
59 Desfontaines *Le Nouveau Gulliver* 144; Samuel Brunt *A Voyage to Cacklogallinia* with an introduction by Marjorie H, Nicolson, published for the Facsimile Text Society by Columbia University Press, Columbia n.d., 30 and 32; [Ludvig Holberg] *A Journey to the World Under-Ground by Nicholas Klimius*, London 1742, 112–3
60 Swift's satire of the tradition that we have been tracing in the earlier chapters of this book is discussed in the unpublished Master's thesis of Lillian Goodhart 'The Universal Character ... A Study of the Background of Swift's Satire on Language in the Voyage to Laputa' 1952. Among articles on Swift's own games with language, the most important, in

addition to that of Pons already quoted, are probably the following: M.W. Buckley 'Key to the Language of the Houyhnhnms in *Gulliver's Travels*' in *Fair Liberty Was All His Cry* edited by A.N. Jeffares, London, New York 1967, 270–8; P.O. Clark 'A Gulliver Dictionary' *Studies in Philology* 50, 1953: 592–624; I. Ehrenpreis 'Swift's "Little Language" in the *Journal to Stella*' *Studies in Philology* 45, 1948: 80–8; E.D. Leyburn 'Swift's Language Trifles' *Huntington Library Quarterly* 15, 1952: 195–200; H.D. Kelling 'Some Significant Names in *Gulliver's Travels*' *Studies in Philology* 48, 1951: 761–78; R.M. Smith 'Swift's Little Language and Nonsense Names' *Journal of English and Germanic Philology* 53, 1954: 178–96; see also Gros [et al.] 'Langues imaginaires et langage secret chez Swift.'
61 The work was republished in 1705 in a second corrected edition and was translated into French in 1707. It appeared as the second volume of the Library of Impostors, London 1926.
62 The most comprehensive accounts of Psalmanaazaar's life and deception are to be found in P.W. Sergeant *Liars and Fakers*, London 1926; A. Chevalley *La bête du Gévaudan; Psalmanazar; L'affaire Overbury*, Paris 1936; J.A. Farrer *Literary Forgeries*, London 1907; R. Aldington *Frauds*, London 1957.
63 *Formosa* 267–8
64 Ibid 269
65 Ibid facing 268
66 Ibid 269
67 Ibid 271
68 Seeber, in 'Ideal Languages,' was the first to point out that close links exist between the ideal languages and earlier schemes of universal language, although he did not pursue the question of the nature of these links.
69 Von der Mühll in his study *Denis Veiras* wrote 'La langue des Sévarambes est purement imaginaire. De toute cette utopie si réaliste, si généralement basée sur des faits et des institutions authentiques, la langue des Sévarambes est, je crois bien, la partie la plus utopique' (233).
70 We are dependent for our knowledge of the life of Veiras on Ascoli 'Quelques Notes biographiques.' Despite Ascoli's assiduous researches, the facts are relatively few.
71 *La Terre australe connue* (1676) 170
72 Ibid
73 Ibid 172
74 Ibid 173
75 For biographical details, see Lachèvre *Les Successeurs* 3–60.
76 *La Terre australe connue* 171
77 Ascoli 'Quelques Notes biographiques'
78 *Histoire des Sévarambes* part 2, 3: 318

79 *Essay* (1668) 385–6
80 *Harmonie universelle* (1636) 'Livre premier de la voix' proposition 47, 65
81 Wilkins *Essay* 386
82 See Mersenne *Harmonie universelle* 'Livre premier de la voix' proposition 50, 75–7.
83 The idea is further amplified, and, incidentally, also criticized, by Comenius in his manuscript *Panglottia*. See Miškovskà 'Panglottie.'
84 Lodwick 'An Essay towards a Universal Alphabet' (1686) *Philosophical Transactions* 16: 126
85 See *The Diary of Robert Hooke 1672–1680* 69 ('Wed. Nov. 12th. 1673. Lent his new Universall alphabet by Fr. Lodwick') and other entries at later dates.
86 On the relations between Veiras and the movement for a universal, rational grammar, see Cornelius *Languages in ... Imaginary Voyages* 119–32.
87 *Voyages* 120
88 *Grammatica* (1663)
89 See Atkinson *The Extraordinary Voyage ... before 1700* and *The Extraordinary Voyage ... 1700–1720* ; E. Von der Mühll *Denis Veiras* ; McKee *Simon Tyssot de Patot* ; Lavender *The 'Histoire des Sévarambes.'*

CHAPTER V

1 See Bodleian Library, Oxford, Aubrey Ms 13. The last letters I note in the series that have a bearing on the revision or total recasting of Wilkins's *Essay* are from 1683. Andrew Paschall then asks Aubrey for news as to whether Wilkins's book is being issued in Latin (f 87).
2 See Gunther *Early Science in Oxford* 12: 181.
3 For example, the anonymous 'Dialogue sur un caractère universel' in the *Journal littéraire de l'année 1720* 2: 81, and Solbrig 'De scripturae oecumenicae' (1723)
4 Seth Ward died in 1689, Lodwick in 1694.
5 Emery in 'John Wilkins' Universal Language' quotes several later references to the *Essay*.
6 See Brunot *Histoire de la langue française* 5: 134–43, 423–31 ; and for the eighteenth century, ibid 8: part 2 *passim*.
7 See *Nouveaux Mémoires de l'académie royale des sciences et belles-lettres de Berlin, 1782*, Berlin 1784, 11.
8 See ibid 65, 67; and volume for 1784, Berlin 1786, 12. A précis in French of Schwab's interesting dissertation is given by Mérian in the *Nouveaux Mémoires* of the Academy for 1785, 371 ff.
9 On the development of German in the eighteenth century, see the excellent study of Blackhall *The Emergence of German*.
10 Lambert discussed this work of Richeri in the *Nova acta eruditorum ad annos 1766 et 1767 publicata*, Leipzig 1768, 334–44.

11 David 'Un témoin des espoirs ... Kalmar.' Other schemes published during the 1770s were a work by Soave, which I have not been able to consult, *Riflessioni* (1774) and Berger's *Plan ... für alle Nationen* (1779).
12 In particular those which appeared in the *Œuvres philosophiques*: see *Nouveaux Essais sur l'entendement humain* 236–8, 363–4, and the *Historia et commendatio lingua characteristicae universalis quae simul sit ars inveniendi et judicandi* 535–40, both printed in the Raspe edition. A number of texts concerning 'la charactéristique universelle' were also printed three years later in the six-volume edition of the *Opera omnia*, Geneva 1768. See in particular 5: 7–8 (a letter to Remond de Montmort), 11, 540; 6: part 2, 8–9.
13 *Nouveaux Mémoires* (1776) 520
14 In his prize-winning essay of 1772 (*Abhandlung über den Ursprung der Sprache*) on the origins of language, Herder had maintained that neither science nor society as a whole could benefit in any way from attempts to form a universal language. For modern reprint with other fragments by Herder, see Herder *Sprachphilosophische Schriften*.
15 See *Nouveaux Mémoires* (1776) 520.
16 See *Œuvres philosophiques* 1: 60; also the Abbé Copineau *Essai synthétique*.
17 Condillac's theory of the origins of language is discussed briefly in Le Roy's introduction to the above edition; and in greater detail in Harnois *Les Théories du langage* chapter 4 and Kuehner *Theories*. Recently, Aarsleff has published an interesting chapter on some of the material dealt with here in his *Study of Language* chapter 1. See also on eighteenth-century ideas on the origins of language two recent articles by Grimsley, 'Some Aspects of "nature" and "language"' and 'Maupertuis, Turgot and Maine de Biran.'
18 *Traité* 'Discours préliminaire' xiv–xv. All references are to the second edition.
19 Ibid xv–xvi
20 Ibid xxii
21 *Nouveaux Mémoires* (1776) 521
22 Ibid 522–3
23 This was first published as the second and third volumes of the *Monde primitif*. It then appeared separately under the title *Histoire naturelle de la parole* in 1776.
24 *Monde primitif* 2: 'Discours préliminaire'
25 *Encyclopédie méthodique ou par ordre de matières par une société de gens de lettres, de savans et d'artistes etc: grammaire et littérature* 3 vols, Paris 1782–6, 2: 456. Faiguet's *langue nouvelle* is discussed by V.T. Miškovskà in a short article, 'La "Langue nouvelle."'
26 De l'Épée's gestural language is discussed more fully below in appendix A.
27 *Nouveaux Mémoires* (1776) 526

28 Thiébault taught general grammar, first in Berlin, then in the 1790s at the École centrale at the rue St-Antoine in Paris; he was also the author of a *Grammaire philosophique*.
29 *Encyclopédie ou dictionnaire raisonné des sciences, des arts et des métiers, par une société de gens de lettres* 7, Paris 1757: 841
30 *Hermes or a Philosophical Inquiry* preface
31 Paris 1751, 4
32 *César Chesneau Du Marsais* 2–3
33 In the *De augmentis scientiarum*, Francis Bacon in 1623 had voiced the possibility that a philosophical grammar might be formed from a study of particular grammars. Wilkins had referred in the *Essay* to several earlier discussions of the subject: e.g. J. Caramuel's *Praecursor logicus*, 1654–5, and T. Campanella's *Philosophiae rationalis*, 1638. For universal grammars prior to that of Port Royal, see Stojan *Bibliografio* 61–2. Even a brief survey of the history of general grammar would clearly be impossible here. I have found the most useful discussion of the Scholastic and Cartesian origins of general grammar, together with an excellent account of the early evolution of the movement, in Sahlin *César Chesneau Du Marsais* chapter 1. The most recent work on the subject is, of course, Chomsky's important *Cartesian Linguistics*. But see also Harnois *Les Théories du langage* chapters 2 and 3; Brunot *Histoire de la langue française* 6: part 2, 899 ff and ibid 10: part 1, 326 ff. Among earlier works of interest on general grammar are F. Thurot's translation of Harris's *Hermes* (*Hermès ou recherches philosophiques sur la grammaire universelle*, see 'Discours préliminaire'); and le Comte Lanjuinais's introduction to Court de Gébelin's *Histoire naturelle de la parole*.
34 *Grammaire philosophique* vii–viii
35 *Élémens d'idéologie: première partie*
36 Brunot *Histoire de la langue française* 9: part 1, 340
37 *Encyclopédie méthodique ... grammaire et littérature* 2: 456
38 *Nouveaux Mémoires* (1776) 522

CHAPTER VI

1 Although only French schemes are considered here, systems of universal writing or language were produced at the same time in Germany, Portugal, England, and America. As examples, we may note the work of Wolke (1797) and of Dantas (1800), and the rather superficial schemes described in the *Memoirs of the Literary and Philosophical Society of Manchester* (1796 and 1798); see checklist (appendix B).
2 See Couturat and Leau *Histoire de la langue universelle* 29–32; Henricy *La Tribune des linguistes* 1: 81; Clark *International Language* 79.
3 *Monthly Review* 24, September-December 1797: article 24, 562
4 Ibid

5 Ibid
6 *La Tribune des linguistes* 1: 81
7 See Ampère *Correspondance* 1: 5–6, letters from Philippon to Ampère.
8 *Biographie universelle ancienne et moderne*, new edition, Paris 1843, 'Ampère' 1: 597. Ballanche is said to have heard Ampère reciting poetry in the new language. See also Launay *Le Grand Ampère* 32.
9 Launay *Le Grand Ampère* 32
10 See on Condorcet's Ms scheme Granger 'Langue universelle' 197. Large extracts from Condorcet's Ms are reproduced in this article with an introductory commentary by Granger. On Condorcet's relations with Condillac, see Baker 'Un "éloge" officieux de Condorcet.'
11 *Esquisse* 357
12 Granger 'Langue universelle' 219
13 Condorcet *Esquisse* 356–7
14 The secretary of the second class of the Institut, Champagne, mentions in his 'Histoire abrégée des travaux de la classe' (*Mémoires de l'institut national: sciences morales et politiques* 3, Paris an IX: ii) the systems submitted to the class by de Maimieux, Zalkind-Hourwitz, Fournaux, and Montmignon. The *Polygraphie* (1800) of Zalkind-Hourwitz is of the familiar type of numerical language, in which all the words of different languages that have the same meaning are represented by a number in a dictionary. Montmignon's *La Clef de toutes les langues*, which appeared in 1811, follows the same principle of enumerating words. Montmignon had, however, in 1785, published a more interesting *Système de prononciation figurée, applicable à toutes les langues, et exécuté sur les langues française et anglaise* in which the quality of a vowel would be shown clearly by placing below the letter a symbol indicating its pronunciation. This, he believed, would aid readers to pronounce foreign languages but would chiefly be useful in correcting divergencies of orthography and pronunciation (see the *Nouvelle Biographie générale* 36, Paris 1861: 334 for details on the Abbé Montmignon). Of Fournaux's scheme there is now no trace and it does not appear to have been published.
15 According to the *Grand Dictionnaire universel du XIXe siècle* 12, Paris 1874, and the *Enciclopedia Italiana* 26: 439, the term *pasigraphie* was first used in the title of the announcement of de Maimieux's scheme: we have found no earlier use of the term.
16 The forthcoming work was announced, for example, in the *Décade philosophique, littéraire et politique* (Paris an IV) 4, i, num. 57, and in the *Magasin encyclopédique; ou Journal des sciences, des lettres et des arts* (1795) 5: 621, a periodical which was at first directed by the Abbé Sicard, the collaborator of de Maimieux. The pasigraphy was also described in a prospectus published along with the *Relation de M. de Chaumeix, échappé aux Massacres d'Aurai et de Vannes*, Paris 1795 (English translation, London 1795).

17 6: 102–14
18 Ibid 114
19 Goupil-Préfelne *Discours* 3
20 Ibid 4
21 On the 19th of pluviôse, year VI (1798), the Lycée des arts 'a couronné un jeune homme, nommé Sureau, qui dans l'espace de huit heures avait appris les douze règles générales auxquelles cet art est borné, et qui en avait parfaitement saisi le mécanisme. Ce jeune homme a expliqué sur-le-champ, à l'aide des tableaux explicatifs, plusieurs phrases pasigraphiques en cinq ou six langues différentes qu'il ignore, ce qui démontre combien cette science, qui serait si utile, pourrait être facilement pratiquée et propagée' (Noel and Carpentier 'La Pasigraphie'). See also *Magasin encyclopédique*, 1797, 4: 389, and 6: 111–2.
22 *Décade philosophique*, an IX, 1, num. 1: 56
23 He was elected a member of the Société Batave des sciences de Haarlem, was president in 1800 of the Société des observateurs de l'homme, and in 1801 was put forward as a candidate for the vacant seat in the grammar section of the third class of the Institut national, to which, ironically, his collaborator, the teacher of the deaf, Sicard, was in the event elected.
24 Of these memoirs only that of Destutt de Tracy is published in the *Mémoires de l'institut national*. Enquiries made of the secretary of the present Académie des sciences morales et politiques and research in the Bibliothèque de l'institut have failed to discover the procès-verbaux of the meetings at which these schemes of universal language were discussed. Moreover, the memoirs of Roederer, which were almost certainly among the papers of the count in the family's possession, were destroyed by fire in 1939 (letter from the present Count Roederer to the author, 17 October 1961). In the case of de Gérando's two memoirs on the subject, the omission is less important, since his ideas are reproduced in the published *Des signes ou de l'art de penser*.
25 Simon *Une Académie* 219
26 They are as follows:

—	∼	ʃ	ζ	C	⊖	⊕	⊃	⊇	ζ	⊄	/
1	2	3	4	5	6	7	8	9	10	11	12

27 *Monthly Review* 24 (September–December 1797): 563, article 25 on de Maimieux's *pasigraphie*.
28 *Pasigraphie* 5
29 De Maimieux insisted upon the geographical nature of his pasigraphical scheme. In the preface to the Épître familière (1802), he asked 'Comment entendre les mots *carte*, *mappemonde*, *zones*, *degrés*, appliqués à une écriture, si l'on ignore que les Pasigraphes adaptent les procédés géographiques à l'intelligence humaine, donnent une longitude et une latitude fixées à chaque idee et la désignent par les signes de cette latitude' (4). See also Firmas-Périés *Pasitélégraphie* 2, 25–6.

30 Sicard regarded this part of de Maimieux's scheme as of the greatest value for the philosopher. 'Ce *Grand Nomenclateur,*' he wrote, 'est pour le métaphysicien-pratique l'entreprise la plus hardie, la plus piquante et la plus nécessaire, comme tendant à former de l'universalité des idées un système clair, simple et facile à retenir, parce que chaque expression y définit les autres, et que toutes y complettent la définition implicite de chacune' (introductory letter to the *Pasigraphie*).
31 De Maimieux *Pasigraphie* 32
32 Ibid
33 Ibid 5
34 De Maimieux claimed to have arrived at his system quite independently of Wilkins's *Essay*; *Pasigraphie* 65.

CHAPTER VII

1 *Projet d'une langue universelle* 2–3. In an article 'Sur la Pasigraphie' in the interesting cosmopolitan review, *Le Spectateur du Nord*, 6 April 1798: 167, we read: 'Le siècle du Magnétisme animal, des Ballons, de la Liberté et de l'Égalité est fait pour produire des choses extraordinaires,' of which 'la pasigraphie' is considered one of the most exceptional.
2 *Discours de Garat sur l'hommage ... du 'Chant de Départ'* 8
3 Garat 'Analyse de l'entendement' 38–9
4 On the establishment of the École normale see Dupuy 'L'École normale de l'an III' and on this and the Écoles centrales, Hippeau *L'Instruction publique*. Chapters 10 and 11 of Fayet *La Révolution française* are devoted to these schools.
5 On the administrative reorganization of France, see, for example, Lefèbvre *La Révolution française* 13: 172–6, 574.
6 An excellent discussion of the creation of the metric system and the reform of weights and measures may be found in Fayet *La Révolution française*, chapters 14–16. Note also Fayet's account of the establishment of the Bureau des longitudes.
7 To the best of our knowledge, this important preoccupation of the Idéologues has not been discussed at any length. Cailliet in *La Tradition littéraire* makes no mention of the subject; Van Duzer in *Contribution of the Idéologues* refers to it in a short footnote only (98); and Picavet in *Les Idéologues* limits himself to a few references. More recently, Acton, in 'The Philosophy of Language,' has touched briefly on the topic. What is perhaps rather more surprising is that the Idéologues' writings in this field have remained completely neglected by historians of the universal language movement. See recent articles on the Idéologues by Moravia 'Logica e psicologia' and 'Aspetti della "science de l'homme."'
8 The word *idéologie* was first used in the sense of 'the science of the analysis of ideas' in Destutt de Tracy 'Mémoire sur la faculté de penser.'

Before the word was chosen for the new science by Destutt de Tracy there are signs of a certain embarrassment as to what it should be called. Laromiguière used the term *métaphysique* in the *Projet d'éléments de métaphysique*, Toulouse 1793, as did Lancelin in the *Introduction à l'analyse des sciences* part 1. Garat, however, in his course at the École normale dismissed this term, as did de Tracy, because it led so often to confusion 'avec cette science ténébreuse des anciennes écoles.' He went on to describe how Condillac had flirted with the term *psychologie*, how Charles Bonnet also had used it, but how he himself preferred a translation of Locke's phrase, his course being entitled 'L'Analyse de l'entendement' (see *Séances des écoles normales* 1: 148–9).

9 Picavet *Les Idéologues* 23
10 For further discussion of these meetings see: Picavet *Les Idéologues* chapter 1; Van Duzer *Contribution of the Idéologues* chapter 1; Alfaric *Laromiguière et son école* 38 ff; Guillois *Le Salon de Mme. Helvétius*.
11 Simon *Une Académie* 219–20
12 As Condillac's treatment of this question, in the course of which many of Locke's points are taken up, developed, or modified, is discussed fully later, Locke's contribution will not be considered here; for a most useful account see Aarsleff 'Leibniz on Locke on Language.'
13 *Œuvres* 3: 86
14 See *Œuvres* 2: 197–218.
15 An excellent article by Politzer, 'On the Linguistic Philosophy of Maupertuis,' considers Maupertuis as a precursor of von Humboldt and the modern linguistic relativists. See also Grimsley 'Maupertuis, Turgot and Maine de Biran.' This has recently been translated into French and published as an introduction to the three essays of Maupertuis, Turgot, and Maine de Biran (*Sur l'origine du langage; étude de Ronald Grimsley suivie de trois textes*, Geneva and Paris 1971).
16 Michaelis *Beantwortung*
17 'The Philosophy of Language' 202–3
18 Condillac *Œuvres philosophiques* 1: 436
19 Ibid 437
20 Ibid 438
21 Ibid 442
22 Ibid 2: 400
23 Ibid 400–1
24 Ibid 401
25 Ibid 395
26 Ibid 404
27 ' ... c'est elle seule [l'analyse] qui corrigera tout ce qui peut être corrigé, parce que c'est elle seule qui peut faire connaître la génération de toutes nos idées. Aussi les philosophes se sont-ils prodigieusement égarés,

lorsqu'ils ont abandonné l'analyse, et qu'ils ont cru y suppléer par des définitions' (ibid 405).
28 See ibid 400–1. Condillac maintained that progress in the experimental sciences had eventually been made 'parce que les philosophes ont mieux observé, *et qu'ils ont mis dans leur langage la précision et l'exactitude qu'ils avaient mises dans leurs observations. Ils ont donc corrigé la langue à bien des égards, et l'on a mieux raisonné*' (ibid 401, italics mine). Meaningless jargon remained a constant threat to be avoided in scientific thinking.
29 Ibid 400
30 Ibid 420
31 Ibid 409
32 Ibid 420
33 Ibid 469
34 Ibid 427
35 Ibid 466
36 Ibid
37 Ibid 428. Granger takes a rather less sceptical view with respect to Condorcet and Leibniz, where the resemblances are striking, 'Langue universelle' 198–9.
38 *Histoire comparée* part 2, 3: 139. The passage in question reads: 'Les mathématiciens ont inventé une sorte de signes, dont ceux de l'algèbre ne sont qu'une partie; par leur moyen, on trouve aujourd'hui des choses où les anciens ne pouvaient atteindre, et cependant cet art ne gît que dans l'usage et l'application exacte de ces signes. Quel bruit ne faisaient point les anciens de leur cabbale? Ils cherchaient les mystères dans les mots. Ils les auraient trouvé dans une langue exacte qui eût servi non-seulement pour les mathématiciens, mais qui eût porté de la clarte dans toutes les sciences, dans tous les arts et dans toutes les affaires de la vie. Ce n'est pas dans les mystères de la langue hébraïque qu'il faut chercher la cabbale; ce n'est pas dans d'autres idiomes, dans la signification arbitraire des caractères; il faut la chercher dans leur vrai sens et dans l'usage exact de leurs mots.' The essay by Leibniz from which this passage is taken was published, we may note, in both French and German in the Dutens edition of 1768, vol 6, part 2: 6–51; this passage appears on pages 8 and 9.
39 See Smeaton 'Contributions' 87 ff.
40 This memoir, together with a second one on the principles of the methodical nomenclature, given by de Morveau to the Académie des sciences on 2 May 1787, an explanation of the tables by Fourcroy, synonyms of the old and new names, and a memoir on the new characters to be used in chemistry by Hassenfratz and Adet, were all published in Lavoisier *Méthode de nomenclature chimique*. McKie, in *Antoine Lavoisier*, quotes large extracts from Lavoisier's memoir, including his explicit

recognition of a debt to Condillac (198–207). See also Daumas *Lavoisier théoricien et expérimentateur* 60–1. The question of the changes in the nomenclature of chemistry is most fully discussed, however, in Crosland *Historical Studies* part 3.

41 As early as 1786, F. Vicq d'Azyr in the *Traité d'anatomie et de physiologie avec des planches coloriées*, published in Paris, had attempted to reform the nomenclature of anatomy and physiology. These efforts to improve anatomical names were continued by F. Chaussier in the *Exposition sommaire des muscles du corps humain suivant la classification et la nomenclature méthodiques adoptées au cours public d'anatomie de Dijon*, Paris 1789, and by C.L. Dumas in the *Système méthodique de nomenclature et de classification des muscles du corps humain*, Montpellier an v.

42 See Alfaric *Laromiguière et son école* 46. See also Marie-Joseph de Chénier *Tableau historique* 22.

43 Condillac *Œuvres philosophiques* 2: 529. In presenting this complete edition of Condillac's work to the Conseil des anciens, Garat wrote: 'Elle [i.e. Condillac's analytical method] la porte sur la seule langue des hommes qui eût de la précision et de l'exactitude sur *la langue des calculs*, sur l'arithmétique et sur l'algèbre; et cette langue, créée et perfectionnée par tant de génies du premier ordre, reçoit d'une méthode si facile et si simple une nouvelle perfection encore; et tous les artifices de cette belle langue sont si bien dévoilés, si bien démêlés, qu'il ne peut plus être impossible à personne de les transporter dans l'expression des idées de tous les genres, de donner à la langue de la morale et des lois la certitude de la géométrie' (*Discours ... en offrant les œuvres de Condillac* 3).

44 The subject is announced in *Mémoires de l'institut national: sciences morales et politiques* 1, Paris an VI: i–iv. This collection of memoirs will subsequently be referred to as *MIN sc. mor. et pol.*

45 See ibid 3, Paris an IX: vi.

46 The influence of Lancelin's work on Stendhal (Henri Beyle) is discussed most fully in F.M. Albérès *Le Naturel chez Stendhal*, Paris 1956, and in V. Del Litto *La Vie intellectuelle de Stendhal: genèse et évolution de ses idées, 1802–1821*, Paris 1959.

47 See volume 1, *Le premier journal*, introduction and 240 ff.

48 *MIN Sc. Mor. et Pol.* 1: i (italics mine)

49 Ibid ii

50 Ibid

51 Ibid iii

52 One of the contestants, de Gérando, points out the difference between the actual title of the essay subject and the intentions of the Institut in setting it (de Gérando *Des signes et de l'art de penser* 1: xxviii).

53 See, for example, Laromiguière *Leçons de philosophie* 1: 21; Maine de Biran *Œuvres* 1: 276–7.

54 See Maine de Biran *Œuvres* 1: 276–8. Maine de Biran is particularly

violent in his attack on Cabanis, saying that one should be surprised at no paradox that comes from someone who maintains that the brain secretes thought: ' ... dire que le cerveau filtre des pensées, c'est bien la plus grande absurdité, la plus grande impropriété du langage qu'on puisse imaginer' (277–8).
55 The mémoire was first published in the *MIN Sc. Mor. et Pol.* 1: 37 ff.
56 *Œuvres philosophiques* 1: 157
57 *Séances des écoles normales* 1: 231
58 De Gérando and Maine de Biran's treatment of this point is more fully discussed in Acton 'The Philosophy of Language' 207–15.
59 'Je me suis bien trompé,' wrote Maine de Biran, 'ou l'analyse fera voir que cette première question est une question de mot, et la solution purement relative au sens que l'on attache à celui d'*idée*. On parlerait plus métaphysiquement en demandant: existe-t-il quelque opération *volontaire* de l'entendement, indépendamment des signes de convention, et sous ce rapport, la question est très importante et me paraît difficile' (Maine de Biran *Œuvres* 1: 247). See also ibid 271, and de Gérando *Des signes et de l'art de penser* 1, chapter 1.
60 Destutt de Tracy *Élémens d'idéologie: première partie* 345–6
61 De Gérando *Des signes et de l'art de penser* 2: 549
62 Maine de Biran *Œuvres* 1: 263
63 Laromiguière *Leçons de philosophie* 1: 4–5
64 Ibid 6
65 Ibid 23–4
66 'Mémoire de la faculté de penser' 416
67 De Gérando *Des signes et de l'art de penser* 1: xii
68 *Élémens d'idéologie: seconde partie* 394
69 Cabanis *Œuvres philosophiques* 2: 162
70 Lancelin *Introduction à l'analyse des sciences* 1: 182

CHAPTER VIII

1 See *Séances des écoles normales* 2: 38
2 As far as we have been able to discover the commission never made its report, unless the 'Réflexions sur les projets de pasigraphie' of Destutt de Tracy can be regarded as the work of the group mentioned above rather than as the contribution of one of its members. No mention of the report can be found anywhere else in the memoirs of the Institut national.
3 Destutt de Tracy 'Réflexions sur les projets de pasigraphie' 551
4 In the second part of the *Élémens d'idéologie*, Destutt de Tracy wrote: 'Je n'ai pas été plus à l'abri qu'un autre du prestige de ces brillantes chimères; mais le lecteur a pu déjà s'appercevoir que j'en suis bien désabusé, au moins en ce qui concerne l'universalité' (394–5).

5 *Une Académie* 219–20
6 Destutt de Tracy 'Réflexions sur les projets de pasigraphie' 548
7 *Des signes et de l'art de penser* 3: 572
8 Destutt de Tracy *Élémens d'idéologie: seconde partie* 402
9 *Introduction à l'analyse des sciences* 1: 315
10 Ibid
11 De Gérando *Des signes et de l'art de penser* 4: 562
12 *Œuvres philosophiques* 2: 164
13 They are, he wrote, 'un vestige des tems grossiers où nous ne savions pas peindre les mots eux-mêmes, ou un effet du goût qui nous entraîne vers la métaphore et l'allégorie, goût dépravé qui nuit beaucoup à la justesse du raisonnement ... Il vaut toujours mieux dire tout simplement sa pensée quand on le peut; nécessairement elle est rendue avec plus d'exactitude' (*Élémens d'idéologie: première partie* 333).
14 Ibid: *seconde partie* 403–4
15 Destutt de Tracy 'Réflexions sur les projets de pasigraphie' 545–6
16 Lancelin *Introduction à l'analyse des sciences* 1: 313
17 Ibid 309
18 *Des signes et de l'art de penser* 3: 584. The same point is made by Maine de Biran; see *Œuvres* 1: 249
19 *Des signes et de l'art de penser* 1: xxi
20 Ibid 4: 562
21 *Œuvres* 1: 245
22 Ibid 256–7. This recognition of the place of irrationality and passion in human life was typical of the whole cast of Maine de Biran's mind. See on this point Huxley's opening essay in *Themes and Variations*, 'Variations on a Philosopher.'
23 Maine de Biran *Œuvres* 1: 252
24 Ibid 266
25 *Élémens d'idéologie: seconde partie* 405
26 Ibid 405–6
27 *Œuvres* 1: 250
28 De Gérando *Des signes et de l'art de penser* 4: 360
29 See David 'Leibniz et le "Tableau de Cébès."'
30 *Élémens d'idéologie: seconde partie* 412
31 *Des signes et de l'art de penser* 4: 380–1
32 Ibid 381
33 Ibid 382
34 Ibid 383–4
35 Ibid 397–8
36 Ibid 405–6
37 Ibid 407
38 Ibid 412
39 Ibid 418

40 Ibid 428
41 Ibid 433
42 Ibid 434
43 Ibid 438
44 François Thurot, a representative of what Picavet called 'the second generation of Idéologues,' agreed that such a language was an impossibility. 'Quelques hommes de beaucoup d'esprit,' he wrote, 'se sont imaginés qu'il serait même utile de faire une langue universelle, dont tous les éléments fussent déterminés avec assez de soin et de précision pour que l'on pût être sûr d'éviter par ce moyen tous les inconvénients des langues usuelles; ce projet est fort beau, mais absolument impossible à exécuter; car il faudrait pour y réussir que celui qui l'entreprendrait eût des idées parfaitement exactes de tous les objets de connaissance humaine, et c'est ce dont les plus habiles sont assurément très loin, ou plutôt ce à quoi il ne sera jamais donné à aucun homme de parvenir' *Œuvres posthumes de M. Fr. Thurot* 295.
45 Such as 'l'algèbre est une preuve bien frappante que les progrès des sciences dépendent uniquement des progrès des langues' *Œuvres philosophiques* 2: 409
46 De Gérando wrote: 'La perfection absolue dans les travaux de l'esprit, comme dans la pratique de la morale, ne peut donc être comparée qu'à ces limites imaginées par les géomètres pour représenter l'infini, limites dont on s'approche plus ou moins sans les atteindre jamais' (*Des signes et de l'art de penser* 4: 569).
47 Ibid 3: 177
48 Ibid 183
49 Ibid 203-4
50 *Élémens d'idéologie: première partie* 392
51 *Des signes et de l'art de penser* 3: 198-9
52 Ibid 4: 568
53 Ibid 3: 343
54 *Œuvres philosophiques* 2: 168-9
55 'Mémoire sur la faculté de penser' 416-7
56 Prévost *Essais de philosophie* 2: 134
57 De Gérando *Des signes et de l'art de penser* 4: 561-2
58 Lancelin *Introduction à l'analyse des sciences* 1: 316
59 *Des signes et de l'art de penser* 4: 564-5

APPENDIX A

1 This section of the book first appeared in the *Journal of the History of Ideas* 26, October-December 1965: 495-508. I am grateful to the Editorial Board for permission to reproduce it here in a slightly modified form.
2 *The Works of Lucian of Samosata* translated by H.W. and F.G. Fowler, 4

vols, Oxford 1905, 2: 256. Classical pantomime was discussed on a number of occasions in the eighteenth century, reference sometimes being made to Lucian's story. See, for example, the Abbé du Bos's *Réflexions critiques sur la peinture et la poésie*, 1st edition 1719, 6th edition, 3 vols, Paris 1755, 3: 282, and, in the nineteenth century, Thomas Reid's *Essays on the Intellectual Powers of Man* in *The Works of Thomas Reid D.D.* edited by Sir William Hamilton, Edinburgh 1846, 5: 449–50.
3 Preface to Hodgson *The Deaf and Their Problems*. See also Paget 'A World Language.'
4 Histories of the universal language movement such as Couturat and Leau *Histoire de la langue universelle*, Guérard *A Short History*, Pei *One Language*, Monnerot-Dumaine *Précis d'interlinguistique*, and Burney *Les Langues internationales* neglect the idea of gesture as the universal language. Stojan *Bibliografio* has, however, a list of gestural languages for the use of the deaf.
5 For a brief treatment of these questions, see Critchley *The Language of Gesture*.
6 *L'Arte de' cenni* 11–2
7 *Chirologia* 3. On Bulwer see Hodgson *The Deaf and Their Problems* 95–7 and Norman 'John Bulwer, The Chirosopher.' The interest of Bulwer's work for an understanding of early seventeenth-century acting technique is discussed in B.L. Joseph's book *Elizabethan Acting*, London 1951.
8 Ibid 7
9 Ibid 5
10 *Philocophus* dedication
11 Hodgson in *The Deaf and Their Problems*, chapter 7, gives an interesting account of the plight of the deaf-mute in the Middle Ages and in the sixteenth and seventeenth centuries.
12 Quoted in ibid 72–3.
13 *Pantagruel* 101–6; see also *Gargantua*, 3rd edition, edited by J. Plattard, Paris 1946, 123–5, and *Le Tiers Livre* edited by J. Plattard, Paris 1948, 81–4.
14 *Discours de la méthode* part 5: 57–8
15 Romans 10: 17
16 *Surdus loquens* preface. The quotation is taken from the English translation, *The Talking Deaf Man*.
17 A number of factors account for this emphasis upon the teaching of conventional language. First, and most obvious, of course, was the desire to reintegrate the deaf into society by teaching them to speak. Secondly, by means of written language, the deaf son of a nobleman (the usual pupil of the early teachers of the deaf) could retain the rights pertaining to his inheritance and successfully administer an estate. Finally, the written

characters of conventional language seemed to offer to the deaf person an instrument of thought that could stand in place of the spoken word and that gestures did not provide.

18 See Hodgson *The Deaf and Their Problems* 82–4.
19 'A Letter of Dr. John Wallis' 359
20 *Reduction de las letras*
21 Ibid 123–4. The quotation is taken from the English translation by H.N. Dixon, *Simplification* 150.
22 *Philocophus* dedication
23 See Bacon *Philosophical Works* 521 ff and Wilkins *Mercury*.
24 We may note that Leibniz also directed attention to the importance of the deaf man for the philosopher in the *Nouveaux Essais sur l'entendement humain* in *Œuvres philosophiques* 2: 94.
25 There is no modern study of the Abbé de l'Épée. See Berthier *L'Abbé de l'Épée* and Dubief *L'Abbé de l'Épée*.
26 *Institution des sourds et muets* 135
27 De l'Épée's solution has obvious affinities with Locke's theory of ideas as expressed in his *Essay Concerning Human Understanding*.
28 *Institution des sourds et muets* part 2: 47–8
29 Ibid 34
30 See *Cours d'études pour l'instruction du Prince de Parme: grammaire* in Condillac *Œuvres philosophiques* 1: 429–30.
31 *Théorie des signes* 1: 4–5
32 *Cours d'instruction* 496
33 De Gérando wrote, for example, in *Des signes et de l'art de penser* 4: 453, that the deaf 'nous offrent donc un terme de comparaison très-favorable pour juger de ce que l'homme doit à l'usage des langues, pour saisir dans ses principes la génération de nos idées, pour apprécier avec exactitude l'influence des signes.'
34 *Leçons de philosophie* 3: 113
35 *De l'éducation des sourds-muets* 1: 509
36 Ibid 517
37 Ibid 564
38 One of its chief virtues, according to de Gérando, was that in order to explain conventional words by signs, strict definitions had to be given, thereby encouraging clear habits of thought. Thus, he wrote, 'le sourd-muet ... apprend les mots par la grammaire, et la grammaire par la métaphysique; on fait raisonner son esprit avant de chercher à guider sa main, et la langue est pour lui le résultat de la science' (*Des signes et de l'art de penser* 4: 473).
39 It is interesting to note that Sir Richard Paget saw a similar omission as one of the major drawbacks to the institution of his own sign language. See 'A World Language.'

Bibliography

The first part of this list contains only important source works used directly for this volume. Schemes of universal writing and language are referred to in the checklist (appendix B). The list of secondary works is made deliberately rather fuller.

MAJOR WORKS

MANUSCRIPTS

British Museum, London:
  Birch 4279 (Pell papers), ff 104–24 (letters of Haack to Mersenne)
  Sloane Ms 427, f 85
  Sloane Ms 897, ff 32–8 (Lodwick Mss)
  Sloane Ms 932, ff 1–20 (Lodwick Mss)
  Sloane Ms 3991, ff 41–67 ('A Language of Real Characters' signed by Daniel Foote and dated AD 1645)
  Add. Ms 4377 (Birch) *Collectanae Grammaticae*, f 4, f 143, f 144, f 148 (Dalgarno Mss and printed prospectus)
Royal Society, London:
  Mss 3131–7, P1, 53–60
  Classified papers 16, no 2, Cave Beck 'Of Memory'
Bodleian Library, Oxford:
  25287, Aubrey Mss 12 and 13
  Ashmolean Ms 788, ff 49–52
  'De clandestino scripto methodica tractatio a Timotheo Brighto Cantabrigiensi ex libro Johannis Baptistae de furtivis literarum notis' Ms 9804, now Cherry Ms 30
Sheffield University Library, Lord Delamere's collection, Hartlib papers:
  Ephemerides (Hartlib's Ms diary) bundles 18, 24, 31, 47, 52, 71

Bibliothèque Mazarine, Paris:
3788 (1948) 2, 3, and 4
Bibliothèque nationale, Paris:
N.A.F. 6206 f 64, f 89, f 91, f 167, f 168

PRINTED VOLUMES

Acosta, J. *The Naturall and Morall Historie of the East and West Indies: Written in Spanish by Joseph Acosta and Translated into English by E.G.* London 1604

Alhoy, L.-F. *De l'éducation des sourds-muets de naissance, considérée dans ses rapports avec l'idéologie et la grammaire: sujet du discours prononcé à la rentrée de l'École nationale des sourds-muets* Paris an VIII

Amman, J.C. *Surdus loquens, seu methodus, qua, qui surdus natus est, loqui discere possit* Amsterdam 1692

– *The Talking Deaf Man, or A Method Proposed, Whereby He Who Is Born Deaf, May Learn to Speak ... Done out of Latin into English by D.F.M.D.* [Daniel Foot] London 1694; facsimile reprint, Menston 1972, *English Linguistics 1500–1800* no 357

Arnauld, A. and Lancelot, C. *Grammaire générale et raisonnee, contenant les fondemens de l'art de parler, expliquez d'une manière claire et naturelle* Paris 1660

Arnauld, A. and Nicole, P. *La Logique ou l'art de penser* Paris 1662

Aubrey, J. *Aubrey's Brief Lives* edited by Oliver Lawson Dick, London 1949

Bacon, F. *The Philosophical Works of Francis Bacon* edited by Ellis and Spedding with introduction by John M. Robertson, London 1905

Beattie, J. *The Theory of Language in Two Parts: Part I, Of the Origin and General Nature of Speech: Part II, Of Universal Grammar* new edition, London 1788

Beauzée, N.S. *Grammaire générale, ou exposition raisonnée des éléments nécessaires pour servir de fondement à l'étude de toutes les langues* 2 vols, Paris 1767

Bergerac, C. de *Histoire comique par M. Cyrano de Bergerac, contenant les états et empires de la lune* Paris 1657

– *Le Libertinage au XVIIe siècle 8: Les Œuvres libertines de Cyrano de Bergerac, parisien (1619–1655) précédées d'une notice biographique par Frédéric Lachèvre* Paris 1921, 1

Bibliothèque des Sciences et des Beaux-Arts 18, October-December 1762 [Article on search for a universal language]

Bonet, J.P. *Reduction de las letras, y arte para enseñar a ablar los mudos* Madrid 1620

– *Simplification of the Letters of the Alphabet and Method of Teaching Deaf-Mutes to Speak* translated from the original Spanish by H.N. Dixon, with a historical introduction by A. Farrar, Harrogate 1890

Bonifacio, G. *L'Arte de' cenni con la quale formandosi favella visibile, si tratta della muta eloquenza, che non è altro che un facondo silentio* Vicenza 1616

Bonnet, C. *Essai analytique sur les facultés de l'âme* Copenhagen 1760

Boxer, C.R., ed. *South China in the Sixteenth Century, Being the Narratives of Galeote Pereira, Fr. Gaspar da Cruz O.P., Fr. Martin de Rada O.E.S.A., 1550–1575* London 1953

Boyle, R. *The Works of the Honourable Robert Boyle* edited by T. Birch, 5 vols, London 1744

Bright, T. *Characterie: An Arte of Shorte, Swifte, and Secrete Writing by Character, Invented by Timothe Bright, Doctor of Phisike* London 1588

Brosses, C. de *Traité de la formation méchanique des langues et des principes physiques de l'étymologie* 2 vols, Paris an IX [1st edition, Paris 1765]

Brunswick, Duke of [Selenus, G.] *Cryptomenytices et cryptographiae, libri IX* Luneburg 1624

Bulwer, J. *Philocophus, or The Deafe and Dumbe Man's Friend by J.B., Surnamed the Chirosopher* London 1648

[Burnet, G.] *The Life of William Bedell, DD, Bishop of Kilmore in Ireland by G.B.* London 1685

Burnet, J. [Lord Monboddo] *Of the Origin and Progress of Language* 6 vols, Edinburgh and London 1773–92

Cabanis, P.J.G. 'Considérations générales sur l'étude de l'homme, et sur les rapports de son organisation physique avec ses facultés intellectuelles et morales' *Mémoires de l'institut national des sciences et arts pour l'an IV de la République: sciences morales et politiques* 1, Paris, thermidor an VI

– *Corpus général des philosophes français* 44: *Œuvres philosophiques de Cabanis* edited by C. Lehec and J. Cazeneuve, 2 vols, Paris 1956

Chénier, M.-J. de *Tableau historique de l'état et des progrès de la littérature française depuis 1789* 3rd edition, Paris 1818 [1st edition, Paris 1815]

Comenius, J.A. [Komenský] *Janua linguarum reserata aurea, sive seminarium omnium linguarum et scientiarum, hoc est compendiosa methodus latinam et gallicam perdiscendi* Paris 1642

– *Linguarum methodus novissima ... latinae linguae exemplo realiter demonstrata* Leszno 1649

– *J.A. Comenii opera didactica omnia, ab anno 1627 ad 1657 continuata* Amsterdam 1657

– *J.A. Comenii orbis sensualium pictus: hoc est, omnium fundamentalium in mundo rerum et in vita actionum, pictura et nomenclatura ... A Work Newly Written by the Author in Latine and High Dutch ... and Translated into English by Charles Hoole* London 1659

– *The Great Didactic of John Amos Comenius* translated into English and edited with biographical, historical, and critical introduction, London 1910 [1st edition 1896]

– *The Analytical Didactic of Comenius* translated from Latin by Vladimir Jelinck, Chicago 1953

- *The Way of Light* translated by E.T. Campagnac, London 1938
Comiers, C. *Traité de la parole, langues et écritures contenant la stéganographie impénétrable* Brussels 1691
Condillac, E.B. de *Corpus général des philosophes français* 33: *Œuvres philosophiques de Condillac* edited by G. Le Roy, 3 vols, Paris 1946–51
Condorcet, A.N. de *Esquisse d'un tableau historique des progrès de l'esprit humain: ouvrage posthume de Condorcet* n.p. 1795
Copineau, Abbé *Essai synthétique sur l'origine et la formation des langues* Paris 1774
Costadau, A. *Traité historique et critique des principaux signes qui servent pour manifester les pensées* 4 vols, Lyons 1717
Court de Gébelin, A. *Monde primitif, analysé et comparé avec le monde moderne, considéré dans son génie allégorique et dans les allégories auxquelles conduisit ce genre* 9 vols, Paris 1773–82, vols 2 and 3
- *Histoire naturelle de la parole ou grammaire universelle à l'usage des jeunes gens par Court de Gébelin, avec un discours préliminaire et des notes, par M. le Comte Lanjuinais* Paris 1816
Dalgarno, G. *Didascalocophus, or The Deaf and Dumb Man's Tutor, to Which Is Added a Discourse of the Nature and Number of Double Consonants* Oxford 1680; facsimile reprint, Menston 1971, *English Linguistics 1500–1800* no 286
Daube, L. *Essai d'idéologie, servant d'introduction à la grammaire générale* Paris an XI
Décade philosophique littéraire et politique; par une Société de Républicains [afterwards *par une Société de Gens de Lettres*] 29 April 1794–16 September 1804 *passim*
Defoe, D. *The Consolidator, or Memoirs of Sundry Transactions from the World in the Moon* London 1705; facsimile reprint forthcoming from Garland Press
Descartes, R. *Œuvres complètes* edited by C. Adam and P. Tannery, 12 vols, Paris 1897–1910, 1: *Correspondance* (1897)
- *Discours de la méthode* edited by E. Gilson, Paris 1930
Desfontaines, P.F.G. *Voyages imaginaires, songes, visions et romans cabalistiques* edited by C.C.T. Garnier, 15: *Le Nouveau Gulliver ou voyages de Jean Gulliver, fils du Capitaine Lemuel Gulliver*, Amsterdam 1787
Deshayer, P.M. *Lettre sur la pasigraphie à Madame ... par Monsieur P.M.D.H.* Paris 1806
Destutt de Tracy, A.L.C. 'Mémoire sur la faculté de penser' *Mémoires de l'institut national des sciences et arts, pour l'an IV de la République: sciences morales et politiques* 1, Paris, thermidor an VI
- 'Dissertation sur quelques questions d'idéologie' *Mémoires de l'institut national des sciences et arts: sciences morales et politiques* 3, Paris, prairial an IX
- 'Réflexions sur les projets de pasigraphie' *Mémoires de l'institut national*

des sciences et arts: sciences morales et politiques 3, Paris, prairial an IX
- *Élémens d'idéologie: première partie, idéologie proprement dite* 2nd edition, *Paris an* XIII [1st edition, Paris an IX]
- *Élémens d'idéologie: seconde partie, grammaire* Paris an XI
- *Élémens d'idéologie: troisième partie, logique* Paris an XIII
- *Principes logiques, ou recueil de faits relatifs à l'intelligence humaine* Paris 1817

Diderot, D. *Diderot Studies* 7: *Lettre sur les sourds et muets* edited by P.H. Meyer, Geneva 1965

Duret, C. *Le Thrésor de l'histoire des langues de cest univers, contenant les origines, beautés, décadences, mutations ... et ruines des langues hébraïque, chanéenne etc. les langues des animaux et oiseaux* Cologne 1613

Dury, J. *The Reformed School* London [1649]; facsimile reprint, Menston 1972, *English Linguistics 1500–1800* no 319

École normale *Séances des écoles normales recueillies par des sténographes, et revues par les professeurs* 13 vols, new edition, Paris 1800–1 [1st edition, Paris an IV]

Épée, C.M. de l' *La Véritable Manière d'instruire les sourds et muets confirmée par une longue expérience* Paris 1784

Falconer, J. *Cryptomenysis patefacta, or The Art of Secret Information Disclosed without a Key* London 1685

Firmas-Périés, A.C.D. de *Pasitélégraphie* Stuttgart 1811

Gallagher, L.J. *China in the Sixteenth Century: The Journals of Matthew Ricci, 1583–1610* translated from the Latin of Trigault by L.J. Gallagher, SJ, New York 1953

Garat, D.J. 'Analyse de l'entendement' *Séances des écoles normales* 13 vols, Paris 1800–1, vols 1 and 2
- *Corps Législatif: Conseil des Anciens: discours prononcé par le c. Garat en offrant les œuvres de Condillac, à la séance du 3 fructidor an VI* Paris an VI
- *Corps Législatif: Conseil des Anciens: discours de Garat sur l'hommage fait au Conseil des Anciens des premières strophes du 'Chant de départ' écrites avec les caractères pasigraphiques, séance du 13 nivôse, an VII* Paris an VII

Gérando, J.M. de *Des signes et de l'art de penser, considérés dans leurs rapports mutuels* 4 vols, Paris an VIII
- *De la génération des connaissances humaines, mémoire qui a partagé le prix de l'académie de Berlin sur la question suivante: démontrer d'une manière incontestable l'origine de toutes nos connaissances* Berlin 1802
- *De l'éducation des sourds-muets de naissance* 2 vols, Paris 1827
- *Histoire comparée des systèmes de philosophie: deuxième partie, histoire de la philosophie moderne, à partir de la renaissance des lettres jusqu'à la fin du XVIIIe siècle* 2nd edition, 4 vols, Paris 1847

[Godwin, F.] *Smith College Studies in Modern Languages* 19, 1937–9: *The Man in the Moone, or A Discourse of a Voyage Thither by Domingo*

Gonsales, the Speedy Messenger London 1638; reprint of text of 1st edition 'The Man in the Moone and Nuncius Inamimatus'
Gonzalez de Mendoza, J. *Historia de las cosas mas notables rites y costumbres, del gran Reyno de la China con un itinerario del nuevo mundo* Rome 1585
- *Histoire du grand royaume de la Chine, situé aux Indes orientales ... faite en espagnol par R.P. Juan Gonçales de Mendoce de l'ordre de S. Augustin ... mise en français avec des additions en marge, et deux indices, par Luc de la Porte* Paris 1588
Goupil-Préfelne, G.F.C. *Corps Législatif: Conseil des Anciens: discours prononcé dans la séance du Conseil des Anciens, le 18 pluviôse de l'an VI de la République française, par G.F.C. Goupil-Préfelne ... en présentant au conseil l'hommage de la pasigraphie, nouvel art littéraire inventé par le citoyen Jean de Maimieux, ancien major d'infanterie allemande* Paris an VI
Hakluyt, R. *The Principal Navigations, Voiages, Traffiques and Discoveries of the English Nation* London 1598–1600
Harriott, T. *Artis analyticae praxis, ad aequationes algebraicas nova methodo resolvendas* London 1631
Harris, J. *Hermes, or A Philosophical Inquiry Concerning Universal Grammar* London 1751; facsimile reprint, Menston 1968, English Linguistics 1500–1800 no 55
- *Hermès ou recherches philosophiques sur la grammaire universelle. ouvrage traduit de l'anglais de Jacques Harris avec des remarques et des additions par François Thurot* Paris, messidor an IV
Herder, J.G. *Sprachphilosophische Schriften* edited by Erich Heintel, Hamburg 1960
Hérigone, P. *Cursus mathematicus, nova, brevi, et clara methodo demonstratus, per notas reales et universales, citra usum cuiuscumque idiomatis intellectu faciles* [in Latin and French] Paris 1633–44
Hobbes, T. *Leviathan, or The Matter, Forme, and Power of a Commonwealth, Ecclesiasticall and Civill* London 1651
Holder, W. *Elements of Speech: An Essay of Inquiry into the Natural Production of Letters, with an Appendix Concerning Persons Deaf and Dumb* London 1669; facsimile reprint, Menston 1969, English Linguistics 1500–1800 no 49
Hooke, R. *A Description of Helioscopes and Some Other Instruments Made by Robert Hooke, Fellow of the Royal Society* London 1676
- *The Diary of Robert Hooke, 1672–1680* edited by H.W. Robinson and W. Adams, London 1935
- [R.H.] 'Some Observations and Conjectures Concerning the Chinese Characters' *Philosophical Transactions of the Royal Society* 24, 1686
Hourwitz, Z. *Origine des langues* Paris n.d.
- *Lacographie ou écriture laconique, aussi vite que la parole* Paris 1811

Hugo, H. *De prima scribendi origine et universa rei literariae antiquitate* Antwerp 1617

Kircher, A. *Reductio linguarum ad unam* Rome 1660

Lancelin, P.F. *Introduction à l'analyse des sciences, ou de la génération, des fondemens, et des instrumens de nos connaissances* 3 parts, Paris an IX–XI

Laromiguière, P. *Paradoxes de Condillac: discours sur la langue du raisonnement par M. Laromiguière* new edition, Paris 1825

– *Leçons de philosophie sur les principes de l'intelligence ou sur les causes et sur les origines des idées* 3 vols, 4th edition, Paris 1826

Lavoisier, A.L. *Méthode de nomenclature chimique, par MM. Hassenfratz et Adet proposée par MM. de Morveau, Lavoisier, Bertholet et de Fourcroy: on y a joint un nouveau système de caractères chimiques adaptés à cette nomenclature* Paris 1787

Leibniz, G. *Œuvres philosophiques latines et françaises de feu Mr. de Leibnitz tirées de ses manuscrits qui se conservent dans la bibliothèque royale à Hanovre, et publiées par ... R.E. Raspe* Amsterdam and Leipzig 1765

– *Opera philosophica* edited by J.E. Erdmann, Berlin 1840

– *Die philosophischen Schriften von G.W. Leibniz* edited by C.J. Gerhardt, 7 vols, Berlin 1875–90

– *Opuscules et fragments inédits de Leibniz, extraits des manuscrits de la bibliothèque royale de Hanovre par Louis Couturat* Paris 1903

Locke, J. *An Essay Concerning Humane Understanding* London 1690

Magasin encyclopédique; ou Journal des sciences, des lettres et des arts, rédigé par Millin, Noel et Warens 1795, 5 [announcement of de Maimieux's *Pasigraphie*]; 1795, 6 'D'une langue universelle, de la nouvelle Pasigraphie; et par rapprochement, de l'art du sténographe et du télégraphe; de l'écriture en chiffre, et de l'art de déchiffrer cette écriture'; 1797, 6 'Nouveau Rapport sur la Pasigraphie'; 1799, 4 'La Pasigraphie de Sicard'

Maine de Biran, M. *Œuvres de Maine de Biran* edited by P. Tisserand, 14 vols, Paris 1920–39

Maupertuis, P. de *Les Œuvres de M. de Maupertuis* 2 vols, Berlin 1753

Mersenne, M. *La Vérité des sciences contre les sceptiques ou Pyrrhoniens* 4 vols, Paris 1625; facsimile reprint, Stuttgart-Bad Cannstatt 1969

– *Harmonie universelle* Paris 1636; facsimile reprint, introduction by F. Lesure, 2 vols, Paris 1963

– *Correspondance du P. Marin Mersenne Religieux Minime* commencée par Mme Paul Tannery, publiée et annotée par Cornélis de Waard, Paris 1932– [12 vols published to 1972]

Michaelis, J.D. *Beantwortung der Frage von dem Einfluss der Meinungen in die Sprache und der Sprache in die Meinungen ... welche den von der konigl. Academie der Wissenschaften für das Jahr 1759 gesetzten Preis erhalten hat von ... Johann David Michaelis* Berlin 1760

– *De l'influence des opinions sur le langage et du langage sur les opinions:*

dissertation qui a remporté le prix de l'académie royale des sciences et belles-lettres de Prusse, en 1759 [translated by de Mérian and Le Guay de Prémontval] Bremen 1762; includes, as well as the prize essay, a 'Dissertation sur le projet de la langue universelle,' translated into English as 'An Enquiry into the Advantages and Practicability of a Universal Language' London 1769

Milton, J. *Of Education: To Master Samuel Hartlib* London 1644

Monthly Review or, Literary Journal enlarged 19, January-April 1796 [annoucement of de Maimieux's *Pasigraphie*]; 24, September-December 1797 [*Projet d'une langue universelle* of Delormel]; 33, September-December 1800 [*Memoria sobre hum projecto de Pasigraphia*]

More, T. *The Utopia of Sir Thomas More* edited by J.H. Lupton, Oxford 1895

Oughtred, W. *The Key of the Mathematics New Forged and Filed: Together with a Treatise of the Resolution of All Kinde of Affected Aequations in Numbers* London 1647

Peiresc, N.F. de *Les Correspondants de Peiresc* 19, *Le Père Marin Mersenne: lettres inédites de Paris à Peiresc, 1633-1637* Paris 1892

Petty, W. [W.P.] *The Advice of W.P. to Mr. Samuel Hartlib for the Advancement of Some Particular Parts of Learning* London 1647

– *The Petty Papers: Some Unpublished Writings of Sir William Petty* edited from the Bowood papers by the Marquis of Lansdowne, 2 vols, London 1927

– *The Petty-Southwell Correspondence, 1676-1687* edited from the Bowood papers by the Marquis of Lansdowne, London 1928

Porta, J.B. *De occultis literarum notis* Strasbourg 1606

Prévost, P. *Des signes envisagés relativement à leur influence sur la formation des idées* Paris an VIII

– *Essais de philosophie, ou étude de l'esprit humain* 2 vols, Geneva an XIII

Purchas, S. *Purchas his Pilgrimes* London 1625

Rabelais, F. *Pantagruel* edited by J. Plattard, Paris 1946

[Renaudot, E.]*Recueil général des questions traitées ès conférences du Bureau d'Adresse sur toutes sortes de matières, par les plus beaux esprits de ce temps* 4 vols, Paris 1655-6, 1

Rivarol, A. de *De l'universalité de la langue française: discours qui a remporté le prix à l'académie de Berlin* Berlin and Paris 1784

Sacy, S de *Principes de grammaire générale, mis à la portée des enfants, et propres à servir d'introduction à l'étude de toutes les langues* Paris an VII

Saint Martin, L.C. de *Essai sur les signes et sur les idées relativement à la question de l'Institut: déterminer l'influence des signes sur la formation des idées* n.p. an VII

Schott, G. *Schola steganographica* Nuremberg 1665

Schwenter, D. [Janum Herculem de Sunde] *Steganologia et Steganographica* Nuremberg [1620]

Sicard, R.A.C. de *Cours d'instruction d'un sourd-muet de naissance pour*

servir à l'éducation des sourds-muets, et qui peut être utile à celle de ceux qui entendent et qui parlent Paris an VIII
- 'Art de la Parole' *Séances des écoles normales* 13 vols, Paris 1800–1 passim
- *Théorie des signes, pour l'instruction des sourds-muets ... suivie d'une notice sur l'enfance de Massieu* 2 vols, Paris 1808
- *Éléments de grammaire générale appliqués à la langue française* 2 vols, Paris 1808, 3rd edition

Sorel, C. *De la perfection de l'homme où les vrays biens sont considérez, et spécialement ceux de l'âme, avec les méthodes des sciences* Paris 1655
- *La Science universelle* 4 vols, Paris 1637–64, 4: *De l'usage des idées, ou de l'origine des sciences et des arts, et de leur enchaînement; du langage, de l'écriture et des chiffres* Paris 1668 [1st edition, Paris 1664]

Spectateur du Nord, Journal politique, littéraire et moral, [Hamburg] 6, April 1798, 'Sur la Pasigraphie'

Sulzer, J.G. 'Observations sur l'influence réciproque de la raison, sur le langage, et du langage sur la raison' *Histoire de l'académie royale des sciences et belles-lettres de Berlin avec les mémoires tirez des registres de cette académie 1767* Berlin 1769

Swift, J. *The Prose Works of Jonathan Swift* edited by H. Davis, Oxford 1939–62, 11: *Gulliver's Travels* 1941

Tallemant des Réaux, G. *Historiettes* 2 vols, Paris 1960–1

Thiébault, D. 'Précis de la grammaire générale de M. de Beauzée, avec quelques observations critiques sur la doctrine de l'auteur' *Nouveaux Mémoires de l'académie royale des sciences et belles-lettres de Berlin 1771* Berlin 1773
- 'Suite de l'examen analytique de la grammaire générale de M. de Beauzée' *Nouveaux Mémoires de l'académie royale des sciences et belles-lettres de Berlin 1773* Berlin 1775
- 'Observations générales sur la grammaire et les langues' *Nouveaux Mémoires de l'académie royale des sciences et belles-lettres de Berlin 1774* Berlin 1776
- *De l'enseignement dans les écoles centrales* Strasbourg an V
- *Grammaire philosophique, ou la métaphysique, la logique et la grammaire réunies en un seul corps de doctrine* 2 vols, Paris an XI

Thurot, F. *De l'entendement et de la raison, introduction à l'étude de la philosophie* 2 vols, Paris 1830
- *Œuvres posthumes de M. Fr. Thurot: leçons de grammaire et de logique: vie de Reid* edited by P.-C.-F. Daunou, Paris 1837

Trigault, N. *De Christiana expeditione apud Sinas suscepta ab Societate Jesu ex P. Matthaei Ricci ... comentariis, libri 5, auctore N. Trigautio* Augsburg 1615
- *Histoire de l'expédition chrestienne au royaume de la Chine entreprise par les PP de la Compagnie de Jésus ... Tirée de comentaires du P.M. Riccius, par le P.N. Trigault* Lille 1616

Tritheim, J. *Poligraphie, et universelle écriture cabalistique ... traduite par Gabriel de Collange* Paris 1561
- *Libri polygraphiae VI* Strasbourg 1600 [1st edition, Oppenheim 1518]
- *Steganographia* Frankfurt [1606]

Turgot, A.R.J. *Œuvres de M. Turgot, ministre de l'état* 9 vols, Paris 1808–11, in vol 3 'Réflexions sur les langues: annexe de l'article "Étymologie"'

Vater, J.S. *Versuch einer allegemeinen Sprachlehre mit einer Einleitung über den Begriff und Ursprung der Sprache, und einem Anhange über die Anwendung der allegemeinen Sprachlehre auf die Grammatik einzelner Sprachen und auf Pasigraphie* Halle 1801

Vigenère, B. de *Traicté des chiffres, ou secretes manières d'escrire* Paris 1586

Vives, J.L. *Vives: On Education, A Translation of the 'De tradendis disciplinis' of Juan Luis Vives* by Foster Watson, Cambridge 1913

Vossius, G. *De arte grammatica, libri septem* Amsterdam 1630

Wallis, J. *Grammatica linguae anglicanae cui praefigitur, de loquela sive sonorum formatione tractatus grammatico-physicus* Oxford 1653; facsimile reprint, Menston 1969, *English Linguistics 1500–1800* no 142

Wallis, J. *A Treatise of Algebra both Historical and Practical, Shewing the Original, Progress, and Advancement thereof, from Time to Time* London 1685

Wallis, J. 'A Letter of Dr. John Wallis (Geom. Prof. Oxon., and F.R.S.) to Mr. Thomas Beverly; Concerning His Method for Instructing Persons Deaf and Dumb' *Philosophical Transactions of the Royal Society* 20, 1698

Ward, S. and Wilkins, J. *Vindiciae academiarum Containing Some Briefe Animadversions upon Mr. Webster's Book, Stiled, The Examination of Academies* Oxford 1654

Webster, J. *Academiarum examen, or The Examination of Academies* London 1654

Willis, J. *The Art of Stenographie ... Whereunto Is Annexed a Very Easie Direction for Steganographie, or Secret Writing* London 1602

SECONDARY WORKS

BOOKS

Aarsleff, H. *The Study of Language in England, 1780–1860* Princeton 1967

Alfaric, P. *Publications de la faculté des lettres de Strasbourg*, 2nd series, 5: *Laromiguière et son école: étude biographique* Paris 1929

Alston, R.C. *A Bibliography of the English Language from the Invention of Printing to the Year 1800* 7: *Logic, Philosophy, Epistemology, Universal Language* Bradford 1967, 8: *Treatises on Short-hand* Leeds 1966

Ampère, A.M. *Correspondance du grand Ampère publiée par L. de Launay* 3 vols, Paris 1936–43, 1

Anderson, F.H. *The Philosophy of Francis Bacon* Chicago 1948

Appleton, W. *A Cycle of Cathay: The Chinese Vogue in England during the Seventeenth and Early Eighteenth Centuries* New York 1951

Atkinson, G. *The Extraordinary Voyage in French Literature before 1700* New York and Columbia 1920

– *The Extraordinary Voyage in French Literature from 1700 to 1720* Paris 1922

– *Les Relations de voyages du XVIIe siècle et l'évolution des idées: contribution à l'étude de la formation de l'esprit du XVIIIe siècle* Paris 1925

Baguenault de Puchesse, G. *de Condillac: sa vie, sa philosophie, son influence* Paris 1910

Berger, R. *La Question d'une langue universelle* Paris 1946

Berthier, F. *Les Sourds-muets avant et depuis l'Abbé de l'Épée* Paris 1840

Berthier, F. *L'Abbé de l'Épée, sa vie, son apostolat, ses travaux, sa lutte et ses succès* Paris 1852

Berthier, F. *L'Abbé Sicard ... précis historique sur sa vie, ses travaux et ses succès, suivi de détails biographiques sur ses élèves sourds-muets les plus remarquables* Paris 1873

Birch, T. *The History of the Royal Society of London* London 1756

Blackhall, E.H. *The Emergence of German as a Literary Language 1700–1775* Cambridge 1959

Boas, G. *French Philosophies of the Romantic Period* Baltimore 1925

Borst, A. *Der Turmbau von Babel* Stuttgart 1960 vol 3

Bréhier, E. *Histoire de la philosophie* Paris 1926–49, 2: *La Philosophie moderne*: i *Le dix-septième siècle*, ii *Le dix-huitième siècle*, iii *Le dix-neuvième siècle: période des systèmes (1800–1850)*

Brown, H. *Scientific Organizations in Seventeenth-Century France, 1620–1680* Baltimore 1934

Brunot, F. *Histoire de la langue française des origines à 1900* 12 vols, Paris 1905–48: 2: *Le Seizième Siècle*; 5: *Le Français en France et hors de France au XVIIe siècle*; 6: *Deuxième Partie: la langue post-classique*; 8: *Le Français hors de France au XVIIIe siècle*; 9: *La Révolution et l'Empire*

Burney, P. *Les Langues internationales* Paris 1962

Bury, J.B. *The Idea of Progress: An Inquiry into Its Origins and Growth* London 1920

Cailliet, E. *Memoirs of the American Philosophical Society* 19: *La Tradition littéraire des Idéologues* Philadelphia 1943

Cajori, F. *William Oughtred, a Great Seventeenth-Century Teacher of Mathematics* Chicago and London 1916

– *University of California Publications in Mathematics* 1 no 8, 'A List of Oughtred's Mathematical Symbols, with Historical Notes' Berkeley 1920

– *A History of Mathematical Notations* 2 vols, Chicago 1928–9

Bibliography 281

Carreras y Artau, J. *De Ramón Lull a los modernos ensayos de formación de una lengua universal* Barcelona 1946
Charma, M.A. *Essai sur le langage* 2nd edition, Paris 1846
– *Sur l'établissement d'une langue universelle, discours prononcé à la rentrée solennelle des facultés de l'académie de Caen, le 15 novembre 1855* Paris 1856
Chomsky, N. *Cartesian Linguistics* New York and London 1966
Clark, W.J. *International Language: Past, Present, and Future with Specimens of Esperanto and Grammar* London 1907
Clarke, M.L. *Classical Education in Britain, 1500–1900* Cambridge 1959
Cornelius, P. *Languages in Seventeenth- and Early Eighteenth-Century Imaginary Voyages* Geneva 1965
Couturat, L. *La Logique de Leibniz d'après des documents inédits* Paris 1901
– *A Plea for an International Language* London 1903
– *On the Application of Logic to the Problem of a Universal Language* translated by F.G. Donnan, London 1910
Couturat, L. and Leau, L. *Histoire de la langue universelle* Paris 1903
Critchley, M. *The Language of Gesture* London 1939
Crosland, M.P. *Historical Studies in the Language of Chemistry* London 1962
Damiron, P. *Essai sur l'histoire de la philosophie en France au XIXe siècle* Paris 1828
Daumas, M. *Lavoisier théoricien et expérimentateur* Paris 1955
David, M. *Le Débat sur les écritures et l'hiéroglyphe au XVIIe et XVIIIe siècles et l'application de la notion de déchiffrement aux écritures mortes* Paris 1965
Drezen, E. *Historio de Mondo-Lingvo* Moscow 1928
Dubief, E. *L'Abbé de l'Épée et l'éducation des sourds-muets* Paris n.d.
Dumesnil, G. *La Pédagogie révolutionnaire* Paris 1883
Durrant, E.D. *The Language Problem: Its History and Solution* Rickmansworth 1943
Duruy, A. *L'Instruction publique et la Révolution* Paris 1882
Espinasse, M. *Robert Hooke* London 1956
Farrar, E. *Language and Languages* London 1878
Fayet, J. *La Révolution française et la science, 1789–1795* Paris 1960
Ferraz, M. *Histoire de la philosophie pendant la Révolution, 1789–1804* Paris 1889
Firth, J.R. *The Tongues of Men* London 1937
Funke, O. *Zum Weltsprachenproblem in England im 17 Jahrhundert: G. Dalgarno's 'Ars Signorum' und J. Wilkins' 'Essay towards a Real Character and a Philosophical Language'* Heidelberg 1929
Funke, O. *Englische Sprachphilosophie im späteren 18 Jahrhundert* Berne 1934

Galland, J.S. *Northwestern University Studies in the Humanities* 10: *An Historical and Analytical Bibliography of Cryptology* Evanston 1945

Gillot, H. *La Querelle des anciens et des modernes en France de 'La Défense et illustration de la langue française' aux 'Parallèles des Anciens et des Modernes'* Paris 1914

Godechot, J. *Les Institutions de la France sous la Révolution et l'Empire* Paris 1951

Gove, P.B. *The Imaginary Journey in Prose Fiction: A History of Its Criticism and a Guide for Its Study, with an Annotated Check List of 215 Imaginary Voyages from 1700 to 1800* new edition, London 1961

Guérard, A.L. *A Short History of the International Language Movement* London 1922

Guillois, A. *Le Salon de Mme. Helvétius: Cabanis et les Idéologues* Paris 1894
– *La Marquise de Condorcet, sa famille, son salon, ses amis, 1764–1822* Paris 1897

Gunther, R.T. *Early Science in Oxford* 14 vols, Oxford 1922–45: 4: *The Philosophical Society* [of Oxford] ; 12: *Dr. Plot and the Correspondence of the Philosophical Society of Oxford*

Guyot, C. and R.T. *Liste littéraire philocophe ou catalogue d'étude de ce qui a été publié jusqu'à nos jours sur les sourds-muets* Groningen 1842

Harnois, G. *Les Théories du langage en France de 1660 à 1821* Paris 1929

Havette, R. *Bibliographie de la sténographie française* Paris 1906

Henderson, P.A. *The Life and Times of John Wilkins, Warden of Wadham College, Oxford* Edinburgh and London 1910

Henricy, C. *La Tribune des linguistes* 2 vols, Paris 1858–9

Hippeau, C. *L'Instruction publique en France pendant la Révolution* Paris 1881

Hodgson, K.W. *The Deaf and Their Problems: A Study in Special Education* London 1953

Huxley, A. *Themes and Variations* London 1950

Iverson, E. *The Myth of Egypt and Its Hieroglyphs in European Tradition* Copenhagen 1961

Jacob, A. [Erdan, A.] *Congrès linguistique: les révolutionnaires de l'A-B-C* Paris 1854

Jesperson, O. *Language: Its Nature, Development and Origin* London 1922

Jesperson, O. *The Philosophy of Grammar* London 1924

Jones, R.F. *Ancients and Moderns: A Study of the Background of the Battle of the Books* Washington 1936, 2nd edition *Ancients and Moderns: A Study of the Rise of the Scientific Movement in Seventeenth-Century England* St Louis 1961

Jones, R.F. [et al] *The Seventeenth Century: Studies in the History of English Thought and Literature from Bacon to Pope by Richard Foster Jones, and Others Writing in His Honor* Stanford [1951]

Jones, R.F. *The Triumph of the English Language* London 1953
Joyau, E. *La Philosophie en France pendant la Révolution, 1789–1795: son influence sur les institutions politiques et juridiques* Paris 1893
Kauppi, R. *Acta philosophica Fennica* fasc. 12: *Über die Leibnizsche Logik* Helsinki 1960
Keatinge, M.W. *Comenius* [an abridged translation of the *Didactica magna*] New York and London 1931
Kennedy, A.G. *A Bibliography of Writings on the English Language from the Beginnings of Printing to the End of 1922* new edition, New York 1961
Keynes, G.L. *John Ray: A Bibliography* London 1951
– *Dr. Timothie Bright, 1550–1615: A Survey of His Life with a Bibliography of his Writings* London 1962
Kneale, W. and M. *The Development of Logic* Oxford 1962
Koester, W. *Geschichtliche Forschungen zur Philosophie der Neuzeit* 2: *Joseph Marie Degérando als Philosoph* Paderborn 1933
Kuehner, P. *Theories on the Origin and Formation of Language in the Eighteenth Century in France* Philadelphia 1944
Lach, D.F. *Asia in the Making of Europe* 1: *The Century of Discovery* Chicago 1965
– *China in the Eyes of Europe: The Sixteenth Century* Chicago 1968
Lachèvre, F. *Le Libertinage au XVIIe siècle* 10: *Les Successeurs de Cyrano de Bergerac* Paris 1922
Launay, L. de *Le Grand Ampère d'après des documents inédits* Paris 1925
Lavender, T.E. *The 'Histoire des Sévarambes' of Denis Veiras* Cambridge, Mass. 1938
Lefebvre, G. *La Révolution française: peuples et civilisations* 13, new edition, Paris 1963
Leigh, C.W. *Catalogue of the Library for Deaf Education* Manchester 1932
Lenoble, R. *Mersenne: ou la naissance du mécanisme* Paris 1943
Lenoir, R. *Condillac* Paris 1924
Le Roy, G. *La Psychologie de Condillac* Paris 1937
Lévy-Bruhl, L. *History of Modern Philosophy in France with Portraits of the Leading French Philosophers* London and Chicago 1899
Lewis, C.I. *A Survey of Symbolic Logic* Berkeley 1918
Ludwig, H. *Marin Mersenne und seine Musiklehre* Berlin 1935
Madinier, G. *Conscience et mouvement: étude sur la philosophie française de Condillac à Bergson* Paris 1938
McKee, D.C. *The Johns Hopkins Studies in Romance Literatures and Languages* 40: *Simon Tyssot de Patot and the Seventeenth-Century Background of Critical Deism* Baltimore 1941
McKie, D. *Antoine Lavoisier: Scientist, Economist, Social Reformer* London 1952

Meister, A. *Die Anfänge der Modernen Diplomatischen Geheimschriften* Paderborn 1902
Migliorini, B. *Lingua e Cultura* Rome 1948
Monnerot-Dumaine, M. *Précis d'interlinguistique générale et spéciale* Paris 1960
Morel, O. *Essai sur la vie et les travaux de Marie-Joseph, Baron de Gérando* Paris 1846
Mornet, D. *Les Origines intellectuelles de la Révolution française, 1715–1787* Paris 1933
Moser, H. *Grundriss einer Geschichte der Weltsprache* Berlin 1888
Mühll, E. Von der *Denis Veiras et son 'Histoire des Sévarambes,' 1677–1679* Paris 1938
Muller, M. *Lectures on the Science of Language Delivered at the Royal Institution of Great Britain in February, March, April, and May 1863* 2nd series, London 1864, lecture 2
Nicolson, M.H. *Smith College Studies in Modern Languages* 17, 1936: *A World in the Moon: A Study of the Changing Attitude towards the Moon in the Seventeenth and Eighteenth Centuries*
– *Voyages to the Moon* New York 1948
Ogden, C.K. *Debabelization: With a Survey of Contemporary Opinion on the Problem of a Universal Language* London 1931
Ogden, C.K. and Richards, I.A. *The Meaning of Meaning: A Study of the Influence of Language upon Thought and of the Science of Symbolism* London 1923
Ornstein, M. *The Role of Scientific Societies in the Seventeenth Century* Chicago 1928
Paget, R. *Human Speech* London 1930
Parker, I. *Dissenting Academies in England* Cambridge 1914
Pei, M. *One Language for the World* New York 1958
Picavet, F. *Les Idéologues, essai sur l'histoire des idées et des théories scientifiques, philosophiques, religieuses ... en France depuis 1789* Paris 1891
Pinot, V. *La Chine et la formation de l'esprit philosophique en France 1640–1740* Paris 1932
Pitman, I. *A History of Shorthand* 3rd edition, London 1891
Pope, W. *The Life of the Right Reverend Father in God, Seth, Lord Bishop of Salisbury and Chancellor of the most Noble Order of the Garter* London 1697
Potter, S. *Language in the Modern World* Harmondsworth 1960
Powell, A. *John Aubrey and His Friends* London 1948
Purver, M. *The Royal Society: Concept and Creation* London 1967
Rambosson, J. *Origine de la parole et du langage parlé* Paris 1881
Rigaud, S. *Correspondence of Scientific Men of the Seventeenth Century,*

Including Letters of Barrow, Flamsteed, Wallis, and Newton 2 vols, Oxford 1841–62
Rossi, P. *Clavis universalis arti mnemoniche e logica combinatoria da Lullo a Leibniz* Milan and Naples 1960
Rowbotham, A.H. *Missionary and Mandarin: The Jesuits at the Court of China* Berkeley and Los Angeles 1942
Sahlin, G. *César Chesneau Du Marsais et son rôle dans l'évolution de la grammaire générale* Paris 1928
[Salisbury Cathedral] *Catalogue of the Books in the Cathedral Library of Salisbury* London 1880
Schapiro, J.S. *Condorcet and the Rise of Liberalism* New York 1934
Scholem, G. *On the Kabbalah and its Symbolism* London 1965
Scott, J.F. *A History of Mathematics from Antiquity to the Beginnings of the Nineteenth Century* London 1958
Sicard, A. *Les Études classiques avant la Révolution* Paris 1887
Simon, J. *Une Académie sous le Directoire* Paris 1885
Spinka, M. *J.A. Comenius, That Incomparable Moravian* Chicago 1943
Sprat, T. *The History of the Royal Society of London, for the Improving of Natural Knowledge* London 1667
Stebbing, L.S. *A Modern Introduction to Logic* London 1930
Stimson, D. *Scientists and Amateurs: A History of the Royal Society* London 1949
Stojan, P.E. *Bibliografio de internacio linguo* Geneva 1929
Streit, R. *Bibliotheca missionum* 11 vols, Munster and Aachen 1916–36, vols 4 and 5
Taylor, F.S. *The Alchemists: Founders of Modern Chemistry* London 1951
Thomson, T. *History of the Royal Society from Its Institution to the End of the Eighteenth Century* London 1812
Turnbull, G.H. *Samuel Hartlib: A Sketch of His Life and His Relations to J.A. Comenius* London 1920
– *Hartlib, Dury and Comenius: Gleanings from Hartlib's Papers* London 1947
Urban, W.M. *Language and Reality: The Philosophy of Language and the Principles of Symbolism* London 1939
Van Duzer, C.H. *The Johns Hopkins University Studies in Historical and Political Science* series 53, no 4: *Contribution of the Idéologues to French Revolutionary Thought* Baltimore 1935
Vaughan, R. *The Protectorate of Oliver Cromwell* 2 vols, London 1839
Vernier, L. *Étude sur Voltaire grammairien et la grammaire au XVIIIe siècle* Paris 1888
Vial, F. *Trois Siècles d'histoire de l'enseignement supérieur en France* Paris 1936
Wallace, K.R. *Francis Bacon on Communication and Rhetoric, or The Art of*

Applying Reason to Imagination for the Better Moving of the Will Chapel Hill 1943
Watson, F. *The English Grammar Schools to 1660: Their Curriculum and Practice* Cambridge 1908
— *The Beginnings of the Teaching of Modern Subjects in England* London 1909
Weld, C.R. *A History of the Royal Society, with Memoirs of the Presidents* London 1848
Willcock, J. *Sir Thomas Urquhart of Cromartie* Edinburgh and London 1899
Williamson, G. *The Senecan Amble* Chicago 1951
Yates, F. *The Art of Memory* London 1966
Yost, R.M. *Leibnitz and Philosophical Analysis* Berkeley 1954
Young, R.F. *A Bohemian Philosopher at Oxford in the Seventeenth Century: George Ritschel of Deutschkahn, 1616–1683* n.p. [1926]
— *Comenius in England* London 1932

ARTICLES

Aarsleff, H. 'Leibniz on Locke on Language' *American Philosophical Quarterly* 1, 1964: 165–88
Abercrombie, D. 'Forgotten Phoneticians' *Transactions of the Philological Society* 1948: 1–34 reprinted in *Studies in Phonetics and Linguistics* London 1965: 47–75
Acton, H.B. 'The Philosophy of Language in Revolutionary France' *Proceedings of the British Academy* 45, 1959: 207–15
Allen, D.C. 'Some Theories of the Growth and Origin of Language in Milton's Age' *Philological Quarterly* 28, 1949: 5–16
Allen, P. 'Scientific Studies in the English Universities of the Seventeenth Century' *Journal of the History of Ideas* 10, 1949: 219–53
Allen, W.S. 'Ancient Ideas on the Origin and Development of Language' *Transactions of the Philological Society* 1948: 35–60
Andrade, E.N. da 'The Real Character of Bishop Wilkins' *Annals of Science* 1, 1936: 4–12
Ascoli, G. 'Quelques Notes biographiques sur Denis Veiras d'Alais' *Mélanges Lanson* Paris 1922: 165–77
Baker, K.M. 'Un "Éloge" officieux de Condorcet: sa notice historique et critique sur Condillac' *Revue de synthèse* 88, 1967: 227–51
Barnett, P. 'Theodore Haak and the Early Years of the Royal Society' *Annals of Science* 13, 1957: 205–18
Bennett, J. 'An Aspect of the Evolution of Seventeenth-Century Prose' *Review of English Studies* 17, 1941: 281–97
Ceñal, R. 'Un anónimo español citato por Leibniz' *Pensamiento* 2, 1946: 201–3

Cherpack, C. 'Warburton and Some Aspects of the Search for the Primitive in Eighteenth-Century France' *Philological Quarterly* 36, 1957: 221–33
Christensen, F. 'John Wilkins and the Royal Society's Reform of Prose Style' *Modern Language Quarterly* 7, 1946: 179–87, 279–90
Clarapède, E. 'Rousseau et l'origine du langage' *Annales de la société Jean-Jacques Rousseau* 24, 1935: 95–120
Cohen, A. 'Jean Le Maire and la musique almérique' *Acta Musicologica* 35, 1963: 175–81
Cohen, J. 'On the Project of a Universal Character' *Mind* 63, 1954: 49–63
David, M. 'De Gérando et le triple problème de l'écriture du xviie au début du xixe siècle' *Revue philosophique* 144, 1954: 401–11
- 'Un Témoin des espoirs du xviiie siècle: Kalmar et sa langue philosophique (1772)' *Revue historique* 215, 1956: 283–9
- 'Leibniz et le "Tableau de Cébès" (*Nouveaux Essais* 1, iv, chapter iii, § 20) ou le problème du langage par images' *Revue philosophique* 151, 1961: 39–50
Davies, H.N. 'Bishop Godwin's "Lunatique Language"' *Journal of the Warburg and Courtauld Institutes* 30, 1967: 296–316
Delsart, A. 'De la pasigraphie ou écriture universelle' *L'Investigateur, journal de l'institut historique* 9, 2nd series, 1849: 78–81
DeMott, B. 'Comenius and the Real Character in England' *Publications of the Modern Language Association of America* 70, 1955; 1068–81
- 'Science versus Mnemonics: Notes on John Ray and on John Wilkins' *Essay towards a Real Character and a Philosophical Language*' *Isis* 48, 1957: 3–12
- 'The Sources and Development of John Wilkins' Philosophical Language' *Journal of English and Germanic Philology* 57, 1958: 1–13
Dieckmann, L. 'Renaissance Hieroglyphics' *Comparative Literature* 9, 1957: 308–21
Elliott, R.W. 'Isaac Newton's "Of an Universall Language"' *The Modern Language Review* 52, 1957: 1–18
Emery, C. 'John Wilkins' Universal Language' *Isis* 38, 1947–8: 174–85
Fargher, R. 'The Literary Criticism of the Idéologues' *French Studies* 3, 1949: 53–66
- 'The Retreat from Voltairianism, 1800–1815' *The French Mind: Studies in Honour of Gustave Rudler* Oxford 1952: 220–37
Freeman, E. 'A Proposal for an English Academy in 1660' *The Modern Language Review* 19, 1924: 291–300
Fisch, H. 'Puritans and the Reform of Prose Style' *English Literary History* 19, 1952: 229–48
Fisch, H. and Jones, H.W. 'Bacon's Influence on Sprat's History of the Royal Society' *Modern Language Quarterly* 12, 1951: 399–406
Funke, O. 'On the Sources of John Wilkins' Philosophical Language (1668)' *English Studies: A Journal of English Letters and Philosophy* 40, 1959: 208–14

Gerhardt, D. 'Zur Problematik der künstlichen Weltsprachen' *Studium Generale* 4, 1951: 192–203

Granger, G.G. 'Langue universelle et formalisation des sciences. Un fragment inédit de Condorcet' *Revue d'histoire des sciences et leurs applications* 7, 1954: 197–204

Grimsley, R. 'Some aspects of "nature" and "language" in the French Enlightenment' *Studies on Voltaire and the Eighteenth Century* 56, 1967: 659–77

– 'Maupertuis, Turgot and Maine de Biran on the origin of language' *Studies on Voltaire and the Eighteenth Century* 62, 1968: 285–307

Gros, L.G., Richer, J., Canseliet, E., Pons, E. 'Langues imaginaires et langage secret chez Swift' *Cahiers du Sud* 46, 1957: 3–44

Hendrich, J. 'Mersenne, Le Maire, Descartes a Komenský' *Český časopis filologický* 2, 1944: 181–4

– 'Umělý jazyk podlé Jana Amosa Komenského' *Jednotná škola* 2, 1946–7: 298–301

Herder, K. 'Sir Thomas Urquhart's Universal Language' *Notes and Queries* 201, 1956: 473–6

Hesse, M.B. 'Hooke's Philosophical Algebra' *Isis* 57, 1966: 67–83

Houghton, W.E. Jr 'The English Virtuoso in the Seventeenth Century' *Journal of the History of Ideas* 3, 1942: 51–73, 190–219

Hunt, H.J. 'Logic and Linguistics – Diderot as "Grammairien-Philosophe"' *The Modern Language Review* 33, 1938: 215–29

Iversen, E. 'Hieroglyphic Studies of the Renaissance' *The Burlington Magazine* 100, 1958: 15–21

Johnson, F.R. 'Gresham College: Precursor of the Royal Society' *Journal of the History of Ideas* 1, 1940: 413–38

Jones, R.F. 'Science and English Prose Style in the Third Quarter of the Seventeenth Century' *Publications of the Modern Language Association of America* 45, 1930: 977–1009

– 'The Attack on Pulpit Eloquence in the Restoration' *Journal of English and Germanic Philology* 30, 1931: 188–217

– 'Science and Language in England of the Mid-Seventeenth Century' *Journal of English and Germanic Philology* 31, 1932: 315–31

Kaye, F.B. 'Mandeville on the Origin of Language' *Modern Language Notes* 39, 1924: 136–42

Knowlson, J. 'A Note on Bishop Godwin's *Man in the Moone*: The East Indies Trade Route and a "Language" of Musical Notes' *Modern Philology* 45, 1968: 357–61

– 'Jean Le Maire, the Almérie, and the "musique almérique": A Set of Unpublished Documents' *Acta Musicologica* 40, 1968: 86–9

Lach, D.F. 'Leibniz and China' *Journal of the History of Ideas* 6, 1945: 436–45

Lawton, H.W. 'Notes sur Jean Baudoin et sur ses traductions de l'anglais' *Revue de littérature comparée* 6, 1926: 673–81

- 'Bishop Godwin's *Man in the Moone*' *Review of English Studies* 7, 1931: 23–55
LeGuin, C.A. 'Roland de la Platière and the Universal Language' *The Modern Language Review* 55, 1960: 244–9
Lenoir, R. 'Psychologie et logique de Destutt de Tracy' *Revue philosophique* 84, 1917: 527–56
- 'Condillac' *Revue philosophique* 95, 1923: 225–75
McColley, G. 'The Pseudonyms of Francis Godwin' *Philological Quarterly* 16, 1937: 78–80
- 'The Date of Francis Godwin's *Domingo Gonsales*' *Modern Philology* 35, 1937–8: 47–60
- 'John Wilkins, a Precursor of John Locke' *Philosophical Review* 47, 1938: 642–3
McCracken, G. 'Athanasius Kircher's Universal Polygraphy' *Isis* 39, 1948: 215–28
McDonald, H. 'Another Aspect of Seventeenth-Century Prose' *Review of English Studies* 19, 1943: 33–43
Merchant, W. 'Bishop Francis Godwin, Historian and Novelist' *Journal of the Historical Society of the Church in Wales* 5, 1955: 45–51
Miškovskà, V.T. 'La Panglottie de J.A. Komenský' *Philologica Pragensia* 2, 1959: 97–106
- 'Langue philosophique et religion au xviie siècle' *Communio Viatorum* 2, 1959: 335–42
- 'Empirisme ou invention à la base lexicale de la Panglottie?' *Acta Comeniana* 20, 1961: 189–97
- 'La "Langue nouvelle" de l'Encyclopédie française' *Philologica Pragensia* 4, 1961: 123–5
- 'Comenius (Komenský) on Lexical Symbolism in an Artificial Language' *Philosophy* 37, 1962: 238–44
Moravia, S. 'Logica e psicologica nel pensiero di Destutt de Tracy' *Rivista critica di storia della filosofia* 19, 1964: 169–213
- 'Aspetti della "science de l'homme" nella filosofia degli idéologues' *Rivista critica di storia della filosofia* 21, 1966: 398–425
Noel, F. and Carpentier, L. 'La Pasigraphie' *Nouveau Dictionnaire des origines, inventions et découvertes ... dans les arts, les sciences, la géographie, le commerce, l'agriculture* 2 vols, Paris 1827, 2: 357
Norman, H.J. 'John Bulwer, the Chirosopher' *Proceedings of the Royal Society of Medicine* 36, 1943: 589–602
Paget, R. 'A World Language' *Nature* 151, 1943: 80
Patrick, J.M. 'A Consideration of *La Terre australe connue* by Gabriel de Foigny' *Publications of the Modern Language Association of America* 61, 1946: 739–51
Politzer, R.L. 'On the Linguistic Philosophy of Maupertuis and Its Relations to the History of Linguistic Relativism' *Symposium* 17, 1963: 5–14

Pons, É. 'Les Langues imaginaires dans le voyage utopique: un précurseur, Thomas Morus' *Revue de littérature comparée* 10, 1930: 592–603
- 'Les Langues imaginaires dans le voyage utopique: les "jargons" de Panurge dans Rabelais' *Revue de littérature comparée* 11, 1931: 185–218
- 'Les Langues imaginaires dans le voyage utopique: les grammairiens, Vairasse et Foigny' *Revue de littérature comparée* 12, 1932: 500–32
- 'Rabelais et Swift: à propos du Lilliputien' *Mélanges offerts à M. Abel Lefranc par ses élèves et ses amis* Paris 1936: 219–28
Pulgram, E. 'An International Language – When?' *Modern Language Journal* 32, 1948: 50–68
Salmon, V. 'Joseph Webbe: Some Seventeenth-Century Views on Language-Teaching and the Nature of Meaning' *Bibliothèque d'humanisme et renaissance* 23, 1961: 324–40
- 'Problems of Language-Teaching: A Discussion among Hartlib's Friends' *The Modern Language Review* 59, 1964: 13–24
- 'Language-Planning in Seventeenth-Century England: Its Context and Aims' *In Memory of J.R. Firth* London 1966: 370–97
- 'The Evolution of Dalgarno's "Ars signorum"' *Studies in Language and Literature in Honour of Margaret Schlauch* Warsaw 1966: 353–71
Schinz, A. 'La Question d'une langue internationale artificielle' *Revue philosophique* 60, 1905: 24–44, 157–72
Seeber, E. 'Ideal Languages in the French and English Imaginary Voyage' *Publications of the Modern Language Association of America* 60, 1945: 586–97
Smeaton, W.A. 'The Contributions of P.-J. Macquer, T.O. Bergman and L.B. Guyton de Morveau to the Reform of Chemical Nomenclature' *Annals of Science* 10, 1954: 87–106
Smith, C. 'Aspects of Destutt de Tracy's Linguistic Analysis as Adopted by Stendhal' *The Modern Language Review* 51, 1956: 512–21
- 'Destutt de Tracy's Analysis of the Proposition' *Revue internationale de philosophie* 82, 1967: 475–85
Stimson, D. 'Dr. Wilkins and the Royal Society' *Journal of Modern History* 3, 1931: 539–63
- 'Puritanism and the New Philosophy in Seventeenth-Century England' *Bulletin of the Institute of the History of Medicine* 3, 1935: 321–34
- 'Comenius and the Invisible College' *Isis* 23, 1935: 377–88
- 'Amateurs of Science in Seventeenth-Century England' *Isis* 31, 1939: 37–47
- 'Hartlib, Haak, and Oldenburg Intelligencers' *Isis* 31, 1939: 309–26
Svoboda, K. 'Komenského názory na řeč' *Český časopis filologický* 1, 1943: 220–33
Syfret, R.L. 'The Origins of the Royal Society' *Notes and Records of the Royal Society of London* 5, 1948: 75–137
Turnbull, G.H. 'Samuel Harlib's Influence on the Early History of the Royal

Society' *Notes and Records of the Royal Society of London* 10, 1953: 101–30

Van Slee, J.C. 'Simon Tyssot de Patot, professeur à l'École illustre de Deventer, 1690–1729: sa vie et ses œuvres' *Revue du dix-huitième siècle* 4, 1917: 200–19

Vinson, J. 'Les Antécédents du Volapuk: l'australien de Jacques Sadeur' *Revue de linguistique* 35, 1902: 41–6

Yates, F.A. 'The Art of Ramon Lull: An Approach to It through Lull's Theory of the Elements' *Journal of the Warburg and Courtauld Institutes* 17, 1964: 115–73

Index

Aarsleff, Hans 13, 86, 143 n17, 164 n12
Académie Royale des Sciences 28, 173
Acosta, Joseph 16, 76 n41
Acton, Harold 5 n4, 163 n7, 166, 178 n58
Adam 9, 12, 13, 67, 72, 136, 212
alchemy and its symbols 76, 79, 117
Alembert, Jean Le Rond d' 142
algebra and its symbols 21–2, 69, 76, 152, 169, 170
Almérie 51
Alsted, Johann-Heinrich 14, 84, 85, 86
Amman, Johann 215
Ampère, André-Marie 151–2, 230
Anderson, James 231
Andreae, Johann Valentin 14, 86
Aquinas, Thomas 79
Arabic numerals 21, 54, 69, 70, 79; as symbols in universal language schemes 48, 59, 61–3, 108, 219
Aristotle and Aristotelian 17, 34, 73, 79, 84, 85, 101; categories of ideas 78
Arithmeticus nomenclator (1654) 74, 108, 226, 227

ars combinatoria (*art combinatoire*) 4, 21, 69–72
Ascham, Roger 31
astrological symbols 45, 54, 79
Aubrey, John 59 n61, 82 n66, 84, 88, 139, 228; on revision of Wilkins's *Essay* (1668) 102–6
Augustine 215
Augustus Caesar 206
Austral continent 112

Babel, confusion of tongues at 4, 9–11, 46, 86, 136, 212, 221
Bacon, Francis 24, 25, 34, 40, 62, 84, 86, 97, 198, 217; on communication 15–16; on Chinese character-writing 44, 56; on imperfections of language 36–7, 41, 164, 169
Ban 52
Baradère 149, 155
Baudoin, Jean 122
Beale, John 20 n48, 81
Beauzée, Nicolas 146, 147, 148
Bébian, Roch-Ambroise 223
Becher, Johann 6, 21, 61, 63, 108, 132, 226
Beck, Cave 11, 21, 23, 25 n74, 41,

42, 61–3, 81, 226
Bedell, William 10, 15, 53, 224
Belon, Pierre 7
Berger, C.G. 141 n11, 230
Bergerac, Cyrano de 70 n17, 112, 122–3
Bergman, Tobern 173
Berlin, Royal Academy of 140, 142, 165
Béthune, Chevalier de 124
Beveridge, William 47, 224
Bibliander, Theodore 44
Bibliothèque nationale, Paris 51 n32, 54 n44
birds, migration 118
Bisterfeld 84
Bodleian Library, Oxford 23 n60, 47 n8, 47 n12–14, 82 n66, 84, 88 n89, 95 n95, 102, 103 n125–8, 104 n130–4, 104 n136, 105 n138–41, 106 n143, 106 n147–8, 139 n1, 224, 228
Boehme, Jacob 14, 86
Bonet, Juan Pablo, on gestural signs 216–7
Bonifacio, Giovanni, on gestural signs 211, 212
Bonnet, Charles 163 n8, 165
Boswell, Sir William 20, 47
botanical character 73, 76, 81
Boyle, Robert 8, 11, 29, 34, 75 n37, 102; on a common writing 9, 21; on verbal ambiguity 37, 40
Bridges, Noah 19
Bright, Timothy 19, 20, 44, 77
British Museum, London 81 n62, 95 n96
Brosses, Charles de 13, 168 n10; on a primitive language 143–5
Brown, William 231
Bruno, Giordano 87
Brunot, Ferdinand 8 n3, 27 n83, 28 n84, 140 n6, 147 n33, 148 n36

Brunt, Samuel 125
Buckingham, Duke of 133
Bulwer, John 212–3, 216, 217, 225; on signs of the deaf 214
Bureau d'Adresse 23, 26
Burnet, Gilbert 10, 53, 224
Burnet, James (Lord Monboddo) 123 n51
Butet, P.R.F. 231

Cabala 13, 14, 76, 77, 78, 84, 85, 86, 88; and Lullism 71 n21, 82–3
Cabanis, Pierre 173, 186; on signs and thought 177–8, 182; on scientific nomenclature 205
Calvin, Jean 27 n83
Campagnac, E.T. 227
Cardano, Girolamo 18
Cavendish, Sir Charles 75
Cavendish, Sir Thomas 117
Cerutti 142
Champagnolle, de la 45 n5, 47, 49, 79 n50, 224
characteristica universalis (caractéristique universelle) 3, 91, 109, 141
Charles I 47
Chinese character-writing 4, 16, 54, 56, 59; and the universal character 18, 19, 23, 24–7, 44, 45, 46, 55, 77; defects of 26–7, 38, 62, 219; tonal system 119
Code civil 163
Colonna, Francesco 23
Combinatorian Jews 84
Comenius (Komenský) 4, 6, 8, 12, 14, 33, 39, 51, 52, 74, 75 n35, 87, 130, 135, 227; on religious harmony 10, 11, 15; reforms in language teaching 31–2, 34, 36; criticisms of Latin 32; and classes of words 77; and John Wilkins 57, 97; and a philosophical

language 55, 88, 96, 132; *Via Lucis* (1668) 10, 11, 32, 43, 56 n48, 57, 74, 75, 84, 88, 102 n119, 132, 227
common ideas 16–17
Condillac, Étienne Bonnot de: on origins of language 143; on signs and thought 163 n8, 164–70, 173, 177, 179, 181, 182, 202, 204, 205, 208, 209; on language and the sciences 173–4, 183, 188, 189, 203; on a philosophical language 170–1, 184, 185, 192, 195; and Leibniz 171–2; and the signs of the deaf man 217, 219, 221
Condorcet, Antoine-Nicholas de 183, 184, 202; on a philosophical language 152–3, 230
Cornelius, Paul 4, 13 n18, 98 n103, 112 n1, 119, 122 n49, 136
Court de Gébelin, Antoine 13, 145
Couturat, Louis 44 n1; on Leibniz 107–10
Cowley, Abraham 35
Cruz, Gaspar da 24
cryptography 25, 54, 57, 70, 77, 122, 132; and a common writing 17–19; and Godwin's musical cipher 119–21
Cyprian 19

Dalgarno, George 3, 11, 15, 43, 72, 74, 75, 76, 85, 91, 95–101 *passim*, 108, 131, 141, 150, 157, 171, 187, 226; *Ars signorum* (1661) 11, 20, 22, 43, 81, 89–90, 96, 131, 226
Dantas Pereira, J.M. 150 n1, 231
Daunou, Pierre 173
David, Madeleine 17, 19 n40, 45 n6–7, 107 n149, 108 n156, 141, 194 n29
deaf man: signs of 15, 95, 96, 214–23; teaching of 215–23

Décade philosophique 155
Defoe, Daniel 125
Delamere, Lord, Mss collection 224, 225
Delormel, Jean 3; universal language 150–1, 162, 230
DeMott, Benjamin 14 n25, 43, 57 n51, 73 n24, 74 n31, 81, 86, 99 n108, 102, 225
Descartes, René 8, 11, 16, 22, 29, 52, 141, 171, 198; on imperfections of language 39; on a universal character 3, 39, 44, 48, 51, 224; on a philosophical language 55, 65–6, 91, 95, 107, 132, 139, 197; and Lull 84, 88; on the deaf 215
Desfontaines, P.-F. Guyot 125
Destutt de Tracy, Antoine-Louis-Claude 5, 149, 173; and *idéologie* 148, 153, 163 n8; on pasigraphy 155, 184–7, 192, 195; on language and thought 164, 178–82, 202, 204, 206, 208
Dialogue sur un caractère universel 229
Diderot, Denis 217, 221
Digby, Sir Kenhelm 75
Doni 51
Douet, Jean 10, 18, 19, 23, 45–7, 49, 54, 55, 79 n50, 224
Dryden, John 118
Dury, John 33, 34, 35

Écoles centrales 148, 155, 163
École normale 162, 163, 183 n1
educational reforms: in seventeenth-century England 30–6; in the 1790s in France 163
Egypt: *see* hieroglyphic writing
Elliott, R.W. 226
Elyot, Sir Thomas 31

emblems 17–18, 23
Emery, Clark 98 n103, 101, 102 n118, 140 n5
encyclopaedia 85, 109, 198
English: prose style 4, 15; development of the language 28
Épée, Charles-Michel de l': on gestural signs 146, 194, 221, 222, 223; methodical signs as a universal language 217–220
Erasmus, Desiderius 30

Faiguet, J. 3, 146, 149, 229
Farce de Pathelin 116
Firth, J.R. 4
Fleurieu 184
Foigny, Gabriel de 112, 114, 129, 228; *langue australienne* 130–2; written character 132–3
Fontenelle, Bernard Le Bovier de 114
Formosan (Psalmanaazaar's fake language) 115, 125–9, 228; alphabet 127; Lord's Prayer in 128–9
Fourcroy, Antoine François de 173
Frederick II 142
French: rise of 30; as an international language 140–1
Frisichius, Joachim 228
Fuller, Dr 54
Funke, Otto 86, 98 n103

Galilei, Galileo 28
Garat, Dominique-Joseph 5, 149, 162, 163 n8, 164; on *pasigraphie* 173, 183, 184; on signs and thought 178, 202
Gassendi, Pierre 8, 52
Gay, John 118
Genesis, divine gift of language 9–14
Gérando, Joseph-Marie de 5, 155, 164, 172; on signs and thought 175, 177 n52, 178, 179, 181, 182, 184, 202, 203, 204, 207, 208; on a philosophical language 184, 185, 187, 188, 189; on literature and science 186; contradictions in the philosophical language 192–3; on a 'hieroglyphic' form of universal character 193–4; on a universal character of root-signs 194–6; on a universal character of simple ideas 196–7; on a universal character based on a division of concepts 197–9; on Wilkins's *Essay* 199–200; on de Maimieux's *Pasigraphie* 200–1; on gestural signs 221 n33, 222–3
German, development of 28
gestural signs 15, 16, 193, 194; in the imaginary voyage 123–4; as a universal language 146, 184, 211–23; as a natural language 212, 216–18
God 9, 71, 84, 86, 136, 215
Godwin, Francis (Bishop) 57, 70 n17, 122; *The Man in the Moone* 56, 112, 117–19
Gonzalez de Mendoza, Juan 24
Goupil-Préfelne, G.F.C. 155
Grammaire générale: *see* universal grammar
grammar: teaching of 30–1; grouping of related words in 77–8
Grammont, Scipion de 31
Gruterus, Janus 19
Guyton de Morveau 173

Haack, Theodore 19, 20 n43, 28, 29, 51, 53, 75
Hakluyt, Richard 113 n8
Hall, John 34 n100, 35
Hall, Joseph 116–17
Hardy, Claude 48
Harriot, Thomas 22, 106 n146
Harris, James 147

Hartlib, Samuel 9, 11, 15, 20 n43, 21, 28 n86, 29, 45 n5, 52 n35, 57, 58, 75, 76, 81, 84, 225; on education 33–5 *passim*; *Ephemerides* 20, 29, 47, 52 n35, 53, 54, 75, 76 n39, 78 n47, 224
Hayne, Thomas 78 n47
Healey, John 117
Hebrew 12, 14, 50, 52, 56, 73, 86, 131, 145
Helvétius 185
Helvétius, Madame 164, 173
Herder, Johann Gottfried 142
Hérigone, Pierre 22, 106 n146
hieroglyphic writing 16, 17, 19, 22–4, 46, 48, 62, 76, 79, 108, 194
Hobbes, Thomas 40, 75 n36
Holberg, Ludwig 112 n3, 122, 125
Holder, William 61
Holmesby, Capt. John 125
Holyband, Claudius 77
Homer 47
Hooke, Robert 11, 35, 228; and Wilkins's *Essay* 100–5 *passim*
Horapollo 23
Hourwitz, Zalkind 153 n14, 231
Hugo, Hermann 24, 25, 44–5; on common ideas 16–17
Huron Indians 113
Huxley, Aldous 190 n22
Huyghens, Christian 52

ideas, classification of 20, 21, 43, 56, 65, 66, 71–4, 76–8, 81, 85, 87, 91, 98, 99–101, 102, 105–7, 108, 109
Idéologues 163; and Condillac 172–3; competition on signs and thought 176–82; on a philosophical language 164, 183–209
Institut national 155, 162, 163, 166, 173, 184; competition on influence of signs on thought 174–82, 184–5, 279

Italian: development of 27–8
Iversen, E. 22 n57, 23
Izquierdo 88

Johnson, Rev. 10, 53–4, 224
Jones, Richard Foster 14, 15 n26, 34 n102, 36, 37 n107, 41 n122, 86
Jones, Row[land] 229

Kalmar, Georgius 141, 229
Keogh, John 139, 228
Kinder, Philip 23, 47–8, 61, 79 n50, 224
King, Sir Robert 53
Kinner, Cyprian 73, 74, 75, 81, 225
Kircher, Athanasius 6, 8, 13, 15, 106 n146, 141; *Polygraphia nova* (1663) 21, 61, 84, 108, 227; and Lullism 84, 88, 107
Klimius, Nicholas 112, 122

Labbé, Philippe 11, 42, 45 n7, 137, 138, 227
Lambert, Jean 141
Lancaster, James 117
Lancelin, P.F. 163 n8, 164, 175, 178, 183, 184, 202, 207; on defects of languages 182; on a philosophical language 186–7
language: revealed 4, 9, 12–14, 23, 55, 124, 136, 143; pansophic 10–11; language-learning 29, 30–1, 33–6; language-teaching reforms 31–6; defects of existing languages 16, 30–4, 36–9, 181–2; origins of language 143–6; and advancement of learning 4, 5, 8, 15, 34–6, 40, 41, 42–3, 55; and thought 164–5; Condillac on 166–72; discussion in the 1790s 172–82; the perfect language, the Idéologues on 183–209; *see* vernacular

langue matrice 49–50, 55, 136
Laromiguière, Pierre 5, 163 n8, 164, 173, 177 n53, 184; on signs and thought 180–1, 202; on gestural signs 184, 221, 222
Latin 28, 29–31, 35, 36, 88, 140; as an international language 7–8; criticisms of 30–3
Launay, Louis de 152
Lavinheta, de 83, 106 n146
Lavoisier, Antoine 173, 203
Le Bret 122
Le Breton, J. 184
Le Maire, Jean 45 n5, 49, 51–2, 68, 79 n50, 225
Le Roy, Georges 172
Leibniz, Gottfried 3, 6, 8, 13, 22, 65 n2, 91, 95, 149, 152, 153, 171, 181, 187, 192, 197, 204, 207, 209, 217 n24; on a universal character 107–11, 132, 139, 141, 142, 194, 219, 227; and Lullism 84, 107; and Condillac 172
lexicons 77–8
lingua humana: *see* language, revealed
Linschoten, Jan Huygen van 117
Lloyd, William (Dr) 99
Locke, John 19, 206, 218 n27; on language and thought 164–6, 169, 181
Lodwick, Francis 11, 38 n112, 72, 74, 75, 76, 131, 225; *A Common Writing* (1647) 57–61, 77, 225; revision of Wilkins's *Essay* 103–5, 228; universal alphabet 136, 139, 228
Lombard, Nicholas 24 n70
Louis XIII 45, 52
Lucian of Samesota 211
Lull, Ramon and Lullism 71 n21, 76, 77, 78, 80, 88 n89, 95, 106, 107; and the Cabbala 82–3; and the universal character 82–91
Luther, Martin 27 n83, 28

McColley, Grant 117 n29, 119
Macquer, Pierre-Joseph 173
Magasin encyclopédique 153, 155 n21
Maimieux, Joseph de, and the *Pasigraphie* (1797) 153–60, 162, 164, 198, 199, 221; judged by de Gérando 200–1
Maine de Biran, M. 5, 164, 165 n15; on signs and thought 175, 177, 178, 179, 184; on a philosophical language 187, 192, 202, 204, 206, 208; on mathematics 188, 189; on moral ideas 190–1
Martin de Rada 24
mathematics 15; and the universal character 21–2; signs of 188–90, 202
Maupertuis, Pierre-Louis Moreau de 165
memory systems 48, 78–82, 87, 102; and universal language schemes 81–2
Mersenne, Marin 4, 8, 11, 19, 22, 25 n74, 28, 29, 39, 44, 45 n5, 48, 49, 50 n24, 50 n26, 51 n27–8, 51 n33, 52 n35, 53, 84 n78, 95, 106 n146, 121, 132, 141, 224, 225; on revealed language 12; and Le Maire 51–2; on a philosophical language 55, 66–72, 139; on a 'natural' language 66–8, 134, 135; and the English language planners 75; on memory 81; and Lullism 84, 88; on a 'combinatory' language 68–72; *Harmonie universelle* (1636) 39, 66, 67, 68, 69, 70, 71, 75, 84, 88, 134, 135
Mexican picture-writing 76, 79, 108, 194

Michaelis, J.D. 165
Milton, John 33
mime 211
Mirandola, Pico della 82
Miškovská, V.T. 68 n10, 135 n83, 146 n25, 227
Monthly Review 151, 156 n27
moon, imaginary voyages to 112, 117–22
moral ideas 190–1, 204
More, Sir Thomas 114–15, 116, 129
musical notation 51, 54, 59, 79; as a cipher 119–22
mysticism, continental 14, 86, 87

Napoleon 155, 164
Newton, Sir Isaac 8, 22, 226
nomenclatures of science 4, 169, 170, 173, 203–4
Northmore, Thomas 230–1

Oldenburg, Henry 29
Olivet, Abbé d' 142
Oughtred, William 22

Paget, Sir Richard 68 n10, 211, 223 n39
Pansophia 10, 11, 84, 97
Paracelsus 117
Pascal, Blaise 225
Paschall, Andrew 84, 88, 139; revision of Wilkins's *Essay* 103–6, 228
Pasigraphie: see Maimieux, Joseph de
Patot, Tyssot de, ideal language of 114, 129, 130, 136–8, 229
Peiresc, Nicholas Claude Fabri de 8, 11, 22, 68, 71, 81
Pell, John 20 n43, 22, 75 n36
Pepys, Samuel 19, 99
Petty, William 8, 11, 34, 35, 37, 40, 42, 47, 73, 75

Picavet, François 163, 164 n10, 202 n44
Pigot, Thomas 82 n66, 84, 88; revision of Wilkins's *Essay* 103–6, 139, 228
Plato 12, 17, 215
Plouquet, Godefroi 141
Pluche, Abbé 147
Ponce de León, Pedro 216
Pons, Émile 112 n1, 114 n10, 115, 116, 125, 129 n68
Pope, Alexander 118
Porta, Joan Baptista 18, 120
Port-Royal, *Grammaire générale* of 136, 147
Prévost, Pierre 164, 175, 178, 206
Psalmanaazaar, George, fake Formosan language of 115, 125–9, 228
Puritanism 4; attitude towards language 33–6, 39; attacks on Latin 33
Pythagorean, 84

Rabelais, François 37, 115, 116, 123, 129, 215
Rambosson, J. 223
Ramus, Petrus 79, 84
Ray, John 8, 78, 82, 99; revision of Wilkins's *Essay* 102–5
Reid, Thomas 211 n2
religious harmony 10–12, 15, 161
Restif de la Bretonne, Nicolas-Edmé 114, 124
Ricci, Matthew 24, 119
Richelieu, Cardinal 49, 51
Richeri 141
Ritchel, George 88 n89, 106
Rivarol, Antoine de 141
rhetoric, in the Renaissance 212
Rochot, Bernard 20 n43, 49
Roederer, Pierre-Louis 155, 184
Romberch, J. Host de 79
Rosicrucian 13, 14

Rossellius, Cosmos 79
Rossi, Paolo 4, 15, 37, 78, 81, 83
    n69, 84 n74, 85 n80, 86, 107 n153
Royal Society of London 4, 11, 28,
    36, 40, 41, 43, 81, 84, 98, 99, 136,
    139; attitude towards language
    36, 40–1, 43; committee for revision of Wilkins's *Essay* 102–7,
    228; *Philosophical Transactions*
    29, 136, 139, 229

Sahlin, Gunvor 147
St Helena, Island of 117
St Petersburg, Imperial Academy of
    140
Salmon, Vivian 5, 7 n1, 12 n16, 18
    n35, 20, 44, 47, 57 n52, 57 n55, 61
    n62, 73 n25, 74 n30, 75 n33–4, 76
    n38–9, 76 n42, 77, 78 n47, 84 n74,
    86, 97, 98 n103, 103 n123
Scholem, Gershom 83
schools in England, reforms 29–36
Schott, Gaspar 74 n29, 108, 132, 227
Schwab, Jean Christophe 141
Schwenter, Daniel [Janum Herculem
    de Sunde] 18, 120
secret-writing: *see* cryptography
Seeber, Edward 112 n1, 114 n10,
    123, 129 n68
Selenus, Gustav, Duke of Brunswick
    18, 120
Shorthand-writing 25, 44, 46, 77;
    and secret-writing 19–20; and a
    universal character 20–1, 95
Sicard, Roch-Ambroise Cucurron de
    149, 153, 155 n23, 156 n30, 194,
    220–2, 223
Sièyes, Emmanuel Joseph 173
Simon, Jules 164, 184
Sinibaldo de Mas, Don 119
Soave, Francesco 141 n11, 229
Solbrig, David 139 n3, 229

Sorel, Charles 23, 45 n5, 48, 49, 50,
    52
Spectateur du Nord 162 n1
Sprat, Thomas 40–1, 100 n113
standardization of weights and
    measures 163
Stendhal 175
Sturm, Johann C. 228
Sudre, Jean 119
Sulzer, J.G. 165
Sumner, Mr 53
Swift, Jonathan 114, 115, 116, 124,
    125, 129
symbolic logic 110

Tallemant des Réaux, Gédéon 48,
    49, 51
Teneriffe 118
Thiébault, Dieudonné: on nomenclature of primitive language 142–6;
    on general grammar 146–9, 230
Thurot, François 202 n44
Tiro 19
Tisserand, Pierre 175
travellers' reports 8, 22, 113, 117
Trigault, Nicholas 24, 38 n112, 113
    n7, 119
Tritheim, Johann 18, 28, 84 n78,
    106 n146
Turgot, A.R.J. 165
Turin, Royal Academy of 140

universal alphabet 136, 139, 225,
    228
universal character: early schemes
    of, *see* Douet, Champagnolle,
    Kinder, Vallées, Le Maire, Johnson; of root-signs 56–61, *see*
    Lodwick; of musical notes 56, 70,
    119–21; of arithmetical numbers
    see Beck, Becher; a philosophical
    language 5, 56, 57, 65, 66, 69–72,
    73, 74, 75, 76, 79, 81, 84, 85, 88,

91, 95, 96, 97, 98, 99, 100, 101, 102, 103, 104, 105–7, 219, see Descartes, Mersenne, Dalgarno, Wilkins, and Leibniz; as a mirror of reality 8, 15, 26, 42–3, 52, 63–4, 73, 74, 76, 87, 88, 96, 97, 100, 101; as an instrument of analysis 9, 43, 91, 96, 106, 108, 109, 110, see also ideas, classification of, and 'technical words'; and the first language of mankind 9–15, 131; and Chinese character-writing 24–7; and mathematics 21–2; and memory systems 78–82; and Lullism 82–91; and Republican ideals 161–2; advantages of 8, 30, 41, 42, 46, 47, 48, 50, 54–5, 65, 68–9, 88, 95–7, 101, 103–4, 109–10, 161–2; criticisms of 50–1, 54, 63, 101–2, 185, 192; de Gérando's criticisms 193–9; de Gérando on Wilkins's *Essay* 199–200; de Gérando on de Maimieux's *Pasigraphie* 200–1
universal grammar 4, 136, 146–9, 182; and logic 147–9
universal language movement, histories of 3, 151, 211
universities, in England 35
Urquhart, Sir Thomas 75, 76, 135, 225, 226; on languages 33, 37; on categories of ideas 73; on memory systems 80–1

Valeriano, Bolzani Giovanni 23
Vallées, des 48–51, 55, 224
Vater, Johann 231
Veiras, Denis, language of Severambians 114, 129, 133–6, 137, 138, 152, 228
verbal disputes, removed 17, 96, 110
vernacular, rise of 27–30; use by the scientist 28
Vienne Plancy, de 25, 26, 61, 139, 228
Vietà, F. 21
Vigenère, Blaise de 17, 120
Villiers, de 45 n7, 52
Vives, Juan 7, 30, 32
Vossius, Gerhard 24
voyages, authentic 8, 22, 113, 117, 129, 137
voyages, imaginary, ideal languages in 112–38
Voyage to the World in the Centre of the Earth 124, 125

Waard, Cornélis de 49
Waite, J. 61
Wallis, John 8, 22, 61, 102, 216
Walton, B. 25 n74
Ward, Seth 8, 11, 20, 47, 73, 75, 131, 197; on primitive language 14, 87, 88; on algebraic symbolism 22; and Wilkins's *Essay* 74, 76, 84, 95, 98; and revision of Wilkins's *Essay* 102–7, 228
Webbe, Joseph 31
Webster, John 14, 25, 34, 35, 42
Wilkins, John 8, 11, 14, 20, 22, 34, 56, 59, 75, 108, 131, 134, 135, 140, 141, 150, 187, 205, 217; on confusion of tongues 10, 17; on common ideas, 17; on Chinese characters 24–7; on defects of Latin 32–3; on defects of language 37–8; and Comenius 56–7; on memory aids 81–2; on a 'natural' language 15, 87–8; on a musical cipher 121; *Mercury* (1641) 18, 24, 56–7, 84 n78, 97, 98, 121, 225; *Essay* (1668) 11–12, 17, 21, 26, 27, 32, 37, 38, 43, 59, 63 n68, 73, 74, 76, 82, 87, 88, 91,

97, 134, 135, 140, 160, 227; revision of *Essay* 102–7; *Essay* judged by de Gérando 199–200
Wilkins, Peter 112, 125
Williams, J. 230
Willis, John 19, 20, 120 n42

Willoughby, Francis 8, 78, 99
Wolke, C.H. 150 n1, 231
Wren, Christopher 102

Yates, Frances 78, 79, 83, 85 n79, 87, 91

UNIVERSITY OF TORONTO ROMANCE SERIES

1 Guido Cavalcanti's Theory of Love
  J.E. SHAW

2 Aspects of Racinian Tragedy
  JOHN C. LAPP

3 The Idea of Decadence in French Literature 1830–1900
  A.E. CARTER

4 Le *Roman de Renart* dans la littérature française et dans les littératures étrangères au moyen âge
  JOHN FLINN

5 Henry Céard: Idéaliste détrompé
  RONALD FRAZEE

6 La Chronique de Robert de Clari: Étude de la langue et du style
  P.F. DEMBOWSKI

7 Zola before the *Rougon-Macquart*
  JOHN C. LAPP

8 The Idea of Art as Propaganda in France 1750–1799: A study in the history of ideas
  J.A. LEITH

9 Marivaux
  E.J.H. GREENE

10 Sondages 1830–1848: Romanciers français secondaires
   JOHN S. WOOD

11 The Sixth Sense: Individualism in French poetry 1686–1760
   ROBERT FINCH

12 The Long Journey: Literary themes of French Canada
   JACK WARWICK

13 The Narreme in the Medieval Romance Epic: An introduction to narrative structures
   EUGENE DORFMAN

14 Verlaine: A study in parallels
   A.E. CARTER

15 An Index of Proper Names in French Arthurian Verse Romances 1150–1300
   G.D. WEST

16 Emery Bigot: Seventeenth-century French humanist
LEONARD E. DOUCETTE

17 Diderot the Satirist:
Le Neveu de Rameau and related works / an analysis
DONAL O'GORMAN

18 'Naturalisme pas mort': Lettres inédites de Paul Alexis à
Émile Zola 1871–1900
B.H. BAKKER

19 Crispin Ier: La Vie et l'œuvre de Raymond Poisson, comédien-poète
du XVIIe siècle
A. ROSS CURTIS

20 Tuscan and Etruscan: The problem of linguistic substratum
influence in central Italy
HERBERT J. IZZO

21 *Fécondité* d'Émile Zola: Roman à thèse, évangile, mythe
DAVID BAGULEY

22 Charles Baudelaire. Edgar Allan Poe: Sa vie et ses ouvrages
W.T. BANDY

23 Paul Claudel's *Le Soulier de satin*: A stylistic, structuralist, and
psychoanalytic interpretation
JOAN S. FREILICH

24 Balzac's Recurring Characters
ANTHONY R. PUGH

25 Morality and Social Class in Eighteenth-Century French Literature and
Painting
WARREN ROBERTS

26 The Imagination of Maurice Barrès
PHILIP OUSTON

27 La Cité idéale dans *Travail* d'Émile Zola
FREDERICK IVOR CASE

28 Critical Approaches to Rubén Darío
KEITH ELLIS

29 Universal Language Schemes in England and France 1600–1800
JAMES KNOWLSON

This book

was designed by

ANTJE LINGNER

under the direction of

ALLAN FLEMING

and was printed by

University of

Toronto

Press

St. John's College
Library · Oxford

St. John's College
Library · Oxford